Encyclopedia of Imaginary
and Mythical Places

Encyclopedia of Imaginary and Mythical Places

THERESA BANE

McFarland & Company, Inc., Publishers

Jefferson, North Carolina

LIBRARY OF CONGRESS CATALOGUING-IN-PUBLICATION DATA

Bane, Theresa, 1969–
Encyclopedia of Imaginary and Mythical Places / Theresa Bane.
p.   cm.
Includes bibliographical references and index.

ISBN 978-0-7864-7848-4 (softcover : acid free paper) ∞
ISBN 978-1-4766-1565-3 (ebook)

1. Geographical myths—Encyclopedias.   2. Legends—Encyclopedias.
3. Mythology—Encyclopedias   I. Title.
GR940.B36 2014   398.23'4003—dc23   2014005176

BRITISH LIBRARY CATALOGUING DATA ARE AVAILABLE

Front cover: road leading into forest © iStock/Thinkstock

Printed in the United States of America

McFarland & Company, Inc., Publishers
Box 611, Jefferson, North Carolina 28640
www.mcfarlandpub.com

For Ryan Hardy.

Without his dedication
and friendship
this book would not
have been possible.

Table of Contents

Preface

This encyclopedia of imaginary places and mythical lands may not be the first of its kind, but I feel it is one of the best available to academics and serious researchers. Other books currently on the market covering the same subject matter as my own book are not geared toward a general and timeless reading audience; these books, apart from naming a handful of places in ASGARD, are filled with locations from works of pure fiction, that is to say, the literary works of authors not only from books but from pop culture movies and television shows. Although it is interesting to know that the small fictitious town of Mystic Falls, Virginia, is the setting for the supernatural drama *The Vampire Diaries* based on the books written by L. J. Smith, who will really be looking for this information five years from now, never mind one hundred? As interesting as I may or may not find the books and the television show, its entry would only be relevant, in my opinion, in a book whose author centered and focused their research on fictional towns in literature published in the twenty-first century. Moreover, as much of a fan as I am of Stella Gibson's *Cold Comfort Farm* (1932), I would never dream of its being an entry in this book. Not only is the novel going on one hundred years old, few people would have heard of it in these modern times; I suspect most would be more familiar, if at all, with the 1995 film rendition. As you can see, based on these examples, it would be impossible for me to hope to mention all the current and relevant fictional settings, let alone those that were named in less popular or self-published books.

Naturally the heavens and hells of the religious afterlife are the locations that most immediately spring to mind when one considers mythological places. However, there are a great number of other locales that are included, such as fairy realms, settings from Arthurian lore, and a few of the kingdoms located "far, far, away," named in fairy tales and relevant political works, such as Sir Thomas More's *Utopia* and Plato's Atlantis from his works *Critias* and *Timaeus*.

Furthermore, I included places named in *Sindbad the Sailor* as well as in *Critias, Timaeus,* and *Utopia* not because they were works of popular fiction in their day but because even after hundreds, and hundreds, and hundreds of years, these stories are still being told to children, taught in schools (even on an academic level), and actively searched for, and because they are still relevant and timely. This is not my decision but rather one society has made, consistently in some cases, for a few thousand years.

With my previous books, *Encyclopedia of Vampire Mythology* (2010), *Encyclopedia of Demons in World Religions and Cultures* (2012), and *Encyclopedia of Fairies in World Folklore and Mythology* (2013), I put my research skills to the test, collecting and collating as many places from all the various folklores, legends, mythologies, and religions I could find. I used not only architectural, artistic, geographic, historical, and religious texts, but also books on the various mythologies from around the world.

To the best of my knowledge, I don't believe there is anyone purporting to be a *mythological geographer*; I would define this as someone who has a broad understanding of the various religious belief systems, folklores, and mythologies, as well as knowledge of the geographic terrain of each area's individual location well enough to support such a job title. It would be quite wonderful if there were. Perhaps such a thing would pave the way for mythological cartographers to emerge, those individuals who would be so bold as to create a visual map laying out the various realms of the heavens above and hells below for readers, researchers, and would be travelers. This is not to be confused, however, with those individuals who are fans of works of fiction and have drawn a map of the terrain covered in the story, such as the many finely crafted maps of J. R. R. Tolkien's Middle Earth and the map of Jim Butcher's Codex Alera. Theses maps, be they constructed by the author or an astute individual, are, as accurate as they may be, the byproduct of a single mind and not a part of regional mythology or the religion of a people.

I have found it a refreshing experience not to write my fourth book on any collection of mythological beings or creatures, but rather on the places they live, when they're not harassing us humans on our mortal realm, of course. As with my previous subjects, the lands I have catalogued and described in this book are not proven to exist. Yet millions of people from all over the world, regardless of social class or economic privilege, believe they do; particularly the heavens and the hells of the world's varied religions. Faith in afterlife destinations, whether a welcoming PARADISE or a tormenting HELL dimension, have been consistent throughout our recorded history. Personally, I find comfort in this notion, knowing all the good I do now will someday present a payoff, while all of the people who escape justice for their crimes of hate and indifference will get what's coming to them eventually, even if it is in the next life and a shade extreme.

As a professional vampirologist—a mythologist who specializes in cross-cultural vampire studies—I compiled information for several books at once while I conducted my basic initial research, cataloging all the different bits of relative data in corresponding file folders, one for demons, one for fairies, one for mythic places, vampires, and the like. Slowly I amassed the material I would ultimately need for the books I already have written, as well as stockpiling information to write future books. It was a time-consuming five years in the making, but I have found it to be well worth the initial trouble and strikingly similar to my belief in an afterlife: work hard now and reap the benefits and rewards later.

I was confident from the outset of this project that I had enough raw materials to write an encyclopedia of imaginary and mythic locations as there are numerous heavens and hells from the varied world religions as well as a plethora of fairy realms and mythological locales, such as from Arthurian lore and time-tested fairy tales. The number of individual entries was not a concern, but I did wonder if the length of some of the entries would be satisfying to my readers; sadly there are some places we are well familiar with, but there is little information fully describing or detailing it from the original source material. The entry of SHEOL is a good example of this, a well-known conceptual location from Rabbinical lore but with little historical and mythological facts to flesh it out as nicely as, say, the description of CAER YS of Breton folklore.

The entry for HEAVEN, to cite another example, was no small task to write. Although it is much longer than most entries in this book, it is short when one considers the scope of what HEAVEN has been purported to be, and attempt to put it into words. Particular care has been taken to give an equal amount of time to the major religions without trying to promote one over the other, using only the information presented in those religions' accepted spiritual texts, while disregarding misconceptions that have been popularized by media over the years. Although it is common to portray HEAVEN as a cloud-filled land where its occupants wear long white unisex gowns and carry a harp they never seem to play, this description is not, by any stretch of the imagination, given in any of the recognized manuscripts I consulted. Yet somehow it is accepted as the Gentile concept of Heaven.

Many times I discovered what I thought to be the truth was in fact a misconception on my part. For instance, prior to writing this book I always assumed, as I am sure many people still do, that Camelot, the legendary court of King Arthur, was the center of the Arthurian world, both as the name of the castle and the land in which it was built. This is only a small part of the truth. In the bulk of Arthurian lore, King Arthur traveled his lands constantly and kept a roaming court. He did not have one fixed location where he heard matters and made political decisions but rather utilized the throne room of the noble's castle where he was currently visiting. Typically the lands of Caerleon, Cardueil, Carilisle, and LOGRES competed for the title of "capitol," but the king never settled in one place long enough to make any such decree. Chrétien de Troyes,

the much famed twelfth century French poet and troubadour, mentions CAMELOT only once in all of his works and in the Welsh Arthurian tradition, Camelot is never mentioned at all, rather Ehangwen was the name of the king's castle, with the capitol located in either KELIWIC, Cernyw, or Gelliwig.

I would like to take this moment to recommend some books I consider to be important and relevant works in the field: Geoffrey Ashe for his books on Arthurian lore; Ebenezer Cobham Brewer whose *Dictionary of Phrase and Fable* is an endlessly useful resource; Sir Richard and Lady Burton's individual translations of *The Seven Voyages of Sinbad the Sailor*; Kathleen N. Daly's books on Greek, Norse, and Roman mythologies; Sir James George Frazer for his works on comparative religion, worship of the dead, and magic; and Ganga Ram Garg for his *Encyclopaedia of the Hindu World*. Each of these authors and their respective works have been extremely important in my work. Likewise, I am partial to Phyllis Ann Karr's book on Arthurian mythology, *King Arthur Companion*. Although this book contains a great deal of her personal opinions and summations, it is well cited and lists scores of characters and places which simply have not been covered in other books. Heilan Yvette Grimes's *The Norse Myths* is a must-have book when delving into the mythology of the Norse gods, rivaled only perhaps by H. A. Guerber's *Myths of the Norsemen*. Either one of these books is rich enough to give its reader a solid working knowledge of the topic, but when used in tandem, the depth of the subject becomes that much more profound.

As I have done in the past, I made use of older books that claim to be the written transcriptions from original oral folklore and tales traditionally told by the people of various nations. This was especially helpful when researching Oceania. Whenever possible, I referenced the oldest edition of each book I utilized because I personally feel earlier editions best reflect the author's original intent. For the sake of my research, it did not matter if the language and spelling was oftentimes antiquated. There are a few books I have relied upon whose date of publication is listed in the mid- to late 1700 and 1800s.

There are two publishing companies reprinting old and out of print books that are public domain, Forgotten Books and Kessinger. I utilized many of their books, as they use the original text exactly as it first appeared in print, typos and all, even though the book itself is newly republished.

After I gathered all of the individual materials I selected for the encyclopedia, I wrote each description making sure everything was taken from the source materials cited for each. Every entry in the book is condensed down to just the essential facts universally agreed upon by the relevant source material. I did not include any information considered to be my own personal opinion or summation. As interesting as some investigators may have found this to be, I felt it would best be left up to each individual to come to their own conclusions, if any, from the information presented without my opinions fouling their research. My goal with each of my encyclopedias has always been to present a brief, yet clear and concise description of the material without any commentary, be it speculation or editorial comment.

I would like to express my deep appreciation to those who assisted me with this undertaking: my absolutely wonderful beta-reader, Angela McGill; Brandon Chandler, whose assistance was essential to completing my *Fairy Encyclopedia*'s index in a timely fashion; Ryan Hardy, who dropped everything and came to my rescue when my laptop crashed while it was backing up my files, saving not only this finished manuscript but everything else stored on my hard drive; and especially my devoted and supporting husband, T. Glenn Bane. Without this dedicated cadre of beloved individuals, this book would not have been possible.

Introduction

It is hard to imagine in our modern times that there was ever cause to wonder what lay on the other side of the mountain. Is that the place where dragons dwell? What would the people be like? What rare and exotic goods may I covet? Now if I find myself truly curious about these answers, I simply pull out my phone to find the appropriate application and, by use of satellite, virtually tour the area in question from the safety and comfort of my home. I might try browsing their online stores. If I'm lucky, I'll get free shipping.

There once was a time when civilized common folks looked up to three classes of people. The first of these was the Warrior. They were the brave men and the occasional women who, by means of brawn and willpower, protected the community from unwanted influences, be they conquering warlords, ancestral curses, or foreign policies. These citizen soldiers left the safety and security of the community and traveled into the unknown to confront an insidious evil. They did so at great personal cost to themselves, oftentimes leaving behind a family without the promise of return. While away, they were forced to complete the Hero's Journey, emerging transformed and victorious. When they did return, they told tales of their epic adventures. The accounts they told for bards to sing were always jampacked with heroic deeds they accomplished,

with amazing descriptions of foreign lands and confrontations with beasts from legends.

Second was the Shaman, a wizened spiritual advisor who safeguarded immortal souls, acted as intermediary to the gods, and blessed the undertakings of the Warrior. This special class of people was always small in number. Entry into this calling was rare; only a select few were chosen to walk this path and the means they were selected from was always wrapped in mystery. Typically the shaman protected his community by traveling, either in body or in astral form, to an Other realm—a place not of this world—where spirit beings, both good and evil, existed. There the Shaman confronted what was wrong and put it right to ensure that the people were safe against otherworldly corruption. The Shaman fought what the Warrior could not, the invisible and intangible threats that afflicted the people and could not be defeated with wit and weapon. If there was plague or drought, only the Shaman could deliver the community from the blight. He (or she) too had fabulous tales of adventures in that Other place, describing a realm the likes of which none have ever seen and could not travel themselves. Only the Shaman could visit the heavens and hells and live to tell the tales.

The third and final class of individuals worthy of the respect of the common man was the Merchant. I know it's hard to imagine, a businessman as a hero, but it's true. Consider this:

The Merchant was the person who wondered not only what was on the other side of the mountain, but also how to turn a profit in returning with the answer. He would, either alone or with a small group, venture into the unknown, or intentionally try to leave the map to procure rare and wondrous objects he could return home and sell to his fellow man for a small profit. Naturally this was dangerous business, and I imagine the revenues were not as consistently sound as intended. When profit margins ran tight, there was a reason and his explanation of a disaster could, with a bit of skill in his storytelling, drive up the price of any object. He could tell you how an item was taken from the hoard of a dragon or plucked from a tree that grew gems rather than fruit. Most people were tethered to their plow and crops nine months out of the year; they were sure never to visit those distant lands, making anything in the merchant's tale possible.

It would also be useful for the Merchant to remember as many of his local tales as possible; this would enable him to trade his hometown goods at a marked-up rate while afar, applying his regional mythology to common enough items he is trying to sell as exotic ones abroad. So long as he was not caught in a lie, it was a wonderful ploy. And even if he was discovered telling a slight mistruth about what he said lay on the other side of the desert, he could always tell the person who was accusing him of being dishonest that they did not travel far enough beyond the desert and into the land of which he spoke. It's not his fault, after all, if they got lost in the wilderness and missed the Loadstone Mountain of which he spoke and from which he nearly did not escape.

Among the three archetypes, one is not better than another; all three are necessary ingredients to society. Each may appeal to a different personality type, but they all are needed and throughout our lives, we will find that at some point, we will play each role at least once, even if only for a little while.

When I began to write this book, it was my intention to create a companion piece to my other encyclopedias; a complete singular volume filled with various imaginary and mythological locations spoken of in our folklore, history, mythology, and religions. I wanted a book filled not with the fictional creations of authors originating from their own imaginations, but of those special locations spoken of, said to be of our world, but cannot and in truth have never been visited by man; places that only exist in our folklore and stories interwoven into our local history and beliefs, places like FAIRY FORTS and IDAVOLD.

While conducting my initial research on the subject, I noticed there were not many books published focusing solely on the subject matter I had chosen. There are the books that guide readers through a particular author's literary world, such as the companion books to J. R. R. Tolkien's Middle Earth or J. K. Rowling's world of Harry Potter, but these types of books were not useful for the academic tome I wanted to write. I intended for my book to cover the allegorical, imagined, and mythological places of our history, only those locales that were visited "once upon a time" by Warriors, Shamans, and Merchants alike. Although interesting in their own right and wonderful books for fans to devour, it was impossible for me to include all literary fictional locations from all books; some method of selecting what was to be included had to be developed or I ran the very serious risk of having fictional locations overrun the mythological ones I was seeking to highlight.

Rather than go down that slippery slope, I made the decision to exclude all fictional literary locales. As much as I may have wanted to include the *Rainbow Bridge*, the setting for the poem of the same name which describes PARADISE-like pasture where our beloved pets go when they die to await being reunited with their owners, it too is a literary creation and albeit sweet, not a part of any mythology or religion I could track down.

The few books available to researchers such as myself are by and large disappointing, such as *The Dictionary of Imaginary Places* by Alberto Manguel and Gianni Guadalupi. This is a massively large and visually impressive tome to say the least. However it is mostly filled with fictional literary locations—and those, more often than not, were locations chosen from books published between 1750 and 1950. Although this is a wonderful resource in the right circumstances, I found it unsatisfactory for my purposes, as neither the authors nor the books used to bulk up its content were relevant, timely, or based on historical mythology. A scant handful of the places mentioned were from works a modern reader would be familiar with, but again, they were pulled from works of fiction. I found it interesting on a personal note to see a map of H. P. Lovecraft's city, Arkham, circa 1943, as I am a fan of his writings, but it was a map I had seen in numerous other locations and in more detail. Perhaps the greatest flaw of this particular book was its title, as it leads readers to assume it contains information it does not.

Other books on the market purporting to be of some use were ultimately not. *The Book of Where: A Gazetteer of Places Real and Imaginary*, for instance, contained a few mythological places but mostly it listed the planets, their moons, the nicknames of many of the world's cities, and a handful of locations from the popular Harry Potter series. Again, nearly all of its entries were places

anyone could visit, point to on a star chart, or were the intellectual creation of an author's work of fiction.

Books about places such as ATLANTIS, EL DORADO, LEMURIA, and MU, are more than plentiful but I needed to be extra careful in their use. For the most part, works on these subjects tend to give the original story or mythology a gratuitous once over, so that it can, as quickly as possible, get on with the speculation of "the truth" of the matter, how ancient aliens are involved, or the rehashing of other people's failed attempts to locate the actual location of these mythical cities. These books are typically filled with uncited sources where the authors make huge and unprecedented leaps in logic, linking together facts with their own unfounded theories. Time will tell if any of these authors were correct in their theories, but until such a time, I did not want to reference any of them in my work.

It was quickly apparent to me that there was no book on the market, past or present, like the one I wanted to write. The book of my vision contained only those places spoken of in our mythologies which do not exist, likely never did, and cannot be reached by travel, but are nevertheless part of our culture and history. For instance, no one will doubt the history, importance, and mystery of the Great Pyramids of Giza and the role they played in the beliefs of the ancient Egyptian people. Hundreds of books have been written on the subject, wondering what they really mean, how they were really built, and the role they played in ancient Egyptian mythos. As amazingly interesting as the pyramids are, they are not in my book because they are real and can be visited and explored by anyone who has the gumption of the archetypical Merchant to visit them. What you will have in my book are entries on AAHAL, the Field of AALU, the ISLAND OF FLAME, and the HALL OF TWO TRUTHS to name but a few. These places exist in the Egyptian afterlife and, literally, only those souls who are fortunate enough to make the journey there will be able to enjoy the eternal pleasures they provide.

As with my other books, it is not necessary for the reader to believe the locations mentioned here are real or to have any faith whatsoever in the locale's corresponding religion. Is it important to have faith in FĀNGZHÀNG, HEAVEN, or the HAPPY HUNTING GROUNDS? Do places such as DAIVER LOGUM and the various NARAKAS actually torment the souls of sinners into retribution? For the sake of reading more about a religion to understand its people, faith is not a requirement; rather understanding the how and why of the necessity of these places. Hopefully my book will contribute to those researchers who are looking to answer those questions; I am merely supplying them with the raw data they need to explore their metaphysical concepts and theories.

The intended purpose of this book is to describe as many of the mythological locations from the varied folklores, histories, and religions as I could responsibly catalogue. Apart from mentioning the original source of the location, I gave as full a description of the topographical land as possible. Sadly, many of the realms found in the afterlife are not as fully described or fleshed out as we researchers would like them to be; mostly I suppose this is because, assuming they are real to begin with, so very few people return from the other side to tell the tale, and of those who do—characteristically the archetypical Shaman—it was in his best interest to control the information. After all, if everyone could travel to LYFJABERG and speak with Menglod, a goddess of healing, what need would they have of the Shaman the next time a pox broke out among the people? Throughout the book, I restrained myself from giving my personal opinion as

to the validity of a place or the role it was said to play in its respective mythology. I did not want to taint my research for future generations with my current "modern world" opinion; what is commonly recognized today as being morally acceptable and "right" may not be in the future. It was not so long ago after all, that the great and ancient city of Troy would have been an entry in this book.

As with all my previous books, I have again utilized a comprehensive cross-referencing system throughout the book; it has been employed so readers and researchers alike can follow the flow of additional information they choose without ever having to reference an outside source for additional details. To highlight these words without becoming tedious or disrupting the flow of readability, all words represented in SMALL CAPS are also entries to be found in the book.

On occasion, a particular location is known by a variety of names or has an assortment of different spellings. Based on my research I chose the most commonly used variation as the title for the main entry and listed all other deviations, in alphabetical order, immediately following under the heading "Variations." These alternate names are also listed independently in the index, as a researcher should not be expected to guess what name variant or spelling I chose to use but should be able to quickly find what he is looking for, no matter his preference for spelling.

This is not a travel guide for a tourist to take with them as they move through dimensions to experience the sights of the various realms provided by our mythologies. However, I am certain academics, researchers, and scholars will be satisfied with what they find here, a book filled with the imaginary and mythological lands from all cultures and societies, catalogued, defined and presented in alphabetical order.

THE ENCYCLOPEDIA

Aab-I-Hamim

A river in HUTAMA, one of the seven HELLS of Islam, Aab-I-Hamim is said to have water so hot that as soon as a sinner drinks from it their lower lip swells up and droops down to their chest while their upper lip balloons up and covers their nose and eyes; the tongue burns, the throat is scorched, and the stomach and intestines are torn apart.

Source: Wagner, *How Islam Plans to Change the World*, 156

Aahla

Variations: the Field of Peace, the Plains of Peace

In the religion of the ancient Egyptians, Aahla ("Field of Peace") was a field of peacefulness reserved for the souls of the redeemed; it was located in one of the four sections of AMENTI in the UNDERWORLD. Similar to the ELYSIUM FIELDS of Greek mythology, here the god Horus dwelled waiting the time for this return to the Earth when he would re-establish the reign of the gods and restore the world to its original glory.

Source: Baskin, *Dictionary of Satanism*, 1; Blavatsky, *Theosophical Glossary*, 1; Bonwick, *Egyptian Belief and Modern Thought*, 46; Cooper, *Horus Myth in Its Relation to Christianity*, 9

Aalu

Variations: Fields of Aalu, Field of AARU

According to the ancient Egyptian legend known as the "Destruction of Mankind" which was first discovered in the tomb of Seti I, the god Ra, tired of ruling over the disobedient people of Earth retired to the sky where he created for himself a place to dwell and rule over. There he created a great field of rest, (AAHLA) and a great field for growing crops, the field of Aalu. The *Book of the Dead* describes says that upon the death of the human body this is the location of the newly formed soul and it is here they will spend their time harvesting the divine crops. The field is surrounded by a wall of iron which has many doors; it is traversed by a river. The barely grows to a height of seven cubits (1.7175197 feet). Aalu has also been compared to the ELYSIUM FIELDS of Greek mythology.

Source: Brodrick, *Concise Dictionary of Egyptian Archaeology*, 3; Dale, *Book of Where*, 9

Aanroo

In the mythology of the ancient Egyptians, Aanroo ("Field of Peace") was one of the four areas of the AMENTI, or UNDERWORLD; it is divided into fourteen sections. Surrounded by an iron wall this wheat field was described as having stalks three, five, and seven cubits tall; disembodied spirits harvested the crop. Aanroo was surrounded by a wall of iron and grew fields of corn, some stalks reached seven cubits tall. Only those who have died knowing the name of the custodians of the seven HELLS will be permitted entry; all others will go to a lower field. Over time the souls of Aanroo will be devoured by Uraeus, the great snake.

Source: Blavatsky, *Secret Doctrine*, 48; Blavatsky, *Theosophical Glossary*, 1

Aaru

Variations: AALU, Iaru, Sekhet-Aaru ("Field of Reeds"), Yaaru

In ancient Egyptian mythology Aaru ("rushes") is the heavenly abode of the god Osiris after he became a part of the pantheon, displacing the god Anubis in the Ogdoad tradition. Only the souls whose weight was exactly measured to that of a feather were allowed to begin the long and dangerous journey east to Aaru; if they survived the ordeal, they would reside there for all eternity in perfect pleasure. To succeeded, they would need to pass through a series of gates, the number of which varies from source to source between 15 and 21. No matter the number of gates, each is guarded by demons armed with knives.

Aaru is described in chapter five of the *Book of the Dead* as an endless field of reeds making up a series of endless islands exactly like those once found along the Nile delta; this PARADISE is an ideal fishing and hunting ground. The occupants of his PARADISE lived an ideal life, much as they would have wanted to in life; there was still a need to eat, drink, and sleep.

Source: Budge, *Egyptian Religion and Magic*, 70–71, 204; Gardiner, *Gateways to the Otherworld*, 231–32

Abaddon

Variations: ALADDON

In Cabalistic lore Abaddon ("Destruction"), the HELL of Perdition, is the second (or sixth, sources conflict) of the seven hells.

Source: Greer, *New Encyclopedia of the Occult*, 1; Mathers, *Sorcerer and His Apprentice*, 24

Abalus, Isle of

Variations: Basilea, Isle of Amber, Isle of the Kings

Roman author, naturalist, natural philosopher, and army and naval commander, Gaius Plinius Secundus, better known as Pliny the Elder wrote of the Isle of Abalus in his book, "*Natural History*"; in it he described it as being large. In the springtime it was said that amber washed up in copious amounts on its shore; the inhabitants use this amber as a fuel source but also sell it to the Teutones, their neighbors.

Source: Kish, *Source Book in Geography*, 70; Pliny the Elder, *Natural History of Pliny*, Volume 1, 341

Abaton

A forever inaccessible town of changing location, Abaton ("a place not to be entered") has never had a visitor inside its wall, although many travelers have claimed to have glimpsed them on the horizon near dusk; the towered walls are variously described as being light blue, fiery red, white, and yellow. Sir Thomas Bulfinch, the American author of *Bulfinch's Mythology* (1881), claimed to have glimpsed Abaton as he travelled through Scotland from Glasgow to Troon; he mentioned hearing what sounded like harpsichord music playing off in the distance.

Source: Manguel, *Dictionary of Imaginary Places*, 1

Abdalles, Kingdom of

The large imaginary kingdom of Abdalles was said to be located along the North African coast near the border of Amphicleocles. The blue-skinned people of this country claim to be the descendants of Abdalles, a son of their sun god, and his union with the first woman, Phiocles.

Many of the laws and customs of Abdalles are seen as being especially cruel to outsiders, such as their favorite form of entertainment, *Lak-Tro Al Dal*, which involves four men insulting and then nearly beating a fifth man to death. Judicial death involves four men flogging the convicted to his demise with iron tipped whips; after the sentence is carried out the skin of the criminal is tanned and used to make dress material for the more fashionable women. It is considered a high offence for anyone but the king to point with his finger; only the king and divinity may do so, all others must point with their elbows.

Source: Manguel, *Dictionary of Imaginary Places*, 2–4; Mouhy, *Lamekis*, 44, 120

Abhasara

Variations: Radiant Realm

Abhasara is the name of the thirteenth HEAVEN of Buddhism.

Source: Garg, *Encyclopaedia of the Hindu World*, Volume 1, 95; Garrett, *Classical Dictionary of India*, 1

Abyla

Variations: Abila

Abyla was the Pillars of Hercules from Roman mythology set on the North African side of the straits of Gibraltar; the other, called CALPE, was on the European side.

Although there are numerous locations said to be Abyla, there is no definitive proof as to where ancient writers were actually referring to. Some ancient authors say the pillars were mountains the god stacked and poured a sea between them while other authors say the "pillars" were actually hills. Other authors describe the pillars actual items, made of bronze standing eight cubits tall (11.8 feet).

Source: Rawlinson, *History of Herodotus*, Volume 3, 29; Smith, *Dictionary of Greek and Roman Geography*, 1055

Abyss

Variations: the BOTTOMLESS PIT, the Pit of the Abyss

In Christian scriptures the Abyss ("the deep") is a domain with a portal opening up to the Earth where some of the spirits who have been condemned there can pass through as they are not bound by the same limitations that regulates the spirits who have been condemned to reside in HELL. For instance, the Abyss is the place where the Antichrist will rise up from although how this will be accomplished is not specified. Satan's chief fallen angels will also rise up from the Abyss according to the Book of Revelation, 9:11; during the fifth Trumpet Judgment supernatural creatures will arise from the Abyss and torment mankind for five months; Satan will be sealed up in the Abyss for 1,000 years only to appear on Earth again at the end of the millennium

for a short while in order to deceive the nations to do battle against God.

In the New Testament there are three Greek words "pit," *abussos*, *bothynor* (or *bothros*), and *phrear*. This refers to the regions which hold the demons which will be released during the time of tribulation.

Source: Kremer, *Chronological Order of the Endtimes*, 98; Wiese, *Hell*, n.p.

Abzu

In Sumerian mythology Abzu was the cosmic temple of the god Enki in Eridu; it represents the realm over which the god presides. The mythical Abzu is located deep within the ocean; to travel to and descend into it is a means by which the god can claim *me* ("divine power").

Abzu is also the word used when the ancient Sumerians were referring to the cosmic water that ran beneath the surface of the earth; it was this water which they believed was the source for all water which was accessible on the surface.

Source: Horowitz, *Mesopotamian Cosmic Geography*, Volume 8, 307–08; Penglase, *Greek Myths and Mesopotamia*, 35, 37

Acheron

Variations: Acharon ("last one" or "later ones")

One of the five rivers of the Greek UNDERWORLD (see HELL, RIVERS OF), Acheron, the river of woe, was the location where the souls of the dead crossed over. If a person was not properly buried, they were not allowed to pass over. In some telling's of the myth, Acheron is described more as a lake or a swamp than a river. Plato, the mathematician and philosopher of classical Greece, claimed Acheron ran underground, deep beneath the deserts and in the opposite direction of the river OCEANUS.

Source: Brewer, *Dictionary of Phrase and Fable*, 596; Dale, *Book of Where*, 12; Evans, *Dictionary of Mythology*, 2

Acherontia

In ancient Greek mythology Acherontia ("pertaining to Acheron") was one of the many realms of the UNDERWORLD ruled over by the god Hades.

Source: Anthon, *Classical Dictionary*, 11

Acherusia Cavern

In the mythology of the ancient Greeks Acherusia was the name of a cave said to be located along the borders of Pontus. It was here the demigod, Hercules, dragged Cerberus, the guardian to the entrance of the UNDERWORLD, to earth.

Source: Anthon, *Classical Dictionary*, Volume 1, 11; Lemprière, *Classical Dictionary*, xxxiii; Smith, *New Classical Dictionary of Greek and Roman Biography*, Volume 1, 7

Acherusian Stream

According to ancient Greek mythology the Acherusian stream was one of the four rivers of the UNDERWORLD (see COCYTUS, OCEANUS and PYRIPHLEGETHON); it ends underground in the Acherusian Lake. Along its shores, human souls wait out their allotted time before being able to be reborn. After standing trial, average souls enter into the lake to be purified of their sins and rewarded for their merit.

Source: Guthrie, *History of Greek Philosophy: Volume 4*, 337; Lemprière, *Classical Dictionary*, xxxiii

Acmonian Wood

In ancient Roman mythology the Acmonian Woods was a location were lovers would rendezvous; it was in this location where the god Mars met with his lover the nymph Harmonia and fathered the race of the Amazons.

Source: Flaum, *Encyclopedia of Mythology*, 28; Hyamson, *Dictionary of English Phrases*, 4; Tripp, *Meridian Handbook of Classical Mythology*, 74

Adamida

Variations: Adam'ida

In the mythology of the early Christians the angel of the sun, Uriel, was ordered by God during the Crucifixion to move the planet Adamida between the sun and the earth in order to create a total eclipse. Upon the planet Adamida resides the unborn souls of believers, martyrs, and saints.

Source: Brewer, *Character Sketches of Romance, Fiction and the* Drama, Volume 1, 8; Daniels, *Encyclopædia of Superstitions, Folklore, and the Occult Sciences*, 942

Adhab-al-Cabr

According to Muslin lore Adhab-al-Cabr ("punishment of the tomb") mankind is judged after death and tormented in their grave until the time of the final resurrection for punishment of their sins.

Source: Brewer, *Dictionary of Phrase and Fable*, 15; Spring, *Giafar Al Barmeki*, 209

Adhab-Algal

In Muslin lore Adhab-Algal is a kind of PURGATORY where wicked souls are tormented by two dark angels, Munkir and Nekir.

Source: de Claremont, *Ancient's Book of Magic*, 104; Spence, *Encyclopedia of Occultism and Parapsychology*, Volume 1, 10

Adhahsiras

Variations: Adhisiras

In Hindu mythology, Adhahsiras is one of the twenty-eight NARAKAS (HELLS) located in a providence in the kingdom of Yama; it is filled with the instruments of torture.

Source: Becker, *Contribution to the Comparative Study of the Medieval Visions of Heaven and Hell*, 14; Wilson, *Vishńu Puráńa*, 215–16

Adhogati

According to the beliefs of Jaina dharma of India Adhogati ("descent" or "downward movement") is a type of ABYSS located in the nethermost regions of HELL. Above Adhogati are seven infernal worlds; above those realms are ten Favanalokas ("PURGATORIES"), purifying worlds, and atop sits the earth.

Source: Garrett, *Classical Dictionary of India*, 6; Hoult, *Dictionary of Some Theosophical Terms*, 3

Adhosiras

Variations: Adhomukha ("head inverted")

In Hindu mythology Adhosiras is a partition in HELL (or NARAKA) ruled over by Yama; it is located beneath the earth and water where souls are punished for the sin of bribery.

Source: Garrett, *Classical Dictionary of India*, 6; Wilson, *Oriental Translation Fund*, Volume 52, 208

Adlivun

Variations: Idliragijenget

In Inuit mythology Adlivun ("those beneath us") is a realm used as a PURGATORY for the deceased; here they are purified for a year before being permitted to pass on into the Land of the Moon (Quidlivun). This realm is ruled by a powerful goddess of sea creatures named Sedna, a hideous one-eyed giant and is described as being dark, dank and shadowy. The psychopomps Anguta and Pinga carry the souls of the dead to Adlivun which lies on the bottom of the sea. Souls here are not tortured, but rather are simply allowed to suffer the loneliness of separation from their loved one and denial of entry into PARADISE.

Source: Grimal, *Larousse World Mythology*, 443; Lynch, *Native American Mythology A to Z*, 2; Van Scott, *Encyclopedia of Hell*, 58

Aeaea

Variations: Eëa

In Greek mythology Aeaea was the name of the emerald wooded island the sorceress Circe lived on; according to Homer's *Odyssey*, she and Odysseus lived together and had a son together named Telegonus. Before he left Aeaea, Circe gave Odysseus instructions on how to cross the ocean and reach the UNDERWORLD.

Source: Evans, *Dictionary of Mythology*, 5; Westmoreland, *Ancient Greek Beliefs*, 149

Aegilips

In Homer's *Iliad*, book II, Aegilips, an obscure and unidentifiable island believed to have located in the Ionian Sea, was a part of the kingdom of Ithaca under the rulership of Odysseus; it was described in the ancient Greek epic poem as being a rugged land (see NERITOS and CROCYLEIA).

Source: Earl of De Edward, *The Iliad*, 50; Page, *History and the Homeric Land*, 163

Aeí

Variations: Plain of Aeí

An Irish mythological site from the epic of *Tain Bo Cuailnge*, Aeí was the location where the two great bulls of the opposing clans fought one another, the white horned bull of Ailell and the brown bull of Quelgny.

Source: Monaghan, *Encyclopedia of Celtic Mythology and Folklore*, 4; Rolleston, *Celtic Myths and Legends*, 224

Aeolia

A FLOATING ISLAND mentioned in Homer's *Odyssey* and Virgil's *Aeneid*, Aeolia was the land where Aeolus, the son of Hippotas lived. A small island, Aeolia was described as being surrounded by an impenetrable wall of bronze. Odysseus is welcomed here by the king and is given a bag containing all the winds that may hinder his trip home.

Source: Johnston, *The Odyssey*, 179; Westmoreland, *Ancient Greek Beliefs*, 149

Aerial Toll Houses

In the belief held by Eastern Orthodox Christians, each person has a personal demon who records their every sin of action and thought. Three days after a person's death the soul separates itself from the body and, escorted by angels, begins to make its way to HEAVEN. Along the way there are twenty tollhouses, each one representing a particular sin and is occupied by demons of that sin. At each stop the demons demand the soul explain their actions by giving a full account of how they rectified their inequities with good deeds. If the soul cannot give a full and proper account, the demons drag the soul to HELL.

The twenty the toll-houses, in order of their appearance are: the sins of the tongue; of lies; of slander; of gluttony; of laziness; of theft; of covetousness; of usury; of injustice; of envy; of pride; of anger; of remembering evil; of murder; of magic; of lust; of adultery; of sodomy; of heresy; and of unmercifulness.

Source: Patapios, *Manna from Athos*, Volume 2, 124; Rose, *Soul After Death*, 254

Aethyr

Variations: Ayres

In the Enochian system of magic the aethyr are thirty planes of existence, each one spanning the distance between the phenomenal and the nominal world. These places are used by initiates of this magical system as a means for traveling in a spirit vision. Each aethyr is presided over by three Governors (except for the thirtieth which has four), one for each sub-aethyr; collectively there are ninety-one Governors. Each aethyr also each teaches a lesson, has its own particular atmosphere, and sexual polarity.

The names of the thirty concentric aethyr, in order, are Lil, Arn, Zom, Paz, Lit, Maz, Deo, Zid, Zip, Zax, Ich, Loe, Zim, Uta, Oxo, Lea, Tan, Zen, Pop, Khr, Asp, Lin, Tor, Nia, Uti, Des, Zaa, Bag, Rii, and Tex.

Source: Whitcomb, *Magician's Companion*, 249–57; W. I. T, *Advanced Enochian Magick*, 76–77

Aetna (ET-nuh)

Variations: Mount Aetna

In the mythology of the ancient Greeks, Aetna was a volcanic mountain whose crater was believed to be the home of the god of craftsmen and blacksmiths, Hephaestus; his workshop was located near his home on MOUNT OLYMPUS. Named after Aetna, the nymph who made her home there, she bore Hephaestus twin sons who were known collectively as the Palici. The Cyclopes, the one-eyed children of the god of the sky, Uranus and the goddess of the earth, Gaia, were often located on Mount Aetna by ancient authors.

In the mythology of the ancient Romans, the god of fire and metalworking, Vulcan, resided within Aetna.

Source: Evslin, *Gods, Demigods, and Demons*, 5–6; Thorburn, *Facts on File Companion to Classical Drama*, 161–62

Agartha

Variations: Agarta, Agartta, Agarttha, Agharti

A legendary city in esoteric lore Agartha has been said to be both located underground in central Asia as well as being a kingdom to be found somewhere in either Afghanistan, north-east Nepal, south Lhasa, Sri Lanka, or Tibet. While some ancient writers claim Agartha and Shambala were the same place, others will tell of the two kingdoms being at odds with one another, the former walking the right-hand path and the later the left-hand path.

Early tales of Agartha were brought to Europe by the French author and occultist Alexandre Saint-Yves d'Alveydre in his book *Mission de l'Inde en Europe* (1885); here he tells of how travelers who visit the remarkable city are unable to remember their visit there. The city contained a university of knowledge called Paradesa where all the occult and spiritual knowledge of mankind was safeguarded. The royal capitol contains a gilded throne decorated with the figures of two million gods. Agartha is also home to birds with teeth, turtles with six feet, stone books, and residents with forked tongues. Guarding the city is a small but powerful army called the Confederates (or Templars) of Agartha.

Associated with Hollow Earth theorists, Agartha can be entered by passing through a Symmes Hole, openings in the earth's crust which can be found, allegedly, at either of the planet's poles. In some esoteric traditions, self-proclaimed emissaries of Agartha's claim a population of twenty-million people and that their libraries date back some fifty-thousand years.

Source: Childress, *Lost Cities of China, Central Asia, and India*, 32–36; Ossendowski, *Beasts, Men and Gods*, 118, 301; Manguel, *Dictionary of Imaginary Places*, 6

Aglaura

A city with no know location Aglaura, as described by the traveler and Venetian merchant

Marco Polo, cannot be spoken of by its residents or visitors alike, for as soon as an attempt is made to so do, words instantly fail and the speaker is resorted to repeat some proverbial description of a city in general. At best, Aglaura can be said as a city to contain both virtue and vice, a few notable eccentric attributes, as well as a basic set of governing rules.

Source: Calvino, *Invisible Cities*, 67–68; Manguel, *Dictionary of Imaginary Places*, 6

Aiaia

In Greek mythology the island Aiaia, believed to be somewhere in the Mediterranean Sea, was the home to the beautiful sorceress Kirke (or Circe), granddaughter of the sea god Okeanos. In the ancient Greek epic poem written by Homer, *The Odyssey*, this island was described as having cliffs and an oak forest. The goddess and her servants lived in a house of polished stone in the center of a valley; the house was encircled by thick shrubs and trees.

After Odysseus visited LAMOS LAISTIYGONIAN TELEPYLOS, he stopped at Aiaia and the witch goddess transformed his crew into a herd of swine. The god Hermes gave the hero a drug called moly which made him immune to her magic. Kirke, impressed with Odysseus's resistance to her magic agreed to transform his men back to their human form in exchange for a year of his love.

Source: Manguel, *Dictionary of Imaginary Places*, 7; Ruck, *World of Classical Myth*, 297–98; Sprague de Camp, *Lands Beyond*, 62

Aiolos

Variations: Aeolus

A FLOATING ISLAND and a neutral port mentioned by the ancient Greek poet Homer in his epic poem *Odyssey*, x, 1–4; Aiolos ("changeful," "glimmering," and "shifty") is described as having a bronze, sheer, unbroken rampart built all around the island. Named after King Aiolos Hippotades, the son of Hippotas, Odysseus stopped there on his way home from Troy; he was given a bag containing all the winds but Zephyr so he would have a direct and speedy trip home.

Source: Bloom, *The Odyssey*, 53; Hansen, *Handbook of Classical Mythology*, 323; Manguel, *Dictionary of Imaginary Places*, 7; Sprague de Camp, *Lands Beyond*, 55

Airctech

Variations: Bountiful Land of Thought-Genesis

The Irish OTHERWORLD, Airctech ("Beautiful Land" or "Bountiful Plain") is where crystals and dragon-stones come from, these items like amber and coral have the ability to both cure the wounds cause by dragons as well as slay them. The island of Airctech give those who visit it the knowledge of how things *are* rather than how they *seem*, it is a realm of truth and abstract thought. It is connected to the OTHERWORLD island MAG RÉIN by a land bridge called CIUIN.

Source: Federation of European Sections, *Transactions of the Third Annual Congress*, 190; Nansen, *Northern Mists*, Volume 1, 354

Ajana-Deva-Loka

In Hindu mythology Ajana-Deva-Loka ("who are devas by birth") is the loka of the Arupa ("formless") Devas, that is, the devas who have no form.

Source: Aiyaṅgār, *Essays on Indo-Aryan Mythology*, Volume 1, 466; Hoult, *Dictionary of Some Theosophical Terms*, 6, 13

Akanithaka

Akanithaka is the name of the twenty-second HEAVEN of Buddhism.

Source: Garrett, *Classical Dictionary of India*, 22; Garg, *Encyclopaedia of the Hindu World: Ak–Aq*, 291

Akashic Record

Variations: Akashic Halls

In occultism the Akashic record is a spiritual realm which contains all the actions, events, feelings, and thoughts which have ever been experienced since the beginning of time. These memories are imprinted on Akasha, an astral light, which exists well outside the range of human senses on the ASTRAL PLANE.

Spiritual medium and those individuals who have the ability to access and utilize their astral bodies are said to be able to access this realm and tap into this power.

Source: Grimassi, *Encyclopedia of Wicca and Witchcraft*, 3; Smith, *Burning Bush*, 295

Aladdon

Variations: ABADDON

According to Jewish Cabalists, there are seven levels to HELL; Aladdon, the GATES OF DEATH, Gebeanom, the MIRE OF CLAY, the PIT OF CORRUPTION, the SHADOW OF DEATH, and SHEOL.

These realms are set one atop the other; ordinary fire is one-sixtieth the heat of the fire of GEBEANOM which is one-sixtieth the heat of the GATES OF DEATH, which is one-sixtieth the heat of the SHADOW OF DEATH, which is one-sixtieth the heat of the PIT OF CORRUPTION, which is one-sixtieth the heat of the Mire of Clay, which is one-sixtieth the heat of Aladdon, which is one-sixtieth the heat of SHEOL.

Source: Brewer, *Dictionary of Phrase and Fable*, 596; Mew, *Traditional Aspects of Hell*, 173

Alakapuri

Variations: Alaka, Alaka-puri, the Curl-City, Prabha ("Splendid"), Vashudhara ("Bejeweled"), Vasu-Sthali ("Abode of Treasure")

In Hindu mythology Alakapuri is said to be the most splendid city in the world; it is ruled by King Kubera, a man described to look like a three-legged white dwarf with a white belly. Many of the occupants of the city were demonic beings known as *yakshas*; they guarded the city with javelins and swords. The palace was created by the divine architect, Visrakarman. Located on the mythical mountain, MANDARA, the king's garden, CHAITRARATHA, was said to be the most beautiful in the world.

Source: Dalal, *Hinduism*, 18, 231; Daniélou, *Myths and Gods of India*, 136

Alcina Island

The island home to the luxury-driven entrances Alcina, she and her lascivious sister Morgana plot against their virtuous half-sister and rightful heir to their father's throne, Logistilla. The palace of Alcina was created with her magic and was described as being splendid in all way except for being in a less than desirable location upon the island.

Alcina lured great numbers of men to her island and after taking them on as a lover would transform them into plants and stones as she tired of them.

Source: Hankins, *Source and Meaning in Spenser's Allegory*, 59; Keightly, *World Guide to Gnomes, Fairies, Elves, and Other Little People*, 452–3; Manguel, *Dictionary of Imaginary Places*, 14

Alcyonian Lake (al-cee-OH-nee-an)

Variations: Bay of Troezen, Lake of Alcyon

The bottomless lake in classical Greek mythology, Alcyonian was said to be in the vicinity of Lerna, the place where the godling Hercules fought the Hydra. Dionysus (Bacchus), the god of wine, used the portal to HADES located within the lake to rescue his mother, Semele, from the UNDERWORLD. The lake was described as being a mere hundred paces in circumference and surrounded by reeds, rushes, and yellow irises.

Source: Pausanias, *Pausania's Description of Greece*, Volume 4, 302–03; Roman, *Encyclopedia of Greek and Roman Mythology*, 138, 435

Alfheim

Variations: Alf-heim, Alfheimr

In Scandinavian mythology Alfheim, located in ASGARD, was the city inhabited by the light elves, the Liosalfar; it was also the location of the home of the god of rain, sunshine, and vegetation, Freyr.

Source: Anderson, *Norse Mythology*, 439; Dunham, *History of Denmark, Sweden, and Norway*, Volume 2, 57, 133; Keightly, *World Guide to Gnomes, Fairies, Elves, and Other Little People*, 64

Alicon

In Islamic mythology Alicon is the name of the seventh and highest HEAVEN; this is where the frightful angel Azrael (Abou Jahi'a) sends the souls of the just.

Source: Brewer, *Dictionary of Phrase and Fable*, 32; More, *Gods and Heroes*, 189; Reddall, *Fact, Fancy, and Fable*, 24

Alphin

The castle Alphin is, according to the thirteenth century French prose, *Vulgate Cycle*, located 30 English miles from CAMELOT.

Source: Karr, *Arthurian Companion*, 34

Al-Salahitah

Variations: Al-Kaláhsitah, Al-Salámit, Al-Seláhitah

According to the ancient Persian fairytale, *Sindbad the Sailor* (750 CE), Al-Salahitah was an island named in the third voyage of the fictional sailor's adventures; it was renowned for its abundance of sandal-wood.

Source: Burton, *Lady Burton's Edition of Her Husband's Arabian Nights*, Volume 3, 490; Burton, *Seven Voyages of Sinbad the Sailor*, 21–29; Sprague de Camp, *Lands Beyond*, 130

Ama-no-Uki-Hashi

Variations: Ama-no-Hashidate

In ancient Shinto beliefs Ama-no-Uki-Hashi ("Floating Bridge of HEAVEN") was the floating bridge connecting the earth to TAKAMA-GA-HAR; it is guarded by a being known as Sarutahiko Ohkami ("Guardian of the Bridge") and it is he who decides who is allowed to pass.

Ama-no-Uki-Hashi was created when the husband and wife, the god and goddess Izangi and Izanami, stirred the brine of primeval chaos with their magical jeweled spear; the drops which fell free created the Japanese archipelago. The very place where the bridge touches the earth branches out into eight roads, leading to places all over the world. According to ancient tradition, the bridge collapsed and fell to earth one day while the gods were all asleep.

Source: Chamberlain, *Handbook for Travellers in Japan*, 401; Roberts, *Japanese Mythology A to Z*, 4

Amano-Iwato

Variations: Ame-no-Ihaya-to ("Door of Heavenly Rock Cavern")

In Japanese mythology the god of the sea, Susanowo, chased Amaterasu, the sun goddess, into Amano-Iwato ("cave of the Sun God"); this caused the sun to hide for a long time casting the world into a period of darkness. The goddess Ama no Uzume performed a lascivious striptease causing the other gods to laugh wildly; Amaterasu emerged from the cave out of curiosity and Susanowo was nowhere to be found.

Source: Jōya, *Quaint Customs and Manners of Japan*, Volume 3, 13, 41; Leviton, *Geomantic Year*, 469

Aman's Land

Aman, a character of Arthurian lore who appears in the *Vulgate Cycle* is typically identified with Malory's King Aniause; he, according to legend, took advantage of the war between Arthur, Ryons, and the Sesnes and attacked Carmelide (Cameliard), the land which bordered his own. Since the lore and mythology tells us the area south of Carmelide is Bertilak de Hautdcsert's territory and Bertilak is allied with Morgan le Fay, Aman's Land is likely north of Carmelide with Merset River to the south and the mouth of the river Ribble in the north.

Source: Karr, *Arthurian Companion*, 36

Amarvavti

In Hindu mythology Amarvavti is the capital city of SWARGA, the domain of the god Indra.

Source: Dowson, *Classical Dictionary of Hindu Mythology and Religion*, 127

Amaurot

In the political novel by Sir Thomas More, *Utopia* (1516), the main city Amaurot is located upon a gently sloping hill and is conveniently located to every other district; it is almost a perfect square in shape. The river Anyder ("waterless") and several streams run past the city and eventually empty out into the ocean. The head of the river has been walled up by the citizens and incorporated into the city proper; if ever the city were to be attacked the enemy would not be able to cut off or poison their water supply. Whenever the national council members of Utopia meet, they do so in Amaurot.

Source: More, *More: Utopia*, 113, 117, 123; Morley, *Ideal Commonwealths*, 69–70

Amaurote

In the political novel by Sir Thomas More, *Utopia* (1516), the main city AMAUROT had a bridge by the name of Amaurote spanning across the river Anyder ("waterless"). It is debated in the story as to whether the bridge is five-hundred paces or three-hundred paces wide.

Source: More, *More: Utopia*, 113, 117, 123; Morley, *Ideal Commonwealths*, 69–70

Amberabâd

Variations: Ambérabad', Amberbad, Amber-city

Amberabâd ("Amber City") is one of the cities or provinces in JINNISTAN, the Persian mythological equivalent of FAIRYLAND.

Source: Keightly, *World Guide to Gnomes, Fairies, Elves, and Other Little People*, 16; Smedley, *Occult Sciences*, 19, 775; Spence, *Encyclopædia of Occultism*, 177; Yardley, *Supernatural in Romantic Fiction*, 53

Ameleouth

In the Old Testament's book of Exodus, the demon Abezi-Thibod claimed to have once resided in Ameleouth, the first HEAVEN, but is currently trapped in a cave under the Red Sea.

Source: Belanger, *Dictionary of Demons*, 15; Conybeare, *Jewish Quarterly Review*, Volume 11, 4

Ameles

The ancient Greek tale, *The Myth of Er*, which appears at the end of Plato's *Republic*, the souls of the dead are said to arrive upon

the PLAINS OF LETHE, along the banks of the river the UNDERWORLD river Ameles ("Careless"); it is from this river where the departed drink from in order to forget their worldly lives. The water from Ameles cannot be contained in any vessel; it must be consumed before a soul is allowed to be reincarnated.

Source: Plato, *Dialogues of Plato*, Volume 2, 116; Rose, *Handbook of Greek Mythology*, 80

Amentet

Variations: Land of No Return, the West

In Egyptian mythology Amentet was the place in the afterlife were the dead waited en-mass for the boat of the sun god, Ra, to pass through. Those individuals who were either lucky enough to have secured the magical words for permission to travel through TUAT or worshiped the god in life were able to secure a seat.

Source: Mercatante, *Who's Who in Egyptian Mythology*, 7–8

Amenthes

According to the classical Greeks, in Egyptian mythology, the process of a soul traveling from AMENTET through TUAT as it sat upon the boat of the sun god, Ra, as it journeyed through the realms of Osiris and Seker was known as *amenthes*.

Source: Cooper, *Archaic Dictionary*, 45; Mercatante, *Who's Who in Egyptian Mythology*, 7–8

Amenti

Variations: Country of Loving Silence, House with No Exit, Ker-neter ("ghostland" or "Land of the Gods"), Land of no Return, Land of the Setting Sun, Neter-xer ("The Funeral Place"), Otamersker, That Which Receives and Gives

In Egyptian mythology Amenti ("the hidden") was the UNDERWORLD; there are fifteen gates which must be passed through to enter into the realm of Osiris; Amenti is the land of deep sleep and darkness, those who stay in this place will remain incorruptible but will not be able to recognize their father or mother, have no feeling or love for their children or wife.

Divided into four regions, Amenti is the location of the Great Judgment; here is where the final separation of good and bad souls is made and fixed forever. There are seven entry gates: Arm of Earth, Concealer of Forms, Destroyer of Conscience, Punishing Spirit, Revealer of Fortune, Sharpening Flame, and Total Darkness. The gate Total Darkness is guarded by a three-headed being (one of a crocodile, a dog, and a lion).

An angry and wrathful god by the name of All-Dead resides here and the residents of Amenti fear him; he accepts no offerings made to him, does not hear prayers made to him.

Source: Blavatsky, *Theosophical Glossary*, 18; Bonwick, *Egyptian Belief and Modern Thought*, 46–50; Cooper, *Archaic Dictionary*, 45–46; Wiedemann, *Religion of the Ancient Egyptians*, 124

Amh

In the Egyptian UNDERWORLD, Amh was the exit gate of the funeral region of AMENTI.

Source: Bonwick, *Egyptian Belief and Modern Thought*, 46–50; Cooper, *Archaic Dictionary*, 47

Amr's Tomb

Variations: Amhar's Tomb, Amir's Tomb

In Welsh Arthurian lore Amr was an illegitimate child or a child from King Arthur's first wife; Other than being one of the four chamberlains who watched over Arthur's bed, little else is known of him. Named as a son of Arthur in *The Mabinogion*, Amr's Tome is said to be located beside a stream known as the "Source Anir"; his is the earelist written story of the King slaying one of his sons.

Source: Manguel, *Dictionary of Imaginary Places*, 22; Tichelaar, *King Arthur's Children*, 13–15

Amsvartnir (am-svärt'nir)

Variations: Amsvartne, Amsvartner, Ams-VArtnir

Amsvartnir ("gloomy" or "red-black") is a lake in NIFLEHEIM, according to Norse lore, that surrounds the lonely island LYNGVI where the wolf Fenrir was bound by the god Odin

and the other Æsir with a silken cord; he will remain captive here until Ragnarok.

Source: Anderson, *Norse Mythology*, 439; Daly, *Norse Mythology A to Z*, 4; Guerber, *Myths of the Norsemen*, 92; Grimes, *Norse Myths*, 254

Andhakupa

According to Hindu and Vedic mythology Andhakupa ("Blind well" or "tenth gate") is the ninth of the twenty-eight NARAKAS (HELLS) located in a providence in the kingdom of Yama; occupants are the souls of those individuals who hurt, killed, or teased creatures of the lower species and those who killed Brahmins or holy people. These unfortunate souls are under constant assault from birds, flies, lice, mosquitoes, snakes, reptiles, worms, and any other creature it hurt or killed during its life. Unable to rest, the souls are condemned to perpetually walk until the time of their punishment has expired or be attacked by the animals they once tormented.

Source: Garg, *Encyclopaedia of the Hindu World: Ak–Aq*, Volume 1, 450; Prabhupāda, *Śrīmad Bhāgavatam*, 903; Parmeshwaranand, *Encyclopaedic Dictionary of Purāṇas*, 721

Andhatamisra

According to Hindu and Vedic mythology Andhatamisra ("Utter darkness of the soul") is the second of the twenty-eight HELL planets created by the Supreme Lord; the occupants here are those individuals who in life cheated, seduced another man's wife, or stole money or possessions. Those who committed suicide were condemned to this HELL, and here the agents of Yama would bind them tightly with cords, increasing the pressure until they blacked out with pain. When the soul regained consciousness and tried to flee Yama's agents would hunt them down and bind them up again. There is or complete darkness in this HELL.

Source: Garg, *Encyclopaedia of the Hindu World: Ak–Aq*, Volume 1, 450; Prabhupāda, *Śrīmad Bhāgavatam*, 903; Parmeshwaranand, *Encyclopaedic Dictionary of Purāṇas*, 721

Andvarafors

The waterfall Andvarafors of Norse mythology was where the dwarf Andvare hid himself in the shape-shifted form of a pike.

Source: Anderson, *Norse Mythology*, 440; Thorpe, *Edda Saemundar hinns Fróda*, 47, 48

Annwfn (an'uvn)

Variations: Annwn, Annwyn, CAER WYDYR

In Welsh lore Annwfn ("great depth," "inner-world," or "non-world") is the OTHERWORLD, a counterpart to the world of man, neither a HEAVEN nor a HELL, but rather a happy place filled with dance, drink, and food. Annwfn has two countries and these two kings are mortal enemies with one another; they often go to war against one another. Although it sometimes appears as an island just over the horizon, it is generally regarded as a lower world, its occupants, who live lives very similar to our own, have access to the upper world where humanity dwells. Additionally the people of Annfwn possessed powers greater than those of mankind. After the introduction of Christianity, Annwfn came to be seen as HELL.

Source: Maier, *Dictionary of Celtic Religion and Culture*, 17; Matson, *Celtic Mythology, A to Z*, 5; Monaghan, *Encyclopedia of Celtic Mythology and Folklore*, 4

Anostos

Variation: Anostus

The historian and contemporary of Plato, Theopsompos once wrote of a conversation between King Midas of PHRYGIA and the satyr Silenos. The satyr told the king the people of the outer continent were twice as large as them and lived twice as long. One region known as Anostos ("Place of No Return") was described as being constantly veiled in a red mist similar to a sunset, as it never experienced total dark or light. Anostos as surrounded by two rivers, Lype ("Greif") and Hedon ("Pleasure"), the banks of each were heavily lined with trees. Those who ate the fruit of the trees which grew off of the river Lype cried constantly thereafter until they wept themselves to death while those who ate the fruit which grew off of the river Hedon all former desires come to rest and begins to age backward.

Source: Manguel, *Dictionary of Imaginary Places*, 26; Nansen, *In Northern Mists*, 17; Sprague de Camp, *Lost Continents*, 15

Antenora

In Dante Alighieri's epic poem *Divina Commedia* ("Divine Comedy") (1320) the river Antenora is located in the second ring of the ninth circle of HELL; it was one of the four tributaries of the river COCYTUS (see CAINA, JUDECCA, and PTOLOMEA). Named for Antenor, the Trojan warrior who turned traitor and betrayed his country and sided with the Greeks in Homer's *Iliad*, traitors to their city or political party are immersed in Antenora's icy waters.

Alighieri utilized names and locations from existing mythologies; many of the demons mentioned in the poem were pulled from established hierarchies for example. Because his work, which was meant to be an allegory for the soul's journey to the path of God was well read and accepted, the names and locations he created for the sake of good storytelling became accepted into mythology as well.

Source: Lansing, *Dante Encyclopedia*, 49; Zimmerman, *Inferno of Dante Alighieri*, 224, 225

Anthemoessa

Variations: Anthemusa

In the mythology of the ancient Greeks, Anthemoessa ("Flowery") was the island home of the sirens.

Source: Evelyn-White, *Hesiod, the Homeric Hymns, and Homerica*, 181; Littleton, *Gods, Goddesses, and Mythology*, Volume 10, 1269; Roman, *Encyclopedia of Greek and Roman Mythology*, 443

Antichthon

A planet created by the Pythagoreans, Antichthon ("opposite earth") was intended to bring the number of movable heavily bodies, the earth, five planets, the moon, the sun, and the sphere of fixed stars, up to the harmonious and perfect number ten. It was expressly stated in their beliefe that Antichthon could not be seen from the earth.

Source: Lewis, *Historical Survey of the Astronomy of the Ancients* 124, 127; Sprague de Camp, *Lands Beyond*, 180

Antillia

Variations: Aira, Anhuib, Ansalli, Ansesseli, Ansodi, Ansolli, Antigla, Antilae, Antilia, Atulae, Con, Isle of the Seven Cities ("*Ilha das Sete Cidades*"), Island of the Seven Cities, Septe Cites, Seven Cities

A legendary island in the Atlantic Ocean, Antillia first appeared on the Beccario map of 1435 due west of Portugal and Spain. According to Iberian legend, seven Christian bishops left Hispania with their respective flocks after the Muslim conquest seeking to avoid persecution. Sailing westward, they eventually came upon an island, named it Antillia, and established seven settlements. This island routinely appeared on maps until the Atlantic was more routinely sailed and accurately mapped.

Because Antillia's shape was originally drawn similar to the later discovered Cuba, geographers assumed an error was made earlier and thereafter to the region as the Antilles.

Source: Babcock, *Legendary Islands of the Atlantic*, 60–73; Carter, *Lost Worlds*, 135–36; Childress, *Lost Cities of North and Central America*, 214–15

Aoncos

One of the many Irish OTHERWORLDS, Aoncos was distinguished from the others by the silver pillar that held it aloft above the ocean waves.

Source: Monaghan, *Encyclopedia of Celtic Mythology and Folklore*, 21

Aornum (a-OR-num)

Variations: Thesprotian Aornum

In Greek mythology Aornum, located near the river ACHERON, was said to be one of the two likely locations where the legendary mu-

sician Orpheus found a cavern which opened up into the UNDERWORLD; he descended into it to retrieve his deceased wife, Eurydice, and return her to the land of the living.

Source: Frazer, *Folk-Lore in the Old Testament*, Volume 2, 526; Graves, *Greek Myths*, 28, 31

Appamana Subha

Appamana Subha, the realm of the infinite aura, is the name of the fifteenth HEAVEN of Buddhism.

Source: Acharya, *Indian Philosophical Terms*, 545; Garg, *Encyclopaedia of the Hindu World: Ak–Aq*, Volume 1, 559; Garrett, *Classical Dictionary of India*, 39

Appamanabha

Appamanabha, the realm of the infinite luster, is the name of the twelfth HEAVEN of Buddhism.

Source: Acharya, *Indian Philosophical Terms*, 545; Garrett, *Classical Dictionary of India*, 39; Garg, *Encyclopaedia of the Hindu World: Ak–Aq*

Apratisht'ba

In Hindu mythology Apratisht'ba ("immeasurably deep" or "supportless") is the fifth of the twenty-eight NARAKAS (HELLS) located in a providence in the kingdom of Yama; it is filled with the instruments of torture. Here, sinners are fastened to wheels and spun for a thousand years, blood flows from their mouths and tears from their eyes.

Source: Garg, *Encyclopaedia of the Hindu World: Ak–Aq;* Garrett, *Classical Dictionary of India*, 40; Wilson, *Vishńu Puráńa*, 215–16

Apsu

Variations: Abzu, Engur

The mythological freshwater ocean from Akkadian, Babylonian, and Sumerian mythology, Apsu was once a great and powerful god, the husband and mate of the dragon, Tiamat; their union created many lesser gods whose restless nature and noisy behavior drove him to seek their destruction. Ea, the chosen champion of the siblings, placed a spell on his father and removed his will, placing him in an un-breakable sleep, effectively killing him. Contained in the underground his watery body becomes the home of Ea Eaku, lord of Apsu.

Source: Leick, *Dictionary of Ancient Near Eastern Mythology*, 11; Lurker, *Routledge Dictionary of Gods and Goddesses, Devils and Demons*, 17

Araboth

Variations: Arabot

In Jewish lore, Araboth ("the clouds") is the seventh of the seven HEAVENS; this is the dwelling place of God as well as the ofanim and seraphim. Ruled over by the angel Cassiel, the angel of dread, fear, grace, and love, lives in this HEAVEN as well as the souls awaiting birth.

Sources: Demy, *Answers to Common Questions About Heaven and Eternity* 83; Webster, *Encyclopedia of Angels*, 85

al A'raf

Variations: Aaraaf, Al Arat, Araf, PARADISE of Fools

The LIMBO of Islamic mythology, al A'raf ("the partition") is described in the Koran as the mystical LIMBO-like domain and wall that separates and lies between Djanna (PARADISE) and JAHANNAM (HELL). The occupants of this region are varied consisting of angels in the form of men; martyrs, the patriarchs and prophets; those individuals who in life were incapable of being morally good or evil, such as infants and the mentally challenged; those who have gone to war, without their parents leave and therein suffered martyrdom; and those whose good and evil works are so equal that they exactly counterpoise each other and therefore deserve neither reward nor punishment. The occupants who will remain here for all eternity have the ability to speak with the occupants in the adjoining domains. Interestingly, the souls in HEAVEN when looking into the al A'raf will only see HELL and those damned souls in HELL who are looking back will only see the individuals who are in HEAVEN.

Source: Hughes, *Dictionary of Islam*, 20–21; Smith, *Century Cyclopedia of Names*, Volume 6, 70;

Stork, *A–Z Guide to the Qur'an*, 32; Van Scott, *Encyclopedia of Hell*, 10

Arallu

Variations: Aralu, Araru, Anduruna, Ganzir, IRKALLA, Kigallu, Mat La Tari ("Land of no Return"), Shualu

The ancient Sumerians believed Arallu was a gloomy and lifeless desart UNDERWORLD where the dead were judge, the wicked punished, and the righteous dwelt; it was a realm of darkness filled with mutated beasts and monsters. It was ruled by Queen Ereshkigal and her royal consort, Nerga. In the west, the place of the setting sun, there are seven entrances with seven gates which lead into Arallu; its gatekeeper was Nedu. Should a person die and not be buried his soul would not be allowed to gain entry into Arallu and would be forced to wander the earth in a state of discontentment.

Source: Budge, *Babylonian Life and History*, 90; *Babylonian Religion and Mythology*, 35, 44; Turner, *Dictionary of Ancient Deities*, 64–65; Van Scott, *Encyclopedia of Hell*, 23

Arberth

A Welsh mythological site, Arberth is a FAIRY FORT said to be in the kingdom of Pwyll; its people are said to have visions.

Source: John, *Popular Studies in Mythology, Romance and Folklore*, Volumes 11–16, 22, 36; Monaghan, *Encyclopedia of Celtic Mythology and Folklore*, 23

Arbray

According to Sir Thomas Malory's *Morte d'Arthur* (1485) Arbray was the location where Sir Sadok, fleeing from Mark's ambush at TENTAGIL, passed LYONESSE and met up with Sir Dinas the seneschal of Cornwall. At Arbray the two men gathered the people together and stocked the town and castle of Cornwall; it seems logical to assume Arbray Castle is within the lands of LYONESSE.

Source: Barber, *Legends of King Arthur*, 426; Karr, *Arthurian Companion*, 43–44

Arbuda

According to Hindu and Vedic mythology Arbuda ("blistering," "a hundred million," and "water-bubble") is a dark, frozen, and vast NARAKA (HELL) surrounded by ice covered mountains; it is constantly in the midst of a blizzard. It is so cold here blisters break out on any exposed skin; all of its inhabitants are naked. The length of time a person is to remain in Arbuda is same time it would take to empty a barrel of sesame seeds if only one seed was removed every 100 years. Occupants of this NARAKA are described as looking like *arbudas* ("first month fetus" or "round mass").

The length of time one stays in the COLD HELLS is very precise if not specific. For each person in the HELL there is a grain room filled with 80 bushels of sesame seeds. Once every 100 years one seed is removed. The length of time for each descending HELL is 20 times the previous.

Source: Dalal, *Hinduism*, 2; Faustino, *Heaven and Hell*, 30; Garg, *Encyclopaedia of the Hindu World: Ar–Az*, 588; Hastings, *Encyclopedia of Religion and Ethics*, Part 7, 133; Mew, *Traditional Aspects of Hell*, 98

Ard Éireann

Variations: Ard Eireann

In Irish lore the mountains in Ireland known as the Slieve Bloom includes a peak called Ard Éireann ("Height of Ireland"). Although this is not the tallest peak in the country the summit was said to be the birthplace of the island of Ireland.

Source: Colum, *Treasury of Irish Folklore*, 213; Monaghan, *Encyclopedia of Celtic Mythology and Folklore*, 23

Argustus

Variations: Arguste

In Arthurian lore, Sir Lancelot, while on the Grail Quest came upon a forest and "saw a fair plain and besides that a fair castle." Upon approach to Argustus the knight noted there was a tournament in progress; half the knights, being sinful, dressed in black and the other half were the good knights of Sir Eliezer

dressed in white. Sir Lancelot joined on the side of the black knights because they were losing but he did not realize they were corrupted. Not only was Lancelot defeated but also shamed. Argustus is believed by Arthurian scholars to be in either northern LOGRES or southern Scotland.

Source: Bruce, *Arthurian Name Dictionary*, 32; Karr, *Arthurian Companion*, 44

Argyre

In ancient Greek and Roman mythology, Argyre ("silver land") was a mythical island located in the east and said to be made of silver.

Source: Lemprière, *Classical Dictionary*, 189

Arimaspi

Roman author, naturalist, natural philosopher, and army and naval commander, Gaius Plinius Secundus, better known as Pliny the Elder wrote of the nation of Arimaspi ("one eye") in his book, "*Natural History*," VII, ii. There, he described the one-eyed people of Arimaspi as being in perpetual war with the local griffins over the gold which is mined.

Source: Anthon, *Classical Dictionary*, Volume 1, 193; Pliny the Elder, *Natural History of Pliny*, Volume 2, 123; Sprague de Camp, *Lands Beyond*, 88

Arroy

Variations: Forest of Adventure

In Arthurian lore and according to Sir Thomas Malory's *Morte d'Arthur* (1485) Arroy is a mysterious country and forest, as any knight who enters into it will happen upon an opportunity for an adventure. For instance, when Sirs Gawine, Marhaus, and Uwaine entered into the forest of Arroy they came upon three damsles near a fountain and chose the women to be their guides.

Source: Manguel, *Dictionary of Imaginary Places*, 36–37; Karr, *Arthurian Companion*, 45; Pyle, *Story of King Arthur and His Knights*, 66, 250

Arsareth

Variations: Ararath

According to the apocalyptic book *Apoca-*

lypse of Ezra (AD 100) (also called *4 Esdras* or *Latin Esdras*) Arsareth ("another land") was the land the Ten Lost Tribes of the Jews were taken to after their capture by King Osea. This land was a year and a half journey to arrive at and apart from the captives, was devoid of mankind.

Source: Brough, *Lost Tribes*, 28–29, 115; Sprague de Camp, *Lands Beyond*, 162–63

Asabru (āsa-bru)

Variations: Asa-bridge, Ásbrú, BIFROST, Bridge of the Æsir

A sacred bridge of the gods in Norse mythology, Asabru ("rainbow") was said to be constructed of air, fire, and water; it was described as having changing and quivering hues. The gods used this bridge to travel to earth or the URDARBRUNNR WELL at the foot of YGGDRASIL. Asabru is an archaic name for BIFROST.

Source: Grimes, *Norse Myths*, 225; Guerber, *Myths of the Norsemen*, 14

Asgard

Variations: Ásegard, Asgaard, Ásgard, Ásgardhr, Asgardr, Ásgardr, Ásgarðr ("Enclosure of the Æsir"), Asgarth, Ásgarth, Ásgarthr, Esageard

In Norse mythology Asgard ("Aser-yard"), one of the NINE WORLDS and located beneath MUSPELHEIM, was the vast city built by Odin and his two brothers after the death of Ymer, it was designed to be well defended against the attacks of the Muspelheim and the Vanir. Asgard was described as being a land more fertile than any other and as equally blessed having a plethora of gold and jewels.

Odin's great hall, GLADSHEIM, was located here as well as the abodes of the twelve principal gods: ALFHEIM was the abode of Freyr, BREIDABLIK was the abode of Baldur, FOLKVANGUR was the abode of Freya, GLADSHEIM was the abode of Odin, GLITNER was the abode of Forsete, HIMMELBIERG was the abode of Heimdal, LANDVIDE was the abode of Vidar, NOATUN was the abode of Niord, SOEQUABECK was the abode of Sage, THRUDEIM was the abode of Thor, THRYMHEIM was the abode of Skada, VALASKIALF was the abode of Vale (Vile), and YDALE was the abode of Uller.

Source: Dunham, *History of Denmark, Sweden, and Norway*, Volume 2, 55; Evans, *Dictionary of Mythology*, 32; Grimes, *Norse Myths*, 255; Guerber, *Myths of the Norsemen*, 11

Ashihara-no-Nakatsukuni

Variations: Ashiwara-no-kuni

In ancient Shinto beliefs Ashihara-no-Nakatsukuni ("Central Land of Reed Plains"), a realm for souls to live out their afterlife, is believed to be located on the earth; it is connected to TAKAMA-GA-HAR and YOMI by an axis called *ame no mihashira*.

Source: Chamberlain, *Handbook for Travellers in Japan*, 402; Swanson, *Nanzan Guide to Japanese Religions*, 132

Asipatravana

Variations: Asi-Patravana, Asi (ta) Patram

In Hindu mythology Asipatravana ("the leaves of whose trees are swords") is the seventh of the twenty-eight NARAKAS (HELLS) ruled over by Yama; it is located beneath the earth and water where souls are punished for the sin of wantonly cutting down trees or leaving the path of the Vedas without an emergency. There is a forest in the center of this HELL; the leaves upon the trees growing here are sword blades. Damned souls are attracted to this place by its offering of cool shade however the wind blows the leaves from their branches and they fall, flaming, to the ground. The sinners of this NARAKAS are those who abandoned their *svadharma* (one's own duty) and accepted another's.

Source: Prabhupāda, *Śrīmad Bhāgavatam*, 903; Parmeshwaranand, *Encyclopaedic Dictionary of Purāṇas*, 721; Wilson, *Oriental Translation Fund*, Volume 52, 209

Asphodel Meadow

Named for the grayish and unattractive plant which grows on barren grounds, the Asphodel Meadow is a bleak and monochrome landscape where the half-life shades who in life were neither evil nor virtuous, live; the majority of the deceased live here. Described by Homer in his epic poem, *The Odyssey*, in this part of TARTATUS game abounds, it is essentially a vast landscape of asphodel flowers, the favorite food of the Greek dead.

Source: Graves, *Greek Myths*, n.p.; Hard, *Routledge Handbook of Greek Mythology*, 109; Westmoreland, *Ancient Greek Beliefs*, 69

Assiah

Variations: Asia, 'Asiyah, Olam Asiyah ("World of Action")

The fourth and densest of the four Cabalistic worlds, Assiah ("action") is the world of action and matter. On the Tree of Life it is represented by the ten celestial spheres and corresponds with Malkuth.

Source: Godwin, *Godwin's Cabalistic Encyclopedia*, 34–35; Greer, *New Encyclopedia of the Occult*, 42

Astolat

Variations: Ascolat, Caer Gwlodd, Calot, Escalot, Gwlodd, Shallott

A legendary city in Arthurian lore, Astolat was the home of Elaine, the Lady of Astolate; her father Sir Bernard; and her two brothers Lavaine and Tirre.

Source: Ashe, *New Arthurian Encyclopedia*, 430; Ashley, *Mammoth Book of King Arthur*, 609–10; Malory, *Le Morte Darthur*, 557

Astral Plane

In occultism the astral plane is a realm of existence which lies next to the physical world near the etheric and mental planes. Having no landscape this white and formless place is filled with astral matter, a substance which can be used by practitioners of magic to create by visualization thought forms which can then manifest in the real world.

The astral plane is divided into two levels, a higher and a lower level. The higher or divine level as it is sometimes called is solar by nature. Containing the blueprint for all things, this level reflects the emotions of individual and the collective unconscious. The lower level is the home of astral beings and the first realm a soul reaches after death.

Source: Greer, *New Encyclopedia of the Occult*, 43; Guiley, *Encyclopedia of Magic and Alchemy*, 21

Astral Temple

In occult philosophy an astral temple is a setting created by a practitioner of magic in the ASTRAL PLANE; within this temple, one is no longer bound by the rules of reality but acts more like a dream experience which can be controlled by the user similar to lucid dreaming. Typically these temples contain doorways to the ASTRAL PLANE as well as the four corners and the four elements and through these portals magical energies can pass through when spells are being cast.

Source: Grimassi, *Encyclopedia of Wicca and Witchcraft*, 33; Rabinowitz, *Encyclopedia of Modern Witchcraft and Neo-Paganism*, 18–19

Aśvakarṇa

Variations: Assakaṇṇa

The Aśvakarṇa Mountains are the sixth mountain chain surrounding SUMERU, the central would mountain in in Hindu cosmology; it is both 2,500 *yojanas* tall and wide. The measure of a single *yojanas* has never been clear, some scholars say it is approximately four and a half miles while other say it ranges between seven and nine miles.

Source: Howard, *Imagery of the Cosmological Buddha*, 66–68; Nagao, *Wisdom, Compassion, and the Search for Understanding*, 192

Atala, Caverns of

In Hindu lore the Caverns of Atala are believed to be the first of the seven underground levels in a vast cavernous system which stretches from Benares, India to Lake Manosarowar, Tibet. In all of the regions (MAHATALA, PATALA, RASATALA, SUTALA, TALATALA, and VITALA), there are beautiful cities built by the architect, Maya. This realm is ruled over by Mahā-Māya.

Source: Dowson, *Classical Dictionary of Hindu Mythology, and Religion*, 233; Parmeshwaranand, *Encyclopaedic Dictionary of Purāṇas*, 1010–1012

Atata

Variations: Ababa, Ata Ta, Hell of Chattering Teeth

The third of the eight cold NARAKA (HELLS) named in Buddhism atata is said to be located two-thousand leagues beneath the continent of JAMBUDVIPA. Occupants of this NARAKA are so tormented with unbearable cold the only sound they can utter is *"at-at,"* the sound of chattering teeth.

The length of time one stays in the EIGHT COLD HELLS is very precise if not specific. For each person in the HELL there is a grain room filled with 80 bushels of sesame seeds; once every 100 years one seed is removed. The length of time for each descending HELL is 20 times the previous.

Source: Alexander, *Body, Mind, Spirit Miscellany*, 150; Faustino, *Heaven and Hell*, 30; Hastings, *Encyclopedia of Religion and Ethics Part*, Part 7, 133; Mew, *Traditional Aspects of Hell*, 98

Atlantis (at-LAN-tis)

The story of Atlantis begins with an old literary device, the narrator assuring the reader that every word they were about to read was true. It first appears in *Timaios*, a treatise on Pythagorean philosophy between Socrates and three of his friends, Hermokrates, Kritias, and Timaios.

A fictitious island-continent first written of by Plato ("broad-shouldered") in his works *Critias* and *Timaeus*, Atlantis ("daughter of Atlas") has a specific beginning going back to the point of its origin by the Greek philosopher in the fourth-century BCE. Prior to the material written about Atlantis in these two dialogues, it did not exist; Aristotle, Plato's own pupil implied in his works that Atlantis was an allegory. In essence the story of Atlantis was a fictionalized version of Plato's *Republic*.

Ruled by a rich communistic military caste, every member of its society was brave, handsome, and virtuous. Five sets of twin boys were the first rulers of Atlantis; Atlas, the eldest of the siblings was the high king and he ruled over the nine lesser kings, his brothers.

The island was divided equally between the brothers; the high king was given the central hill and its surrounding areas. It was in the palace here where the kings would meet to discuss laws, pass judgment, and pay tribute to their patron god, Poseidon.

Although the land was fertile growing fruits, nuts, and other vegetation it also provided ample crops as the climate was such it allowed for two full harvests each year. Many animals, including elephants, roamed freely on the island. In spite of its over-abundance of food stores, Atlantis did not trade with its Greek neighbors.

The island-continent was described as being larger than Asia Minor and Libya combined and was set in the Atlantic Ocean, somewhere west of the Pillars of Hercules.

To enable trade more easily amongst themselves a water canal was dug through the rings of the island running south towards the sea for five and half miles. The main city of Atlantis was located just outside of the outer ring and covered a circle of eleven miles across the plains. This region was the most densely populated area, home to the bulk of its citizenry. Beyond lay a fertile plane 330 miles long and 110 miles wide.

Its natural resources from the towering mountains in the north were gold, orichalc, and silver; mineral resources it was overly abundant with. Lakes, meadows, rivers, and villages dotted the mountainsides.

The architecture was described as nothing less than marvelous; it had drill grounds, harbors, parks, racetracks, and many public works. The shipyards of Atlantis were filled with triremes and chariots ran up and down its paved streets. High walls with towers protected the main city, though it had never been attacked; its castle was complicated yet elaborate sporting a grand temple to Poseidon with a hot and cold running spring.

For generations the people of Atlantis lead virtuous lives but over time they began to become corrupted by greed and power. When the god Zeus saw what had become of these people he grew angry and called an assembly of the gods in order to pass judgment on them.

It was decided to destroy the island and in a single blast of violence lasting a day and a night, Atlantis and all of its people were consumed by the sea.

Although there is no evidence to support the idea that Plato's Atlantis was ever anything more than a bit of literature, archeologist and treasure hunters have been actively looking for it ever since the discovery of the location of the Battlefield of Troy in 1871 by amateur archaeologist and German chemist Heinrich Schliemann. It was during this frenzy in 1891 when Sir Arthur Evans discovered what he called the Palace of King Minos proving beyond a doubt that Minoan civilization was real. As both men also believed Atlantis once existed, the hunt to find it only increased. In spite of the fact Plato clearly tells his readers almost exactly where the lost city once stood, it has been rumored to be discovered in over forty different locations, including the Azores, the Caucasus Mountains, north of Scandinavia, Santorini, South Africa, southern Sweden,the straits of Gibraltar, Svalbard Archipelagos, and the island of Crete.

Source: Dale, *The Book of Where*, 20; Evans, *Dictionary of Mythology*, 36; Sprague de Camp, *Lands Beyond*, 9–14, 29, 32, 34–35, 41–42

Attapa

Attapa is the name of the nineteenth HEAVEN of Buddhism.

Source: Garg, *Encyclopaedia of the Hindu World: Ar–Az,* Volume 1, 796; Garrett, *Classical Dictionary of India*, 64

Atziluth

Variations: Olam ha-Atziluth

The first and highest of the four Cabalistic worlds Atziluth ("nearness"), the world of nobility, is the divine world of archetypes. Attributed to Kether, Atziluth's element is fire; it is also the residence of God and the superior angels.

Source: Godwin, *Godwin's Cabalistic Encyclopedia*, 37; Greer, *New Encyclopedia of the Occult*, 42

Aukumea

In Maori mythology, Aukumea is the eighth of the ten divisions of HEAVEN; in one version of the telling of the demigod Tawhaki there are twelve divisions but sometimes there are as many as fourteen and as few as two named. Aukumea is where the spirits live for a short while.

Source: Craig, *Dictionary of Polynesian Mythology*, 56; Grey, *Maori Lore*, 12; Mead, *Tāwhaki*, 58

Aulis

In Greek mythology, Aulis was the port city from where the Achaean fleet assembled just before the expedition sailed for Troy. Calchas the seer announced the only way Artemis would lift the wind was if Agamemnon offered his daughter Iphigenia up in sacrifice in exchange for a favorable wind.

Source: Evans, *Dictionary of Mythology*, 38; Westmoreland, *Ancient Greek Beliefs*, 692

Aurvangar

Aurvangar ("the gravelly wetlands") was home to the dwarves, collectively known as the Lovarr, who traveled from Svarin's grave mound; their names were Ai, Alf, Eikinskjaldi, Fal, Fio, Frosti, Ginnar, Ingi, Skafio, Skirvir, and Virvir. Alternate names for the Lovarr are: Ai, Alfr, Dolgthrasir, Draupnir, Eikinskialdi, Glofnn, Har, Haugspori, Hlaevangr, Skafdr, Virvir, and Yngvi.

Source: Sturlusonar, *Prose Edda of Snorri Sturluson*, 42; Wägner, *Asgard and the Gods*, 311

Autoia

In Maori mythology, Autoia is the seventh of the ten divisions of HEAVEN; in one version of the telling of the demigod Tawhaki there are twelve divisions but sometimes there are as many as fourteen and as few as two named. Autoia is where the human soul is created.

Source: Craig, *Dictionary of Polynesian Mythology*, 56; Grey, *Maori Lore*, 12; Mead, *Tāwhaki*, 58

Avalon

Variations: Affallon, Apple Island, Insuls Avallonis ("Isle of Apples"), Avillion

In the Welsh Arthurian tradition the Island of Avalon was the land of the dead, a place where no one ever grew old and their needs were fulfilled by thought. According to Geoffrey of Monmouth, one of the major figures in the development of British historiography it was ruled by Morgan le Fey who lead a sisterhood of nine. Avalon was associated with Glastonbury Tor a hill near Somerset, England was once nearly encircled by water. Since 1191 the hill has been considered a FAIRY ISLAND.

Source: Ashliman, *Fairy Lore*, 16; Evans, *Dictionary of Mythology*, 39–40; Keightly, *World Guide to Gnomes, Fairies, Elves, and Other Little People*, 45; Lacy, *Arthurian Encyclopedia*, 32–35

Avata-Nirodhana

According to Hindu and Vedic mythology Avata-Nirodhana ("a dark well") is a dark NARAKA (HELL) described as being a well filled with poisonous fumes and thick smoke. The souls here are those who had in life confined others in granaries, mountain caves, or wells; these evil-doers constantly choke and suffer.

Source: Garg, *Encyclopaedia of the Hindu World: Ar–Az*, 836; Prabhupāda, *Śrīmad-Bhāgavatam*, Volume 5, Part 2, 441, 472

Avernus (un-VUR-nuhs)

Variations: Aornos

According to ancient Roman mythology Avernus was a small lake in a volcanic crater; its underwater caves were believed to open lead to the entrance of the UNDERWORLD, TARTARUS.

Source: Evans, *Dictionary of Mythology*, 40; Evslin, *Gods, Demigods, and Demons*, 23

Avici

Variations: Avīci, Avichi, Avívhi

According to Hindu and Vedic mythology Avici ("waterless") is the twentieth of the twenty-eight NARAKAS (HELLS) located in a providence in the kingdom of Yama; described as being made of solid stone which is in the form of ocean waves, but not so large as to offer shelter. The souls here are those individ-uals who in life bore false witness or outright lied during a business transaction or while offering charity. Here, the souls are taken to the top of a mountain and thrown, head first, 100 *yojans* (2,400,000 feet/930 miles) into the ocean of stone, shattering the body upon impact; the soul is instantly restored and the act is repeated over and over again.

In Buddhist lore, Avici is the lowest of the 136 UNDERWORLDS, it is reserved for the most egregious offenders, those who rejected Buddha and his holy teachings. Souls here are purged of their sins to prepare them for reincarnation; each "hell-year" is fifty earth years long and arriving at this HELL is a minimum sentence of 500 hell-years.

In Indian Buddhism, Avichi ("Uninterrupted") the eighth and lowest of the EIGHT HOT HELLS; it is the HELL of Incessant suffering. The souls here are the ones who committed one of the five great premeditated sins: killing an Arhat, killing one's father, killing one's mother, disrupting the Sangha, or harming the Buddha.

Source: Garg, *Encyclopaedia of the Hindu World: Ar–Az*, 841; Mew, *Traditional Aspects of Hell*, 41; Parmeshwaranand, *Encyclopaedic Dictionary of Purāṇas*, 722; Van Scott, *Encyclopedia of Hell*, 25

Awiha

Awiha ("not thinking") is the name of the eighteenth HEAVEN of Buddhism.

Source: Eitel, *Hand-Book for the Student of Chinese Buddhism,* 21; Garrett, *Classical Dictionary of India*, 68

Ayahpana

According to Hindu and Vedic mythology Ayahpana is the twenty-first of the twenty-eight NARAKAS (HELLS) located in a providence in the kingdom of Yama. Here, those who belong in the first three classes—the brahmanas, the ksatryas, and the vaisyas—who drink Soma. For punishment, these sinners are forced to drink smelted iron.

Source: Parmeshwaranand, *Encyclopaedic Dictionary of Purāṇas*, 722; Rengarajan, *Glossary of Hinduism*, 67

Babel, Tower of (bay'bul)

In the Old Testament Book of Genesis (11, 1–10) at one time all the people of the earth spoke the same language; on a plain in the land of Shinar it was decided to bake bricks and make a city that had a tower so tall it touched the HEAVENS. This plan was conceived so the builders would have fame and a sense of community. The Lord saw the city and its tower and how the people were working as a single unit. Concerned the people of the world would be able to achieve any goal they set their mind to, the Lord confused their language and scattered the people over the planet.

Zagguarts, or towers as they were called in Babylon were common place; in Mesopotamia, the most famous of these, Etemenanki, as actually called the Tower of Babel.

Source: Dale, *Book of Where*, 21; Mills, *Mercer Dictionary of the Bible*, 81

Babiagora

Lakes which lie between Hungary and Poland which have a gloomy and melancholy nature are often used for hydromancy, a type of divination.

Source: Spence, *Encyclopædia of Occultism*, 58; Waite, *Occult Sciences*, 138

Balanton

Variations: Baranton

A marvelous cold spring in Arthurian lore Balanton was said to bubble or boil up from beneath a pine tree; it was described as having a golden basin hanging from the tree's branches; the slap beside the spring was made of emerald and had four bright rubies underneath it. On the other side of Balanton was a small but pretty chapel. Sometimes Balanton is said to be located within BROCÉLIANDE where Merlin was entrapped by his lady, Vivien.

Source: Karr, *Arthurian Companion*, 59; Leslie, *Early Races of Scotland and Their Monuments*, 167

Balbec

In ancient Persian lore Balbec and CHILMI-NAR were two cities built by the power of a djinn who was acting under the orders of Jan ben Jan, the individual who ruled the world before the creation of Adam. These two cities were intended to be locations suitable for the djinn to hide in.

Source: Brewer, *Dictionary of Phrase and Fable*, 161

Baltia

Variations: ABALUS, Balcia, Basilia, Basileia, Baunonia, Isle of Abalus

In Greek mythology Baltia was a legendary island, immense in size, said to be located somewhere in northern Europe. Amber was said to wash up on the shore in the spring time; this amber was used as a fuel and was sold to the neighboring people, the Teutones. Baltia was described by Pliny the Elder in his *Natural History* (4.27; 37.11); he paraphrases the testimony of Xenophon of Lampsacus who called the island Balcia, Pytheas and Timaeus who called it Basilia, and Pytheas who referred to it as ABALUS, all of their original writings have been lost.

Source: Cunliffe, *Extraordinary Voyage of Pytheas the Greek*, 149–50; Pliny the Elder, *Pliny's Natural History*, Volumes 1–3, 32

Banoic

Variations: Benwick

Ruled by King Ban, the brother of King Bors and the father of Sir Lancelot, Banoic of Arthurian lore, was said to be located near western Gaul.

Source: Manguel, *Dictionary of Imaginary Places*, 56; Taylor, *Coming of the Saints*, 317

Bar Shasketh

Variations: Bar Shachath, the Pit of Ruin

In Cabalistic lore Bar Shasketh, the Pit of Destruction is one of the seven HELLS.

Source: Greer, *New Encyclopedia of the Occult*, 60

Barahoot, Valley of

Variations: Bal'a'hoot, Borhut

In the province of Hadramot, the Valley of

Barahoot is where a certain well resides; its water is black and fetid. Each evening the souls of idolaters and infidels are taken to the well and made to drink from it. The valley is filled with owls and black serpents.

Source: Lane, *Manners and Customs of the Modern Egyptians*, 531; Merrick, *Hayât al-qulûb*, 165

Baralku

Variations: Bralgu

In the Yolngu mythology of Australia, Baralku was a mythological island located to the east of Arnhem Land; this place of the dead is where the Barnumbirr creator-spirit and the Djanggawul siblings were said to originate. It is believed that souls return to Baralku after the body dies.

Source: Berndt, *Djanggawul*, 1; Macintyre, *Concise History of Australia*, 9

Barenton

Variations: Belenton, Bellenton, Berenton, Spring of Barenton

According to the Breton people of Brittany Barenton, the fountain that could make rain was located in the very heart of the legendary forest BROCÉLIANDE; when water was drawn from the well and sprinkled around it unleashed violent storms.

Source: Collectif, *Classical Mythology and Arthurian Romance*, 47; Monaghan, *Encyclopedia of Celtic Mythology and Folklore*, 36, 278

Barrey

Variations: Barey, Barri

In Norse mythology Barrey ("leafy") was a cool and pleasant grove within a forest; it was here the giantess Gerd met with divine servant, Skirner, to make arrangements to rendezvous with the Vanir god, Frey, who had been in love with her for a long time.

Source: Anderson, *Norse Mythology*, 441; Daly, *Norse Mythology A to Z*, 11

Barzakh

In Islam, Barzakh ("barrier" or "obstruction") is a type of LIMBO; the faithful rest in comfort while sinners are punished until the day of resurrection. The barzakh is also described as a barrier separating the living from the dead; although mentioned in the Koran three times, it is not described in detail.

In eschatology, the barzakh is the word used to describe the barrier between the world of man (which contains the earth, HEAVENS, and nether regions) and the realm of spirits and God.

Source: Glassé, *Concise Encyclopedia of Islam*, 78; Houtsma, *E. J. Brill's First Encyclopaedia of Islam*, 668

Bay of Trespasses

Variations: Baie de Trepasses, Bay of the Dead, Bay of Lost Souls, Bay of Regrets

In the folklore of Brenton regarding the city of CAER YS, the Bay of Trespasses was the location where the sorceress Dahut would discard the bodies of her lovers; once in the water the men would become a plaything for her true husband and his attendants.

Source: Ellis, *Celtic Myths and Legends*, 517; Matson, *Celtic Mythology, A to Z*, 123

Bedegraine

Variations: Bedingan, Bedingham, Bedingram, Bedingran, Bedinham, Brandigan ("born of the raven"), Bredigan, Brekenho, Brekingho

In some tellings of Arthurian lore, Bedegraine was said to be the battlefield where King Arthur first solidified his reign by defeating a cadre of rebel kings. First mentioned in the Vulgate *Merlin*, this event became a major event in Sir Thomas treatment.

Source: Ashley, *Mammoth Book of King Arthur*, 611; Bruce, *Arthurian Name Dictionary*, 61; Manguel, *Dictionary of Imaginary Places*, 64

Bhur-Loka

Variations: Bhoor-Loka, Buh Loka

One of the eight regions of heavenly existence in Hindu mythology, Bhur-Loka is the earth.

Source: Dowson, *Classical Dictionary of Hindu Mythology and Religion*, 179

Bhuvar-Loka

Variations: Bhuvar loka

One of the eight regions of heavenly existence in Hindu mythology, Bhuvar-Loka is the space between the earth and the sun.

Source: Dowson, *Classical Dictionary of Hindu Mythology and Religion*, 179

Bibbu

In Sumerian mythology Bibbu ("wild sheep") was either a comet or possibly a planet.

Source: Kovacs, *Epic of Gilgamesh*, 111; Muss-Arnolt, *Concise Dictionary of the Assyrian Language*, Volume 1, 142

Bifrost (BEE-frost)

Variations: Asabridge, Asa Bridge, Asbrú ("bridge"), Bifröst, Bilröst, Bridge of the Gods ("Asbru")

The Rainbow Bridge of Norse mythology, Bifrost ("the trembling way") spans the sky connecting MIDGARD (Earth) to ASGARD. According to the *Prose Edda*, written in the 13th century by Snorri Sturluson, the bridge ends at the residence of the god Heimdallr (Heimdal) in HIMINBJÖRG; it is he who guards it preventing the jötnar from crossing.

Made of air, fire, and water, it looks to be three fragile strands of matter but it is actually impossibly strong. It has been prophesied Bifrost will be destroyed by the forces of Muspell. Until that time, each day the gods ride on horseback over the bridge to URDARBRUNNR WELL where they sit in judgment, all except for Thor who must go on foot, wading through the rivers KORMT, and ORMT and the stream KERLAUG; being the god of thunder, his passage would shatter Bifrost. Heimdall was appointed watchman of the bridge as not only does he have magnificent senses but also a horn called Giallarhorn which when blown will sound out an alarm through the NINE WORLDS.

Source: Anderson, *Norse Mythology*, 189; Daly, *Norse Mythology A to Z*, 12; Evans. *Dictionary of Mythology*, 44; Guerber, *Myths of the Norsemen*, 153

Bigfish

Variations: Big Fish Island

According to the ancient Persian fairytale, *Sindbad the Sailor* (750 CE), Bigfish was an island named in the first voyage of the fictional sailor's adventures. The story says that far in the southeast a merchant ship came upon an islands lush and "green as PARADISE." The crew and passengers went ashore where they cooked, washed, and walked the island. Unfortunately, the fires lit for cooking and washing disturbed the gigantic resting fish, which began to move and descend back into the ocean.

Source: Burton, *Lady Burton's Edition of Her Husband's Arabian Nights*, Volume 3, 16; Burton, *Seven Voyages of Sinbad the Sailor*, 8–14; Sprague de Camp, *Lands Beyond*, 117

Bilskinir (bil'sker-nir)

Variations: Bilskirner, Bilskirnir

In Norse mythology Bilskinir ("lightening" or "storm serene") is the name of the home of the god of thunder, Thor; this hall located in THRUDEIM, the Land of Strength, was described as being covered with studded shields which glowed red and inside it was a gleaming purple. Having 540 rooms, Bilskinir was equal in size to VALHALLA; although Snorri Sturluson in his edition of the *Prose Edda* says the *Lay of Grimnir* claims there were 640 floors.

Source: Bennett, *Gods and Religions of Ancient and Modern Times*, Volume 1, 384; Grimes, *Norse Myths*, 258; Guerber, *Myths of the Norsemen*, 59; Sturlusonar, *Prose Edda of Snorri Sturluson*, 50

Bimini

An island believed to exist in the Bahamas, Bimini of Arawak folklore was thought to be the location of the fabled Fountain of Youth, a well whose waters would give immortality to any who drank from it. Described as lying far beyond the reach of mortal man just beyond the horizon, lovely Bimini may be reached only by the strongest of rowers in the fastest of canoes. Bimini was also the name of a goddess in Arawak mythology who rose from the primal waters to give birth to the entire world.

As time passed the idea of the island of Bimini being an earthy PARADISE akin to the GARDEN OF EDEN; as the Arawak tradition began to fade Bimini became linked to ATLANTIS, now described as once having been the height of human technology and culture before the Arawaks arrived.

Source: Curran, *Lost Lands, Forgotten Realms*, 189, 191–93; Joseph, *Atlantis Encyclopedia*, 71–72

Birds, Isle of

Variations: Insula Avium, Ylonde of Byrdes
Described in the tales of Saint Brendan the legendary Isle of Birds was located off the British coast on old maps; According to the *immram*, (Irish navigational story) *Navigatio Sancti Brendani* ("The Voyage of St. Brendan") as holding "*a fayre tree, bull of bowes, and on every bough sate a fare bird, and they sate to thick on the tree that unnethe only lefe of the tree might be seen.*" According to legend, the birds of the island were fallen angels, but these particular angels had not committed any particularly serious sin.

Source: Bevan, *Mediæval Geography*, 172–73; Magasich-airola, *America Magica*, 138

The Black Chapel

Variations: The Ancient Chapel
In the thirteenth century French poem, *Vulgate Cycle*, the Black Chapel was the name of the chapel where the last of King Arthur's knights, Girflet and Lucan, carried his wounded body after their last battle. In the morning, Arthur and his last knight left the Black Chapel to travel to the sea where at noon, his knight was sent to throw the sword, Excalibur, into the lake on the other side of the hill.

Source: Bruce, *Arthurian Name Dictionary*, 69; Karr, *Arthurian Companion*, 73

Blank, Castle

Sir Lancelot, after having been tricked into having sexual relations with Elaine of Escalot went insane in a fit of anger after he was accused of faithlessness by his beloved, Queen Guinevere; for two years he wandered a forest in a distraught state until he was found by Sir Bliant, the brother of Slivant, lord of Castle Blank ("White"). It was here the knight was tended to, well cared for and fed; although his body was restored to full health and his handsome appearance returned his mind was still in a state of torment.

Source: Karr, *Arthurian Companion*, 76–77; Malory, *Le Morte Darthur*, 16; Manguel, *Dictionary of Imaginary Places*, 81

Blessed, Islands of the *see* Islands of the Blessed

Blest, Isle of the

Variations: Hy-Brasail, O'Brazil
A FAIRY ISLAND from Irish lore, the Isle of the Blest is similar to the ELYSIAN FIELDS of ancient Greece; it is only by special favor from one of the fay that a mortal may travel to this island.

When the Isle of the Blest is able to be seen by mortals it is glimpsed only just after sunset and is seen rising out of the Atlantic Ocean. Upon the island there is a city which can be seen; it has been said the population of the city have need for lamps, the moon, or the sun.

Source: Burke, *South Isles of Aran*, 63; McCoy, *Witch's Guide to Faery Folk*, 43

Bliant, Castle of

Variations: Bryaunt
Not to be confused with CASTLE BLANK, Castle Bliant was one of Pellam's castles in Arthurian lore; it was located on an island, surrounded in iron. Lord Pellam gave the castle and its lands to Sir Lancelot after he recovered from his madness. Lancelot was able to defend it against all jousters and named the land Joyous Island (see JOYOUS GARD); he lived there with Pellam's daughter, Elaine.

Source: Bruce, *Arthurian Name Dictionary*, 74; Karr, *Arthurian Companion*, 78–79

Boiling Well, Forest of the

A perilous forest of Arthurian lore the Forest of the Boiling Well was the location of King

Lancelot's murder by beheading; he was the grandfather of Sir Lancelot. During the assassination the head of the king fell into the well; when the killers attempted to remove the severed head from the well, it boiled up and scorched their hands.

Source: Karr, *Arthurian Companion*, 79–80

Booyan

In Russian lore there is a magical island called Booyan; it is named in incantations and in spellwork. Described as being located in the middle of the ocean, the holy men who live there have access to a healing stone called Alatyr ("father of all stones").

Source: Cotterell, *Encyclopedia of World Mythology*, 110; Littleton, *Gods, Goddesses, and Mythology*, Volume 1, 1271

Bottomless Pit

In the *Bible* the phrase bottomless pit is used to describe the realm of the dead and demonic forces. The disembodied spirits who are forced to dwell here are filthy and unclean seeking opportunity to embed themselves into the bodies of mankind.

Used interchangeably with the Hebrew word ABYSS ("the deep") in some versions of the Bible, the bottomless pit was used by the Near Eastern cultures to signify the opposite of the vault of HEAVEN, later it came to be used as a metaphor for the grave. The phrase is most often used in the Book of Revelation as the abode of scorpion-like locusts. Under the absolute control of God, a key will be given to an angel so that it will be unlock it allowing the Beast to ascend to perdition. The bottomless pit is not a place of torment or torture but rather a source for all that is evil.

Source: Elwell, *Tyndale Bible Dictionary*, 234; Larkin, *Book of Revelation*, 74

Bower of Bliss

Variations: Bowre of Blisse

The Bower of Bliss is a FLOATING ISLAND and the home of the enchantress Acrasia the enemy of temperance in Edmund Spencer's unfinished epic poem, *The Fairy Queen* (1590). The island is presented as an earthly PARADISE but this is ultimately revealed to be untrue. Acrasia lures men to the Bower of Bliss with the promise of sex and then using her magic transforms them into various beasts. The guardian of the island is a character named Genius; he is described as being aligned with women, effeminate, and unmanly. At the end of Book II, the enchantress is destroyed by the knight, Sir Guyon.

Source: Hamilton, *Spenser Encyclopedia*, 273; Tambling, *Allegory*, 59

Bragman, Isle of

Variations: Land of Faith

Said to be located somewhere in the Indian Ocean, the isle of Bragman is populated by people who all live good and moral lives and have no personal faults; there is no murder, prostitution, theft, or crime of any sort, nor is there any hunger or war. The weather on Bragman is always pleasant. Because of these ideal conditions, the citizens typically die of old age. Although the people are not Christians they live only by the Ten Commandments; they are led by their king and high teacher, Prester John, likely a title rather than a name. When Alexander the Great was informed of this land and how its people lived, he refused to conquer it.

Source: Manguel, *Dictionary of Imaginary Places*, 87; Morris, *A to Z of Utopianism*, 83

Brahma-Loka

Variations: SATYA-LOKA

One of the eight regions of material existence in Hindu mythology, Brahma-Loka ("World of Brama") is the realm of the superior deities. The souls who reside here are exempt from re-birth and no longer have to descend into the physical world. In the seven spheres of the earth, Brahma-Loka is the seventh.

Source: Dasa, *Swedenborg the Buddhist*, 109; Dowson, *Classical Dictionary of Hindu Mythology and Religion*, 179; Wilson, *Vishńu Puráńa*, 48

Brahmaloka

Variations: Satya Loka

The highest HEAVEN in Buddhism, Brahmaloka ("Brama's land in Heaven") is a realm of infinite truth and wisdom; inhabitants here never die, some await reincarnation while others anticipate final liberation.

Source: Wilson, *Vishńu Puráńa*, 48

Brandigant, Castle

The castle of King Evrain of Arthurian lore, Castle Brandigant was said to be located on an island four leagues across and in a river which was approximately 30 Welsh leagues (about 90 miles) from Castle Guiviet the Little in Penevric.

Source: Karr, *Arthurian Companion*, 85; Newell, *King Arthur and the Table Round*, Volume 2, 245–46

Breidablik (brade-a-blick)

Variations: Baldr's Brow, Breidablik, Breroablik

In Norse mythology Breidablik ("vast splendor") is the name of the home of the god Balder; nothing unclean can enter into its halls and nothing unclean can be found there; it was constructed in the land of least evil in ASGARD. Baldur lives in Breidablik with his wife the goddess Nanna Nepsdottr; their hall, FEIKSTAF was made of shining gold and silver. Chamomile flowers grow here in such abundance it is sometimes called Baldr's Brow because of its medicinal powers. Breidablik is considered to be *gridastadr* ("a sacred place").

Source: Anderson, *Norse Mythology*, 186, 279; Daly, *Norse Mythology A to Z*, 13–14; Dunham, *History of Denmark, Sweden, and Norway*, Volume 2, 55; Grimes, *Norse Myths,* 19, 200, 215; Sturluson, *Younger Edda*, 77, 84, 259

Brendan Isle

Variations: Promised Land of the Saints, Saint Brendan Isle

A traditional mythical FLOATING ISLAND said to be in the Atlantic Ocean, Brendan Isle appeared on the map of the famous cartographer, mathematician, and philosopher, Geradus Mercator's *Chart of the World* of 1569.

Source: Sprague de Camp, *Lands Beyond*, 203; Van Duzer, *Floating Islands*, 174; Westwood, *Mysterious Places*, 202

Bresquehan

A forest in Arthurian lore, Bresquehan was said to be located near the river Saverne ("Seven"); a river running through Bresquehan formed one of the boundaries between Cambenic and Norgales.

Source: Karr, *Arthurian Companion*, 87

Brí Léith

An Irish FAIRY FORT in the center of Ireland, Brí Léith was said to be the home of the great fairy king, Midir.

Source: Macleod, *Celtic Myth and Religion*, 53; Monaghan, *Encyclopedia of Celtic Mythology and Folklore*, 60

Briah

The second of the four Cabalistic worlds Briah ("creation"), the world of creation, is the divine realm of archangels and eternal patterns. Briah's element is water; it's Hebrew letter Heh.

Source: Godwin, *Godwin's Cabalistic Encyclopedia*, 218; Greer, *New Encyclopedia of the Occult*, 180

Briestoc

A subkingdom in Arthurian lore, Briestoc was said to be located in the vicinity of the DOLORUS TOWER of Dolorus Gard (see JOYOUS GARD). All of the knights of Briestoc were lost in battle when its lady sent them to rescue Sir Gawaine from Carados.

Source: Bruce, *Arthurian Name Dictionary,* 277; Karr, *Arthurian Companion*, 89–90

Brig of Dread

Variations: Bridge of Dread

An old belief allude to by Sir Walter Scott, the Brig of Dread must be traversed by a soul immediately after leaving the body. Narrow as a thread the Brig of Dread crosses a chasm; to successfully cross the bridge allows entrance into HEAVEN wherein to fall from the Brig is to land in HELL.

Source: Baring-Gould, *Book of Folklore*, 34; Spence, *Encyclopædia of Occultism*, 80

Brimer

In Norse mythology Brimer is the ale hall located in OKOLNER where the giants will meet after Ragnarok. Good and virtuous beings currently enjoy Brimer as it is well known for its plentiful good drink.

Source: Anderson, *Norse Mythology*, 430, 434; Bennett, *Gods and Religions of Ancient and Modern Times*, Volume 1, 395; Daly, *Norse Mythology A to Z*, 39

Brittia

Variations: Isle of the Blessed

According to the Byzantine scholar Procopius of Caesarea (AD 500–AD 565) in his work *History of the Gothic War* (550) the island of Brittia was where the souls of the dead were transported to once leaving the body. Said to be located between the islands of Brettania and the legendary island, THULE, the farmers and fishermen of the island take turns ferrying the souls from the mainland to the island, a distance of some 25 miles. At midnight, a knock will sound of the ferryman's door and he will hear muffled voices but see no one. At the shore he will then see an unfamiliar boat; this vessel, although it appears empty once it is adrift will handle as if it is heavily burdened. Upon arriving on the shore of Brittia an hour later, the boat's invisible passengers quickly disembark; the ferryman will hear a loud voice repeatedly asking for names and country of origins.

Source: Grimm, *Teutonic Mythology*, Volume 2, 832–33; Lewis, *Historical Survey of the Astronomy of the Ancients*, 494

Brocéliande

Variations: Broceliande, Forest of Brocéliande

In Arthurian lore Brocéliande first appeared in the verse chronicle *Roman de Rou* (1160),

by Wace. Known for its unusual weather, Brocéliande most notable feature is a magical fountain from which hunters will take its icy water and wet a stone in order to summon rain; it is also the location where Merlin made a spring appear creating the GARDEN OF JOY for his lady, Vivien in order to please her as well as the location of the oak tree Vivien later trapped Merlin within.

Source: Archibald, *Cambridge Companion to the Arthurian Legend*, 47; Lacy, *Arthurian Encyclopedia*, 67; Monaghan, *Encyclopedia of Celtic Mythology and Folklore*, 61

Brug Maic ind Oc

Variations: Sid

Brug Maic ind Oc ("enchanted palace of the sons of the young") was one of the two palace homes of the god, Dagda which was specially built for him; BRUGH NA BOINNE was the other. Brug Maic ind Oc was located underground.

Source: Arbois de Jubainville, *Irish Mythological Cycle and Celtic Mythology*, 154; Evan-Wentz, *Fairy Faith in Celtic Countries*, 292

Brugh

Variations: Bru, Bruighean, Bruighin Sithein

In Irish fairy lore a brugh ("fairy place") is a hill, natural or man-made, where a collection of fairies live. Many burial mounds are also considered to be a brugh, especially if it is where one of the Tuatha de Danann are said to be buried.

Source: Briggs, *Encyclopedia of Fairies*, 50; Evans-Wentz, *Fairy Faith in Celtic Countries*, 327; Mahon, *Ireland's Fairy Lore*, 85–6; McCoy, *Witch's Guide to Faery*, 42

Brugh na Boinne

Brugh na Boinne ("castle of the Boyne") was one of the two residence of King Dagda; this palace contained three trees which always bore fruit, a vessel always full of excellent drink, and two pigs, one of which was always nicely roasted and ready to eat. In this castle no one ever died. Located underground,

Brugh na Boinne was given by Dagda to his son, Oengus for a day and a night but in his son's cleverness was able to lay claim to it forever. The steward of Brugh na Boinne was named Dichu and the smith was named Len Linfiaclach. BRUG MAIC IND OC was Dagda's other palace.

Source: Evan-Wentz, *Fairy Faith in Celtic Countries*, 292; Gregory, *Gods and Fighting Men*, 78

Brunnaker (broon-na-ker)

Variations: Brunnaker's Grove, Glasir

In Norse mythology Brunnaker was the apple grove which became the home of Bragi and Idunn; it was located near the southern edge of ASGARD near GLADSHEIMR.

Source: Grimes, *Norse Myths*, 260; Guerber, *Myths of the Norsemen*, 102

Bulotu

In Tongan mythology, Bulotu is a PARADISE where the souls of chiefs and great people live in a realm of fruit trees laden with a plentiful bounty; it is overseen by the goddess Hikuleo and lays "beyond the horizon." Souls reach Bulotu by flying through the sky to the west.

Source: Collocott, *Journal of the Polynesian Society*, Volume 30, 153; Williamson, *Religious and Cosmic Beliefs of Central Polynesia*, 271

Bulu (Mbúlu)

In Fijian mythology, Bulu ("burial" or "covering") is the UNDERWORLD realm of the gods and all the departed souls of mankind. It is believed that sometimes when angered the gods will snatch a person up, body and soul, and send them to Bulu; only after offerings are made by family and friends will the missing person be returned. Of all the native tribes only one, the Kai Taliku, do not go to Bulu when they die; rather these souls float up to the sky.

Source: Freese, *Philosophy of the Immortality of the Soul and the Resurrection of the Human Body*, 70; Hazlewood, *Fijian and English and an English and Fijian Dictionary*, 17; Waterhouse, *King and the People of Fiji*, 406, 408

Bumbaran

In the folklore of the Philippines, Bumbaran was said to be a beautiful earthly PARADISE which sunk into the sea.

Source: Galang, *Encyclopedia of the Philippines*, 26, 28

Buss Island

Variations: Sunken Land of Buss

An island said to be located in the Atlantic Ocean, Buss Island was alleged to have been discovered in 1578 by an expedition attempting to find the legendary Northwest passage, a short-cut to China. In the fleet, one of the ships, a fishing vessel known as a *busse* came into ill-repair and was sent back to England. On its return it logged that it came upon a large and previously undiscovered island. For three days they sailed along its coast; the land looked to be fruitful and wooded. For decades this PHANTOM ISLAND, placed somewhere between Friesland and Ireland, was charted on maps but was seen less and less frequently. Interestingly, the Hudson's Bay Company had in 1673 laid claim to *Buss Island*, even though Henry Hudson had been unable to locate it. In 1745 a Dutch map proposed the island had sunk and was now a dangerous sand bar.

Source: Babcock, *Legendary Islands of the Atlantic*, 175–77; Latta, *Franklin Conspiracy*, 237

Buyan

In Slavic mythology, Buyan is an island with the ability to appear and disappear; it figures prominently in many myths. A sort of proto-UNDERWORLD with a silent and subterranean city, Koschei the Deathless is said to keep his soul carefully hidden here—inside a needle, inside an egg, inside an oak tree. The brothers, Northern, Western, and Eastern Wind live here and they are the source of all weather.

Source: Kennedy, *Encyclopedia of Russian and Slavic Myth and Legend*, 48; Stanton, *Mythology*, 258

Cabbalusa (kah-ba-LU-sa)

According to Lucian of Samosata, the ancient Greek rhetorician and satirist (AD 125–

180) the island of Cabbalusa ("horse") was not especially large but it was populated entirely by young and beautiful Greek speaking women, attired as courtesans in long robes; it main city was called HYDRAMARDIA and its streets are covered with human bones and skulls.

The story claims that as soon as the men disembarked from their ship the women rushed up to meet them, immediately pairing off with the men, and taking them into their homes. If one was inclined to observe the women more carefully before entering into their home, one would notice they had the legs and feet of asses. These beings, known as ass-shanks or sea-women, feed upon travelers. First these creatures make their prey drunk, then either during or after intercourse, over-power the victim. When captured, the ass-shanks have the means to transform them-selves into water to escape their bonds or con-finement.

Source: Lucian of Samosata, *Works of Lucian of Samosata*, 172; Verma, *Word Origins: Volume 15*, 187

Caer Arianrhod

In Welsh mythology the great rocky island Caer Arianrhod ("Castle Silver Wheel") was destroyed by a flood cause by the sinful nature of its inhabitants, much like in the story of CAER YS; the story is likely a post-pagan belief of the goddess Arianrhod who had affairs with mermen. There is a rock off the coast of north Wales about a mile out to sea that is said to be the wreckage of Arianrhod's castle.

Source: Melrose, *Druids and King Arthur*, 79, 82; Monaghan, *Encyclopedia of Celtic Mythology and Folklore*, 67–68

Caer Gwydion

Caer Gwydion ("Milky Way") is the name of the celestial home of the Fairy King, Gwydion ab Don, and his wife, the Fairy Queen Gwenhidw; it was said to be located among the stars.

Source: Evan-Wentz, *Fairy Faith in Celtic Coun-tries*, 152; Monaghan, *Encyclopedia of Celtic Mythol-ogy and Folklore*, 235

Caer Nefenhir

In Welsh mythology Caer Nefenhir ("Cas-tle of High HEAVEN") was a mysterious OTH-ERWORLD location; it appeared in several an-cient texts including the story of *Kulhwch and Olwen*.

Source: Monaghan, *Encyclopedia of Celtic Myth-ology and Folklore*, 68

Caer Wydyr

In Welsh lore, Caer Wydyr ("Glass Castle") was another name for the OTHERWORLD, AN-NWFN; it was mentioned in the old Welsh Arthurian poem, *Preiddiau Annwfn*.

Source: Koch, *Celtic Culture*, 147; Monaghan, *Encyclopedia of Celtic Mythology and Folklore*, 68

Caer Ys

Variations: City of Is, City of Ys, Is, Ker Iz, Ker Ys ("City of the Depths"), Lynonnesse, Ys ("lower")

There are a number of legends connected with the Brenton folklore of the city of Caer Ys, some claim it was destroyed by the devil while others say it was God who destroyed the city; other stories say it was the caused by Dahut, a sorceress and the daughter of the rul-ing king.

Basically, the story tells the tale of how a king named Gradlon marries a beautiful and powerful fairy sorceress named Malgven who used her magic to support her husband and make him a great conqueror; she gave her hus-band a winged horse from the sea by the name of Morvarch. Together the royal couple had a daughter named Dahut the Golden.

St. Gwenole visited the kingdom and con-verted the king to Christianity enraging his fairy bride; she took her daughter and aban-doned her husband. One day Dahut returned claiming she rejected her mother's magic and as she was the most beautiful woman in world her father did not suspect her of any treachery. As powerful as her mother they had plotted the downfall of the king.

First she convinced her father to build the most beautiful city the world had ever seen and call it Caer Ys; it was constructed actually jetting out of the ocean but was kept safe by a massive dike with a pair of golden doors. The city appeared to be the perfect Christian city however it was the home of a cult that practiced human sacrifice; Dahut was its leader and married to the god of the sea, an evil entity who one day, when the city was full of foreigners, ordered his wife to unlock the dike. King Gradlon tried to escape the flood on his winged horse with his daughter but Morvarch could not handle their combined weight. Just when it looked like all three would crash into the ocean St. Gwenole appeared to his Christian king and told him to let the demonic princess fall into the sea. Gradlon did, as he suddenly realized the true nature of his child.

Although the king founded a new capital, remarried, and had a son who years later succeeded him, Dahut and her husband, the evil god of the sea lived happily in their underwater city, Caer Ys.

Source: Ellis, *Celtic Myths and Legends*, 516–21; Farrar, *Witches' Goddess*, n.p.; Matson, *Celtic Mythology, A to Z*, 121–22

Caesars, City of the *see* City of the Caesars

Caf

Variations: Mount Caf

In Mohammedan lore Caf is an exceptionally large mountain which encircles the earth. Resting upon a foundation of emerald known as Sakhrat; its reflection is what is said to give the sky its azure hue. Giants and fairies live upon the mountain and each stony grain of Caf is believed to hold magical powers.

Source: MacKey, *Encyclopedia of Freemasonry 1909*, 685; Partington, *British Cyclopaedia of the Arts*, Volume 3, 344

Caina

In Dante Alighieri's epic poem *Divina Commedia* ("Divine Comedy") (1320) the river Caina is located in the first ring of the ninth circle of Hell; it was one of the four tributaries of the river Cocytus (see Antenora, Judecca, and Ptolomea). Named for Cain, the character who, in the Bible, slew his brother Able in a fit of anger and jealously; traitors to their family or kill anyone of their bloodline protrude from Caina's icy waters from the neck up, their teeth constantly chatter and their tears freeze in their eye sockets.

Alighieri utilized names and locations from existing mythologies; many of the demons mentioned in the poem were pulled from established hierarchies for example. Because his work, which was meant to be an allegory for the soul's journey to the path of God was well read and accepted, the names and locations he created for the sake of good storytelling became accepted into mythology as well.

Source: Lansing, *Dante Encyclopedia*, 135; Zimmerman, *Inferno of Dante Alighieri*, 36, 224

Cakravāḍa

Variations: Cakkavāḍa

The Cakravāḍa Mountains are the circular edge of the world which encases the seven seas and seven mountain ranges surrounding Sumeru, the central would mountain in in Hindu cosmology. Cakravāḍa is both 312.5 *yojanas* tall and wide. The measure of a single *yojanas* has never been clear, some scholars say it is approximately four and a half miles while other say it ranges between seven and nine miles.

Source: Howard, *Imagery of the Cosmological Buddha*, 66–68

Calpe

Variations: Calpë

Calpe was the Pillars of Hercules from Roman mythology set on the European side of the straits of Gibraltar; the other, called Abyla, was on the North African coast.

Although there are numerous locations said to be Calpe, there is no definitive proof as to where ancient writers were actually referring to. Some ancient authors say the pillars were mountains the godling stacked and poured a sea between them while other authors say the "pillars" were actually hills. Other authors describe the pillars actual items, made of bronze standing eight cubits tall (11.8 feet).

Source: Rawlinson, *History of Herodotus*, Volume 3, 29; Smith, *Dictionary of Greek and Roman Geography*, 1055

Calydon

Variations: Aledon, Caledon, Caledonia, Calidoine, Celadon, Celyddon, Cylyddon

In Arthurian lore Calydon was a forest said to cover the northern portion of England and southern Scotland. This forest was believed to be the location of King Arthur's seventh successful battle against the Saxons. In the Vulgate *Estoire del Saint Graal* we are told Calydon is the home to the Papagustes serpent.

Source: Archibald, *Cambridge Companion to the Arthurian Legend*, 38; Ashley, *Mammoth Book of King Arthur*, 263–43; Bruce, *Arthurian Name Dictionary*, 96

Camelot

Variations: Camaalot, Camaaloth, Camaelot, Camahaloth, Camalahot, Camalat, Camallate, Camalot, Camchilot, Camehelot, Cameloth, Camelotto, Camilot, Chamalot, Damolot, Gamalaot, Kaamalot, Kaamelot, Kamaalot, Kamaaloth, Kamaelot, Kamahalot, Kamahaloth, Kamelot, Kameloth, Schamilot

The legendary court of King Arthur, Camelot was the location of many adventures and tournaments. In most tales of the king, Caerleon, Cardueil, Carilisle, and LOGRES competed for the position of his capitol; likely this is because the court moved around the country quite often. In fact, there is no definitive fixed location or idea of exactly what Camelot was. Some authors described it strictly as the name of the king's castle while others say it was the name of the town the castle was located in. Most scholars regard Camelot as being entirely fictional. The name Camelot has come to mean something of an ideal kingdom in spite of the downfall of its king.

Although what and where Camelot stood is in question what it stood for is not: Camelot

under Arthur's rule was always a place where ambitious knights would go to prove themselves and increase their honor and renown. The king created a code of courtliness and encouraged his people to live by these courtly ideals and high standards of chivalry.

In the Vulgate *Estoire del Saint Graal* we are told of an evil pagan king named Agrestes in the time of Joseph of Arimathea, killing many of his followers before God struck him down with madness.

The French poet and trabodur Chrétien de Troyes who wrote extensively on Arthurian stories and invented the character of Lancelot in his 12th century *Arthurian Romances* only used Camelot once in his works; however he described it as a timeless land with enchanted forests and people who could utilize magic.

In the Welsh tales of Arthur, there is no mention of Camelot at all, rather Ehangwen ("expansively white") is the name of his palace and his capitol was located in KELIWIC, Cernyw, or Gelliwig.

Source: Archibald, *Cambridge Companion to the Arthurian Legend*, 9; Ashley, *Mammoth Book of King Arthur*, 196; Bruce, *Arthurian Name Dictionary*, 98; Castleden, *King Arthur*, 149; Evans, *Dictionary of Mythology*, 50; Lacy, *Arthurian Encyclopedia*, 75–76; Monaghan, *Encyclopedia of Celtic Mythology and Folklore*, 73

Camlan

Variations: Camlann, Camlaun

In Welsh lore Camlan was said to be the location of the final battle of King Arthur, where he was defeated by his son, Mordred, and then taken to the OTHERWORLD by the Lady of the Lake.

Source: Koch, *Celtic Culture*, 121; Monaghan, *Encyclopedia of Celtic Mythology and Folklore*, 73

Campacorentin, the Forest

Variations: La Forest Perilleuse

In the Forest Campacorentin of Arthurian lore an unnamed knight came upon two damsels bathing; one of the ladies shot the knight in the thigh with a magical arrow, for only the best knight in the land would have the ability to pull it free. Campacorentin is believed to be located somewhere in Scotland.

Source: Karr, *Arthurian Companion*, 100

Canadian Floating Islands *see* Floating Islands, Canadian

Canguin, Rock of

Variations: Chanpguin, Roche de Canguin, Sanguin

Located near the border, the Rock of Canguin was the castle of Queen Ygerne (Igraine); it was constructed after the death of Uther Pendragon and she lived there with her granddaughter, Clarissant. Sir Gawain once confronted the PERILOUS BED here. The Rock of Canguin was used in Arthurian lore as an OTHERWORLD connection.

Source: Bruce, *Arthurian Name Dictionary*, 101; Karr, *Arthurian Companion*, 100

Canoel

In the medieval epic *Tristan and Iseult*, Canoel was the capital city of Parmenie, homeland of Tristan. A port town located on the English Channel, King Rivalin of Parmenie took his family name, Canelengres, from here.

Source: Bruce, *Arthurian Name Dictionary*, 101; von Strassburg, *Tristan and Isolde*, 23, 73

Cantre'r Gwaelod

Variations: Cantref Gwaelod, Cantref y Gwaelod, Maes Gwyddno ("Plain of Gwyddno")

A legendary city said to have sunk, Cantre'r Gwaelod ("Lowland Hundred") was first record in the thirteenth century tome *Llyfr Du Caerfyrddin* ("*Black Book of Carmarthen*") telling the story of how a well maiden failed to properly perform her duties.

The more modern version of the legend came into being in the seventeenth century; according to it Cantre'r Gwaelod was a fertile region ruled by sixteen noblemen who were overseen by King Gwyddno Garanhir ("Longshanks"). Its capital was Caer Wyddno ("fort of Gwyddno" or "Palace of Gwyddno"). This low-lying kingdom, 40 miles long and 20 miles wide, was protected from the sea by dikes and sluices, but one night its overseer, Seithennin, became drunk at a banquet and left them open. The floodwaters rushed in and drowned every soul in all sixteen cities which made up Cantre'r Gwaelod; only the poet Taliesin survived. Some people claim to be able to hear the sunken city's church bell ring.

Source: Gwyndaf, *Chwedlau Gwerin Cymru*, 24, 68; Haughton, *Haunted Spaces, Sacred Places*, 94–97

Caphar Salama

A triangle-shaped island in the Academic Sea, Caphar Salama, with its approximate perimeter of thirty miles, is said to be rich with grains and pasture lands which are fed by brooks and rives filled with fish; it has only one city, Christianopolis. A Christian land there is no compulsion or hypocrisy among the people; the citizens, all here by choice, volunteer to live by the principals of Christian religion. City officials are respected and all events, meetings, and schoolroom classes are started off with a prayer.

Shipwreck survivors who find themselves on its shores are carefully scrutinized by three city officials before they are taken into the utopian city. The first examiner guard against the entrance of beggars and tramps; the second asks questions regarding their family, health, history, manner of life, and so forth; the third asks questions testing their knowledge on art, charity, church, investigation, language, natural history, science, and theology.

Source: Andreä, *Johann Valentin Andreae's Christianopolis*, 20, 30–31, 37; Manguel, *Dictionary of Imaginary Places*, 112

Carbonek Castle

Variations: Caer Belli, Caer Sidi, Castle of Eden, Castle of Joy, Castle of King Pelles, Castle of Souls, Castle of Wonders, Chateau Marveil, CORBENIC CASTLE, Corbin, Corbenic, Grail Castle, Grail Mountain, Munsalvaesche, Spinning Castle

According to medieval legend, Carbonek

Castle was where the Holy Grail was once housed in a tiny chapel in the heart of the castle. Although there are as many descriptions of the castle as there are variations of the legend, the construction of Carbonek was attributed in one text to Titurel the first king of the Grail, who claimed he received the construction plans through divine intervention.

Source: Leviton, *Encyclopedia of Earth Myths*, n.p.; Malory, *Le Morte Darthur*, 2, 16, 19; Manguel, *Dictionary of Imaginary Places*, 117

Cardigan

Variations: Caradigan, Cardican, Kardigan, Karidagan

According to the French poet and trabodur Chrétien de Troyes, Cardigan was one of the places where King Arthur would hold court; he only used CAMELOT once and gave it a vague description. In the lore of Sir Thomas Malory, Cardigan was mentioned as a place where Sirs Aglovale and Percivale lodged while looking for Sir Lancelot.

Source: Bruce, *Arthurian Name Dictionary*, 104; Karr, *Arthurian Companion*, 103

Carlisle

Variations: Cardoile, Cardol, Carduel

According to Sir Thomas Malory Carlisle was of the cities where King Arthur would hold court. The French poet and trabodur Chrétien de Troyes used Carlisle as Arthur's capital rather than CAMELOT in his stories; it was the location where Erec spoke with Gunret the Little about finding Arthur's court, where Percival entered into Arthur's court, and where the romance of Yvain took place. It was also where Queen Guinevere was taken for execution.

Source: Bruce, *Arthurian Name Dictionary*, 104; Karr, *Arthurian Companion*, 103

Carteloise Castle and Forest

Variations: Carcelois, Carteloise

In Arthurian lore Carteloise Castle was ruled by the Earl of Hernox but he lost control of it to his three wicked sons; they imprisoned their father and then raped and murdered their sister. Sir Galahad and his companions managed to defeat the sons and free the Earl who soon thereafter died from his wounds.

The forest of Carteloise was described as a "waste forest" but it was the place where Galahad and his companions saw a mystical white hart walking through the woods with an entourage of four lions.

The location of Carteloise Castle and its surrounding forest has been placed at various locations up and down the English and Scottish borderlands.

Source: Cox, *Popular Romances of the Middle Ages*, 195; Karr, *Arthurian Companion*, 105–106

Caseossa

Variations: Milk Island

According to Lucian of Samosata's parody travel tales *True History* (second century AD) Caseossa was said to be located in the Atlantic Ocean and surrounded by milky-white waters; it was decried as being a round island, about twenty-five miles wide, and its land having the consistency of mature cheese. The grapes that grow on the island, when pressed, do not produce wine but rather milk. Although there are no inhabitants living upon the island there is a temple dedicated to the nymph Galatea.

Source: Davis, *Don't Know Much About Geography*, 48; Manguel, *Dictionary of Imaginary Places*, 118

Castle Blank *see* **Blank, Castle**

Castle Brandigant *see* **Brandigant, Castle**

Castle Corbenic *see* **Corbenic, Castle**

Castle Cubele *see* **Cubele, Castle**

Castle Dangerous *see* **Dangerous, Castle**

Castle Edyope *see* **Edyope, Castle**

Castle of Bliant *see* **Bliant, Castle of**

Castle of Ercildoune *see* **Ercildoune, Castle of**

Castle of Indolence
From the popular eighteenth century allegorical poem *Castle of Indolence* by James Thomson, the castle was said to be located in the clouds of the land of Drowsiness. The owner of the keep was a sorcerer who would drain anyone who entered of their energy and free-will.
Source: Hager, *Encyclopedia of British Writers*, 249

Castle Terabil *see* **Terabil, Castle**

Cauldron, Lake of the
In Irish lore the Lake of the Cauldron earned it name when a gigantic man with yellow hair named Llassur Llaesggyvnewid, fished a cauldron out of it. If a deceased man was placed within the vessel it would restore his life to him but he would never again be able to speak; it is said that those who are thus restored make excellent warriors.
Source: Guest, *The Mabinogion*, 37–38; Manguel, *Dictionary of Imaginary Places*, 123

Cauther (caw'ther)
A lake of PARADISE named in the Koran, Cauther's water is said to be as clear as crystal, cold as snow, and sweet as honey. Any believer who drinks of its water will never suffer from thirst again.
Source: Bechtel, *Dictionary of Mythology*, 53; Brewer, *Dictionary of Phrase and Fable*, 230

Caverns of Atala *see* **Atala, Caverns of**

Caverns of Mahatala *see* **Mahatala, Caverns of**

Caverns of Rasatala *see* **Rasatala, Caverns of**

Caverns of Sutala *see* **Sutala, Caverns of**

Caverns of Talatala *see* **Talatala, Caverns of**

Caverns of Vitala *see* **Vitala, Caverns of**

Ceallapacha
Variations: Tuutaycpacha
In the Incan mythology, Ceallapacha is the age of darkness, the beginning of the world.
Source: Osborne, *South American Mythology*, 74

The Cedar Forest
Described in tablets four through six in the *Epic of Gilgamesh*, the gloriously beautiful Cedar Forest is the realm of the gods in ancient Mesopotamian mythology. Guarded by the demigod and demonic Humbaba, it was entered by the questing hero, Gilgamesh, who dared to cut trees from its virgin stands in his search for immortality.

Tablet four tells us the story of Gilgamesh's six-day journey to the Cedar Forest; each day he prayed to the god Shamash and each night the god gave the hero an oracular dream. The first, fourth, and fifth dreams has been lost to us; the others foretell his success in battle and divine protection. Humbaba is wearing only one of his seven coats of armor and therefore is particularly vulnerable. Enkidu, Gilgamesh's companion, become afraid and wants to leave but after a short fight between them, Gilgamesh convinces him that they must stand against Humbaba together.

In the fifth tablet Gilgamesh and Enkidu cut down some of the trees drawing out Humbaba; after much taunting from both sides, they break out into a fight. With the assistance of Shamash, the hero is able to win. Defeated, with his last breath the demon curses Enkidu to an early death; soon thereafter the companion become ill and dies a slow and painful death.

Source: Kovacs, *Epic of Gilgamesh,* 40–43; Shaffer, *Journal of the American Oriental Society,* Volume 103, pp. 307–13

Celaenea (sel-AY-nee-a)

In the mythology of the ancient Greeks, Celaenea was a mountain in Asia where the god Apollo fled with the satyr, Maryas.

Source: Bell, *Bell's New Pantheon or Historical Dictionary of the Gods, Demi Gods, Heroes and Fabulous Personages of Antiquity 1790,* 162

Celidon

Variations: Cellydon, Coit Celidon

A dense wood of Arthurian lore, Celidon, like the legendary forest BROCÉLIANDE, appears in many stories, among which was an important battle which led to a victory for King Arthur's knights. The magician Merlin was said to wander the forest of Celidon during his years of madness.

Source: Melrose, *Druids and King Arthur,* 6; Monaghan, *Encyclopedia of Celtic Mythology and Folklore,* 80

Chaitraratha

Variations: Caitra-ratha ("Colorful-Chariot"), Saugandhika ("the Fragrant")

Within the mythical city of ALAKAPURI located upon Mount MANDARA, according to Hindu lore is Chaitraratha, the most beautiful garden in the world. Here, faun musicians, known collectively as the *kinnaras,* play beautiful music for their king, Kubera.

Source: Dalal, *Hinduism,* 231; Daniélou, *Myths and Gods of India,* 136

Chaneph

François Rabelais (1494–April, 9 1553) a doctor, French Renaissance writer, Greek scholar, monk, and Renaissance humanist, describes in his best known book, *Gargantua and Pantagruel,* the island of Chaneph ("hypocrisy"); it is occupied by friars who lived by begging, mumblers of *ave marias,* religious hypocrites, sham saints, and tellers of beads.

Source: Chesney, *Rabelais Encyclopedia,* 33; Rabelais, *Five Books of the Lives, Heroic Deeds and Sayings of Gargantua and His Son Pantagruel,* 317–19

Charaxio

In the Sethian work, Holy Book of the Great Invisible Spirit, Seth leaves his tome on the mythical Mount Charaxio ("mountain of the worthy") where it will be rediscovered at the end of time.

Source: Meyer, *The Nag Hammadi Scriptures,* 269; Smith, *Dictionary of Gnosticism,* 56

Charybdis (kuh-RIB-dis)

Charybdis is the lethal whirlpool named in Homer's *Odyssey* (xii, 101–110); it is located on one side of a narrow channel. Three times a day this whirlpool was said to suck down tremendous amounts of water. Charybdis is directly opposite the home of the frightful sea monster, Scylla; the only way to safely pass the whirlpool is to sail directly beneath the overhang of the multi-headed creature's lair.

Together Charybdis and Scylla are oftentimes used by authors to show two equally distressing alternatives, one of which must ultimately be selected.

Source: Sprague de Camp, *Lands Beyond,* 67; Evans, *Dictionary of Mythology,* 56

Chelm (KHELM)

Variations: Town of Fools

In Jewish folklore oral tradition, Chelm is a proverbial town said to be inhabited by fools; in the story the Wise Men of Chelm, it describes the model of a foolish Jewish community where life, logic, and religion were all inverted.

Source: Ben-Amos, *Folktales of the Jews,* 453; Dale, *Book of Where,* 32

Chemmis

The earliest ancient Roman geographer, Pomponius Mela who wrote around AD 43 described Chemmis as a FLOATING ISLAND in

Egypt; it moved whenever the wind blew. It was described as having sacred groves and a temple to the god Apollo upon it.

Plutarch, a Greek biographer, essayist, and historian tells us the Egyptian goddess Isis loosened Chemmis from the Earth and set it adrift to protect Horus, her son, from their enemy, Seth.

The ancient Greek historian Herodotus described Chemmis as being located in the middle of a broad and deep lake and having a grand temple to Apollo upon it. Palm trees grew upon the island in great abundance as did fruit trees. According to him, Latona, one of the eight gods of the first order received Apollo from the goddess Isis and hid him upon the island. The movements of the searching god Typhon cause the island to move and float and consequently prevented him from being able to find the infant god.

Source: Anthon, *Classical Dictionary*, 337–38; Faber, *Origin of Pagan Idolatry*, 221; Herodotus, *Herodotus*, Volume 2, 99; Van Duzer, *Floating Islands*, 56

Chiconamictlan

In Aztec mythology Chiconamictlan ("Nine Hells") was the final stop on a souls four year journey through the UNDERWORLD. After crossing the Chiconahuapan River ("Nine Rivers") they are received by the god Mictlantecutli. Upon reception, the soul forgets all its attachments to the earth and disappears into nothingness; immortality is only for those who are destined to reside in one of the other HEAVENS.

Source: Leon-Portilla, *Aztec Thought and Culture*, 124; Moreno, *Handbook to Life in the Aztec World*, 165; Spence, *Introduction to Mythology*, 211

Chilminar

Variations: Forty Pillars, Tchemurtaeskoi

In ancient Persian lore BALBEC and Chilminar were two cities built by the power of a djinn who was acting under the orders of Jan ben Jan, the individual who ruled the world before the creation of Adam. These two cities were intended to be locations suitable for the djinn to hide in.

Source: Brewer, *Dictionary of Phrase and Fable*, 161

Chinwad Bridge

Variations: al-Sirat, Bridge of the Requiter, Chinavat Bridge, Chinvar Bridge, Chinvat Bridge, Cinvat Bridge

In Zoroastrian mythology, after a person dies, their soul remains with the body for three days; on the fourth day it arrives at the Chinwad Bridge; ("bridge of judgment" or "beam-shaped bridge"); it is described as being finer than a single hair and sharper than the edge of a sword. Legend says the bridge is located in the far North, in a place of filth where the damned are tortured.

The bridge spans a chasm filled with horrific monsters and the Gate of HELL where Ahriman dwells in his dark ABYSS. On the far side of the bridge is the entrance to PARADISE but at the top of the bridge two angels, Mihr ("Covenant") and Rashn ("Justice"), write down its accounts. Sometimes a third angel, Sraosha ("Obedience") is said to be present. If the soul has more good to it than not, it is allowed to move on, if not it falls into the pit; once a soul has fallen it cannot leave of its own power. Infidels cannot cross the bridge, they immediately fall.

Source: Mehr, *Zoroastrian Tradition*, 109; Van Scott, *Encyclopedia of Hell*, 58

Chryse

Variations: Khrýsē ("Golden")

A small island said to have been in the Aegean Sea and mentioned by the Greek geographer and traveler Pausanias and Sophocles, the Greek tragedian playwright; its main feature was a temple to Apollo and its patron deity was the goddess, Chryse, for whom the island is named for. The oracle Onomacritus predicted it would sink beneath the waves and after the second century it seemed to have disappeared.

Source: Gillies, *History of Ancient Greece*, 249;

Martínez, *Fakes and Forgers of Classical Literature*, 225

Cibaciba

In Fijian mythology there are two caves entrances which lead to the UNDERWORLD, Cibaciba and DRAKULU. This is the place where the souls of the departed descend into BULU, or the invisible world. Every town will have its own cibaciba, and the area is typically chosen for having some particular topographical feature.

Source: *King and the People of Fiji*, 411; Hazlewood, *Fijian and English and an English and Fijian Dictionary*, 24

Cíbola

Variations: ANTILLIA, the Seven Cities of Cíbola

A legendary city said to be in the American southwest, Cíbola was one of the Seven Cities of Gold sought after by Spanish conquistadors. These cities were sought after in part because Catholic lore claimed that after the Muslim invasion of the Iberian peninsula of AD 714, seven bishops crossed the Atlantic Ocean with their flock and founded a Christian UTOPIA; these cities were referred to as *Ilha das Sete Cidades* ("Isle of the Seven Cities").

Source: Hendrickson, *Facts on File Dictionary of American Regionalisms*, 461; Smith, *Discovery of the Americas, 1492–1800*, 76, 107

City of the Caesars

Variations: City of the Patagonia, Elelín, Lin Lin, Trapalanda, Trapananda, Wandering City

A mythical land, the City of the Caesars was said to be in South America located between a mountain of diamonds and a mountain of gold somewhere in the Andes between Argentina and Chile. The city of the Caesars was described as being prosperous, filled with cultured people, having paved streets, being surrounded by a moat, and only accessible by drawbridge. One story of its founding claims it was founded by the survivors of a Spanish

shipwreck while another says it was built by Romans fleeing civil unrest after the assassination of Julius Caser. Sometimes folklore tells of the city being enchanted and only appearing at certain times or under certain conditions by uses of the magic of its benign and enlightened king.

Source: Childress, *Lost Cities and Ancient Mysteries of South America*, 187–88; Magasich-airola, *America Magica*, 77–79, 96

Ciuin

Variations: Ciùin

The Irish OTHERWORLD, Ciuin ("Gentle Land" or "Mild Land") is a land bridge of sorts connecting the island of AIRCTHECH with the island MAG RÉIN; wealth and treasure of every hue is found in this beautiful realm filled with sweet music and the best of all wine. Ciuin is occupied by fairies and they linger on the sub-plain or land bridge as Heimdal would on the BIFROST.

Source: Federation of European Sections, *Transactions of the Third Annual Congress*, 190; Matthews, *Encyclopaedia of Celtic Myth and Legend*, 113; Nansen, *Northern Mists*, Volume 1, 354

Clas Myrddin

According to Arthurian lore, the entire island of Britain was the palace of the magician Merlin before it was inhabited and during this time the land was known as Clas Myrddin ("Merlin's Enclosure").

Source: Matson, *Celtic Mythology, A to Z*, 81–82; Monaghan, *Encyclopedia of Celtic Mythology and Folklore*, 90

Clashing Rocks

Variations: Cyanean Rocks, SYMPLEGADES

In the ancient Greek story of Jason and the Argonauts, the Clashing Rocks were a pair of coastal peaks near the northern end of the Bosporos that would rush together with tremendous force and crush anything passing between them. Not to be confused with the WANDERING ROCKS, the Clashing Rocks needed to be successfully navigated on the outset of the Argonaut's journey.

In the story the Argonaut, Euphemes released a bird, setting it into flight so it would pass between the crags; the bird triggered the Clashing Rocks into action losing only the smallest bit of its tail feathers, a sign taken as a good omen from the gods and permission to proceed with their plan. As the rocks began to separate and reset, they sailed the Argo quickly and safely through the pass losing only the smallest part of the rear of their ship, the same as the dove.

Source: Hard, *Routledge Handbook of Greek Mythology*, 188–89; Stanton, *Mythology*, 142

Cloud Cuckoo Land

Variations: Cloudland, Nephelokoygia

In the ancient Greek play *The Birds* by Aristophanes, a comic playwright of ancient Athens, Cloud Cuckoo Land was located between earth and HEAVEN and constructed by the birds at the request of Euelpides ("Plausible") and his friend, Pisthetaerus ("Hopeful") as they were tired of the hustle and bustle of Athens and sought a better life. Things turn badly quickly, as all sorts of people the friends sought to avoid, astrologers, informants, and poets, arrive on their doorstep. Additionally, the city was unintentionally built in a location in the sky where it blocked the smoke from the burnt offering ever reaching the gods and starves them.

Source: Dale, *Book of Where*, 34; Macrone, *It's Greek to Me*, 111

Cockaigne

Variations: Cocaigne ("Land of Plenty"), Cockayne, Cokaygne, Coquaigne, Cucagna, Cuckoo-Land, Kuchenland ("Cake Land"), Land of Cockaigne, Lubberland, Lubberland, LUILEKKERLAND ("Lazy Luscious Land"), *País de Cucaña* ("Fools' PARADISE"), *Schlaraffenland* ("Land of Milk and Honey") Schlaraffenland ("Sluggard's Land"), Topsy-Turvydom

A UTOPIA from Greek and Latin literature that flowed into medieval legend and oral traditions, Cockaigne was a mythical land of extreme luxury and plenty where all physical comfort was instantly at hand; it was a parody of PARADISE where gluttony and idleness were practiced and encouraged. Writing about Cockaigne was commonplace as it represented the resentment of the strictures of self-discipline and want as well as living out wish fulfillment fantasies.

A food-lover's PARADISE, fences are made of sausage, floors and steps of candied molasses, houses of cake and roofed with bacon, rivers of wine, roads of pastry, roasted fowl fly low in the air, and streams of porridge roll slowly downstream. In this land of plenty, where the necessity of food has been alleviated, there is the belief prosperity can flourish as dreams are fulfilled.

Unlike other Utopian societies, the Land of Cockaigne was open to anyone who could find it. The animals here exist only to serve mankind, boar, deer, and rabbits are tame and easily caught, sometimes even cooking themselves. Other wonders of Cockaigne are abbots beaten by monks, fish leaping out of the water to be eaten, free food, grilled geese flying right into your mouth, horses born with saddles, mild weather, nuns raising their habits, open sexuality, people enjoy eternal youth, roasted pigs with knives in their back to make carving easy, sex readily available, skies that rain of cheese, tarts that cook themselves, and wine that flows freely.

Source: Lindahl, *Medieval Folklore*, 186; Merriam-Webster, Inc., *Merriam-Webster's Encyclopedia of Literature*, 254; Pleij, *Dreaming of Cockaigne*, 168–69; Simpson, *Corn Palaces and Butter Queens*, 9–10, 16

Cocytus

Variations: Kokytos

According to ancient Greek mythology Cocytus ("Lamentation"), the river of wailing, was one of the four rivers of the UNDERWORLD (see ACHERON, OCEANUS, and PYRIPHLEGETHON).

The human souls who after their trial are deemed evil but curable spend about a year in TARTARUS before being sent up through both Cocytus and PYRIPHLEGETHON, passing thorough the water seeking forgiveness for the crimes the committed in life, the people they murdered, or wronged.

In Dante Alighieri's epic poem *Divina Commedia* ("Divine Comedy") (1320) the Cocytus is located in the ninth and lowest region of Hell and is referred to more as a frozen lake than a river; the source of its water is the same as all the rivers of Hell, the tears of a statue called the Old Man of Crete. Cocytus is where traitors and those who commit complex acts of fraud are tortured. In the Italian epic poem Cocytus has four icy tributaries, Antenora, Caina, Judecca, and Ptolomea.

Source: Evans, *Dictionary of Mythology*, 60; Guthrie, *History of Greek Philosophy: Volume 4*, 377; Zimmerman, *Inferno of Dante Alighieri*, 216–17

Colchis (COL-chis)

Variations: Kolkhis

In ancient Greek mythology Colchis was located in the kingdom of Aeetes on the island of Rhodes. Within a grove sacred to the god Ares, Aeetes hung the Golden Fleece from a tree which was guarded by a fierce dragon. Here the fleece remained until it was retrieved by Jason and the Argonauts.

Source: Anthon, *Classical Dictionary*, 364; Daly, *Greek and Roman Mythology, A to Z*, 3; Evans, *Dictionary of Mythology*, 5

Connla's Well

Variations: Cóelrind's Well

Although Irish lore does not tell us for whom Connla's Well is named or where it is located, it does describe it as having nine hazel trees growing around the well with its branches hanging over it. The nuts from the trees drop into the well and the salmon (or trout, sources vary) who lives there eats them all getting fat; each one of the nuts adds a mottled spot to its scales. If the well can be found it is believed that by drinking the water, eating one of the nuts or the fish will grant inspiration and wisdom.

Source: Matson, *Celtic Mythology, A to Z*, 34; Monaghan, *Encyclopedia of Celtic Mythology and Folklore*, 97

Corbenic, Castle

Variations: Adventurous Castle, Grail Castle

In Arthurian lore Corbenic ("Blessed Body") is the name of the castle of the Fisher King; it is situated on a river. It was dangerous place to stay the night, as any who did was found dead in the morning. Corbenic was the residence of Pelles, a maimed Fisher King and the father of Sir Galahad's mother, Elaine. In some versions of Arthurian tales Sir Perceval and not Sir Galahad becomes the Fisher King of Corbenic castle.

Source: Darrah, *Paganism in Arthurian Romance*, 225–26; Monaghan, *Encyclopedia of Celtic Mythology and Folklore*, 97

Corcyra (KOR-sy-ruh)

Variations: Kérkyra

Both modern Corfu and mythical Corcyra are steeped in legend. According to Greek mythology and local folklore, sickle-shaped Corcyra was formed when Cronus flung his sickle after he dismembered his father, Uranus. The bloodstained weapon became a fertile island. Named for the nymph Corcyra who was loved by the god of the sea, Poseidon, he gave the land mass to her as a gift.

Corcyra is also mentioned in the story of the Odyssey; according to Homer, Odysseus's ship wrecked upon its reef. In the story of Jason and Medea, the couple conducted their nuptials in one of the island's caves.

Source: Evslin, *Gods, Demigods, and Demons*, 41–42; Smith, *Dictionary of Greek and Roman Geography*, 671; Westmoreland, *Ancient Greek Beliefs*, 239

Cornouaille

According to the folklore of Breton the kingdom of Cornouaille was home to the dissolute princess Dahut; it was also the country to where Tristan brought the fair Iseult to.

Source: Monaghan, *Encyclopedia of Celtic Mythology and Folklore*, 98–99

Court of Hefeydd Hen

Variations: Hyfaidd Hen

Located in the Kingdom of the Immor-

TALS, the Court of Hefeydd Hen of Welsh medieval folklore was described in the *Mabinogion* as the location of two important feasts. The first was for the wedding feast of Pwyll and Rhiannon and the second for the union of Gwawl and Rhiannon. The palace here was described as being beautiful, impregnable, immense, and strong with seven gates.

Source: Morus, *Fates of the Princes of Dyfed 1914*, 86; Sullivan, *Mabinogi*, 179, 231

Crocyleia

In Homer's *Iliad*, book II, Crocyleia, an obscure and unidentifiable island believed to have located in the Ionian Sea, was a part of the kingdom of Ithaca under the rulership of Odysseus (see AEGILIPS and NERITOS).

Source: Earl of De Edward, *The Iliad*, 50; Page, *History and the Homeric Land*, 163

Crossroads

Variations: Fork-roads

Since ancient times the crossroads, an intersection of two or more roads meeting, have been a place of magic. Symbolically, it represents a place where worlds meet, where the supernatural and the mundane touch. Historically, demons, fairies, and all sorts of spirits linger there; they are places were witches and sorcerers congregate.

There is a plethora of beliefs involving the crossroads and the sort of magic that can be invoked there. German necromancers in the middle ages summoned spirits at the crossroads. Hoodoo, which involves conjuration and root-work, also relies on performing certain rites at the crossroads. In ancient Rome the god Mercury was said to be a guardian of the crossroads as was Bhairava, an ancient god of India. Shrines to Hecate were placed at crossroads where three roads meet; offerings of garlic were left for her. Stone markers commemorating the god Hermes were placed here by the ancient Greeks. The Catholic Saint Simon is depicted in art as sitting in a chair at the crossroads. There was a tradition in Britain to bury criminals, suicides, and alleged vampires at the crossroads. During the middle ages it was believed sorcerers went to these locations to summon the Devil.

In addition to summoning spirits and preforming magic at crossroads they are also said to be locations to utilize against the forces of evil. Possessed objects can be buried here to diffuse their energy. If ever being pursued by a supernatural force it is also believed that running into a crossroads will confuse and occasionally disperse the spirit.

Source: Greer, *New Encyclopedia of the Occult*, 115; Guiley, *Encyclopedia of Demons and Demonology*, 44; Rabinowitz, *Encyclopedia of Modern Witchcraft and Neo-Paganism*, 62

Cubele, Castle

Variations: Nobel, Tubelle

Located in a valley about two days ride from the castle of King Aman's daughter near Cameliard, Sir Thomas Malory says that Castle Cubele was the host of a tournament between the Earl of the Plains and the Lady of Hervin's nephew.

Source: Karr, *King Arthur Companion*, 121; Sommer, *Vulgate Version of the Arthurian Romances*, Volumes 1–8, 28

Cuilenn, Grey Lake of *see* Grey Lake of Cuilenn

Cwensea

Variations: Bella More

In Scandinavian folklore Cwensea ("fæminæ") was a gulf occupied by Amazons, a nation populated entirely of women. Anundr, the son of Emundr, during his campaign against the warrior-women, he was killed after drinking water from a well the Amazons poisoned.

Source: Ingram, *Inaugural Lecture on the Utility of Anglo-Saxon Literature*, 96; Pritsak, *Origin of Rus'*, 401

Daiver Logum

Variations: Sorgum

An UNDERWORLD of Hindu mythology Daiver Logum is the dwelling place of prophets not yet fit for entry into the PARADISE of Shiva or Vishnu and the three hundred and thirty million daivers, a species of djinn. Ruling over this realm is the daiver, King Daivuntren (Indiren). The occupants of this UNDERWORLD are feed by the milk of the sacred, winged cow, Kaumaden.

Source: Kindersley, *Specimens of Hindoo Literature*, 143; Smedley, *Occult Sciences*, 51; Spence, *Encyclopædia of Occultism*, 113

Dàiyú

Variations: Dai Yu

A mythological island PARADISE in the East China Sea, Dàiyú is one of four FLOATING ISLANDS the Immortals are believed to live upon (see FĀNGZHÀNG, YÍNGZHŌU, and YUÁNJIĀO). Each of these islands is 70,000 li apart from one another; each has a mountain on it rising 30,000 *li* (49,215,000 feet) high and at its top is a plain 90,000 *li* (147,645,000 feet). The palaces on each of these mountains are constructed of gold. At one point the islands were fixed into place on the back of 15 celestial sea turtles. When two of the celestial turtles were killed and eaten by a giant from Longhuo, Dàiyú and YUÁNJIĀO became too unstable, drifted to the North Pole and eventually sank into the sea leaving more than 100 million immortals homeless.

Source: Chen, *Chinese Myths and Legends*, 26–27; Roberts, *Chinese Mythology: A to Z*, 60

The Dancing Place of the Goblin

The Dancing Place of the Goblin is a named fairy circle in British fairy lore; it is located near a magical yew tree which grows exactly in the middle of the Forests of the Yew (*Ffridd yr Ywen*).

Source: Bevan-Jones, *Ancient Yew* 128; Sikes, *British Goblins*, 72

Dandasukam

Variations: Dandasuka

According to Hindu and Vedic mythology Dandasukam is the twenty-fifth of the twenty-eight NARAKAS (HELLS) located in a provi-

dence in the kingdom of Yama. Here, those who persecuted venomous creatures, such as snakes, are cast here. Hooded snakes and wild beasts that live in this NARAKAS attack and consume the sinners they come across.

Source: Parmeshwaranand, *Encyclopaedic Dictionary of Purāṇas*, 723; Veṭṭaṃmāṇi, *Purāṇic Encyclopaedia,* Volume 2, 369

Dangerous, Castle

Variations: Castle Perilous

Not to be confused with Castle Perilous written about by Sir Thomas Malory, Dangerous Castle was the home of Dame Lyonors (Lioness); it was once besieged by Sir Ironside. Castle Dangerous was described as being "beside the Isle of Avillion."

Source: Bruce, *Arthurian Name Dictionary*, 110; Cox, *Popular Romances of the Middle Ages*, 131; Karr, *King Arthur Companion*, 123–24

Daru 'l-baqa'

In Islamic lore Daru 'l-baqa' ("abode which remains") is used as a synonym for HEAVEN.

Source: Hughes, *Dictionary of Islam*, 69

Daru 'l-Bawar

The term Daru 'l-Bawar ("The Abode of Perdition") is used in the Korran (Surah xic 33) as a synonym for HELL.

Source: Hughes, *Dictionary of Islam*, 69; Temple, *Glossary of Indian Terms Relating to Religion*, 15

Dáruna

In Hindu mythology, Dáruna is one of the twenty-eight NARAKAS (HELLS) located in a providence in the kingdom of Yama; it is filled with the instruments of torture.

Source: Garrett, *Classical Dictionary of India*, 157; Wilson, *Vishṅu Puráṅa*, 215–16

Davy Jones' Locker

Variations: Davy's Locker, Jonah's Locker

In modern nautical lore Davy Jones' Locker is a common name for the ocean. Scholars have suggested the name arose in part from a Celtic god Tavy ("stream") who entered into his

OTHERWORLD kingdom through the water; these scholars propose the name may have been Christianized into the name Devy. To explain the last name, they point out a Scottish god of the ocean with a similar sounding name, Shoney; he was said to take those who have drowned at sea and keep them imprisoned on the ocean floor.

Source: Farmer, *Slang and Its Analogues Past and Present*, 258; Monaghan, *Encyclopedia of Celtic Mythology and Folklore*, page 118; Spence, *Minor Traditions of British Mythology*, 115

Day, Land of *see* Land of Day

The Dead, Land of *see* Land of the dead

Delos

Variations: Ortygia

In the mythology of the ancient Greeks, Delos was the FLOATING ISLAND on which the goddess Leto, upon discovering she was made pregnant by the god Zeus, found sanctuary from his vengeful wife, the goddess Hera. After the birth of Leto's twins, Apollo and Artemis, the god of the sea, Poseidon, fixed Delos in place, fastening it to seafloor.

According to Pindar, a lyrical poet from ancient Greece, Delos was once a heavenly body which was set upon the sea; after the arrival of Leto it gained stability by having four pillars rise up from the seafloor and act as its foundation.

Source: Evans, *Dictionary of Mythology*, 69; Munn, *Mother of the Gods, Athens, and the Tyranny of Asia*, 211; Van Duzer, *Floating Islands*, 5–6

Demons, Isles of

Variations: Islands of Demons, Y. de Demones

Generally shown as two islands in the Newfoundland and Labrador region the Isles of Demons were believed to be populated by demons, monsters, and wild animals who lived to do nothing by assault passing ships and anyone who was foolish enough to land on its

shores. The islands first appeared on a Ruysch map in 1507; when they became more popularly known they then appeared on maps by Mercator and Ortelius in the 1560s, however by the mid–1600s the Isles of Demons no longer appeared any map, and rightfully so, as there are no islands off the coast of Newfoundland.

Source: Babcock, *Legendary Islands of the Atlantic*, 178–80; Johnson, *Phantom Islands of the Atlantic*, n.p.; Sylvester, *Indian Wars of New England*, 92

Dendain

Variations: Dudain, Dunayin ("invisible")

According to the *Book of Enoch*, Dendain ("the land of Naid") is the vast mountainous wilderness where the male monster, Behemoth, will be re-born; it is the mythical abode of the descendants of Cain, east of the GARDEN OF EDEN. Behemoth is so large the desert, which is invisible, only covers its belly. The story says God created this monster on the fifth day but did not want it to reside in the oceans with its female counterpart, the Leviathan, so he placed the Behemoth on that part of the Earth which was dried up on the third day of creation.

Source: Conway, *Demonology and Devil-Lore*, Volume 1, 409; Leviton, *Encyclopedia of Earth Myths*, n.p.

Deva-Loka

Variations: Devaloka

In Hindu mythology Deva-Loka is the six celestial worlds located between the earth and the BRAHMA-LOKAs; it is the location where the gods and devas live.

Source: Garrett, *Classical Dictionary of India*, 163; Hoult, *Dictionary of Some Theosophical Terms*, 65

The Devil's Road

Variations: Chemins au Deable

A road in Arthurian lore said to be haunted by devils, Sir Lancelot was shaken as he traveled down the Devil's Road through the FOREST OF MISADVENTURE, as he was hearing strange voices but never saw their source. The Devil's Road was said to be located not so far from the castle of Gais on the Thames.

Source: Bruce, *Arthurian Name Dictionary*, 145; Karr, *King Arthur Companion*, 126

Di Fu

Variations: Difu ("Earth Mansion")

Di Fu ("earth court") is the UNDERWORLD place of judgment where a soul's fate is decided by the four Si Wang Pan Guan (Death-Lords, or "death-judges").

Source: Brown, *China, Japan, Korea*, 93

Di Yu

Variations: DIYU ("earth prison" or "UNDERWORLD prison")

In Chinese mythology Di Yu is an UNDERWORLD realm much like a prison as the souls here are not allowed to pass on because of the transgressions they made in life; only ascension into HEAVEN or reincarnation will enable a soul to leave.

Source: Brown, *China, Japan, Korea*, 94

Dia (DYE-uh)

Variations: Naxos

In Greek mythology the island of Dia ("made of") was where Theseus mysteriously and quickly abandoned Ariadne after she rescued him from the Labyrinth; fortunately she was saved by the god Dionysus who took her up into the HEAVENs and married her.

Source: Coale, *Mystery of Mysteries,* 108; Grant, *Routledge Who's Who in Classical Mythology*, 325

Diamonds, Valley of *see* Valley of Diamonds

Dinas Affaraon

In Welsh lore the city of Dinas Affaraon ("the palace of higher powers") is mentioned so frequently by bards in their poetry that some scholars are lead to believe it once existed; it was also mentioned in the *Black Book of Caermarthen*. Dinas Affaraon was described as laying atop the summit of a "panting" cliff

near a main road which ran to Lleyn. It had a triple wall and a hundred towers at least six feet thick surrounding the city.

Source: Hartley, *Western Mystery Tradition*, 94; Spence, *Mysteries of Britain*, 80

Dionysus's Island

According to Lucian of Samosata's parody travel tales *True History* (second century AD) Dionysus's Island had grape vines which were shaped like women and could not only speak but hold entire conversations. It was advised however not to engage in dialogue with the vines, as speaking with them cause drunkenness. If sexual intercourse was attempted with one of these plants, the transgressor risked being transformed into a grapevine himself.

Source: Davis, *Don't Know Much About Geography*, 48; Manguel, *Dictionary of Imaginary Places*, 118

Dis

The city of Despair in Dante Alighieri's epic poem *Divina Commedia* ("Divine Comedy") (1320), Dis was found in the sixth circle of HELL. Described as an iron-walled city guarded by fallen angels and surrounded by the Stygian marsh, it is overrun with tombs. The Furies, Alecto, Medusa, and Megaera live here with those souls who have committed active sins, were followers of the philosophy of the Epicureans, Heretics, and some Muslims. Dis marks a division in HELL, separating the upper and lowers portions, those who commit sins of incontinence and those of violence.

Source: Dante, *Dante Alighieri's Divine Comedy*, 117; Dante, *The Inferno*, 128

Diyu

According to Buddhism, traditional Chinese folk religion, and Taoism, Diyu ("earth prison" or "UNDERWORLD prison") is a PURGATORY serving to both punish and renew souls for their preparation of reincarnation. Described as an underground maze with numerous chambers and levels souls revisit and stone for the sins they committed in life.

Source: Bokenkamp, *Early Daoist Scriptures*, 235; Menegon, *Ancestors, Virgins, and Friars*, 299

Djahannam

Variations: Djahannum, Jahannum

A HELL in Muslim mythology, Djahannam is a place of boiling water and pus; those found here are the nonbelievers and those who follow other religions no matter the quality of life they lived. Wearing clothes of unquenchable fire and shackled in heavy irons, these individuals receive lashings from red-hot irons while boiling water and molten brass is poured over their head until the skin blisters and falls off. There is no salvation for those who are condemned to Djahannam but all Muslims are said to quickly pass through here, except for those who perished while attacking the enemies of Islam.

Source: Gibb, *Concise Encyclopedia of Islam*, 81

Djinnestan (jin'nes-tin')

Variations: Jinnestan, Jinnistan, Jinnestân

In Oriental mythology, Djinnestan ("jinni land") is the name of the realm of the djinn. Said to be located in the Kaf mountain chain which encircles the earth, the capital city is called the City of Jewels and its main district is called the Country of Delight. Outside of their homeland they live in abandoned buildings, caves, graveyards, places of darkness, and underground. All djinn were ruled by a succession of seventy-two kings or "Suleyman."

Source: Gilman, *New International Encyclopædia*, Volume 6, 117; Hughes, *Dictionary of Islam* 135; Wheeler, *Explanatory and Pronouncing Dictionary of the Noted Names of Fiction*, 101

Doloreuse Chartre

Variations: Dolorus Gard, Dolorous Gard

A small but strong castle located near Dolorus Gard (see JOYOUS GARD), the lord of Doloreuse Chartre was the villainous Sir Brandus des Illes; he was the lord of Dolorus Gard until it was conquered and liberated by Sir Lancelot.

Source: Bruce, *Arthurian Name Dictionary*, 286; Karr, *King Arthur Companion*, 129

Dolorus Tower

In the earliest versions of the Arthurian tale of Guinevere's abduction, Dolorus Tower was ruled by Madoc; the castle could only be entered by two bridges which were guarded by the warriors Burmalt and Caradoc. Sir Gawain manages to fight his way into the castle and rescue the queen. In later versions of the stories the castle was ruled by the evil giant, Sir Carados who collected the knights he defeated in combat and kept them imprisoned in his dungeon until Sir Lancelot defeated and killed him. Lancelot then renamed the castle La Bele Garde (or La Bele Prise). In the thirteenth century French poem, *Vulgate Cycle*, Sir Melians Li Gai and his wife became the lord and lady of the castle.

Source: Bruce, *Arthurian Name Dictionary*, 150–51; Karr, *King Arthur Companion*, 130

Dragon's Hill

A dragon's hill is a location where an act of *dracocide*, the slaying of a dragon, has taken place. According to legend the hill in England where Saint George slew his dragon would be one such location; another would be where the Saxon hero, Cedric, slew the dragon, Naud.

Source: Brewer, *Reader's Handbook of Allusions, References, Plots, and Stories*, 271; Dale, *Book of Where*, 41

Drakulu

Variations: Drakusi

In Fijian mythology there are two caves entrances which lead to the UNDERWORLD, CIBACIBA and Drakulu ("having the skin knocked or chaffed off"). This is the place where the souls of the departed descend into BULU, or the invisible world. It is believed the soul of a married man can reach it easier than one who was not married.

Source: Hazlewood, *Fijian and English and an English and Fijian Dictionary*, 35; Reed, *Myths and Legends of Fiji and Rotuma*, 21

The Dreamtime

Variations: Alchera

In the mythology of the Australian Aboriginal, the Dreamtime refers to the dawn of time when the ancient beings imagined or dreamed the universe into being; this long ago time also co-exists with current, modern time as well and is still an on-going process. Although the stories of the Dreamtime vary from tribe to tribe, and there are more than 500 recognized ones, they consider it to be a reality which shapes their daily lives; many of these stories contain the Rainbow Serpent, the oldest of the ancient Aboriginal ancestors, the world's oldest religious symbol. Originally passed on through the oral tradition the stories of the Dreamtime are largely retellings of the primordial creation epoch featuring one or more of the different Aboriginal ancestors.

Dreamtime is also a state of being which individuals can enter into through the use of ritual magic. Participates are believed to briefly enter into this realm and participate in one of the Dreamtime stories taking on the role of one of the ancestors.

Source: Belanger, *Nightmare Encyclopedia*, 46; Tresidder, *Complete Dictionary of Symbols*, 158

Drogeo

Variations: Droceo, Drogio

An island described by the Zeno Brothers' map (1558), Drogeo, a PHANTOM ISLAND, was reported to be inhabited by cannibals; however, fishermen who claim to have visited his island say it was a "great country."

Source: Babcock, *Legendary Islands of the Atlantic*, 132; Johnson, *Phantom Islands of the Atlantic*, 47; White, *Exploration in the World of the Middle Ages*, 124

Duat

Variations: Akert, Amenthes, Dat, Dwat, Neter-khertet, TUAT

Located west of the Nile River, beneath the earth, Duat ("HEAVEN by night" or "the zone of twilight") is the UNDERWORLD of the ancient Egyptian's mythology. Described as a dark and dangerous realm filed with lakes, marshes, and rivers, there were also numerous carnivorous animals, evil spirits, and monsters; this is where a soul went to for its judgment after death. It is a dangerous journey to arrive at Duat, as the soul must combat monster, traverse lakes of fire, ferry a ride with the god Cherti, and have the magical spell which will open the gates.

The abode of many deities, including Anubis and Osiris, Duat was where the god Ra retired to each evening after he pulled the sun across the sky; it was the duty of the god Thoth to record the names of all who entered.

Source: Crisafulli, *Go to Hell*, 20–25; Pinch, *Egyptian Mythology*, 122–23; Wilkinson, *Myths and Legends*, 246

Duku Kä Misi

Variations: Old Woman

In the belief system of the Yąnomamö people of Venezuela and Brazil Duku Kä Misi is the first and topmost of the four layers of HEAVEN. Considered to be pristine this layer is largely a void now but was the point of origin for many things in the distant past. Duku Kä Misi does not play a role in the lives of the Yąnomamö people or shamans, it is merely recognized as something that exists and once upon a time was important; whatever vague function it once had this realm is now considered to be empty and infertile.

The four essential layers of Yąnomamö belief each lay horizontal to one another and are separated by an undefined but small space. The layers are shaped like inverted serving plates, gently curved, rigid, round, thin, and having both a top and a bottom. Beyond the four essential layers, Duku Kä Misi, HEDU KÄ MISI, HEI KÄ MISI, and HEI TÄ BEBI, there are additional, less important and unnamed layers. Some of these lesser layers are considered as being fragile or rotten, as if simply by walking upon one would destroy it; however a great deal of magic occurs in these dangerous places which are dominated by spirits.

Source: Chagnon, *Yąnomamö*, 102–03; Eller, *Introducing Anthropology of Religion*, 45

Dún Bolg

Dún Bolg ("fortress Bolg") was the location where the warriors of Leinster showed their objection to the *bó rama* ("cow tribute") they had been forced to pay to the king of Tara. Similar to the ancient Greek story of the Trojan Horse, the Leinsters hid themselves in baskets they hung about the necks and backs of the cows; at a predetermined moment the warriors revealed themselves and fought the king's men into submission.

Source: Monaghan. *Encyclopedia of Celtic Mythology and Folklore*, 141

Eanna

Variations: E-Anna ("House of An"), House of the Sky, the Pure Treasury

In Sumerian mythology Eanna ("House of the Sky") was the temple of the god Anu and the goddess Ishtar; it was the location where Anu stayed on his rare visits to Earth. Eanna was said to be located atop a ziggurat in Uruk, the mythological capital city of the hero Gilgamesh.

Source: Dalley, *Myths from Mesopotamia*, 41; Kovacs, *Epic of Gilgamesh*, 111

Echtrae, plural: echtrai

Variations: Eachtra, Eachtrai

An echtrae ("adventure") is, in Irish folklore, an excursion to the OTHERWORLD; this sort of journey is typically undertaken by a lone hero who has encountered the supernatural. Often times theses stories are triggered by the request of a beautiful maiden or a great warrior of the Tuatha de Danann. Echtrae should not be confused with an *immrama*, which is a voyage tale and typically contains maritime themes and heavy Christian overtones.

Source: Koch, *Celtic Culture*, 646; Matson, *Celtic Mythology, A to Z*, 48

Edyope, Castle

This castle from Arthurian lore was located in the "waste forest" in Wales or in the waste lands of LISTENEISE according to the thirteenth century French prose, *Vulgate Cycle*.

Source: Karr, *King Arthur Companion*, 137

The Eight Cold Hells

According to Indian Buddhism there are eight cold Hells believed to lay thousands of miles beneath the continent of JAMBUDVIPA next to the EIGHT HOT HELLS. Generally, the cold hells deal with those souls who were cold-hearted in life and are now suffering for the sins of omission they committed in life.

The length of time one stays in the cold hells is very precise if not specific. For each person in the HELL there is a grain room filled with 80 bushels of sesame seeds; once every 100 years one seed is removed. The length of time for each descending HELL is 20 times the previous. The hells, in the order of their descent are ARBUDA, NIRARBUDA, ATATA, HAHAVA, HUHUVA, UTPALA, PADMA, and MAHAPADMA.

Source: Hastings, *Encyclopedia of Religion and Ethics Part*, Part 7, 133; Mew, *Traditional Aspects of Hell*, 98

The Eight Hot Hells

According to Indian Buddhism there are eight hot Hells believed to lay thousands of miles beneath the continent of JAMBUDVIPA next to the EIGHT COLD HELLS. Generally, the hot hells deal with those souls who committed sins in life. Each of the hot hells has an entrance on of each of its four sides which leads to their *utsada* ("sub-hell"), making the total number of hot hells actually 128.

The length of time one stays in the cold hells is very precise if not specific. For each person in the HELL there is a grain room filled with 80 bushels of sesame seeds; once every 100 years one seed is removed. The length of time for each descending HELL is 20 times the previous. The hells, in the order of their descent are SAMJIVA, KALASUTRAM, SAMGHATA, RAURAVA, MAHARAURAVA, TAPANA, PRATAPANA, Avichi (see AVICI).

Source: Blo-gros-mtha'-yas, *Treasury of Knowledge*, 114; Mew, *Traditional Aspects of Hell*, 38–41

Eikin

Variations: Ækin, Ekin

According to Norse mythology Eikin

("oaken") was one of rivers which ran from AS-GARD to MIDGARD. It was created from the water dripping off of the antlers of Eikthryir as he stood atop the roof of VALHALLA eating leaves off YGGDRASYLL.

Source: Grimes, *Norse Myths*, 263; Guerber, *Myths of the Norsemen*, 13, 263

Ekur

Variations: E-Kur

Similar to Mount OLYMPUS from the mythology of ancient Greece, ekur ("mountain house") is a Sumerian word for the location where the gods would meet in the GARDEN OF GODS, the Sumerian PARADISE. This building is described as being a lofty dwelling place made of lapis-lazuli; it is beautiful inside and from there the god Enli could watch over all of Sumer. The god Ninurta was born here.

Source: Dalley, *Myths from Mesopotamia*, 320; Leviton, *Encyclopedia of Earth Myths*, n.p.; Penglase, *Greek Myths and Mesopotamia*, 73

El Dorado

The legendary city of El Dorado ("the guilded one") was believed to be a city of gold existing somewhere deep in the rain forest of the Amazon; it was thought to be the location to where the Inca escaped with their gold when fleeing the Spanish invader explorers. Apart from it being the name of the city, El Dorado also referred to the name of the ruling king and the city's god.

As a human king, El Dorado would cover his body in gold dust and each year wade out into the center of the city's lake where he would wash his body clean.

Source: Bingham, *South and Meso-American Mythology A to Z*, 46; Sprague de Camp, *Lands Beyond*, 251

Elaea ('EAam)

Variations: Elaia

Roman author, naturalist, natural philosopher, and army and naval commander, Gaius Plinius Secundus, better known as Pliny the Elder wrote of the island of Elaea in his book, "*Natural History*," Volume 32. It is unsure

where this ancient was or if it was a chain of islands rather than a single location.

Source: Pliny the Elder, *Pliny's Natural History*, 20, 97; Smith, *Dictionary of Greek and Roman Geography*, Volume 1, 809

Elean nam Ban

Variations: Eilean nam Ban Mora ("Isle of Big Women")

In Scottish folklore Elean nam Ban ("Isle of Women") is an island said to be located "off the coast" on which a green well was believed to mark the edge of the world. This island's residents were female giants.

Source: Monaghan. *Encyclopedia of Celtic Mythology and Folklore*, 150

Elephant Graveyard

Variations: Elephant's Graveyard

A popular misconception, the elephant graveyard was alleged to be the place where elderly pachyderms went to die; leaving the heard an old elephant was said walk alone to this secret place and die amongst the bones of the hundreds of thousands who have gone before him.

Although such a place does not exist it is not uncommon to discover large piles of elephant bones in one place, likely a herd who has succumbed to starvation or illness together.

Source: Christensen, *Deadly Beautiful*, 225; Cottae, *Best of Field and Stream*, 252–53

Elfland

Variations: ALFHEIM, Alfheimr ("ELF home"), FAIRYLAND

Elfland is one of the many names given to the mythical homeland of the elves and fairies; it is very often associated with the land of the dead. According to folklore descriptions, there is no sun or moon, no day or night, only perpetual twilight. All cultures have elves and fairies in their mythology also have an equivalent of Elfland.

On very rare occasions the fay will invite a human there and treat them well, as an honored guest. Of those who make the trip to

Elfland, few do it of their own free will. Typically mortals who enter into Elfland are kidnapped and taken there or have been tricked in going. Humans who are taken are only released if they are able to perform some task or valuable service for the fairies. Few make the trip back home. Sightings of people who have died and ghosts are said to be from Elfland.

Those who visit are subject to a distorted sense of time, what seemed to be the passing of a few minutes or an evening is later revealed to have been hours, weeks, or even years. Most unfortunate is once a human leaves Elfland, the lost time catches up to them, ageing them appropriately, even if they are to turn instantly to dust.

There are many and varied stories describing the entrance to Elfland as being both celestial and terrestrial; the entry is speculated to be located in an "other-space," in-between dimensions, or in a parallel dimension. The actual doorway to Elfland has been in numerous places, in the forest, the hills, upon stone, up in the mountains, off on an island, over the sea, beneath the earth, and under the water.

Elfland itself has been described as a land of unequaled beauty. The nobility's court is a splendid place, filled with music and dancing.

Source: Brewer, *Dictionary of Phrase and Fable*, 413; Guiley, *Encyclopedia of Magic and Alchemy,* 99; Henderson, *Scottish Fairy Belief*, 44–7; Vallee, *Other Worlds, Other Universes*, 84–6

Elidner

Variations: Eliudnir, Éljúðnir, Eljúonir, Elvidner, Elvidnir

The estate of the Norse goddess Hela, Elidner ("Home of Storms") was located in the worst section of NEFLHEIM, NEFHEL. The doors of this hall face due north so that sunlight will never fall upon them and there entwined serpents covering the walls.

Source: Grimes, *Norse Myths*, 264; Guerber, *Myths of the Norsemen*, 264, 291

Elivager (el-i-vag-ar)

Variations: Elivagar

Elivager is the collective name for the streams of venomously cold ice water which flowed from HVERGELMIR WELL, the seething cauldron, which sits in the exact center of NIFLEHEIM, according to Norse mythology.

Source: Bennett, *Gods and Religions of Ancient and Modern Times*, Volume 1, 385; Brewer, *Dictionary of Phrase and Fable*, 414; Guerber, *Myths of the Norsemen*, 2

Eljudnir

Variations: Éljúðnir, Elvidnir, Elvidna ("misery")

The Hall of the Dead in Norse mythology, Eljudnir ("damp with sleet") is overseen by the goddess Hel, ruler of the Nine Worlds; it is located in NEFLHEIM. Eljudnir is described as being iron-bared, having high walls and banisters, a huge gate, and is staffed by a maidservant named Ganglot ("idler") and a manservant named Ganglati ("lazy-goer"). The goddess received here the souls of not only an array of criminals and perjurers but also those who were unfortunate enough to die or disease, old age, or without shedding blood.

Many items in her home named: her *arsal* (bed-hangings), Glittering Evil; her curtains, Misfortune; her knife, Starvation; her plate, Famine; her bed, Sickness; her table, Hunger; and her threshold, Stumbling-block.

Source: Belloni Du Chaillu, *Viking Age*, 33; Daly, *Norse Mythology A to Z*, 25, 48

The Elysian Fields (ee-LEE-zhun) (ee-LIHZ-ih-uhn FEELDZ)

Variations: Elysium

According to the mythology of the pre–Helenistic Greeks the Elysian Fields were a part of the UNDERWORLD region, TARTATUS; here, is where the souls of heroes, those with the favor of the gods, and those with the proper connections went to after their death; there was no moral requirement for admittance. It was ruled over by originally by Rhadamanthus, but later jointly with Cronos.

The Elysian Feilds always enjoyed pleasant weather and spectral game abounded. Demons, Furies, Harpies, and other creatures of HADES were barred from entering.

Although described as a wonderful place, one of the few reports of Elysium that exists is actually negative. The late Achilles told Odysseus as he was traveling through, he would rather be the slave of the poorest peasant than rule over the dead.

Source: Daly, *Greek and Roman Mythology, A to Z*, 50; Evans, *Dictionary of Mythology*, 81; Evslin, *Gods, Demigods, and Demons*, 61

Emain Ablach

Variations: Abhlach, Eamhain, Emhain, Emhain Ablach, Emhain

In Irish mythology Emain Ablach ("Island of Apples") was the location of an OTHER-WORLD, a place of everlasting beauty and summer whose residents danced the days away; it was here the hero Bran mac Febail traveled to, lured by the vision of a woman who left him a silver branch. Upon reaching Emain Ablach Bran found the mysterious woman, Niamh of the Golden Hair, and taking her as his lover, they spent many happy years together. As in many tales involving the OTHERWORLD, time moves more slowly in Emain Ablach.

Believed to be located off the coast of either Ireland or Scotland, Emain Ablach was an entryway into the OTHERWORLD; its capitol was Cruithin na Cuan and it was ruled by King Manannan Mac Lir, the Irish god of the sea.

Source: Koch, *Celtic Culture*, 146, 147; Monaghan. *Encyclopedia of Celtic Mythology and Folklore*, 173

Emne

The Irish OTHERWORLD, Emne has been described as a beautiful and hospitable island without death, debility, grief, sickness, or sorrow.

Source: Matthews, *Encyclopaedia of Celtic Myth and Legend*, 113, 115

Empyrean

According to Ptolemy, a Greco-Roman astrologer, astronomer, geographer, mathematician, poet, and writer, Empyrean was the fifth of the five HEAVENs; it was described as a plain of elemental fire, unapproachable light, and the seat of God.

Source: Bunson, *Angels A to Z*, 92

Enchanted Castles

The French playwright and writer Germain-François Poullain de Saint-Foix (February 1698–August 1776) explained the origins of enchanted castles in his "Historical Essays"; according to De Saint Foix females were the subject of abduction and violence as they passed an abbey or feudal castle. When these victims were sought after by their family and demanded to be returned; the monks who held them would begin a siege rather than release the women. When pressure to release the hostages increased the monks would bring to the walls a holy relic which would cause the assailants to desist rather than violate a holy item. This act, he claims, is the origin of enchanters, enchantments, and enchanted castles.

Source: Brewer, *Dictionary of Phrase and Fable*, 418; Disraeli, *Curiosities of Literature*, Volume 2, 188

Ephyra (EF-i-ruh)

Variations: Cornith

Founded by the ancient Greek king, Sisyphus, the city of Ephyra was said to have been originally populated by people who were grown out of mushrooms. One of its citizens was Bellerophon, the man who sought to tame the flying horse, Pegasus; he found the animal at the spring of Peirene, a landmark of the city. The fountain was said to have been formed by the tears of a mother who so cried over the accidental death of her son by the goddess, Artemis.

Source: Cahill, *Paradise Rediscovered*, 961; Grant, *Routledge Who's Who in Classical Mythology*, 98

Ercildoune, Castle of

Variations: Rhymer's Tower

Thomas the Rhymer who, according to the thirteenth century ballad of "True Thomas" visited the queen of the fairies in her castle,

Ercildoune. In Arthurian times this castle was seen as a gateway to the OTHERWORLD.

Source: Karr, *King Arthur Companion*, 145

Erebus (air'-i-buhs)

Variations: Erebos

In classical mythology Erebus ("darkness," "deep blackness," "shadow," and "sunset") was the mysterious place of darkness under the Earth through which the newly deceased arrived; these souls needed to pass through this realm of HADES order to reach the land of the god Pluto. Erebus was also the name of the father of Charon, the Ferryman who carried the souls of the deceased across the river STYX.

Source: Daly, *Greek and Roman Mythology, A to Z*, 51; Evans, *Dictionary of Mythology*, 84

Eridanus

Eridanus was a legendary river which was said to have flowed through the ELYSIAN FIELDS; its banks were fringed with laurel.

Source: Daly, *Greek and Roman Mythology, A to Z*, 51; Doane, *Bible Myths and Their Parallels in Other Religions*, 389

Erymanthus (air ih MAN thih uhn)

Variations: Mount Erymanthos

In Greek mythology Mount Erymanthus was the location where Heracles' fourth labor took place; there the demigod was sent to confront and defeat the monstrously large, vicious, and wild erymanthian boar.

Source: Evans, *Dictionary of Mythology*, 86; Morford, *Classical Mythology*, 421

Erytheia

Variations: the Red Island

A mythological island in Greek lore, Erytheia, located in the far west, was said to be the home of the giant Geryon and his herd of red cattle. The demigod, Heracles was sent to retrieve one of these cows for this tenth labor; he traveled to Erytheia in a golden boat he borrowed from the sun god, Helios.

Source: Huber, *Mythematics*, 30; Morford, *Classical Mythology*, 423

Estotiland

An island described by the Zeno Brothers' map (1558), Estotiland was charted as being located 1,000 miles west of FRISLAND. Those who claimed to have visited the island, six fisherment who were shipwrecked there said the natives were of European descent but spoke their own language; had books written in Latin but did not know how to read, although the locals were clearly intelligent. Estotiland was reputed to be developed enough to have cities, gods, and trade with Greeland brimstone, furs, and pitch.

Source: Babcock, *Legendary Islands of the Atlantic*, 128; White, *Exploration in the World of the Middle Ages*, 124

Eubcea, Island of (u-be-ah)

The coral cave home of the god of the sea, Neptune in Greek mythology, Eubcea was filled with nymphs.

Source: Guerber, *Myths of the Norsemen*, 359; Lemprière, *Classical Dictionary*, 121

Fahfah

According to Muslim beliefs, Fahfah is one of the rivers of al JANNA (PARADISE); it sources from the roots of the tree, Tuba. The waters of these rivers are described as being like honey, milk, water, and wine and along the banks are precious gems.

Source: Brewer, *Wordsworth Dictionary of Phrase and Fable*, 413, 1097

Fairy Fort

Variations: Barrow Mound, Burghs, Cashel, Fairy Mound, Forth, Lios, Place of the Fairies, RATH, Ring Fort, Rusheen, Stone Fort, Taigh Shidhe ("fairy house")

Found all over Ireland a fairy fort was the remains of a hill fort or some other circular dwelling; most of these locations date back to the Iron Age. At one time there was said to be as many as sixty-thousand such locations over the country; fairies were said to frequent these locations, thereby giving the name. It was believed damage to these ancient sites would anger the fairies who dwelt within and would cause some disaster to befall the perpetrator. Fairy forts were also believed to the entryway to FAIRYLAND.

Source: Bord, *Fairies*, 49; Eason, *Complete Guide to Faeries and Magical Beings*, 123–4; Illes, *Encyclopedia of Spirits*, 909; Narváez, *Good People*, 314

Fairy Island

A fairy island is an island only visible or able to be seen part of the time. In areas where these islands are said to appear sailors make a point to be cautious; landing on one of these islands is never considered to be a good idea, although in conflicting reports it is also believed anyone who goes to one of these islands will enjoy a lifetime of joy and pleasure. Examples of a fairy island would be AVALON and Anglesey of England; GRESHOLM of Wales; and ISLE OF THE BLEST, HY BRASIL of Ireland.

Source: Degidon, *New Catholic World*, Volume 85, 98; Froud, *Faeries*, 24–25; McCoy, *Witch's Guide to Faery Folk*, 43; Olcott, *Book of Elves and Fairies*, 91

Fairyland

Variations: ELFLAND, Faërieland, Faeryland, Fairy Kingdom, Fairy-Land, Faylinn ("fairy kingdom"), Feerieland, Tir Nan Og ("land of the young"), MAG MELL ("Plain of Honey"), Mag Mon ("Plain of Sports"), MAG MOR ("Great Plain"), Mag Rein ("Plain of Sea"), Tir fo Thuinn ("Land Under Waves"), Tir na nOg ("land of perpetual youth"), Tir Tairngiri ("Land of Promise")

The homeland of the fairies, Fairyland is described as being an enchanting place where happiness abounds; there is no illness or death, time stands still. It is not uncommon for a mortal who travels to Fairyland never to return, as in many mythologies the homeland of the fay is not merely located underground but is actually some sort of afterlife destination, perhaps even and alternative or parallel universe.

Although the entryways into the realm of the fay are located here on earth Fairyland said sometimes said to be underground or under-

water while other times it is described as being in some other nearby dimension or in-between place. These entry ways are usually located in a cave, in the side of a hill, or under the water. On the occasion Fairyland is said to be actually located on our world, it is described as being on top of a hill, but invisible to the human eye.

Unlike other designated lands, Fairyland is almost always described as being ruled over by a fairy queen, rather than a king, although there are many named fairy kings, few have been the king of Fairyland.

Source: Board, *Fairies*, 5–6, 122; Keightly, *World Guide to Gnomes, Fairies, Elves, and Other Little People*, 8, 56, 289; Monaghan. *Encyclopedia of Celtic Mythology and Folklore*, 348; Stepanich, *Faery Wicca*, Book One, 23, 87

The Fairy's Mirror

Within the forest of BROCÉLIANDE, there was, according to Arthurian lore, a place was known as PERILOUS VALLEY and here was the location of a lake known as the Fairy's Mirror; it was said that from here, nightmares rose up rom it like mist.

Source: Monaghan. *Encyclopedia of Celtic Mythology and Folklore*, 379

Falias

One of the four cities the legendary Tuatha de Danann of Celtic lore are said to originate, Falias is where the Lia Fail, the Stone of Destiny, came from; it was protected by the druid, Morfessa (see FINDIAS, GORIAS, and MURIAS).

Source: Ellis, *Brief History of the Druids*, 73, 124; Monaghan, *Encyclopedia of Celtic Mythology and Folklore*, 179

Fāngzhàng

Variations: Fanghu, Fang Hu

A mythological island PARADISE in the East China Sea, Fāngzhàng ("Square Kettle") is one of four FLOATING ISLANDS the Immortals are believed to live upon (see YÍNGZHŌU and YUÁNJIĀO). Each of these islands is 70,000 li apart from one another; each has a mountain on it rising 30,000 *li* (49,215,000 feet) high and at its top is a plain 90,000 *li* (147,645,000 feet). The palaces on each of these mountains is constructed of gold. The birds and beasts alike wear silk robes and the trees grow both fruit and pearls. Anyone who eats of them will never die. At one point the islands were fixed into place on the back of 15 celestial sea turtles.

Source: Chen, *Chinese Myths and Legends*, 26–27; Roberts, *Chinese Mythology: A to Z*, 60

Feather Mountain

Variations: Place Where Many Feathers Are Shed

A mythological mountain Feather Mountain was associated with the flood lore of Chinese folklore. Kun who was the first to try and stop the floodwaters, failed and died there.

Source: Christie, *Chinese Mythology*, 87; Porter, *From Deluge to Discourse*, 37, 81

Feikstaf

Variations: Feiknastafr

In Norse mythology Feikstaf is the hall of the god Baldur and his wife Nanna Nepsdottr; it was located on his estate, BREIDABLIK and was described as being made of a shining gold roof and silver pillars.

Sources: Grimes, *Norse Myths,* 19, 265

Fensalir

Variations: Fensal

In Norse mythology Fensalir ("Bog Hall") is the hall of the goddess Frigg, wife of the god Odin; in this place of mist the goddess spends her time at her spinning wheel with her eleven handmaidens. Some scholars believe Fensalir was located in a bog or swamp because followers of Frigg worshiped near a spring.

Source: Andrews, *Dictionary of Nature Myths*, 75; Bennett, *Gods and Religions of Ancient and Modern Times*, Volume 1, 386; Daly, *Norse Mythology A to Z*, 29

The Fields of Asphodel (ASS-fuh-del)

Variations: ASPHODEL MEADOWS

In Greek mythology and as described in the ancient Greek epic poem written by Homer, the *Odyssey* (xi), the Fields of Asphodel was a region of HADES where the spirits of heroes wander aimlessly among other and lesser spirits. The majority of the deceased dwell here. The landscape is described as a gloomy and monochromatic grey plain of nearly barren ground where the plant for whom the region is named after, asphodel, grows in abundance; the plant is unattractive and blooms with either white or yellow flowers that have no scent. The three judges of the UNDERWORLD Aeacus, Minos, and Rhadamanthys, rule here although HADES rules the entire Underworld.

If a libation of blood in offered up to one of these deceased heroes they will reawaken and experience their humanity in the Fields of Asphodel for a period of time.

Source: Graves, *Greek Myths*, n.p.; Hard, *Routledge Handbook of Greek Mythology*, 109; Westmoreland, *Ancient Greek Beliefs*, 69

Fields of Food

A PARADISE realm in the mythology of ancient Egyptian, the Fields of Food is ruled over by the god, Anup.

Source: Bunson, *Encyclopedia of Ancient Egypt*, 209; Massey, *Ancient Egypt, the Light of the World*, 512

Fimbulthul

Variations: Fimblethul, Fimbuthul

According to Norse mythology Fimbulthul ("Mighty Speaker" or "Mighty Wind") was one of rivers which ran from ASGARD to MIDGARD. It was created from the water dripping off of the antlers of Eikthryir as he stood atop the roof of VALHALLA eating leaves off YGGDRASYLL.

Source: Anderson, *Norse Mythology*, 444; Bennett, *Gods and Religions of Ancient and Modern Times*, Volume 1, 386; Guerber, *Myths of the Norsemen*, 13, 263; Lindow, *Norse Mythology*, 115, 189

Findias

Variations: Findrias, Finias

In Irish mythology Findias ("Blessed" or "Bright") was one of the cities of the Tuatha de Danann; it was ruled by a druid called

Uscias. The unerring sword of King Nuadd was forged in Findias (see FALIAS, GORIAS, and MURIAS).

Source: Macleod, *Celtic Myth and Religion*, 92, 93; Monaghan. *Encyclopedia of Celtic Mythology and Folklore*, 187

Fire, Lake of *see* Lake of Fire

Fjorm

According to Norse mythology Fjorm was one of rivers which ran from ASGARD to MIDGARD. It was created from the water dripping off of the antlers of Eikthryir as he stood atop the roof of VALHALLA eating leaves off YGGDRASYLL. The collective name for these rivers was ELIVAGER.

Source: Daly, *Norse Mythology A to Z*, 24; Guerber, *Myths of the Norsemen*, 13, 263

Flame, Island of

Variations: Island of Fire, Island of Peace, Khemenu ("Town of Eight")

In the mythology of the ancient Egyptians, the Island of Flame was the location of the birth of the sun god, Osiris. A region of the kingdom of Osiris, the Island of Flame was associated with the rising sun; it was a magical place said to lay far to the east, beyond the limits of the mortal world. The Island of Flame was a realm of everlasting light where the gods were born.

Source: Cahill, *Paradise Rediscovered*, 327; Malkowski, *Before the Pharaohs*, 229

Floating Island

Variation: Phantom Island, Sailing Island, Vanishing Island

Popular in Chinese, Gaelic, Greek, Mesopotamian, Norse, and Scottish mythology, although they appear in other mythologies as well, floating islands were most often reported by ancient sailors, especially after a storm. Commonly a floating island was described as being a PARADISE and the home of a divinity or a divine treasure, such as the Well of Immortality. These islands are sometimes used

in folklore as a symbol of death or the afterlife.

Source: Andrews, *Dictionary of Nature Myths*, 103; Nunn, *Vanished Islands and Hidden Continents of the Pacific*, 92

Floating Islands, Canadian

In Lake Superior there is said to be a group of FLOATING ISLANDS ruled by a vexatious god to whom the local Indian population would pay tribute to by tossing ornaments and tobacco into the water. The islands are described as being covered with beautiful flowers and trees, melodic birds, sparkling crystals, and sweet fruits. Because the god who watched over these islands is extremely jealous he will throw up banks of thick fog to prevent travelers from landing upon the shore and causing them to wreck into the rocky shoreline.

Source: Manguel, *Dictionary of Imaginary Places*, 109; Skinner, *Myths and Legends of America*, 189

Flowers, Lake of *see* Lake of Flowers

Folkvang (fok'vang)

Variations: Fólkvangr, Folkvangr, Folkvangur

In Norse mythology Folkvang ("Battlefield" or "field of folk" or "People Field") was the realm of the goddess, Freya; her dwelling place in ASGARD was the great hall known as SESSRYMNIR ("the roomy-seated"). The goddess welcomed half of those slain in battle into Folkvang each day; the other half were sent to Oden's VALHALLA.

Source: Daly, *Norse Mythology A to Z*, 30; Dunham, *History of Denmark, Sweden, and Norway*, Volume 2, 55; Guerber, *Myths of the Norsemen*, 77, 131; Lindow, *Norse Mythology*, 118

Food, Fields of *see* Fields of Food

Fools, Paradise of *see* Paradise of Fools

The Forest Campacorentin *see* Campacorentin, the Forest

Forest of Cedars

In Akkadian mythology the Forest of the Cedars was the home of the goddess Irmina, a form of Ishtar; it was guarded by Humbaba (Huwawa, Khumbaba), a monstrous giant. The forest was described as covering "ten thousand double-hours" (70,000 miles) worth of land.

Source: Chisholm, *Encyclopedia Britannica*, Volume 12, 19; Malkowski, *Before the Pharaohs*, 104

Forest of Mandara *see* Mandara, Forest of

Forest of Misadventure

The Forest of Misadventure from Arthurian lore was the location of the DEVIL'S ROAD; on the other side of the forest was the VALLEY OF NO RETURN.

Source: Bruce, *Arthurian Name Dictionary*, 145

Forest of the Boiling Well *see* Boiling Well, Forest of the

Fortunate Isles

There have been several FLOATING ISLANDS sighted just off the coast of Ireland and Scotland which have been called Fortunate Isles, a reference likely to the fay, the gods, or the Tuatha de Danann.

Source: Ashe, *Mythology of the British Isles*, 247; Monaghan. *Encyclopedia of Celtic Mythology and Folklore*, 199

Fountain of Changing Colors

Believed to be located near La Tour Quaree on the Salerne River, the Fountain of Changing Colors of Arthurian lore was so named because its water would change colors whenever a sinner or unclean person would approach; it was also where Josephe once preached. There is an inscription upon the rock at the base of the fountain left there by Josephe, it reads: "*The adventure of the Fountain will be achieved by the great lion with the marvelous neckband.*"

Source: Karr, *King Arthur Companion*, 108

Franangrs-Fors

Variations: Franangrs-Force

In Norse mythology Franangrs-Fors was the waterfall in which god Loki in the shape-shifted form of a salmon swam; it was here the gods caught him and bound him up.

Source: Anderson, *Norse Mythology*, 445; Rydberg, *Teutonic Mythology*, 1020

Frisland

Variations: Fixland, Freezeland, Friesland, Frischlant, Frislandia

An island which appeared on nearly all maps made between 1560 and 1600, rectangular shaped Frisland was at first thought to be Iceland but the Zeno Brother's map (1558) placed it as an island south of Iceland.

Source: Babcock, *Legendary Islands of the Atlantic*, 142

Frodi, Mill of (fro'de)

Variations: Grótti

In Norse mythology the Mill of Frodi was said to have belonged to Peace Frodi, a king who ruled Denmark when there was believed to peace throughout the world; it was given to him by Hengikiaptr ("hanging jaw"). His mill was enchanted and could easily grind up anything he wished including gold, peace, and prosperity.

Source: Guerber, *Myths of the Norsemen*, 128; Thorpe, *Northern Mythology*, Volume 1, 207

Fu Sang

Variations: Fousang

A mythical island in Chinese lore Fu Sang was the seat of a great civilization according to a Buddhist monk named Hui-Shen who claimed to have spent several years there. He described it to the Imperial Chinese court in AD 502 where he was received as an ambassador; according to the priest, in AD 458 five Buddhist monks first arrived there and taught their religion to the people.

Fu Sang did not have any iron but was rich in copper; it had no citadels, fixed prices, implements of war, tariff, walled cities, or warfare.

Homes were made of cedar beams and reed mats. Criminals were judged in excavated locations and if found guilty would be covered in ash; such a stigma could last for generations, especially if the guilty party was a person of social rank. The people enjoyed domestic bison, deer, and horses, ate mulberries, and knew how to create fabric and paper; they were ruled by a chief and his cadre of advisors.

Source: Davis, *Weird Washington*, 55–56; Rees, *Secret Maps of the Ancient World*, 48, 94

Galafort Castle

Variations: Galeforf, Grand St. Graal

The first British castle Joseph of Arimathea, along with his followers, entered, Castle Galafort, named after Sir Galahad,was ruled by Duke Ganor, who, under the influence of Celidoine, Nascien's son, converted to Christianity. A Christian stronghold, Galafort was where the Holy Grail was kept until Sir Alan and Joshua left to found CARBONEK CASTLE.

Source: Bruce, *Arthurian Name Dictionary* 197; Karr, *Arthurian Companion*, 168; Rhys, *Studies in the Arthurian Legend*, 328

Gandharva-Loka

Variations: Gandharvaloka

One of the eight regions of material existence in Hindu mythology, Gandharva-Loka, is the realm of the heavenly spirits; it is ruled by King Chitraratha. Living in beautiful cities these bird- and horse-headed beings sing the praises of the gods. In the seven spheres of the earth, Gandharva-Loka is the fourth.

Source: Dowson, *Classical Dictionary of Hindu Mythology and Religion*, 180; Wilson, *Vishńu Puráńa*, 48, 140

Gaora

According to the traveler and English writer Richard Hakluyt (1553–1616), Gaora was a land where the people had no head; their eyes were located in their shoulders, and their mouths in their chests.

Source: Dale, *Book of Where*, 49

Garden of Eden

Variations: Eden, Field of Souls, Gan Eden

Perhaps one of the most ancient and venerable names of mythology, the Garden of Eden was not only the location of the creation of mankind but also the only place and time when man did not know pain, suffering, or want and all knowledge was freely given to him.

According to Biblical mythology, in the first book of the Bible, chapter two of Genesis, it was said God created an idyllic place with ample food and water; this location was known as the Garden of Eden; it was a place of ease, fertility, and harmony as disease and death were unknown here. A river was described as flowing through it and after leaving the garden branching out into four streams, the Euphrates, GIHON, PISON, and the Tigris.

Tended after by the first man, Adam, and his wife, Eve, God put in this idealized birthplace of humanity "every beast of the field and every fowl of the air" in the garden. Also located here was the Tree of Knowledge and so long as neither of the humans ever ate of its fruit they would have a peaceful existence. Eventually Eve was tempted by the serpent to eat the fruit; she in turn then tempted Adam to follow suit. Upon discovery of their crime God banished the couple from the garden, "to the east and into the land of Nodd." Guarding the entrance to the garden now are cherubim with fiery swords.

Source: Frankel, *Encyclopedia of Jewish Symbols*, 45–46; Greer, *New Encyclopedia of the Occult*, 144; Leviton, *Encyclopedia of Earth Myths*, n.p.; McClintock, *Cyclopaedia of Biblical, Theological, and Ecclesiastical Literature*, Volume 3, 52–53

Garden of Joy

Variations: Joie de la Cort, Joy of the Court, Schoydelakurt

In Arthurian lore Sir Mabonagrain fell in love with one of Enide's cousins, Elena, and the couple retreated to Evtain's castle, BRANDIGANT. There, Mabonagrain swore to his lady love to remain with her in the castle's garden, which they named the Garden of Joy, until such a time as another knight could defeat him in honest combat. Mabonagrain defeated all comers and perhaps as a deterrent to others, placed the decapitated heads of his opponents on pikes throughout the garden he and his lady lived in. As gruesome as this token of his victory was, no one in the story seemed to think it harsh, brutal, or in any way disgusting or inappropriate. The Garden of Joy was described as being perfectly suited for lovers secret hideaway, as it was magically enclosed allowing every kind of bird, fruit, and herb to prosper there all year round. The story, *Erec*, by French poet and trabodur Chrétien de Troyes, is the origin of this tale.

Source: Bruce, *Arthurian Name Dictionary*, 285; Karr, *Arthurian Companion*, 253

Garden of the Gods

In the mythology of the ancient Sumerians the Garden of the Gods was the PARADISE home of the Annanuki. In the *Epic of Gilgamesh*, the hero travels through the FOREST OF CEDARS to arrive at the Garden of the Gods; little description of this place remain as the lines of text concerning events here have been damaged beyond translation. The text we have says the garden is the source of a river and lies next to a mountain covered in cedars. Within the garden Gilgamesh discovers an array of precious stones such as agate, lapis lazuli, and pearls.

Source: Kluger, *Archetypal Significance of Gilgamesh*; 162–63; Kramer, *The Sumerians*, 293; Maier, *Gilgamesh*, 144

Garden of the Hesperides

The Garden of the Hesperides of Greek mythology was the sacred garden of the goddess Hera occupied by her nymphs, the Hesperides; it was from here the gods received their immortality from the Apples of Joy. Described by the renowned Greek author and explore Scylax of Caryanda as being enclosed on all sides by a wall ten *stadia* tall and wide the Garden of the Hesperides was densely filled with a wide array of fruit trees. Originally the Greeks said the garden was located close to

Mount Atlas but later it was said to be in West Africa.

One of the trees in the garden produced golden fruit, the Apples of Joy, which bestowed immortality upon any who ate them; this tree was guarded by a fierce serpent known as Ladon.

Source: Anthon, *Classical Dictionary*, 615; Illes, *Encyclopedia of Spirits*, 484; Spence, *Encyclopaedia of Occultism, reprint*, 319

Gastropnir

In Norse mythology Gastropnir ("guest squeezer") was the home of the giantess Menglad; it was made from the limbs of Leirbrimir ("clay giant") and was believed to be strong enough to last until the end of time. This stronghold prevents unwanted visitors by entrapping uninvited guests in its walls of clay.

Source: Bellows, *Poetic Edda*, 242; Lincoln, *Death, War, and Sacrifice*, 113

The Gates of Death

According to Jewish Cabalists, there are seven levels to HELL; ALADDON, the Gates of Death, GEBEANOM, the Mire of Clay, the Pit of Corruption, the Shadow of Death, and SHEOL.

These realms are set one atop the other; ordinary fire is one-sixtieth the heat of the fire of GEBEANOM which is one-sixtieth the heat of the GATES OF DEATH, which is one-sixtieth the heat of the SHADOW OF DEATH, which is one-sixtieth the heat of the PIT OF CORRUPTION, which is one-sixtieth the heat of the Mire of Clay, which is one-sixtieth the heat of ALADDON, which is one-sixtieth the heat of SHEOL.

Source: Brewer, *Dictionary of Phrase and Fable*, 596; Mew, *Traditional Aspects of Hell*, 173

Gazewilte

In the thirteenth century French poem, *Vulgate Cycle*, an Arthurian Romance, castle Gazewilte is ruled over by Sir Persides; it is here where the lord of the castle imprisons his wife, Helaine, for five years until Sir Ector de Maris defeats him and rescues the lady.

Source: Karr, *Arthurian Companion,* 193, Sommer, *Vulgate Version of the Arthurian Romances,* 391

Gebeanom

According to Jewish Cabalists, there are seven levels to HELL; ALADDON, the GATES OF DEATH, Gebeanom, the MIRE OF CLAY, the PIT OF CORRUPTION, the SHADOW OF DEATH, and SHEOL.

These realms are set one atop the other; ordinary fire is one-sixtieth the heat of the fire of GEBEANOM which is one-sixtieth the heat of the GATES OF DEATH, which is one-sixtieth the heat of the SHADOW OF DEATH, which is one-sixtieth the heat of the PIT OF CORRUPTION, which is one-sixtieth the heat of the Mire of Clay, which is one-sixtieth the heat of ALADDON, which is one-sixtieth the heat of SHEOL.

Source: Brewer, *Dictionary of Phrase and Fable,* 596; Mew, *Traditional Aspects of Hell,* 173

Gehenna

Variations: Gai ben–Hinnom ("Valley of Hinnom's son") Ge Hinnom ("Valley of Hinnom"), Geenna, Gehennem, Gehenom, Gehinnam, Gehinnon, Gehinnom ("Valley of the Hinnom"), Gehinnom, Gehinom, JAHANNAM

Originally, Gehenna was a valley west of Jerusalem where King Solomon built temples where child sacrifices were made to the gods Chemosh and Moloch. Later the same area was used as the city's garbage dump where perpetual fires were continuously burning down the trash. Since that time, the name Gehenna has become synonymous with evil and has since been imagined to be a gateway to HELL.

The *Book of Enoch* describes Gehenna as a burning HELL filled with coal, pitch, and sulpher, where the wicked are tethered and set ablaze in a furnace. Rabbinic lore describes Gehenna as a place of punishment alternating between fire and ice. Souls are said to be divided into three categories, the Beinonim ("in-between"), the Righteous, and the Wicked; each of these groups must spend some time in Gehenna to purify their soul. Most rabbis

teach that a soul's stay in Gehinnon is typically one year long but no more than twelve years in all, except for blasphemers and heretics whose souls will face total annihilation. During their time in Gehinnon, a sort of PURGATORY, the souls is purged of the sins committed in life.

Gehenna came into being on the second day of Creation; it has three gates, each guarded by an angel, Kipod, Nasagiel, and Samael; one gate opens up to a desert, another opens up to the sea and the third opens to Ben Hinnom located just outside Jerusalem.

Source: Brener, *Mourning and Mitzvah,* 138–39; Dennis, *Encyclopedia of Jewish Myth, Magic, and Mysticism,* 103–04; Mathers, *Sorcerer and His Apprentice,* 24

Geirridr's Garth

Variations: Geirödhsgard, Geirridsgard, Geirroðargardar, Geirrodr's Garth, Geirródr's Garth, Gerrodr's Gard

Geirridr's Garth was the hrymthursar home of Geirridr, according to Norse mythology; the river VIMER ran near it. Geirridr's Garth is described as looking like a large mountain with a massive chimney sticking out of its top.

Source: Grimes, *Norse Myths,* 140, 269

Geirvimul (GAYR-vim-ul)

Variations: Geirvimul

According to Norse mythology Geirvimul ("quick with spears" or "Spear-Teeming") was one of rivers which ran from ASGARD to MIDGARD. It was created from the water dripping off of the antlers of Eikthryir as he stood atop the roof of VALHALLA eating leaves off YGGDRASYLL.

Source: Anderson, *Norse Mythology,* 446; Grimes, *Norse Myths,* 263, 269; Guerber, *Myths of the Norsemen,* 13, 263

Gevurah (geh-voor-AH)

Variations: Geburah

The fifth of the ten sephirot in the Kabbalistic tree of life, Gevurah is the second emotive attributes of the sephirot. Located above Hod, below Binah and across from Chesed, Gevurah typically is drawn with four paths to each of its neighbors. Associated with the color red, Gevurah is known as "concealment," "judgment," "power," "restraint," and "strength." Said to be the Left Hand of God, Gevurah is understood as to how God judging humanity and punishes the wicked with absolute adherence to the letter of the law and a strict meting out of justice.

Source: Kaplan, *Innerspace*, 41, 61; Samuel, *Kabbalah Handbook*, 114

Ghayy

In Islamic lore Ghayy ("destruction") is a chamber or valley in HUTAMA, one of the seven Hells; within, the souls there are punished so severely the souls on the other levels of HELL pray 400 times a day in order to avoid being moved there.

Source: Chopra, *Encyclopaedic Dictionary of Religion: G–P*, 313; Wagner, *How Islam Plans to Change the World*, 156

The Ghuls, Kingdom of

Variations: Kingdom of the Ghouls

According to the ancient Persian fairytale, *Sindbad the Sailor* (750 CE), the kingdom of the Ghuls was an island named in the fourth voyage of the fictional sailor's adventures. In the tale, after his ship was wrecked, he and the survivors washed ashore upon an island and were immediately taken captive by the unclad natives. The prisoners were force-fed food laced with a drug that stupefied them so they could be fattened up before being slaughtered and eaten. Sindbad alone refused to eat and was therefore able to escape.

Source: Burton, *Seven Voyages of Sinbad the Sailor*, 30–39; Sprague de Camp, *Lands Beyond*, 132

Giallar Bridge (gyal'lar)

In Norse mythology the Giallar Bridge crossed over the GIOLL River in NIFLHEIM. Described as being made of arched crystal it was suspended by a single hair in place. Guarding this bridge was a grim looking skeleton named Modgud; each spirit who would pass would have to pay her a toll of blood. The spirits that crossed the Giallar on the horses or wagons which were burnt in their funeral pyres as the journey through this region was a painful one over the roughest roads in the coldest and darkest region of the North.

Source: Brewer, *Dictionary of Phrase and Fable*, 514; Guerber, *Myths of the Norsemen*, 180–81

Giants, Land of *see* Land of Giants

Gihon (gi'HON)

The second of the four rivers described as flowing through the GARDEN OF EDEN, Gihon ("Gushing Forth"), whose entomology indicates it was a fast running river, was said to then "encircle the land of Cush," a geographic impossibility since the two of the other rivers named, the Euphrates and the Tigris are in Mesopotamia; biblical and secular scholar alike heavily debate which modern river, if any, could be the biblical Gihon and PISON (Pishon) have been.

Source: McClintock, *Cyclopaedia of Biblical, Theological, and Ecclesiastical Literature*, Volume 3, 861–62

Gimle

Variations: Vingolf

In Norse mythology, Gimle was one of the Nine Worlds and the residence of the eternal being, Alfadur; after the destruction of the universe, Ragnarok, this was meant to be the home of those souls considered to be good.

Source: Dunham, *History of Denmark, Sweden, and Norway*, Volume 2, 52; Evans, *Dictionary of Mythology*, 104

Gimli (geem-lee)

Variations: Gimil, Gimill, GIMLE, Gimlé, Gîmle, Gimlir

In Norse mythology Gimli ("HEAVEN") was a golden-roofed hall in ASGARD. The highest of the heavenly abodes, Gimli will be the resting place and refuge of the virtuous after the battle of Ragnarok.

Source: Anderson, *Norse Mythology*, 446; Grimes, *Norse Myths*, 270; Guerber, *Myths of the Norsemen*, 339

Ginnunga-Gap (gi-noon' ga-gap or ghin-un-ga-gap)

Variations: Ginnunggap

In Norse mythology Ginnunga-Gap ("yawning gap") was the primeval ABYSS located in the center of space; it was the nothingness before the start of time. Ginnunga-Gap was so deep no one could see its bottom; it was in a perpetual state of twilight with calm and mild air. North of Ginnunga-Gap is NIFLEHEIM a land of misty ice; to the south lays the fiery realm of MUSPELHEIMR.

Source: Daly, *Norse Mythology A to Z*, 39; Evans, *Dictionary of Mythology*, 104; Guerber, *Myths of the Norsemen*, 2

Gioll (gyoll)

Variations: Gjoll

In Norse mythology, Gioll was the great rock the gods found in the center of the earth; from it they forged the chains Gelgja to which they tied the fetters Gelgia to the god Fenris to the boulder THVITI.

Source: Bennett, *Gods and Religions of Ancient and Modern Times*, Volume 1, 387; Daly, *Norse Mythology A to Z*, 39; Guerber, *Myths of the Norsemen*, 93

Giöll (gyel)

In Norse mythology, Giöll ("resounding") was a river which forms one of the boundaries of NIFLHEIM. Over this river is the bridge, GIALLAR (GJALLARBRU). This river which runs the closest to the hall of the goddess Hel, separates the land of the living from the afterlife. Giöll was one of the rivers which came forth from the fountain HVERGELMIR WELL.

Source: Bennett, *Gods and Religions of Ancient and Modern Times*, Volume 1, 387; Daly, *Norse Mythology A to Z*, 39; Grimm, *Teutonic Mythology*, 803; Guerber, *Myths of the Norsemen*, 181

Gipul

According to Norse mythology Gipul was one of rivers which ran from ASGARD to MIDGARD. It was created from the water dripping off of the antlers of Eikthryir as he stood atop the roof of VALHALLA eating leaves off YGGDRASYLL. Other sources claim Gipul was one of the rivers which came forth from the fountain HVERGELMIR WELL located in NIFLHEIM.

Source: Guerber, *Myths of the Norsemen*, 13, 263; Sturluson, *Younger Edda*, 279

Gjallarbru Bridge (gyall-ar-broo)

Variations: GIALLAR, Gjallarbrú, Gjallar-Bridge

In Norse mythology Gjallarbru ("Resounding Bridge") was the bridge which spanned across the river GIÖLL connecting the lands of the living and the deceased. This was the bridge the god Hermod crossed to enter into the land of Hel, NIFLHEIM, to search for the soul of the god Balder. Gjallarbru was described as being made of crystal, having a golden roof, and suspended by a single hair, as the weight of the dead do not require more support. The far side of the bridge is blocked by a gated wall known by many names including Corpse Gate, HELGRINDR, NAGRINDR, and Valgrindr.

Source: Anderson, *Norse Mythology*, 446; Bennett, *Gods and Religions of Ancient and Modern Times*, Volume 1, 387; Daly, *Norse Mythology A to Z*, 39; Grimes, *Norse Myths*, 73

Gladsheimr (glädz-him)

Variations: Gladsheim, Glads-heim, Glaosheimr, Gludsheim ("Home of Brightness")

In Norse mythology Gladsheimr ("Gleaming Home" or "Happy Home") was a magnificent hall in VALHALLA, ASGARD containing twelve seats, one for each of the primary gods. This hall was the location where the Æsir meet for council. It was described as being made out of a solid piece of gold which had been carved and crafted into a grand palace; it was said to be the most beautiful of all the Asgardian palaces.

Source: Bennett, *Gods and Religions of Ancient and Modern Times*, Volume 1, 388; Dunham, *History of Denmark, Sweden, and Norway*, Volume 2, 55; Evans, *Dictionary of Mythology*, 105; Guerber, *Myths of the Norsemen*, 260; Leviton, *Gods in Their Cities*, 69

Glasir Grove (gla'sir)

Variations: Brunnakr Grove, BRUNNAKER Grove, Glaser, Glaser Grove

In Norse mythology Glasir Grove, located near the southern ridge of ASGARD, was an orchard of apple trees that had leaves made of red gold; it was near both GIMLI and GLADSHEIMR. In the middle of this forest, the god Odin had a third palace. Many of the horses of ASGARD grazed here including Falhofnir, Gering, Gisl, Glenr, Gyllir, Hafeti, Hjalmtheer, Jor, Lettfeti, Lungr, Silfrintoppr, Sinir, Skaevadr, Skeidbrimir, Soti, Tjaldari, and Vigg.

Source: Bennett, *Gods and Religions of Ancient and Modern Times*, Volume 1, 388; Grimes, *Norse Myths*, 260; Guerber, *Myths of the Norsemen*, 18

Glitnir (glit'nir)

Variations: Glitner

Glitnir ("glittering"), located in ASGARD, was the palace of the just and righteous god and lawgiver of the Æsir, Forseti (Forsete), the son of the gods Balder and Nanna. Located in ASGARD, Glitnir was described as being radiant and having a silver thatched roof which was supported by pillars of gold. Forseti would sit enthroned in Glitnir and acting as the lawgiver of the gods would everyday listen to their complaints and make settlements so fair none ever complained.

Source: Dunham, *History of Denmark, Sweden, and Norway*, Volume 2, 55; Grimes, *Norse Myths*, 19, 271; Guerber, *Myths of the Norsemen*, 142

Gloevant

Variations: Gloant, Glocuen, Gloevant Bohort, Gloeven, Gloevent, Gloovent, Golant

In the thirteenth century French poem, *Vulgate Cycle*, Gloevant was a forest, likely located near Stanggore.

Source: Karr, *Arthurian Companion*, 196; Sommer, *Vulgate Version of the Arthurian Romances*, 44

Glouchedon

Variations: Glevum, Glocedon, Godelone

In the thirteenth century *Vulgate Cycle*, Sir Gawaine wins a warhorse in a tournament named Gringolet; so impressed with the mount he declares to his brothers and father "I have won such a horse that I would never exchange it for the castle of Glouchedon."

Source: Karr, *Arthurian Companion*, 196; Sommer, *Vulgate Version of the Arthurian Romances*, 343

Gnipahellir

Variations: Gnipa

A cave from Norse mythology, Gnipahellir ("Gnipa-Cave"), located in HEL, is guarded by a fierce and howling dog with a blood-stained chest known as Garm.

Source: Anderson, *Norse Mythology*, 387; Daly, *Norse Mythology A to Z*, 40; Lindow, Norse Mythology, 147

Gnita

Variations: Gnita-heath ("Glittering Heath"), Gnitaheior

In Norse mythology Gnita ("Glittering") is the home of Fafner in his monstrous dragon-form and where he kept the treasure known as Andvarenaut.

Source: Bennett, *Gods and Religions of Ancient and Modern Times*, Volume 1, 388; Anderson, *Norse Mythology*, 377, 447

Godhava

Variations: Apara-Godana, Apara-Godaniya, Godana

In Hindu mythology, Godhava was one of the four continents located in the outermost concentric circles surrounding Mount MERU (see JAMBUDVIPA, VIRAT-OLEHA, and UTTARA KURU). Located to the west, it was said to be the home of round faced beefeaters.

In in Buddhist cosmology Godhava was known as Godana and was described as being the shape of a half-moon and lying directly west of SUMERU.

Source: Howard, *Imagery of the Cosmological Buddha*, 66; Kern, *Manual of Indian Buddhism*, 57; Sprague de Camp, *Lands Beyond*, 282

Goloka Vrindavana

Variations: Krishnaloka

The personal abode of Lord Krishna, Goloka Vrindavana is described as being shaped like a giant lotus flower; upon each leaf of the flower a different pastime is enjoyed. Here, Krishna partakes in transcendental ecstasy while his devotees offer their service to him.

Source: Knapp, *Heart of Hinduism*, 235, 589

Gomel

According to Norse mythology Gomel was one of rivers which ran from ASGARD to MIDGARD. It was created from the water dripping off of the antlers of Eikthryir as he stood atop the roof of VALHALLA eating leaves off YGGDRASYLL.

Source: Grimes, *Norse Myths*, 263; Guerber, *Myths of the Norsemen*, 13, 263

Gomorrah *see* Sodom and Gomorrah

Gomul

Variations: Gömul

According to Norse mythology Gomul was one of sixteen rivers which ran from ASGARD to MIDGARD.

Source: Anderson, *Norse Mythology*, 447; Bennett, *Gods and Religions of Ancient and Modern Times*, Volume 1, 388; Grimes, *Norse Mythology*, 271; Guerber, *Myths of the Norsemen*, 13

Gopul

Variations: Göpul

According to Norse mythology Gopul was one of rivers which ran from ASGARD to MIDGARD. It was created from the water dripping off of the antlers of Eikthryir as he stood atop the roof of VALHALLA eating leaves off YGGDRASYLL.

Source: Bennett, *Gods and Religions of Ancient and Modern Times*, Volume 1, 388; Grimes, *Norse*

Mythology, 271; Guerber, *Myths of the Norsemen*, 13, 263

Gorias

One of the four cities the legendary Tuatha de Danann of Celtic lore are said to originate from, Gorias was a city said to be located in the OTHERWORLD (see FALIAS, FINDIAS, and MURIAS); it was the site of the creation of the Spear of Lugh. It was from where the druid, Urias of the Noble Stature came from.

Source: Ellis, *Brief History of the Druids*, 73, 124; Monaghan, *Encyclopedia of Celtic Mythology and Folklore*, 224

Gorsedd Arberth

A mound in the kingdom of ARBERTH, Gorsedd Arberth is said to be blessed with magical properties; anyone of high birth sitting upon it is either beaten soundly by invisible hands or has a vision of a wonderful marvel.

Source: John, *Popular Studies in Mythology, Romance and Folklore*, Volumes 11–16, 22; Koch, *Celtic Culture*, 1610

Gotham

In British folklore, Gotham is a proverbial town said to be inhabited by fools and men who play idle pranks; it is similar to CHELM and SCHILDBURG.

Source: Ben-Amos, *Folktales of the Jews*, 453; Hodgson, *Beauties of England and Wales*, 188–89

Grad

Variations: Graad, Gráð, Gráth, Grod, Groth

According to Norse mythology Grad was one of rivers which ran from ASGARD to MIDGARD.

Source: Bennett, *Gods and Religions of Ancient and Modern Times*, Volume 1, 388; Grimes, *Norse Mythology*, 271; Guerber, *Myths of the Norsemen*, 13

Grao

According to Norse mythology Grao ("Greedy") was one of sixteen rivers which ran from ASGARD to MIDGARD.

Source: Guerber, *Myths of the Norsemen*, 13; Sturlusonar, *Prose Edda of Snorri Sturluson*, 65

Great Below

Variations: "The Country Unseen" and "The Place of Darkness"

According to Sumerian mythology the Great Below (*"Ki-Gal"*), a HELL, was under the dominion of the goddess Irkalla and the home of the UNDERWORLD deities. Described as a having a cave entrance this realm was surrounded by seven walls, each of which had a gate; the watchman of all the gates was Nedu. Any who wished to enter must first perform an ancient ritual. It was to the Great Below the goddess Ishtar traveled to in search for her spouse, Tammuz.

Source: Kramer, *Sumerian Mythology*, 41, 76, 88

Great Ireland

Variations: Hibernia Major, Hvítramanna-land ("White-men's-land"), Irland it mikla ("Ireland the Great")

A little known PHANTOM ISLAND in the Atlantic ocean near eastern Canada, Great Ireland was first mentioned in the *Landnámabók* (circa 1300) as being six days sailing due west of Ireland. In the *"Saga of Erik the Red"* it was described as having no houses, its population living in caves or dugouts, speaking Erse, and wearing white robes.

Source: Baring-Gould, *Curious Myths of the Middle Ages*, 284–85; Woolf, *From Pictland to Alba*, 285

Greek Rivers of the Underworld *see* Underworld, Greek Rivers of the

Green Chapel

The Green Chapel of Arthurian lore said to be located not two miles from the court of CAMELOT, was described as being an ancient and overgrown hollow barrow or cave on the ootherside of a hill. There is a rocky path that leads to the craggy valley where there is a rushes stream running alongside the Chapel. Upon finding it Gawaine suspects the Green Knight uses this location to partake in unchristian devotions.

Source: Hill, *Looking Westward*, 100–101; Karr, *Arthurian Companion,* 208

Green Isle

Variations: Isle of Apples

A FLOATING ISLAND off the Scottish coast, Green Isle was believed to be part of FAIRY-LAND, filled with beautiful orchards growing magical fruits; in many tales it is said to be populated only by women.

Source: Monaghan. *Encyclopedia of Celtic Mythology and Folklore*, 228

Gresholm

Variations: Gresholme, Isle of Gwales

A FAIRY ISLAND from Welsh lore, Gresholm was once described by Captain John Evanz, as being a large tract of land covered in thick, waving grass, laying two or three feet below the surface of the English Channel; the effect of looking upon Gresholm made the Captain feel dizzy. According to George Owen's *History of Pembrokeshire* (1602) it lay eight miles off the mainland.

Source: McCoy, *Witch's Guide to Faery Folk*, 43; Rhys, *Studies in the Arthurian Legend*, 394; Squire, *Celtic Myth and Legend*, 394–95

Grey Lake of Cuilenn

Variations: Culann, Cullen

In Irish mythology the Grey Lake of Cuilenn was under the dominion of the fairy king, Cuilenn. The lake, which would turn anyone who swam in it grey, was located on the summit of a mountain called SLIEVE GULLION. According to legend, when the hero Finn bathed in the lake to gain wisdom it robbed him of his strength and youth transforming him into an old man. Only when the fairy King presented him with a golden challis filled with the same lake water did his strength and youth return; additionally, he was granted the wisdom and supernatural knowledge he sought.

Source: Lincoln, *Death, War, and Sacrifice*, 56; Monaghan, *Encyclopedia of Celtic Mythology and Folklore*, 109

Grippia

In the German metrical romance of the twelfth century, "*Herzog Ernst von Schwaben*" ("*Duke Ernst of Swabia*") Grippa was a land described as being as large as England, cultivated and fruitful, having grain fields, orchards, and vineyards; it lay somewhere in the Mediterranean sea, about a three day sail from Syria. Its people, called Agrippians, were generally villainous with sub-human moral standards, killing anyone who visited their land with poison arrows. In addition to this, the Agrippians had the heads of birds; men had the heads of cranes and wore red tunics, each one carrying a bow, buckler, and knife. The women of Grippia had the heads of swans.

Source: Blamires, *Herzog Ernst and the Otherworld Voyage*, 29–40; Sprague de Camp, *Lands Beyond*, 99, 102–03

Groclant

First appearing on maps in the late 1500s, Groclant is typically drawn as being on the western side of Greenland; one of the first maps it appeared on was a Mercator map from 1569. This area of the Atlantic was heavily explored and soon after its appearance, Groclant disappeared. One of the last maps to mark its location was a Quadus map of 1608.

Source: Enterline, *Erikson, Eskimos and Columbus*, 52; Nansen, *In Northern Mists*, 130

The Grove of Nemi

Sacred to the goddess Diana, the grove at Nemi was also the home of two lesser divinities, the nymph of clear water, Egeria and Virbius, a handsome hero and hunter. Diana was worshiped as a goddess of childbirth in the grove.

The grove was ruled by a runaway slave who gained office by first cutting a bough from a particular oak tree in the grove and then killing in one-on-one combat, the priest-king, entitled Rex Nemorensis (the King of the Woods), who overseen the grove. The killer then became the new priest-king until he was slain by his successor.

Source: Evans, *Dictionary of Mythology*, 106–07; Frazer, *Golden Bough*, 14, 20

Guindoel

Variations: Castel d'Orvale, Gindiel, Grandiel, Granidel, Guidel, Raginel

In the thirteenth century poem, *Vulgate Cycle*, Guindoel Castle was ruled by Lady Oruale. Although Sir Marigart was in love with her, when she refused to marry him, the knight invaded Guindoel, killed her cousin and rapped the lady he claimed to love. After the castle's conquest, Marigart dishonored the maidens of her village, vanquished her knights, and imprisoned Lady Oruale in a cave which was guarded by two lions. Four years later Sir Ector arrived at Castle Guindoel and killed Marigart; rescued Lady Oruale and restored her to power promising to be her knight always and everywhere.

Source: Karr, *Arthurian Companion*, 222; Sommer, *Vulgate Version of the Arthurian Romances*, 46

Guinee

Variations: Guinée

In the Vodou belief Guinee is the spirit world, the homeland of the loa; it is located *en bas de l'eau* ("under the waters"); this realm is indescribable and obscure.

Source: Olmos, *Sacred Possessions*, 17; Oswald, *Vodoo*, 38

Gunnthorin

Variations: Gunnthrain

According to Norse mythology Gunnthorin was one of rivers which ran from ASGARD to MIDGARD.

Source: Grimes, *Norse Myths*, 13; Guerber, *Myths of the Norsemen*, 13

Gunnthra

According to Norse mythology Gunnthra was one of rivers which ran from ASGARD to MIDGARD. It was created from the water dripping off of the antlers of Eikthryir as he stood atop the roof of VALHALLA eating leaves off YGGDRASYLL.

Source: Grimes, *Norse Myths*, 13, 263; Guerber, *Myths of the Norsemen*, 13, 263

Hades (Hay'-deez)

Variations: Aides, Dwellings of Hades, Erebus, Hades, Haides, Halls of Dis, House of Hades, Realm of Haides

Greek and Roman mythologies describe Hades ("Unseen") as the UNDERWORLD place of the dead; this was a concept that developed over time. Originally Hades, the location, was a dark, gloomy, and mist filled endless plain where mortal souls went to after their bodies died. It was under the dominion of the god Hades who lent his name to the realm. The Greek UNDERWORLD was the collective name used to refer to the realms that lay beneath the earth or beyond the horizon, such as ACHERONTIA, ASPHODEL FIELDS, EREBUS, STYGIA, and TARTARUS, the prison holding the Titians. There are five rivers in Hades, the ACHERON ("Sorrow"), COCYTUS ("Lamentation"), LETHE ("Forgetfulness"), PYRIPHLEGETHON ("Fire"), and STYX ("Hate"); they form the boundary between upper and lower worlds.

It was in HOMER'S *The Iliad* where the idea of Hades as a dark place of endless night located somewhere beneath the Earth was first introduced; a single river needed to be crossed in order to enter; and this river was guarded by a hound. Once across, souls were judged by the king and queen of the realm.

The Odyssey added more details, expanding on the description of Hades, claiming it lay beyond the western horizon, in fact, Odysseus reaches it by ship. The process by which a soul is judged was also expounded upon.

The epic *Minyad* introduces Charon, the Ferryman of the dead. The Roman poet, Virgil (70–19 BCE described the ferryman as being frightful, having fiery eyes, a filthy cloak, and an unkempt beard. He placed Elysium (see ELYSIAN FIELDS, The) under the earth and makes it the place where the blessed and favored souls reside.

Hesiod in this works *Catalogues*, *Theogony*, and *Works and Days* added even more topographic details, defined TARTARUS, and introduced the ISLANDS OF THE BLESSED.

Source: Littleton, *Gods, Goddesses, and Mythology*, Volume 5, 605–08; Seigneuret, *Dictionary of Literary Themes and Motifs*, 11–12

Hahava

Variations: the Groaning Hell

The fourth of the eight cold NARAKA (HELLS) named in Buddhism Hahava ("Lamentation") is a realm of lamentation. Described as being a cold, cavernous area thousands of miles beneath the earth, a perpetual snowstorm is raging there. The land of Hahava is made of ice, the mountains are covered in snow, there is no light source, and the air carries swarms of misquotes and plague. This NARAKA is filled with those souls who have committed sins of omission, those who did not do what should have been done, and the cold-hearted.

The length of time one stays in the cold hells is very precise if not specific. For each person in the HELL there is a grain room filled with 80 bushels of sesame seeds. Once every 100 years one seed is removed. The length of time for each descending HELL is 20 times the previous.

Source: Faustino, *Heaven and Hell*, 30; Hastings, *Encyclopedia of Religion and Ethics Part*, Part 7, 133; Kern, *Manual of Indian Buddhism*, 58

Hall of Two Truths

One of the many mystical halls in AMENTI, the Egyptian UNDERWORLD the Hall of Two Truths was where a soul was weighed and measured. *The Book of the Dead*, an ancient text written for the deceased, contained instructions on how to enter and what to expect in the hall; as the deceased recited a specific speech he must be anointed in myrrh oil, dressed in a clean clothes, wearing green or black eyeliner and white sandals. Within the hall the creature Ammut sits next to the scales of justice where the weight of the deceased heart will be weighed against a feather. Should the sins committed in life cause the heart to off-balance the feather the heart was tossed to

Ammut who would eat it; this would prevent the person from continuing on with their journey into the afterlife.

Source: Bonwick, *Egyptian Belief and Modern Thought*, 46–50; Remler, *Egyptian Mythology, A to Z*, 10, 45

Hamistagan

Variations: Hamēstagān

A LIMBO-like realm in Zoroastrian mythology, Hamistagan ("in equilibrium" or "stationary") was a neutral location where souls who did not fall into the category of "evil" or "good" awaited for Judgment Day. Similar to the Roman Catholic idea of PURGATORY, it is located somewhere between HEAVEN and HELL and the souls here are not punished or purification in any way. Originally there was no sensation experienced here but in later texts it was said the souls lived in an environment similar to the earth but they were cold during the winter and hot in the summer months.

Source: Ara, *Eschatology in the Indo-Iranian Traditions*, 205; Chopra, *Encyclopaedic Dictionary of Religion: G–P*, 336

Hanan Pachua

In Incan mythology nobility and good people who earned the right would spend their afterlife in Hanan Puchua, a HEAVEN-like realm where there they would enjoy an existence of comfort and ease.

Source: Roza, *Incan Mythology and Other Myths of the Andes*, 17

Happy Fields

Variations: Place of the Heroes, Resting Place of Nergal

Similar to the ELYSIAN FIELDS from the mythology of Ancient Greece, the Happy Fields from the Assyrio-Chaldean beliefs was the UNDERWORLD realm of the god Hea and the goddess Nin-Kigal. According to their ancient beliefs, "good" souls were rewarded with eternal happiness, living on in this realm "drinking pure liquor ... feeding on rich foods [and] ... reclining on couches." Warriors who went to the Happy Fields were additionally surrounded by all of the treasures they amassed in life while his captives are paraded back and forth before him.

Source: Blavatsky, *Theosophical Glossary*, 134; Society of Biblical Archæology of London, England, *Transactions of the Society of Biblical Archæology*, Volume 5, 565

Happy Hunting Grounds

Variations: Happy Lands, Happy Regions

The Happy Hunting Grounds of Native American Indian lore is described as an idealized PARADISE, having glorious stars, a mild moon, pure air and sunshine, and welling streams. Each of the different Indian nations has its own section in the Hunting Grounds, as they were not able to co-exist on earth they also will not co-exist here as an insurmountable barrier is separating each region and no war-minded brave may pass between them. The souls of dogs walked the same trail to enter into the Hunting Grounds of the master it served in life so together they may hunt the plentiful animal spirits. As a means to ensure one's soul would enter into the Happy Hunting Grounds after death offering of tobacco would be tossed in fire as a means to thank the Great Spirit for all he gives.

Source: Jones, *Traditions of the North American Indians*, 225–26; Lowenstein, *Native American Myths and Beliefs*, 69, 124

Hau-Ora

Variations: the Living Waters of Thane

In Maori mythology, Hau-Ora is the fourth of the ten divisions of HEAVEN; in one version of the telling of the demigod Tawhaki there are twelve divisions but sometimes there are as many as fourteen and as few as two named. Hau-Ora is the HEAVEN where the souls of new-born children are created.

Source: Craig, *Dictionary of Polynesian Mythology*, 54, 56; Grey, *Maori Lore*, 12; Mead, *Tāwhaki*, 58

Haviya

The sixth of the seven Islamic HELLS, Haviya is reserved for Christians.

Source: Wagner, *How Islam Plans to Change the World*, 156

Hawaiki

Variations: 'Avaiki, Habai, Haiva, Havai'i, Havaiki, Havahiki, Hawaiiki, Hawaiki, Hou'eiki ("chiefs"), Sauali'i ("spirits")

A mythological island from Polynesian lore, Hawaiki isfrom where the Polynesian people trace their origin from and to where their souls will return after death. Very often Hawaiki is used as the word to refer to the UNDERWORLD location where souls go after death. Details of Hawaiki are vague and confusing, as the oral traditions among the tribes of people, such as the Hawaiians, Marquesans, Rarotongans, Samoans, and the Tongans to name but a few, freely interchanged actual distant islands as being Hawaiki, a distant, faraway place which cannot be visited by mortals.

Common people needed to have a proper burial and funeral rites said for the deceased otherwise the souls would not be able to reach the lowest and most desirable level of Hawaiki. If the rites were not performed or done incorrectly, the soul would remain on the earth and haunt the living. Entry in Hawaiki could also be made by traveling through Aki (HEAVEN); is believed by many traditions the lowest level of Hawaiki is also, or at least overlaps to some degree, the highest level of Aki.

Source: Craig, *Handbook of Polynesian Mythology*, 131; Kirch, *Island Societies*, 87; Orbell, *Concise Encyclopedia of Māori Myth and Legend*, 31–32

Hawiyah

Variations: Hawiya

The final and seventh of the HELLS of Islamic mythology, Hawiayah ("Abyss") is a deep pit whose bottom cannot be reached. This level, traditionally, is reserved for hypocrites but it was only used once in the Koran; here sinners will constantly have their cheeks ripped off of their face. The souls here are those in life who professed to be a member of a religion but in their heart did not believe the teachings.

In some sources, Hawiyah is said to be the third of the seven Islamic HELLS and is reserved for hypocrites (see AL HUTAMA, JAHANNAM, AL JAHIM, LAGAM, SA'IR, and SAQAU).

Source: Hughes, *Dictionary of Islam*, 170–71; Maberry, *Cryptopedia*, 38; Netton, *Popular Dictionary of Islam*, 101; Wherry, *Comprehensive Commentary on the Quran*, 148

Heaven

Variations: PARADISE

In nearly all of mankind's religions Heaven is the realm of the gods or God. Generally speaking Heaven is said to be located in a distant, infinite space inaccessible to living mortals where an omnipresent deity or deities are in a continual state of manifesting their glory or existing in their natural state of being. When this divinity leaves its realm it often has to alter its form in order to interact with mankind. After a mortal body dies and releases the soul it contained the spirit eventually ascends into Heaven where it enjoys according to various religions an afterlife ranging between an eternity of blissfulness happiness to a state of general contentment; a place free of evil, perfect in its holiness, filled with all knowledge, and where the company of a god and the heavenly hosts can be enjoyed.

Christianity, Judaism, and Islam all share a similar view of heaven where it is the realm of God and the final destination of the souls of believers. In Buddhism and Jainism many heavens exist and in Hinduism not only are there many different heavens but also many different universes.

Heaven is used in three different ways in the Bible, as an atmospheric place in the material world, a celestial location, and as the dwelling place of God. Atmospheric heaven is the place where clouds float and birds fly; where dew, frost, rain, snow, thunder, and wind originates. The celestial heaven is where the moon, planets, stars, and sun are; this is the universe. Paul referred to the dwelling place of God as the third heaven in 1 Corinthians 12:2; it is the very specific location where God sits enthroned, renders judgment, and dispenses blessings.

In the Ptolemaic (ancient Egyptian) belief system, there are five types of heavens, a planetary heaven, a sphere of fixed stars, the vibrating crystalline, the primum mobile, and the empyrean where the deities dwell.

In the Islamic tradition there are seven heavens. The first is made of pure silver and it is where the stars are located; it is the dwelling place of Adam and Eve; the second heaven is made of polished steel and is where Noah resides; the third heaven is made of some many precious stones it is too dazzling for the eyes of a mortal man to look upon; it is where the angel Azrael writes names into and out of the Book of Life. The fourth heaven is made of the finest silver; dwelling here is the Angel of Tears who endlessly cries for the sins of man. The fifth heaven is made from the purest gold; residing here is Aaron and the Avenging Angel who presides over elemental fire. The sixth heaven is made of hasala, a type of carbuncle; dwelling here is Moses and the guardian angel of earth and heaven. The seventh heaven, made of divine light, is the abode of God and where Abraham dwells. Each inhabitant here is larger than the earth and has 70,000 heads, each head has 70,000 mouths, each mouth has 70,000 tongues, and each tongue speaks 70,000 languages; for all time the inhabitants sing the praises of the God.

When Heaven is styled as being a PARADISE it is typically described as a lush garden where the blessed or saved go. In Islamic believe it is a garden of unparalleled beauty where there is abundant water and beautiful women doting on men.

Source: Buck, *Theological Dictionary*, 209–12; Enns, *Moody Handbook of Theology*, 386; Hexham, *Concise Dictionary of Religion*, 101, 167

Hedu Kä Misi

Variations: Hedu

In the belief system of the Yąnomamö people of Venezuela and Brazil Hedu Kä Misi ("sky layer") is the second highest of the four consistent and major layers of HEAVEN. This realm is like the earth in all ways containing gardens, plants, and wildlife but rather than being occupied with humans it is the dwelling places of the dead; the occupants do everything a living person would do including copulating, eating, hunting, and practicing witchcraft. Everything existing on earth has a counterpart here. The bottom of this layer is visible to the mortals of earth; the celestial bodies, such as the moon, planets, stars, and the sun, are attached to it and hang down.

The four essential layers of Yąnomamö belief each lay horizontal to one another and are separated by an undefined but small space. The layers are shaped like inverted serving plates, gently curved, rigid, round, thin, and having both a top and a bottom. Beyond the four essential layers, DUKU KÄ MISI, HEDU KÄ MISI, HEI KÄ MISI, and HEI TÄ BEBI, there are additional, less important and unnamed layers. Some of these lesser layers are considered as being fragile or rotten, as if simply by walking upon one would destroy it; however a great deal of magic occurs in these dangerous places which are dominated by spirits.

Source: Chagnon, *Yąnomamö*, 102–03; Eller, *Introducing Anthropology of Religion*, 45

Hefeydd Hen, Court of *see* Court of Hefeydd Hen

Hei Kä Misi

In the belief system of the Yąnomamö people of Venezuela and Brazil Hei Kä Misi is the third of the four consistent and major layers of HEAVEN; it is relatively close to DUKU KÄ MISI and was created when a section of HEDU KÄ MISI broke off and fell downward.

The four essential layers of Yąnomamö belief each lay horizontal to one another and are separated by an undefined but small space. The layers are shaped like inverted serving plates, gently curved, rigid, round, thin, and having both a top and a bottom. Beyond the four essential layers, DUKU KÄ MISI, HEDU KÄ MISI, HEI KÄ MISI, and HEI TÄ BEBI, there are additional, less important and unnamed layers. Some of these lesser layers are considered as being fragile or rotten, as if simply by walking upon one would destroy it; however a great deal of magic occurs in these dangerous places which are dominated by spirits.

Source: Chagnon, *Yąnomamö*, 102–03; Eller, *Introducing Anthropology of Religion*, 45

Hei Tä Bebi

In the belief system of the Yąnomamö people of Venezuela and Brazil Hei Tä Bebi is the fourth of the four consistent and major layers of HEAVEN; it was created when a section of HEDU KÄ MISI broke off and came crashing downward, through another layer, and eventually settled. Almost entirely barren a version of the Yąnomamö people, called the Amąhiriteri. The part of HEDU KÄ MISI which struck and moved on only contained the Amąhiriteri and their gardens, not the jungles they hunted in. Having no game, they eventually became cannibals; they send their spirits upwards to capture the souls of children which they eat.

The four essential layers of Yąnomamö belief each lay horizontal to one another and are separated by an undefined but small space. The layers are shaped like inverted serving plates, gently curved, rigid, round, thin, and having both a top and a bottom. Beyond the four essential layers, DUKU KÄ MISI, HEDU KÄ MISI, HEI KÄ MISI, and HEI TÄ BEBI, there are additional, less important and unnamed layers. Some of these lesser layers are considered as being fragile or rotten, as if simply by walking upon one would destroy it; however a great deal of magic occurs in these dangerous places which are dominated by spirits.

Source: Chagnon, *Yąnomamö*, 102–03; Eller, *Introducing Anthropology of Religion*, 45

Hel

Variations: Halja, Helgardh, HELHEIM ("Home of Hel" or "House of Hel"), HELL, Helle, Hölle, Khalija ("one who covers up or hides something")

In Norse mythology Hel is the name of the land ruled by the goddess of death, Hel, from her hall, ELIDNER; it is situated beneath one of the roots of the tree, Ygdrasil, the lowest of the nine worlds it rests below NIFLHEIM and is encircled by the river GIÖLL. A downward path called HEL-WAY must be traveled to reach Hel; it is long, taking as few as nine days to traverse; its barren gates HELGRINDR (Hel-Gate) slowly creek and grinded open making a horrible noise. The land is surrounded by a wall with a few gates, such as NAGRINDR ("Corpse Gate") and Valgrind ("Carrion Gate"). Hel has bleak and gloomy rivers traversing the landscape. The magical ring, Draupner, cannot use its powers of fertility here.

The occupants of this realm are those individuals, be they good or evil in life, who died of old age or disease; however there is a region set apart called NIFLHEL for the truly evil to go.

None who enter Hel can ever leave again; one of the first signs of Ragnarok approach will be when the Sooty-Red the rooster who sits atop HELGRINDR leaves its root and Hel.

Source: Anderson, *Norse Mythology*, 387–88, 449; Daly, *Norse Mythology A to Z*, 48; Lindow, *Norse Mythology*, 172

Hel-Way

According to Norse mythology, Hel-Way is a downward path that must be traveled to reach the realm called HEL; it is long, taking as few as nine days to traverse; it ends directly in front of a set of barren gates known as HEL-GRIND.

Source: Anderson, *Norse Mythology*, 387; Lindow, *Norse Mythology*, 172

Helgrindr

Variations: Corpse Gate, Gates of Hel, Hel Gate, Helgrind, NAGRINDR, and Valgrindr

In Norse mythology Helgrindr (HEL-Gate) is the gated wall which stands on the far side of GJALLARBRU BRIDGE; the bridge which spans between the world of the living and the deceased. The primary gate which leads into HEL, the realm of the dead who die of disease or old age, it is located at the end of HEL-WAY. Sitting atop the gate is a rooster named Sooty-Red whose call stirs the dead; on the other side of this gate is the *hrímthurs* (ice giant) Hrim-grimnir.

Source: Anderson, *Norse Mythology*, 449; Bennett, *Gods and Religions of Ancient and Modern Times*, Volume 1, 389; Grimes, *Norse Myths*, 73; Lindow, *Norse Mythology*, 172

Helheim

In Norse mythology Helheim ("Home of Hel" or "House of Hel") is the home of the goddess, Hel. Those who were wicked in life or died of old age or disease reported to HEL in Helheim. One of the nine worlds of Norse cosmology, Helheim is located directly below MANNAHEIM and between NIFLHEIM and SVARTALFAHEIM.

Source: Anderson, *Norse Mythology*, 187, 391, 449; Bennett, *Gods and Religions of Ancient and Modern Times*, Volume 1, 389

The Heliades

Variations: The Isles of the Sun

The Heliades was believed to a chain of seven PARADISE-like islands located in the far south, somewhere in the ocean beyond India. Peaceful with forests of fruit-bearing trees the inhabitants who called themselves the Heliades (People of the Sun) were a beautiful, hairless, and tall race of people with rubbery bones.

Each of the seven islands was ruled by a king, the oldest man on the island; upon reaching the age of 150 years, he was euthanized by means of a magical plant and the next oldest person took his throne. As a nation, there was no idea of family, children were raised in common and were denied any knowledge of who their parents were.

Source: Diodorus Siculus, *Historical Library of Diodorus the Sicilian*, 335

Heljar-ran

In Norse mythology Heljar-ran is the name of the castle where the Asmegir, Lif, and Lifthraser, live with their descendants. Located

on a grassy plain the keeper of Heljar-ran is Delling, the Red Elf of the Dawn. Located at the eastern gate is the gravesite of a *vale* (prophetess).

Source: MacKenzie, *Teutonic Myth and Legend*, 148

Hell

Variations: the Abyss, al-Nar, Arka, Furnace of Fire, GEHENNA, HADES ("the unseen world"), Heklafell, Helan ("to cover"), Infernus, JAHANNAM, LAKE OF FIRE, NARAKA, the Pit, Place of Torments, Pool of Fire, SHEOL, Shi Ba Chen Di Yu, TARTARUS

In nearly all of the world's religions and belief systems there is a hell, a place of punishment a person's soul is sent to after their death to atone or be punished for the sins committed in life; depending on the belief system, being sentenced to Hell is not necessarily a sentence for all eternity, as some religions propose the pain and suffering undertaken is a means of removing sin and purifying the soul to then either graduate up into HEAVEN or prepare it for rebirth and reincarnation. Generally speaking, in monotheistic religions, hell is ruled by demons while in polytheistic religions, the politics of hell are as complicated those here on earth.

Scripture describes Hell as a BOTTOMLESS PIT, dark, filled with fire, a place of torment with varying degrees of suffering. Punishment is not eternal or everlasting but rather unspecified although it is implied to be decisively long.

In the Old Testament we are assured that while all men do go to SHEOL, the grave, all the souls do not go to the same place; in the New Testament the word HADES was used to reference the afterlife as well as a state of death. At one time it was taught that HADES and SHEOL each were divided into two regions, one where the righteous awaited the resurrection of Christ and the other was reserved for the wicked. Also, GEHENNA was also used as a destination for eternal punishment and not annihilation.

According to Buddhist traditions, a soul's

stay in Hell is not eternal but rather very long. Each person is sent to a specific NARAKA ("hell") depending on the sins committed during their life until their karma is balanced after which the person is reborn to a different plane of existence. There are 136 places of punishment a sol may be sent to. Physically, NARAKA is believed to a great cavernous area deep beneath the earth.

The place of final judgment for the wicked the HELL of the Christians is filled with those souls who have died with final forgiveness. The Bible describes this realm as a place of everlasting fire prepared for the Devil and his followers. There is no broadly accepted agreement as to the size and location of Hell, nor is there a unified agreement as to what quantifies a damned soul.

To the ancient Greeks, Hell was called TARTARUS a fiery section of HADES where the evil and wicked were punished. Classical authors have described there as being five rivers of Hell.

In Islamic belief, Hell is a raging pit where all the non-believers and evil-doers are sent; there are a variety of punishment offered as different crimes have different levels of punishment. It is described in the Quran as being a place of eternal fire filled with black smoke, boiling water, crackling flames, and scorching winds; boiling water is poured over their heads, scorched skin which has burned off with quickly grow back so the pain may be begin again anew and iron hooks lash out of nowhere and ensnare anyone who tries to escape. The lightest sentence a person can receive is to be made to wear boots filled with fire, this will cause their brain to boil (Quran 46: 18–20; 50:30). There are seven layers to the Islamic hell, AL NĀR: JAHEEM, JAHANNAM, SA'IR, SAQAR, NATA, HAWIYA, and HUTAMA.

Jewish Cabalists say there are seven levels to Hell, the Gates of Death, the Shadow of Death, the PIT OF CORRUPTION, the Mire of Clay, ALADDON, and SHEOL.

There are seven NARAKAS (HELLS) in Jainas; those who are in the seventh and lowest realm have a stature of 500 poles; each of the hells residing above are each half the height of the one below. The NARAKAS in order of descent are Ratnaprabhâ, 'Sarkarâprbhâ, Vâlukâprabhâ, Pankaprabhâ, Dhûmaprabhâ, Tamaprabhâ, and Tamatamaprabhâ.

The structure of Hell is remarkably complicated in Chinese and Japanese religion where as those who practice the Bahá'ís faith do not believe in Hell being a place but rather a state of being, "HEAVEN *is nearness to me and* HELL *is separation from Me.*"

Source: Brewer, *Dictionary of Phrase and Fable*, 596; Buck, *Theological Dictionary*, 212–13; Bühler, *On the Indian Sect of the Jainas*, 45; Enns, *Moody Handbook of Theology*, 292–93; Esposito, *Oxford Dictionary of Islam*, 111; Hexham, *Concise Dictionary of Religion*, 102; Van Scott, *Encyclopedia of Hell*, 59

Hell Planets, Twenty-Eight

Variations: NARAKAS

According to Hindu and Vedic mythology there are twenty-eight (or twenty-one; sources conflict) HELL planets or NARAKAS created by the Supreme Lord; each one is designed to punish the living entities who dwell within them. These HELL planets are ruled over by Yamarja who resides in Pitriloka with his assistants the Yamadutas. Immediately upon the death of a sinful man the Yamadutas carry him directly to Yamarja who then judges the individual and selects which of HELL planets is best suited for him to reside in. Once they are placed in their NARAKAS, the person can begin to work off their bad Karma.

The names of the twenty-eight HELL planets are: ANDHATAMISRA, ANDHAKUPA, ASIPATRAVANA, AVATA-NIRODHANA, AVICI, AYAHPANA, DANDASUKA, KALASUTRAM, KRIMIBHOJANA, KSHARAKARDAMA, KUMBHIPAKA, LALABHAKSHA, MAHARAURAVA, PRANARODHA, PARYAVARTANA, PUYODA, RAKSHOGANA-BHOJANA, RAURAVA, SANDAMSA, SARAMEYADANA, SUCIMUKHAM, SULAPROTA, SUKARAMUKHA, TAPTASURMI, TAMISRA, VAITARANI, VAJRAKANTAKA-SALMALI, and VISASANA.

Source: Knapp, *Secret Teachings of the Vedas*,

N.p.; Parmeshwaranand, *Encyclopaedic Dictionary of Purāṇas*, 720–23

Hiiela

Variations: Manala

In Estonian mythology Hiiela is the land and the dwelling place of the dead; it is located directly beneath sacred oak groves where the dead are buried.

Source: Kõiva, *Using Estonian/American Based Culture Models*, 60; Paulson, *Old Estonian Folk Religion*, Volume 108, 195

Himinbiorg

Variations: Himinbjor ("HEAVEN Defender"), Himmelbierg

The palace of the god Heimdal was called Himinbiorg ("Cliffs of HEAVEN"), according to Norse mythology. It was found on the highest point of BIFROST; the other gods would visit here often as the mead of Heimdal was especially delicious.

Source: Bennett, *Gods and Religions of Ancient and Modern Times*, Volume 1, 389; Daly, *Norse Mythology A to Z*, 49; Grimes, Norse Myths, 17; Guerber, *Myths of the Norsemen*, 148

Hindarfiall (hin'dar-fyal)

Variations: Hindfell

In Norse mythology Hindarfiall is the place where Odin took the valkyrie Brunhild where, after piercing her with the Thorn of Sleep, surrounded her with a wall of fire known as the Vafurloge. As she lay awaiting the arrival of a worthy husband brave enough to pass through the flames, she retained her beauty and youth. Hindarfiall is described as being a tall mountain whose cloud-top summit also had a halo of flames.

Source: Guerber, *Myths of the Norsemen*, 280, 284; Sturluson, *Prose Edda*, 134

Hnitbjorg

Variations: Skaldskaparmal

The mountain stronghold Hnitbjorg was where the giant Sattung kept three containers of the Mead of Poetry after he stole it from

the dwarfs, Falar and Galar, according to the ancient Norse poem, *Havamal*.

Source: Daly, *Norse Mythology A to Z*, 50; Sturlusonar, *Prose Edda*, 94

Hodmimir (hod-me'mir)

Variations: Hoard-Mímir's Holt, Hoddmim's Holt, Hoddmimir's Holt, Hoddmimir's Wood, Hodd-Mimir's Holt, Hoddmímis Holt, Hoddmimishold, Hoddmimisholt, Hodmimer's Forest, Hodmimer's Grove, Hodmimer's Holt, Hodmimer's Wood, Hodmimir's Holt

Hodmimir ("Mimir's Forest") was, in Norse mythology, where the human woman, Lif ("Life"), and a human man, Lifthrasir ("Stubborn Will to Live"), took refuge there to survive the three-year long winter of Fimbulvetr ("Mighty Winter"), the worst possible winter imaginable which occurs just prior to Ragnarok as well as during the time when Surtr had set fire to the world during Ragnarok.

Source: Bennett, *Gods and Religions of Ancient and Modern Times*, Volume 1, 390; Grimes, Norse Myths, 278; Guerber, *Myths of the Norsemen*, 337

Holl

Variations: Höll

According to Norse mythology Holl was one of rivers which ran from ASGARD to MIDGARD.

Source: Guerber, *Myths of the Norsemen*, 13; Sturlusonar, *Prose Edda of Snorri Sturluson*, 65

Hollow Earth

An idea of a hollow earth was first put forth by the British astronomer Edmund Halley in the late 17th century; Halley proposed the earth was made of four concentric spheres, and the interior of the planet is populated. Openings located at the North and South poles allow the Agartha, an advanced race of people, to fly their UFOs to and from their home; the gases released from these openings, Halley suggested was the cause of aura borealis.

In the 19th century, the American Army officer John Symmes so heavily promoted the idea of these internal concentric spheres the alleged openings at the poles were called, during that time, Symmes Holes. After Rear Admiral Richard Evelyn Byrd, Jr. Flight over the North Pole in 1926 and the South Pole in 1929 did not reveal any openings advocates of the theory refused to be dissuaded.

The 1913 privately published *Journey to the Earth's Interior* by Marshal B. Gardner, claimed inside the earth the sun was 600 miles in diameter and the openings at the poles were 1,000 miles wide.

Source: Carroll, *Skeptic's Dictionary*, 160; Gardner, *Journey to the Earth's Interior*, 422

Hronn

Variations: Hr∂nn, Hrön, Hrönn, Ronn

Hronn ("billowing" or "rising wave") was one of the nine rivers from Norse mythology which flow from MIDGARD to NIFLHEIM. It is also listed as one of sixteen rivers which ran from ASGARD to MIDGARD.

Source: Grimes, *Norse Myths*, 14, 280; Guerber, *Myths of the Norsemen*, 13; Sturlusonar, *Prose Edda*, 52

Huángquán

A mythological realm of the dead in Chinese mythology, Huángquán ("Yellow Springs") first appeared in ancient texts in the eight century BCE This vaguely described realm is said to be located beneath the earth and to be cast into darkness. Huángquán is reference in *Taipngjing*, stating there "those who are good go up, their fate belonging in HEAVEN as the living belong in HEAVEN; those who are bad go downward, and their fate belongs to the earth and for this reason they go down and return to the Yellow Springs."

Source: Olberding, *Mortality in Traditional Chinese Thought*, 110

Hufaidh

A mythological island said to be located in the mashes of southern Iraq Hufaidh is something of a PARADISE, growing palms and pomegranates and having large buffaloes. Anyone who ever went to Hufaidh, if they returned, would be cursed by the djinn, making the person unable to have their words understood.

Source: Lebling, *Legends of the Fire Spirits*, 134; Thesiger, *Marsh Arabs* 84–85

Huhuva

The fourth of the eight cold NARAKA (HELLS) named in Buddhism, Huhuva ("Chattering Teeth") is described as being so cold its occupants sit, teeth chattering making the sound "hu hu."

The length of time one stays in the cold hells is very precise if not specific. For each person in the HELL there is a grain room filled with 80 bushels of sesame seeds; once every 100 years one seed is removed. The length of time for each descending HELL is 20 times the previous.

Source: Alexander, *Body, Mind, Spirit Miscellany*, 150; Mew, *Traditional Aspects of Hell*, 98

al Hutama

Variations: al Hutamah

The third (or fourth, sources vary) of the seven Islamic HELLS, Hutama ("that which shatters, wrecks, or smashes") is reserved for hypocrites and Christians. In other sources it is listed as the first of the seven Islamic HELLS and is reserved for the Jewish people (see HAWIYAH, AL JAHIM, LAGAM, SA'IR, and SAQAU).

Source: Hughes, *Dictionary of Islam*, 170–71; Netton, *Popular Dictionary of Islam*, 108; Wagner, *How Islam Plans to Change the World*, 156; Wherry, *Comprehensive Commentary on the Quran*, 148

Hvergelmir Well

Variations: Hveigilmer ("Old Kettle"), Hvengelmir, Hvergelmen, Hvergelmer Well, Hvergelmin, Hwergelmr, Kvergjelme, Vergelmir

In Norse mythology, Hvergelmir Well ("roaring kettle") is one of the three wells which nourish the ash tree, YGGDRASIL (see MIMIRSBRUNNR WELL and URDARBRUNNR WELL). Located in NEFLHIM, the well was so swollen it spawned thirty-six separate rivers, twelve flowed to MIDGARD, twelve flowed to NIFLHEIM, and twelve flowed into ASGARD. Entwind around the base of the well was a nest of poisonous snakes which were constantly gnawing upon the roots of YGGDRASIL.

Source: Bennett, *Gods and Religions of Ancient and Modern Times*, Volume 1, 390; Grimes, *Norse Myths*, 14; Guerber, *Myths of the Norsemen*, 14

Hy Brasil

Variations: Brasil, Brazil Rock, Brazir, Green Island, Hy-Brasil, Hy-Brazil, Hy Breasal, Hy Breasail, Hy-Breasil, Hy-Breasal, Hy na-Beatha (Isle of Life), I Breasil, Isle of Maam, Mag Mell ("Plain of Honey"), O'Brasil, Tir fo-Thuin ("Land Under the Wave"), Tir nam-Buadha ("Land of Virtue"), Ysole Brazil

A PHANTOM ISLAND of Celtic folklore and mythology, Hy Brasil was originally an earthly extension of the UNDERWORLD; over time and as man began to venture out and chart the sea, its location and description have changed. It was last sighted in 1908, it was said to be in the Atlantic Ocean off the coast of west Ireland, near Innishmurray.

Typically Hy Brasil faded away as ships sailed towards it; there are very few stories of anyone actually having been on the island. Nevertheless between 1385 and 1865 a number of maps charted the island as being southwest of Galway Bay. Drawn as a near perfectly circular island with a central river running right through the middle of it, Hy Brasil's topography was given as being hilly with small mountains along its coastline. Of the few reports of sailors or explorers actually making a landing, it was also said to be very thickly wooded. In the 19th century its location was moved to the south of Rathlin Island.

Source: Babcock, *Legendary Islands of the Atlantic*, 65, 91; Evan-Wentz, *Fairy Faith in Celtic Countries*, 334; Curran, *Lost Lands, Forgotten Realms*, 63–75; Monaghan. *Encyclopedia of Celtic Mythology and Folklore*, 252–53

Hydramardia

According to Lucian of Samosata, the ancient Greek rhetorician and satirist (AD 125–180) the city of Hydramardia, located on the island of island of CABBALUSA, was not especially large but was entirely populated by beautiful and young Greek speaking women; its streets were covered with the human bones and skulls of the men who were devoured by the city's cannibalistic women.

Source: Lucian of Samosata, *Works of Lucian of Samosata*, 172; Verma, *Word Origins:* Volume 15, 187

Hylech

Variations: Apheta, Hyleg, Yleg

In ancient Chaldean astrology Hylech was a planet or a place in the HEAVENs which influenced a person's entire life.

Source: Lilly, *Christian Astrology,* Book 3, 527; Owen, *New and Complete Dictionary of Arts and Sciences*, Volume 2, 1702

Hyperborea

Variations: Hyperborei

According to ancient legends Hyperborea ("beyond the north wind") lay far to the northwest, beyond the Pillars of Hercules; he ancient Greek historian Herodotus and Pliny the Elder, a Roman author and naturalist each believed it to be a real land. The people of the realm were known as Hyperboreans and were described as living exceedingly long lives dying only after having lived a full life by jumping off a certain cliff into the sea; they never knew disease, hard labor, or war. These people were living in a delightful climate and never suffered cold or ice in the winter months; Hyperborea was said to be the winter home of the god Apollo.

Source: Agrippa von Nettesheim, *Three Books of Occult Philosophy,* 334; Pliny the Elder, *Pliny's Natural History*, 29

Icaria

Variations: Island Caria

An island described by the Zeno Brothers' map (1558), Icaria was drawn about the size of the Shetland Islands; if a straight line is drawn from Iceland to ESTOTILAND and another from Friesland to Cape Hwarf, Icaria lay at the intersection.

Source: Babcock, *Legendary Islands of the Atlantic*, 142

Ice Realm

In the folklore from Denmark the Ice Realm is the domain of the Snow Queen, ruler of the fairies.

Source: Rose, *Spirits, Fairies, Leprechauns, and Goblins*, 296–7, 351

Ida

Variations: Idavold, Iðavölir, Plains of Ida

In Norse mythology, the ninth root of YG-GDRASIL ends in the plains of Ida; it is here that Mount Idavallr, the center most and highest peak in MIDGARD is located. This land was claimed by the Æsir and they called it AS-GARD.

Source: Anderson, *Norse Mythology*, 182; Grimes, *Norse Myths*, 13

Idavold (eda'vold)

Variations: Idavoll, Idawold, Ithavoll

In Norse mythology Idavold ("Plains of Ida") was a broad plain located far above the earth in the center of ASGARD, where the god Odin encouraged the other gods and their descendants to gather; it was here the young gods played games, Odin's throne Hlidskjalf sat, and where Balder was slain by his blind brother, Hodur.

This sacred place was said to be on the other side of the river IFING; it is in this place where ASGARD is located. After Ragnarok, Idavold will become green again; new halls will be constructed there by the surviving gods.

Source: Anderson, *Norse Mythology*, 182, 187; Bennett, *Gods and Religions of Ancient and Modern Times*, Volume 1, 391; Daly, *Norse Mythology A to Z*, 55; Guerber, *Myths of the Norsemen*, 11

Ifing (e'fing)

In Norse mythology Ifing is the river of AS-GARD which surrounds the plain of IDAVOLD and separated JOTUNHEIM and MIDGARD; its

water never freezes and thereby the Jotuns had no way to cross over into MIDGARD.

Source: Anderson, *Norse Mythology*, 451; Bennett, *Gods and Religions of Ancient and Modern Times*, Volume 1, 391; Guerber, *Myths of the Norsemen*, 11, 12

Ilara

In the mythology of the Tiwi people there are four layers which make up the universe, Ilara, the subterranean world, the earth, JU-WUKU the sky world, and the upper world known as TURIRUNA. In Ilara, it is always dark.

Source: Mountford, *The Tiwi*, 170

Ildathach

When the OTHERWORLD was imagined to be a FLOATING ISLAND in Irish lore, it was sometimes called Ildathach ("many-colored land") because of the breathtaking and unearthly hues of the land.

Source: Monaghan. *Encyclopedia of Celtic Mythology and Folklore*, 255

Ilium (IHL-ih-uhm)

Variations: Tros, Troy

Ilium is the ancient name for the city Troy; it was named after its fourth king, Ilvs. "*Iliad*" means "*story of Ilium*." According to Greek legend Ilium was founded by Ilus, the son of Callirhoe.

Source: Daly, *Greek and Roman Mythology, A to Z*, 76–78; Evslin, *Gods, Demigods, and Demons*, 111

Imchiuin

The Irish OTHERWORLD, Imchiuin ("Very Mild Land") was mentioned in the 50 quatrain poem "The Voyage of Bran, son of Febal, and his Expedition."

Source: Matthews, *Encyclopedia of Celtic Myth and Legend*, 116; Nansen, *Northern Mists*, Volume 1, 354

The Immortals, Kingdom of

Variations: Country of the Immortals

Homeland of the COURT OF HEFEYDD HEN, the Kingdom of the Immortals of Welsh medieval folklore had a palace described as un-equaled in beauty, hospitality, impenetrable strength, kindness, and loftiness. It had seven wide, stone-paved ramparts. Upon each rampart were 147 giants, the least of which could break an oak tree over its knee. There were seven large gates made of granite and seven watch-dogs guarding them. Between each gate were seven flights of 140 stairs. On the seven towers were seven raised spears with seven beautiful silk banners.

Source: Morris, *Fates of the Princes of Dyfed*, 33–34

Indolence, Castle of *see* Castle of Indolence

Indra-Loka

Variations: Indraloka, Swarga

One of the eight regions of material existence in Hindu mythology, Indra-Loka ("World of Indra"), the HEAVEN of the god Indra, is the realm of inferior deities. It is described as being 800 miles in circumference and forty miles high; its pillars are constructed of solid diamonds, all of the palaces and the furniture contained within is made of gold. Beautiful gardens and relaxing pools surround Indra-Loka and its audience chamber is large enough to hold all 330,000,000 of the celestials, the 48,000 rishis, and all of the accompanying servants. In the seven spheres of the earth, Indra-Loka is the second.

Source: Dowson, *Classical Dictionary of Hindu Mythology and Religion*, 127, 180; Garrett, *Classical Dictionary of India*, 268; Wilson, *Vishńu Puráńa*, 48, 71

Inis Subai

The Irish OTHERWORLD, Inis Subai ("Isle of Delight") where its citizenry do nothing but laugh and make foolish faces all day. This island was visited by the hero Bran; he had one of his men disembark from their vessel and set foot upon the island. As soon as the man touched the ground, he became as all the other islanders.

Source: Nansen, *Northern Mists*, Volume 1, 355

Innishmurray, the Invisible Island of

Variations: Inis Muireadheach ("Muireadheach's Island")

An enchanted and invisible island, Innishmurray lies just off of Ireland; it can be seen once every seven years.

Source: Begg, *On the Trail of Merlin*, 131; Evan-Wentz, *Fairy Faith in Celtic Countries*, 49

The Invisible Island of Innishmurray *see* Innishmurray, the Invisible Island of

Ioavallr

Variations: Idavild, Plains of Ida

A plain in Norse mythology Ioavallr is where the god first assembled, established their heavenly homes, and decided where to regroup after the battle of Ragnarok.

Source: Anderson, *Norse Mythology*, 451

Iram of the Pillars

Variations: Aram, City of the Tent Poles, Erum, Iram, Iram of the Tent-Poles, Irem, Irum

A lost city or tribe mentioned in the Koran, Iram of the Pillars was said to be somewhere south of Arabia. It has been speculated the ancient people known as Ad, the tribe who were the recipients of the Divine message given to them by the prophet Hud, may be the people of Iram of the Pillars.

Source: Burton, *Lady Burton's Edition of Her Husband's Arabian Nights*, 515: Glassé, *Concise Encyclopedia of Islam*, 26

Irama

The city of Irama from Swahili lore is said to be full of springing fountains; its columns were solid gold and set with rubies, the walls were covered with silver plaques and trimmed in gold; it was only visible at night.

Source: Knappert, *Myths and Legends of the Swahili*, 58

Irkalla

Variations: Arali, ARALLU, Gizal, Ir-Kalla, Irkalia, Kigal, the Lower World

In Babylonian mythology the subterranean UNDERWORLD Irkalla ("Great City") is ruled by the goddess Ereshkigal ("Queen of the Great Below") and her consort, the death god, Nergal. Originally the goddess was known as Irkalla and her name was lent to her domain, just like in Greek mythology the god Hades resides and has dominion over HADES. Like SHEOL, Irkalla is neither a place of punishment nor reward but rather a mundane version of earthy life; here Erishkigal is perceived as a guardian or warden of her domain overseeing the monotonous activities.

Source: Budge, *Babylonian Life and History*, 114; Heidel, *Gilgamesh Epic and Old Testament Parallels*, 121, 17–72

Iron Wood

Variations: Jarnvror, Jarnved

Located east of MIDGARD, the Iron Wood forest was home to a witch named Jarnvids, the mother of the wolves Hati, Maanagarm ("Moon-Swallower"), and Skoll who will devour the sun and moon during Ragnarok. The trees here had leaves of iron.

Source: Anderson, *Norse Mythology*, 179, 451; Bennett, *Gods and Religions of Ancient and Modern Times*, Volume 1, 391; Daly, *Norse Mythology A to Z*, 47–48

Iṣadhara

Variations: Isadhara

The Iṣadhara Mountains are the third mountain chain surrounding SUMERU, the central would mountain in in Hindu cosmology; it is both 20,000 *yojanas* tall and wide. The measure of a single *yojanas* has never been clear, some scholars say it is approximately four and a half miles while other say it ranges between seven and nine miles.

Source: Howard, *Imagery of the Cosmological Buddha*, 66–68; Nagao, *Wisdom, Compassion, and the Search for Understanding*, 192

Island of Buss *see* Buss Island

Island of Eubcea *see* Eubcea, Island of

The Island of Joy *see* Joy, the Island of

Island of Lessoe *see* Lessoe, Island of

Island of Lyngvi *see* Lyngvi, Island of

Island of Pankhaia *see* Pankhaia, Island of

Island of the Satyrs *see* Satyrs, Island of the

Island of Turning *see* Turning, Island of

Islands of the Blessed

Variations: FORTUNATE ISLES, ISLE OF THE BLEST

In Greek mythology the Islands of the Blessed was an earthly realm located far beyond the Pillars of Hercules. A very few highly favored mortals are taken, body and soul, to this pre–Hellenic island PARADISE which is ruled over by the god Rhadamnthys; according to the ancient Greek poet Homer only elite heroes were taken here. There is perfect happiness on the Island of the Blessed and no one ever dies; replete with flowers and favored with sweet smelling ocean breezes, all activities of leisure may be enjoyed here.

Source: Daly, *Greek and Roman Mythology, A to Z*, 50; Rose, *Handbook of Greek Mythology*, 80

Isle of Bragman *see* Bragman, Isle of

Isle of Mam *see* Mam, Isle of

Isle of Sheep *see* Sheep, Isle of

Isle of Silo *see* **Silo, Isle of**

Isle of the Blest *see* **Blest, Isle of the**

Isle of Wails *see* **Wails, Isle of**

Isle on the River Renemar

According to John de Mandeville, a fourteenth century author and doctor, the Isle on the River Renemar was located in the Kingdom of PRESTER JOHN is populated by feathered men.

Source: Sprague de Camp, *Lands Beyond*, 153

Isles of Demons *see* **Demons, Isles of**

Ithaka

Variations: Ithake

According to Odysseus, his island home of Ithaka was one of many islands located to the west of Greece. A rugged place not fit for driving horses but having many open places appropriate for growing corn and grape vines suitable for wine in great abundance. Ithaka was also said to have good pasture land for goats, plentiful woods, and many watering holes. A tree-covered mountain called Neriton is on the island.

Source: Connolly, *Ancient Greece of Odysseus*, 76; Sprague de Camp, *Lands Beyond*, 78

Jade Mountain

A mythological mountain in Chinese lore Jade Mountain is the home of Xiwangmu ("Queen Mother of the West"). Once, a huge amount of water poured out of the mountain flooding the area causing Emperor Wang to order Pieh Ling to dredge the mountain.

Source: Birrell, *Chinese Mythology*, 198; Yang, *Handbook of Chinese Mythology*, 162

Jahannam

Variations: Jahim ("Burner")

Jahannam is a PURGATORY-like HELL in

Muslim lore through which all believers in the faith will pass through; it is described as having seven divisions to it. Jahannam is the fourth of the seven HELLS of Islam (see AL HUTAMA, HAWIYAH, AL JAHIM, LAGAM, SA'IR, and SAQAU).

In other sources Jahannam is the first or second of the seven Islamic HELLS and is reserved for idolaters who were polytheists. Souls who are in this HELL will be asked if they were ever approached in life by a warner; they will respond they did but admit rejected the warning. When this realm is no longer needed, Jahannam will be obliterated.

Source: Hughes, *Dictionary of Islam*, 170–71; Netton, *Popular Dictionary of Islam*, 133, 178; Wagner, *How Islam Plans to Change the World*, 156; Wherry, *Comprehensive Commentary on the Quran*, 148; Wilcockson, *Student's Guide to A2 Religious Studies*, 150

al Jahim

Variations: Jaheem

The sixth of the seven HELLS of Islamic mythology, al Jahim is, traditionally, where the souls of idolaters are sent (see AL HUTAMA, HAWIYAH, JAHANNAM, LAGAM, SA'IR, and SAQAU).

Source: Hughes, *Dictionary of Islam*, 170–71; Wagner, *How Islam Plans to Change the World*, 156; Wherry, *Comprehensive Commentary on the Quran*, 148

Jambudvipa

In Hindu mythology, Jambudvipa was one of the four continents located in the outermost concentric circles surrounding Mount MERU (see GODHAVA, VIRAT-OLEHA, and UTTARA KURU). Located to the south, it was also the name of one of the Hot Hells (see EIGHT HOT HELLS).

Source: Kern, *Manual of Indian Buddhism*, 57; Sprague de Camp, *Lands Beyond*, 282

Jana-Loka

Variations: Janaloka

One of the eight regions of heavenly existence in Hindu mythology, Jana-Loka, is the heavenly home to Brahma's sons Sanaka, Sananda, and Santa-kumara; it is located twenty-million leagues above Dhruva, the polar star and pivot of the atmosphere. In the seven spheres of the earth, Jana-Loka is the fifth.

Source: Dowson, *Classical Dictionary of Hindu Mythology and Religion*, 179; Garrett, *Classical Dictionary of India*, 285; Wilson, *Vishńu Puráńa*, 48

al Janna

Variations: al Jannah

In the Koran al Janna ("the garden") is the most common name by which PARADISE is referred; the word suggest an enclosed garden, one with plentiful foliage, tall shade trees, and shelter from storms.

Source: Glassé, *Concise Encyclopedia of Islam*, 237; Netton, *Popular Dictionary of Islam*, 134

Jeraspunt

According to Medieval lore and first appearing in the ancient German work compiled in the fifteenth century by Kaspar von der Rhon, *Book of Heroes*, Jeraspunt was said to be the palace of the fairy queen, Virginial. Here the queen was guarded over by the dwarf Bibung but was still kidnapped by the magician Ortgis.

Sources: Guerber, *Legends of the Middle Ages*, 113–14; Rose, *Spirits, Fairies, Leprechauns, and Goblins*, 40; Wägner, *Epics and Romances of the Middle Ages*, 114

Jotunheim (yot-oon-hame or ye'toon-him), plural: Jotunheimar

Variations: Jotunheimer

The home of the Frost Giants in Norse mythology, Jotunheim was founded by Bergelmir and his wife. Located on the edge of the ocean far to the north east of MIDGARD, the forest Jotunheim is home to the well of wisdom, Mimir. The river Iving which separates Jotunheim from ASGARD never freezes over, no matter how cold the region becomes. Ruled by Thrym ("uproar") the fearsome king of the ice giants, his stronghold Utgard is the chief primary of Jotunheim; other strongholds

in this realm are GASTROPNIR, the home of the giantess Menglad, and THRYMHEIM ("house of uproar"), the mountain stronghold of the giant Thiazi.

Source: Anderson, *Norse Mythology*, 451; Avant, *Mythological Reference*, 205; Evans, *Dictionary of Mythology*, 147; Guerber, *Myths of the Norsemen*, 5

Joy, the Island of

Variations: Inis Subai

From the Celtic literary poem "*The Voyage of Bran, son of Feba*"; the Island of Joy was the first island Bran encountered. The inhabitants of this island laughed at Bran and his companions as they sailed around the island, never conversing with them.

In Arthurian lore the Island of Joy was under King Pelle's rule; it was the location to where Sir Lancelot retired in shame to after his five years of insanity. The island received it named because after the knight had hung his shield from the limb of a tree, maidens would come daily and dance and sing about it. After Lancelot was coaxed into returning to court by Sir Hector, the island fell into ruin and was renamed Dry Island.

Source: Bruce, *Arthurian Name Dictionary*, 277; Evan-Wentz, *Fairy Faith in Celtic Countries*, 339; Matthews, *Encyclopaedia of Celtic Myth and Legend*, 121

Joyous Gard

Variations: Dolorus Gard, Gioiosa Guardia, Joieuse Garde, Joyeuse Garde

The castle of Sir Lancelot of Arthurian lore, DOLORUS GARD was under the effects of an evil spell; once Lancelot captured the castle, the spell was broken. Within the castle's crypt the conquering knight discovered an empty tomb with his own named engraved upon it; this was interpreted as an omen the castle was destined to be his and the location of his final resting place. King Arthur and his queen, Guinevere were among the first guest invited to visit the newly renamed castle, Joyous Gard.

When Guinevere is taken to CARLISLE for execution, Lancelot rescues her and they both return to Joyous Gard; sadly the strife that becomes of this causes the happy castle to revert back to its original name, DOLORUS GARD. After the death of Lancelot, his body was said to be taken to Joyous Gard and entombed there.

The thirteenth century French poem, *Vulgate Cycle*, places Joyous Gard in northern England, someplace near Humber but the English preference is to have the castle's location as the site of a known castle in Northumberland.

Source: Bruce, *Arthurian Name Dictionary,* 286; Lacy, *Arthurian Encyclopedia,* 309

Judecca

In Dante Alighieri's epic poem *Divina Commedia* ("Divine Comedy") (1320) the river Judecca is located in the fourth and lowest ring of the ninth circle of HELL; it was one of the four tributaries of the river (see ANTENORA, COCYTUS, and PTOLOMEA). Named for Judas Iscariot, the character who, in the New Testament of the Bible, betrayed Jesus Christ to the Romans for thirty pieces of silver; traitors to their benefactors are immersed in Judecca's icy waters.

Alighieri utilized names and locations from existing mythologies; many of the demons mentioned in the poem were pulled from established hierarchies for example. Because his work, which was meant to be an allegory for the soul's journey to the path of God was well read and accepted, the names and locations he created for the sake of good storytelling became accepted into mythology as well.

Source: Lansing, *Dante Encyclopedia,* 544; Zimmerman, *Inferno of Dante Alighieri,* 225, 239

Juherbâd

Variations: Gouherbad, Gauher-abad, Gauher-ábád

Juherbâd ("Jewel City") is the capital city of SHAD-U-KAM, one of the cities or provinces in DJINNESTAN, the Persian mythological equivalent of FAIRYLAND. Juherbâd is ruled over by two kings.

Source: Keightly, *World Guide to Gnomes, Fairies, Elves, and Other Little People,* 16; Smedley, *Occult Sciences,* 19, 775; Spence, *Encyclopædia of Occultism,* 177; Yardley, *Supernatural in Romantic Fiction,* 53

Juwuku

In the mythology of the Tiwi people there are four layers which make up the universe, ILARA, the subterranean world; KALUWARTU, the earth; Juwuku, the sky world, and the upper world known as TURIRUNA. Juwuku is the dome that encompasses the flat disk of the earth.

Source: Campion, *Astrology and Cosmology in the World's Religions,* 29; Mountford, *The Tiwi,* 170

Kâf

Variations: Jabal Kâf

The mountain rage Kâf, home to the divs, djinn, and peries, surrounded the flat, circular earth like a ring; outside of it there was a great ocean. Described as being made of green chrysolite, the reflection of Kâf gave the sky its greenish tint; it was said to be 2,000 miles in height.

Source: Hanauer, *Folklore of the Holy Land,* 140; Keightly, *World Guide to Gnomes, Fairies, Elves, and Other Little People,* 15, 16

Kalapa

According to Tibetan Buddhist legend Kalapa is the capital city of the SHAMBHALA; it is where the Kulika king, Suchandra, has his lion throne. Described as being an exceedingly beautiful city Kalapa has a sandalwood grove with a huge three-dimensional Kalachakra mandala; its palace is made of solid gold and silver and is embedded with coral, emeralds, moon crystals, pearls, and turquoise.

To each side of the capital city is a lake, each filled with jewels; one is shaped like a crescent moon and the other like a half moon. To the north are the shrines to the gods and saints and due south is a magnificent wooded park of sandalwood trees.

Source: Lepage, *Shambhala;* 24; Znamenski, *Red Shambhala,* 1

Kalasutram

Variations: Kalasutra, Kālasūtra, Krishnasutra

According to Hindu and Vedic mythology Kalasutram ("black rope") is the sixth of the twenty-eight NARAKAS (HELLS) located in a providence in the kingdom of Yama; it is filled with the instruments of torture for those who did not respect their elders, mothers, and fathers. Here sinners run about in the unbearable heat until they pass out; upon revival, the punishment is repeated.

In to Indian Buddhism, Kalasutram is the second of the EIGHT HOT HELLS; it is known as the Black Rope Hell and the souls here are punished for the sins of theft. Here the souls are tied with black fetters to all the objects they once stole.

Source: Mew, *Traditional Aspects of Hell*, 38–41; Prabhupāda, *Śrīmad Bhāgavatam*, 903; Parmeshwaranand, *Encyclopaedic Dictionary of Purāṇas*, 721; Wilson, *Vishṅu Purāṅa*, 215–16

Kale-Thaungto

In Burma Kale-Thaungto is a town fully occupied by wizards.

Source: Spence, *Encyclopædia of Occultism*, 242

Kalichi

In Hindu and Vedic mythology Kalichi is the huge palace where the god Yama lives; it is located in the city of YAMAPURI in PITRI-LOKA. It is here in the city of Kalichi where Yama sits upon his throne of judgment, Vichāra-bhū.

Source: Dalal, *Religions of India*, 398; Dowson, *Classical Dictionary of Hindu Mythology*, 374

Kaluwartu

In the mythology of the Tiwi people there are four layers which make up the universe, ILARA, the subterranean world; Kaluwartu, the earth; JUWUKU the sky world, and the upper world known as TURIRUNA. Kaluwartu is described as being a flat disk surrounded by water and covered by a solid dome, the JU-WUKU.

Source: Campion, *Astrology and Cosmology in the World's Religions*, 29; Hiatt, *Australian Aboriginal Concepts*, 165

Karma-Deva-Loka

In Hindu mythology Karma-Deva-Loka is the loka of Rupa Devas who dwell in one of the four lower divisions of the mental world.

Source: Aiyaṅgār, *Essays on Indo-Aryan Mythology*, Volume 1, 466; Hoult, *Dictionary of Some Theosophical Terms*, 67, 116

Kasil

According to the ancient Persian fairytale, *Sindbad the Sailor* (750 CE), Kasil was an island named in the first voyage of the fictional sailor's adventures; the sounds of drums and tambourines were heard all throughout the night. Kasil is said to be the homeland of al-Dajjal, the Muslim antichrist who will lay waste to the world leading an army of 70,000 Jews. In the waters around this island was said to be a fish some 200 cubits (300 feet) long.

Source: Burton, *Lady Burton's Edition of Her Husband's Arabian Nights*, Volume 3, 372; Burton, *Seven Voyages of Sinbad the Sailor*, 8–14; Lane, *Sindbad the Sailor*, 22; Sprague de Camp, *Lands Beyond*, 119

Kattigat

Variations: Catte grat, Cattegat, Kattegat, Kattigut, Hlesey, Hlessey

In Norse mythology Kattigat ("Cat's Throat") was an island where the god of the sea Ægir (Hler) and his wife the goddess Ran's hall was located. The coral cave palace of Ægir is surrounded by mermaids, nixies, and undines.

Source: Daly, *Norse Mythology A to Z*, 41; Grimes, *Norse Myths*, 283; Guerber, *Hammer of Thor*, 245

al-Kawthar

According to Muslim beliefs, al-Kawthar (abundance) is traditionally identified as being one of the rivers of al JANNA (PARADISE) although the Koran does not specifically say that it is. As a river Kawthar would source from the roots of the tree, Tuba. The waters of these rivers are described as being like honey, milk, water, and wine and along the banks are precious gems. Only the righteous will be allowed to drink from it.

Source: Netton, *Popular Dictionary of Islam*, 142

Keliwic

Variations: Celliwic, Gelliwig, Killiwic

In the Welsh tales of Arthur, there is no mention of CAMELOT but rather three tribal thrones to the land of Britain located at places where Arthur would hold court. A Northern tradition claims one of the thrones was located at Pen Rhionydd; the Welsh throne was at Saint David's, and the Cornish one at Keliwic ("Woodland"). It is interesting to note Keliwic was mentioned as an Arthurian residence before any recorded ideas about Caerleon or CAMELOT.

Source: Ashley, *Mammoth Book of King Arthur*, 196; Lacy, *Arthurian Encyclopedia*, 314

Kerlaug (kor'loug)

Variations: Kerlaugar, Kerlaung, Kerlögar

In Norse mythology Kerlaug was the stream the god Thor had to wade through daily in order to attend the meetings which took place at URDARBRUNNR WELL; a poisonous mist rises up from it.

Source: Bennett, *Gods and Religions of Ancient and Modern Times*, Volume 1, 392; Guerber, *Myths of the Norsemen*, 60; Guerber, *Hammer of Thor*, 42

Kerneter

In Egyptian mythology, Kerneter ("good place") is one of the gates in AMENTI, the UNDERWORLD; it is a PARADISE and described as being a subterranean sphere with its own blindly brilliant sun.

Source: Brown, *Great Dionysiak Myth*, 317; Cooper, *Archaic Dictionary*, 45

Khadiraka

Variations: Karavīka

The Khadiraka Mountains are the fourth mountain chain surrounding SUMERU, the central would mountain in in Hindu cosmology; it is both 10,000 *yojanas* tall and wide.

The measure of a single *yojanas* has never been clear, some scholars say it is approximately four and a half miles while other say it ranges between seven and nine miles.

Source: Howard, *Imagery of the Cosmological Buddha*, 66–68; Nagao, *Wisdom, Compassion, and the Search for Understanding*, 192

Kherani Mountain

According to the Kurdish author, geographer, governor of Hamāh, historian, and prince of the Ayyubid dynasty, Abu al-Fida, Kherani Mountain juts out of the sea; this large island is well known for its inland iron mines and load stones.

Source: de Camp, *Lands Beyond*, 144

Khubur

In the belief of the ancient Babylonians, Khubur ("Assembly") was a river in the north which needed to be crossed, as it was the first obstacle a soul needed to traverse in its journey through ARALLU, the UNDERWORLD. The ferryman, Khumuttabal was described as having a bird's head and four arms and feet.

Source: Budge, *Babylonian Life and History*, 90; Clay, *Origin of Biblical Traditions Hebrew Legends in Babylonia*, 96–97

Kibu

Variations: Boigu

The Mabuiag people of the Torres Strait believe the spirits of the deceased travel to an island, Kibu ("Sun-down") thought to be located over the horizon far to the north-west where no canoe or man has ever been. All spirits, be they bad or good, reside in Kibu; they reunite with friends who have passed before them and those who come from the same village live together in the same rooms in the great long house of ghosts.

Source: Frazer, *Belief in Immortality and the Worship of the Dead*, 175–76, 213; Ward, *Hung Society*, 25

Kikorangi

Variations: Kiko-rangi

In some versions of the Maori legend of

Tawhaki, Kikorangi is the first of the twelve layers of HEAVEN; typically there are only ten named divisions but sometimes there are as many as fourteen and as few as two named. Kikorangi is presided over by the god Toumau and it is one of three HEAVENs presided over by the war god Maru.

Source: Craig, *Dictionary of Polynesian Mythology*, 114, 347; Grey, Maori Lore, 12; Mead, *Tāwhaki*, 58

Kimmerioi

According to Homer's *Odyssey*, Kimmerioi was a land located somewhere in the far west *"hidden in darkness and in the clouds"* (II.13). It has been hypothesized the Kimmerioi were ancient Celts who settled in Western Europe and Asia Minor.

Ephorus (400–330 BC), the ancient Greek historian described the people of Kimmerioi as living underground called *argillai*; these people made their living by mining and by those who came to consult with their oracle.

Source: Guest, *Origines Celticae*, 7, 8, 13; Sprague de Camp, *Lands Beyond*, 74

Kingdom of Abdalles *see* Abdalles, Kingdom of

Kingdom of Prester John *see* Prester John, Kingdom of

Kingdom of Saguenay *see* Saguenay, Kingdom of

Kingdom of the Ghuls *see* The Ghuls, Kingdom of

Kingdom of the Immortals *see* The Immortals, Kingdom of

King's Hill

Variations: Kongsbjerg

In Danish fairy-lore King's Hill was where the promontory-king (*klintekonger*) lived; these kings keep watch over the country and in the event of war draw up their armies to defend the land.

Source: Keightly, *World Guide to Gnomes, Fairies, Elves, and Other Little People*, 91

Kmibhojanam

According to Hindu and Vedic mythology Kmibhojanam ("food for worms") is the tenth of the twenty-eight NARAKAS (HELLS) located in a providence in the kingdom of Yama; depraved brahmans who take food without first asking the blessings of the gods are located here. Insects, snakes, and worms bit and sting these sinners slowly eating them up. Once consumed, the soul is restored and the punishment begins anew.

Source: Parmeshwaranand, *Encyclopaedic Dictionary of Purāṇas*, 721

Kormt

One of the two rivers which ran beneath the BIFROST BRIDGE, the god Thor would wade across it, the river ORMT, and the stream KERLAUG each day to attend the daily meeting the gods held at the URARD FOUNTAIN.

Source: Anderson, *Norse Mythology*, 451; Bennett, *Gods and Religions of Ancient and Modern Times*, Volume 1, 392; Guerber, *Myths of the Norsemen*, 60

Krimibhaksha

In Hindu mythology Krimibhaksha ("where worms are his food") is a partition in HELL (or NARAKA) ruled over by Yama; it is located beneath the earth and water where souls are punished for the sin of hating the Brahmas, his father, or the god and spoiling precious gems.

Source: Wilson, *Oriental Translation Fund*, Volume 52, 208

Krimibhojana

Variations: Krmibhojana

In Hindu mythology Krimibhojana is one of the twenty-eight NARAKAS (HELLS) located in a providence in the kingdom of Yama; it is filled with the instruments of torture.

Source: Garrett, *Classical Dictionary of India*,

340; Prabhupāda, *Śrīmad Bhāgavatam*, 903; Wilson, *Vishńu Puráńa*, 215–16

Krimisa

In Hindu mythology Krimisa ("lord of worms" or "that of insects") is a partition in HELL (or NARAKA) ruled over by Yama; it is located beneath the earth and water where souls are punished for the sin of using magic for the sake of hurting others.

Source: Garrett, *Classical Dictionary of India*, 340; Wilson, *Oriental Translation Fund*, Volume 52, 208; Wilson, *Vishńu Puráńa*, 215–16

Krishana

In Hindu mythology, Krishana is one of the twenty-eight NARAKAS (HELLS) located in a providence in the kingdom of Yama; it is filled with the instruments of torture.

Source: Das, *Journal of the Buddhist Text Society of India*, Volumes 1–3, 69; Wilson, *Vishńu Puráńa*, 215–16

Krishna

In Hindu mythology Krishna ("black") is a partition in HELL (or NARAKA) ruled over by Yama; it is located beneath the earth and water where souls are punished for the sin of causing impotence, lives by fraud, is generally impure, or trespasses on another's land.

Source: Wilson, *Oriental Translation Fund*, Volume 52, 209

Ksharakardamam

Variations: Ksharakardama

According to Hindu and Vedic mythology Ksharakardamam is the twenty-second of the twenty-eight NARAKAS (HELLS) located in a providence in the kingdom of Yama. Here, those who brag and insult those born of a noble birth are kept upside down and tortured in various ways.

Source: Parmeshwaranand, *Encyclopaedic Dictionary of Purāṇas*, 722

Ksuramarga

Variations: Ksuradharamarga

One of the four kinds of sub-hells (*utsada*)
to the EIGHT HOT HELLS in Indian Buddhism, Ksuramarga ("Razor Road") is described as a great road either covered with or made of razor blades; each time a step is made the flesh of the foot is painfully destroyed only to be fully healed as it is raised.

Source: Nāgārjuna, *Nāgārjuna's Letter*, 107; Sadakata, *Buddhist Cosmology*, 51–52

Kukula

One of the four kinds of sub-hells (*utsada*) to the EIGHT HOT HELLS in Indian Buddhism, Kukula ("Fire-pit" or "Heated by Burning Chaff"), is described as a vast plain of smoldering red-hot embers where suffers are immersed up to their knees and made to walk.

Source: Nāgārjuna, *Nāgārjuna's Letter*, 103; Sadakata, *Buddhist Cosmology*, 51–52

Kumari Kandam

Variations: Kumari Nadu

A lost continent named in ancient Tamil literature Kumari Kandam was described in the fifteenth century text *Kamtapuranam* as a place free of barbarians; it was described as stretching south of India, from Africa in the west to Australia in the east with culture flourishing as early as 30,000 BCE as the first civilized society, according to Tamil tradition, the people of Kumari Kandam were ruled by fair and just leaders and enjoyed many artistic and technological advances and had four distinctive *kunams* ("traits"): a good work ethic, rational thought (*pakuttarivu*), struggled courageously, and shared eating.

After the ice age and the rising of the ocean's levels some 16,000 years ago, the continent was lost forcing its inhabitants to flee to the surrounding lands.

Source: Douglas, *Forbidden History*, 84, 182; Wellington, *Recipes for Immortality*, 90, 97

Kumbhipaka

Variations: Kumbhi-pakah

According to Hindu and Vedic mythology Kumbhipaka is the fifth of the twenty-eight NARAKAS (HELLS) located in a providence in the kingdom of Yama; it is filled with the instruments of torture. Described as being an 8,000 mile wide cauldron of boiling oil, this HELL is filled with sinner who cooked animals while they were still alive and then ate them.

Source: Prabhupāda, *Śrīmad Bhāgavatam*, 903; Parmeshwaranand, *Encyclopaedic Dictionary of Purāṇas*, 721

Kunapa

One of the four kinds of sub-hells (*utsada*) to the EIGHT HOT HELLS in Indian Buddhism, Kunapa ("Corpses and Dung") is described as a swamp of filth and putrid with odor filled with wild animals who pierce the skin with their sharp beaks; maggots eat their way into the skin and chew their way down and into the marrow of the bones. Upon arrival, sinners immediately sink into the muck up to their head.

Source: Nāgārjuna, *Nāgārjuna's Letter*, 107; Sadakata, *Buddhist Cosmology*, 51–52

Kunlun Mountains

A Taoist PARADISE in Chinese mythology, the Kunlun Mountains was the earthy residence of the immortals and supreme deities; it is one of the pillars keeping the sky from crashing down upon the earth as well as a ladder to ascend into the HEAVENS.

In its earliest descriptions Kunlun was described as being a huge mountain, 248 miles square and 80,000 feet high, located in the North West. Atop its summit were nine gates guarded by a beast called Kaiming ("Enlightened"); nine wells made of jade, and a crop of magical grain growing 40 feet tall and five spans wide.

To the west of Kulun flew phoenixes; to the north grew the Jade Tree, the Pearl Tree, Tree Grain, the Shirou ("Seeing Flesh") Tree, the Sweet Spring, and the Tree of Immortality.

Source: Lepage, *Shambhala*, 19; Yang, *Handbook of Chinese Mythology*, 160

Kur Kurnugi

Variations: Kur-Nu-Gi-A

A subterranean HELL of Sumerian mythology, Kur Kurnugi ("Mountain of no return") was described as a dark place from which no one ever returned, the road to it lead only in one direction; occupants of Kur Kurnugi have dust for food and clay plates for bread.

Source: Dalley, *Myths from Mesopotamia*, 324; Dowden, *Companion to Greek Mythology*, 390

Labyrinth

Variations: Maze

A labyrinth is a complex path of some description, be it a two-dimensional pattern or a three dimensional structure. Although the word *maze* is used interchangeably with labyrinth, there is an argument to be made that the two are separate ideas. A maze, generally speaking, is a tortured branched path with some routes leading to dead-ends; having more than one entrance and exit, the maze is specifically designed to challenge and confuse those who seek to reach the goal to which it leads. A labyrinth only has one means of entrance which is also the eventual exit; its single path has many twists and turns but never branches off (unicursal); eventually it leads to the objective.

The oldest structure to which the word labyrinth was applied was in the northern Egyptian city Crocodilopolis ("City of Crocodiles").

In Greek mythology the Labyrinth was the structure King Minos of Crete had the artesian Daedalus design and construct to contain the Minotaur, the monstrous offspring of his wife, Queen Pasiphae and a sacrificial white bull; this compound was so elaborate and difficult to navigate, anyone who entered it would become hopelessly lost.

Source: Daly, *Greek and Roman Mythology A to Z*, 87; Evans, *Dictionary of Mythology*, 151; Matthews, *Mazes and Labyrinths*, 2, 7

Ladhwa

The second of the seven HELLS of Islamic mythology, Ladhwa is reserved for the souls of the Jewish people.

Source: Wherry, *Comprehensive Commentary on the Quran*, 148

Ladon

A river in western Arcadia in Greek mythology, Landon was the location where the demigod Hercules captured the sacred Cerynitian hind, an immortal stag sacred to the goddess Artemis, after a year-long pursuit. Just as the golden antlered stag was about to leap across the river Hercules took it to ground, without injuring it, with an arrow.

Source: Evans, *Dictionary of Mythology*, 151; Hard, *Routledge Handbook of Greek Mythology*, 259; Westmoreland, *Ancient Greek Beliefs*, 235

Lagam

Variations: Ladha, Latha ("Flamer"), Nata

The fifth of the seven Islamic HELLS, Lagam is reserved for Christians (see AL HUTAMA, HAWIYAH, JAHANNAM, AL JAHIM, SA'IR, and SAQAU).

Source: Hughes, *Dictionary of Islam*, 170–71; Wagner, *How Islam Plans to Change the World*, 156

Laiabhaksam

Variations: Puyoda ("Having Fetid Water")

According to Hindu and Vedic mythology Laiabhaksam is one of the twenty-eight NARAKAS (HELLS) located in a providence in the kingdom of Yama. Here those lustful men who allow their wives to swallow semen find themselves submerged in an endless sea of semen.

Source: Garg, *Encyclopaedia of the Hindu World: Ar–Az*, 841; Parmeshwaranand, *Encyclopaedic Dictionary of Purāṇas*, 722

Lake of Cuilenn *see* Grey Lake of Cuilenn

Lake of Fire

Variations: Sea of Fire (Christian)

Appearing in both the religions of the Ancient Egyptian as well as Christian mythology the imagery of a lake of fire has become synonymous with HELL or a place where evil people are sent to be endless punished, tortured, or destroyed.

In the Egyptian mortuary relief entitled "*The Book of Gates*" tell us the Lake of Fire was located in the UNDERWORLD in the Sacred Cavern of Sokar. This sunless region was the destination for damned souls; any who entered here were never to return.

The Lake of Fire in Christian belief is a place of continual suffering, the destination of those who die without knowing Christ, the Devil, and fallen angels. The suffering caused in the Lake of Fire is twofold; there is the punishment of separation, as those who are here are forever withheld from the presence of God without hope of reconciliation. The second takes the form of actual pain and torment from the infernal atmosphere and blazing environment.

Source: Bunson, *Encyclopedia of Ancient Egypt*, 209; Lockyer, *All the Doctrines of the Bible*, 292

Lake of Flowers

A PARADISE realm in the mythology of ancient Egyptian, the Lake of Flowers was filled with beautiful flowers, cool breezes, and refreshing water. Once admitted, residency in the Lake of Flowers was *shenu* ("eternal"), an everlasting continuation of an idealized life on earth, similar to the Field of Reeds (see AARU).

Source: Bunson, *Encyclopedia of Ancient Egypt*, 209; Najovits, *Egypt, Trunk of the Tree*, Volume 2, 30

Lake of the Cauldron *see* Cauldron, Lake of the

Lalabhaksha

In Hindu mythology Lalabhaksha ("where saliva is his food") is a partition in HELL (or NARAKA) ruled over by Yama; it is located beneath the earth and water where souls are punished for the sin of eating his meal before making offerings to the gods, his guests, or the manes.

Source: Source: Wilson, *Oriental Translation Fund*, Volume 52, 208; Wilson, *Vishńu Puráńa*, 215–16

Land of Cockaigne *see* Cockaigne

Land of Day

Variations: Udlormiut

According to Inuit legend the Land of Day is a large village located in the Land of the Moon; it is where the souls of the deceased engage in endless sport activity where they are free from cold and hunger as they await reincarnation. The Land of Day could only be reached by traveling the "dangerous pathway," the aurora of the Northern Lights; only the deceased and ravens can safely make this journey. The individuals who reside here never broke a taboo in life and died a violent death.

Source: Grimal, *Larousse World Mythology*, 444; Leenaars, *Suicide in Canada*, 197; Logan, *Firebridge to Skyshore*, 10

Land of Giants

Variations: Tir na Fathach

The Land of Giants is an OTHERWORLD in Welsh mythology; it is ruled over by the great giant chieftain, Isbaddaden (Ysbaddaden).

Source: Monaghan, *Encyclopedia of Celtic Mythology and Folklore*, 478; Mountain, *Celtic Encyclopedia*, Volume 5, 763, 1339

Land of Pantoroze *see* Pantoroze, Land of

Land of Promise

Variations: Tir na Tairngire, Tir Tairngiri

An OTHERWORLD in Celtic mythology, the Land of Promise has been the home to an Irish divinity of the sea, Manannan Mac Lir; in the romantic tale of Clidna the Land of Promise is where she was courted by the womanizing outcast of the Fianna, Ciabhan.

Source: Monaghan, *Encyclopedia of Celtic Mythology and Folklore*, 90, 311; Mountain, *Celtic Encyclopedia*, Volume 5, 1339

Land of Shadows

Variations: Tir na Scath

A Celtic Otherworld kingdom, the Land of Shadows was the dwelling place of Skatha (Scathach), a mighty female warrior who taught young heroes the art of combat.

Source: Matson, *Celtic Mythology A to Z*, 115; Mountain, *Celtic Encyclopedia*, Volume 5, 1339

Land of Summer

Variations: Gwâld yr Hâv, Tir na Samhraidh

In Welsh lore the Land of Summer was an OTHERWORLD; it was the place where the ancestors of the Cymri came from.

Source: Mountain, *Celtic Encyclopedia*, Volume 5, 1339; Squire, *Celtic Myth and Legend*, 119

Land of the Dead

Variations: Tir na Mairbh

In Celtic lore the Land of the Dead was oftentimes said to be located out in the western sea as a FLOATING ISLAND. The deceased rested peacefully in their graves until occasion called for them to rise. The Death Coach of Irish lore came from the Land of the Dead to retrieve a person who was slated to die. Once a person crosses over into the Land of the Dead they are no longer human and are subject to a set of taboos not applied to mankind.

Source: Monaghan, *Encyclopedia of Celtic Mythology and Folklore*, 120; Mountain, *Celtic Encyclopedia*, Volume 5, 1339; Spence, *Magic Arts in Celtic Britain*, 80

Land of the Living

Variations: Tir Inna Beo, Tir na mBeo

A PARADISE of Celtic lore where a person's soul retires to upon death, the Land of the Living has music issuing forth from the ground; its inhabitants never again know the effects of age or sickness and drink and food appear at will from magical vessels.

Source: Mountain, *Celtic Encyclopedia*, Volume 5, 1339; Osborne, *Civilization*, 37–38

Land of the Moon

Variations: Quidlivun

According to Inuit mythology after as soul spends a year being purified in ADLIVUN, they are allowed to pass onto the Land of the Moon where they find eternal rest. Also here are those individuals who died a violent death.

Source: Grimal, *Larousse World Mythology*, 443; Lynch, *Native American Mythology A to Z*, 2

Land of the Western Paradise see Pure Land of the Western Paradise

The Land of Women

Variations: Tir na mBan, Tír na mBean

From the Celtic literary poem "*The Voyage of Bran, son of Feba*"; the Queen draws Bran and his followers ashore and to her island, the Land of Women, and entertains. Bran and company believe they have been on the island for a year but in truth many years had passed.

In Arthurian lore the Land of Women is an OTHERWORLD ruled over by the Lady of the Lake; in Irish lore it is an UNDERWORLD or FLOATING ISLAND where the fairy queen Niamh of the Golden Hair rules.

Source: Evan-Wentz, *Fairy Faith in Celtic Countries*, 339; Monaghan, *Encyclopedia of Celtic Mythology and Folklore*, 279; Mountain, *Celtic Encyclopedia*, Volume 5, 1339

Land of Youth

Variations: Tir na h-Oige, Tir na nOg, Tír na nOg

A popular name for the OTHERWORLD in Irish and Scottish mythology, the Land of Youth, emphasizes the eternal and unfading beauty of its fairy occupants.

Source: Monaghan, *Encyclopedia of Celtic Mythology and Folklore*, 347; Mountain, *Celtic Encyclopedia*, Volume 5, 1339

Land Under the Waves

Variations: Tir fo Thuinn

The domain of the fairy Fiachna, the Land under the Waves, as its name implies, is a country and OTHERWORLD located under the sea. It also refers to any city which has been consumed by the sea, such as with CAER YS.

Source: Ellis, *Celtic Myths and Legends*, 516–21; Mountain, *Celtic Encyclopedia*, Volume 5, 1339

Landvide (land-ve'di)

Variations: Landvidi

In Norse mythology Landvide ("the wide land") located in ASGARD, was the home of the god Vidar. The palace here was situated in the middle of an impenetrable primeval forest and was described as being decorated with boughs of greenery and fresh flowers.

Source: Bennett, *Gods and Religions of Ancient and Modern Times*, Volume 1, 392; Dunham, *History of Denmark, Sweden, and Norway*, Volume 2, 55; Guerber, *Myths of the Norsemen*, 158, 160

Langarrow

Variations: Langona

According to local lore, there once stood on the northern shores of Cornwall a city called Langarrow which held seven churches, each one well known for both its beauty and size; the population was generally wealthy as the land was fertile and the fishing plentiful. One day it was decided to construct a port area (or develop a mine, sources vary) and the town hired a labor force of convicted criminals; these individuals were housed in caves and huts just outside the city, but unfortunately not far away enough from the general population. As construction went on the citizens and the convicts began to intermingle; several marriages took place. Over time the morality of the people of Langarrow became corrupt; divine retribution was delivered upon the town, as a violent three-day long storm stirred up great sand hills and buried the town completely.

Source: Courtney, *Cornish Feasts and Folk-Lore*, 67; Dyer, *Church-Lore Gleanings*, 86

Langchen Khabab

Variations: Langchen Khabap

In Hindu mythology Langchen Khabab ("River from the Elephant Mouth") is one of the four rivers which runs out of MAPHAM YUMTSHO, the lake located at the bottom of Mount MERU; it flows to the west.

Source: Chodag, *Tibet, the Land and the People*, 148, 156; McCue, *Trekking in Tibet*, 207

Lavana

Variations: Sabala, Savana

In Hindu mythology Lavana ("salt") is a partition in HELL (or *Naraka*) ruled over by

Yama; it is located beneath the earth and water where souls are punished for the sin of being abusive to his better, associating with women who are in a prohibited degree, disrespectful to his spiritual guide, or reviles in or sells the Vedas.

Source: Wilson, *Oriental Translation Fund*, Volume 52, 208; Wilson, *Vishńu Puráńa*, 215–16

Leipter (lip'ter)

Variations: Leift, Leipt, Leiptr

A sacred stream in Norse mythology Leipter ("Quick as Lightening"), along its magical banks solemn oaths were sworn which could not then be broken. Leipter was found in the realm of the goddess, Hel, NIFLEHEIM.

Source: Grimes, *Norse Myths*, 285; Guerber, *Myths of the Norsemen*, 182, 385

Lemnos

An island in the Aegean Sea, Lemnos was the island where the godling Hephaestus landed after he was literally thrown from Mount Olympus by one of his parents, Hera or Zeus, for having been born with a weak body and a club foot. The natives of the islands, the barbaric Sintians, raised the child in secret for fear the gods would seek to finish him off. The women of Lemnos offended the goddess Aphrodite by neglecting their religious duties to her; the goddess punished the women causing them to have an offensive odor.

Source: Evans, *Dictionary of Mythology*, 157; Westmoreland, *Ancient Greek Beliefs*, 54

Lemuria

A zoologist by the name of Philip Sclater proposed a hypothesis in 1864 to explain how similar animal fossils could be found on India and Madagascar but not on Africa; he suggested a landmass once existed he called Lemuria, whose center submerged and thereby created the space between India and Madagascar. Next, a German evolutionary scientist named Ernst Haeckel suggested that man, *Homo sapiens*, came into being on that massive land bridge before it sank. Some paelogeologist put forth the idea Lemuria was a part of the super continent Gondwanaland and did not sink but was a victim of the landmass' break-up.

Helena P. Blavatsky, the founder of Theosophy Incorporated, assimilated the idea of Lemuria into her occult practices; this is likely the reason the idea of Lemuria exists today. Blavatsky claimed there would be seven races of mankind and the third race, an advanced civilization of seven-foot tall, egg laying hermaphrodites who practiced bestiality and black magic lived on Lemuria. The gods, offended by their actions destroyed the island and created the fourth race of man and the island of ATLANTIS. After the publication of her book, *Secret Doctrines* (1889) other Theosophical visionaries began to claim to have interactions with the surviving Lemurians who now live in secret on Mount Shasta.

Source: Clark, *Hidden Realms*, 6–13; Feder, *Encyclopedia of Dubious Archaeology*, 157–58; Sprague de Camp, *Lands Beyond*, 20–21

Lerad (la-rad)

Variations: Lædr, Læraδ, Læradi, Læradr, Læraδr, Lærath, Lærδr, Lärad, Leding, Leraδ, Leradur

Atop of the ash tree YGGDRASIL of Norse mythology, Lerad ("the peace giver") was the name of its top-most bough. Lerad overshadowed GLADSHEIM the hall of the god Odin while the other branches of YGGDRASIL spread out and covered the nine worlds. There was an eagle that made a nest on Lerad; in-between the eyes of the eagle sat the falcon Vedfolnir who with his keen eyesight would watch over everything and report to Odin all he saw. The great she-goat of Odin, Heidrun, continuously grazes upon the leaves and twigs of Lerad and by doing so she is able to produce enough mead for all the heroes who would drink of it.

Source: Anderson, *Norse Mythology*, 263; Grimes, *Norse Myths*, 284; Guerber, *Myths of the Norsemen*, 13, 19

Lessoe, Island of

The Island of Lessoe was one of the two dwelling places of the Norse god of the sea, Ægir (Hler).

Source: Blumetti, *Book of Balder Rising*, 228; Guerber, *Myths of the Norsemen*, 185

Lethe (LEE-thee)

Variations: PLAINS OF LETHE

One of the five rivers in HADES (TARTARUS), the UNDERWORLD in Greek and Roman mythology, Lethe ("Forgetfulness," "Oblivion") is the beautiful and sparkling river from which the dead were obligated to drink from so they would forget the lives they once had on earth (see ACHERON, COCYTUS, PYRIPHLEGETHON, and STYX). The banks of the river were known as the PLAINS OF LETHE.

Source: Daly, *Greek and Roman Mythology A to Z*, 87; Evslin, *Gods, Demigods, and Demons*, 124–25; Rose, *Handbook of Greek Mythology*, 23, 88

Lethe, Plains of *see* Plains of Lethe

Leuke

An island from Greek lore, Leuke ("White Island") was the PARADISE-like island home of the blessed dead. The hero, Achilles, was said to have gone to Leuke after death, but various sources also claim he went to ELYSIUM FIELDS, HADES, and the ISLANDS OF THE BLESSED. According to lore, after the battle of the Trojan War the Amazons launched a campaign against the island of Leuke, said to be located at the mouth of the Danube river; upon arrival they saw the ghost of Achilles which so terrified their horses the women warriors were forced to abandon their mission.

Sources: Burgess, *Death and Afterlife of Achilles*, 41; Littleton, *Gods, Goddesses, and Mythology*, Volume 1, 64

Lich-Way

The path by which a funeral takes to the church is known as a lich-way; this route is typically not a well-traveled road and will deviate from commonly used thoroughfares.

Source: Donald, *Chambers's English Dictionary*, 468; Sprague, *Burial Terminology*, 168

Lily Lake

A PARADISE realm in the mythology of ancient Egyptian, Lily Lake, located in the eastern sky, must be crossed by the deceased Pharaoh in order to be separated from the sun god; to cross the lake he must maintain the favor of a ferryman named "Face-Behind" as he needed to stand facing backward to pole the boat from the stern.

Source: Bunson, *Encyclopedia of Ancient Egypt*, 214; Spence, *Mysteries of Egypt*, 73

Limbo

Variations: Limbus infantium ("Children's Limbo")

Limbo ("Boarder" or "Hem") is an intermediary location situated between HEAVEN and HELL; this is the temporary location for those souls who died pure of sin yet were otherwise excluded from the vision of God until Christ's ascension into HEAVEN as well as the permanent place for those unbaptized who died without grievous personal sin.

Although the concept of limbo is not a part of Roman Catholic belief, does not appear in the bible, nor is it taught as being a part of the religion, there is a wide-spread belief in it. The idea came about in the thirteenth century as an answer for what happened to the souls of newborn infants who died unbaptized and carrying the weight of Original Sin.

Some scholars taught there were four divisions to Limbo: *Limbus Fatuorum* for fools and the mentally disabled who are not responsible for the sins they commit; *Limbus Patrum* who were the good patriarchs who lived before the time of Christ and never had the means or opportunity to convert to Christianity; *Limbus Puerorum* for unbaptized children; and *Limbus Purgatorius* where the better sort are cleansed of their sins.

Source: Demy, *Answers to Common Questions About Heaven and Eternity*, 58–59; Hexham, *Concise Dictionary of Religion*, 137; Walsh, *Handy-book of Literary Curiosities*, 381

Listeneise

Variations: Listenoise

The name of the land of the Holy Grail in some Arthurian lore, Listeneise is also the location of the Grail Castle. In the *Prose Tristan*, Listeneise is the name of the kingdom of King Pellinore; in Sir Thomas Malory's *Le Morte d'Arthur*, it is the kingdom of Pellam, the Maimed King.

Source: Karr, *King Arthur Companion*, 130; Spence, *Dictionary of Medieval Romance and Romance Writers*, 130

The Living, Land of *see* Land of the Living

Lizard Islands

In Torquemada's "*Garden of Flowers*" the Lizard Islands are where women who were outcast from the rest of the world were welcomed and received.

Source: Brewer, *Dictionary of Phrase and Fable*, 520

Loadstone, Mountain of

Variations: MAGNETIC MOUNTAIN, MURUKEYYIN

First described by Claudius Ptolemy, the second century Egyptian geographer, he claimed the Mountain of Loadstone lay in the Far East near the ISLAND OF THE SATYRS; however, it was popularized in the third adventure of Duke Ernest in the German metrical romance "Herzog Ernst von Schwaden." in the German story Loadstone was said to be an island in the Mediterranean Sea; his ship wrecked upon its shores because the mountain pulled out the nails which held the vessel together. He and his companion survived and managed to escape by using the griffins that came to the island daily to feed off of the bodies of the dead. Arabic folklore also tells of a mountain of loadstone located on an island in the Indian Ocean. As in other tales, any ship which sails too close to the island will have all its iron fitting pulled free and fly to the mountain.

Source: Lane, *Thousand and One Nights*, 340; Sprauge de Camp, *Lands Beyond*, 105, 142

Loc Lann

Variations: Lochanns ("Black Calls"), Lochlannach ("Men of Lochlann")

The name of the northern land the mythical race known as the Fomorians came from in Irish lore was called Loch Lan; their capitol city of Berva is mentioned in some tales but nothing else is known of it.

Source: Monaghan. *Encyclopedia of Celtic Mythology and Folklore*, 293; Squire, *Celtic Myth and Legend Poetry and Romance*, 205

Logres

The setting for Chrétien de Troyes's *Chevalier da la Charrete* and *Perceval*, as well as much of the thirteenth century French poem, *Vulgate Cycle*, Logres, a poetic creation, is typically identified as the country of England but it is sometimes a vague focus of adventure and romance.

Source: Ashley, *Mammoth Book of King Arthur*, 381; Lacy, *Arthurian Encyclopedia*, 339

Logrum (lo'grum)

Variations: Lake Malar, Löer, Lögrin, Logrinn, Lögrinn, Lör, Mälar

A lake in Norse mythology, Logrum ("the sea") was said to be created when Danish Zealand was carved away from Sweden by Gefjun.

Source: Grimes, *Norse Myths*, 285; Guerber, *Myths of the Norsemen*, 50

Loka

A *loka* is a division of the universe, and in the Hindu Sankhya and Vendanta schools of philosophy there are three such *lokas*, an earth, a HEAVEN, and a HELL. The seven material or earth worlds are BRAHMA-LOKA, GANDHARVA-LOKA, INDRA-LOKA, PISACHA-LOKA, PITRI-LOKA, RAKSHASA-LOKA, SOMA-LOKA, and the YAKSHA-LOKA. There are also seven heavenly worlds: BHUR-LOKA, BHUVAR-LOKA, JANA-LOKA, MAHAR-LOKA, SAWR-LOKA, SATYA-LOKA, and TAPAR-LOKA.

Source: Dowson, *Classical Dictionary of Hindu Mythology and Religion*, 179; Garrett, *Classical Dictionary of India*, 362

Lost City of Z *see* Z, Lost City of

Lost Island

Variations: Cephalonia, Hidden Island

In Greek lore Lost Island received its name because it was only by luck anyone who had ever visited this small island in the Ionian chain could find it again.

Source: Gould, *Miscellaneous Notes and Queries with Answers in All Departments of Literature*, Volume 2, 536; Skyes, *Who's Who in Non-Classical Mythology*, 44

Lover's Leap

A rocky outcrop in various folklores, from ancient Greece to Native Americans, from which aggrieved or rejected lovers jump to their death.

Source: Brewer, *Wordsworth Dictionary of Phrase and Fable*, 687; Watts, *Encyclopedia of American Folklore,* 92

Loycha

A FLOATING ISLAND on a lake in Ireland Loycha was said to grow herbs that could cure any illness but only one person at a time could land on it. For seven years Loycha would drift along the lake's surface then permanently attach to the shore; after which, there would be a great clap of thunder as a new FLOATING ISLAND would appear.

Sources: Larson, *King's Mirror*, 107–08; Van Duzer, *Floating Islands*, 203

Ludr

Ludr was the name of the mill which in Norse mythology the giant Bergelmir and his wife climbed upon during the deluge, thereby saving themselves and creating the race of Jotuns.

Source: Grimes, *Norse Myths*, 7; Guerber, *Myths of the Norsemen*, 286

Luilekkerland

Unlike the Land of COCKAIGNE which was open to anyone who could find it, to gain entry into Luilekkerland ("lazy-and-licker-ish land" or "lazy luscious land") one had to want to get very badly and be willing to perform an incredible feat, such as eating a mountain of buckwheat oatmeal. Once this task is complete, every possible delight is awaiting. Animals here live only to serve man, so tame they can be caught by hand and will in many cases cook themselves.

Source: Capers, *Images and Imagination*, 7–8; Pleij, *Dreaming of Cockaigne*, 81

Lupercal

The place where the mythical founders of Rome, Romulus and Remus, were suckled by the she-wolf, Lupercal is a sacred grotto said to be located at the foot of the Palatine; it was described as having ample drinking water, large trees, and thick bushes.

Source: Bell, *Bell's New Pantheon*, 46; Burn, *Rome and the Campagna*, 156–57

Lycia (LISH-ee-a)

An ancient kingdom in Greek mythology, Lycia was said to have been plagued by a fire-breathing monster known as the Chimaera. King Iobates sent the hero, Bellerophon, after the monster who by use of his flying horse Pegasus was able to defeat the monster.

Source: Daly, *Greek and Roman Mythology A to Z*, 34; Westmoreland, *Ancient Greek Beliefs*, 759

Lyfjaberg (LEV-ya-berg)

In Norse mythology the hill Lyfjaberg ("Hill of Healing") in JOTUNHEIM is where Menglod, a goddess of healing, lives.

Source: Blumetti, *Book of Balder Rising,* 351; Crossley-Holland, *Norse Myths*, 124, 247; Guerber, *Myths of the Norsemen*, 286

Lymdale (lim'dal)

Variations: Hunaland

In Norse mythology Lymdale was the home

of the valkyr Brunhild; it could be seen from the top of HINDARFIALL.

Source: Guerber, *Myths of the Norsemen*, 280

Lyngvi, Island of

Variations: Lyngri, Lyngve

In Norse mythology, Lyngvi was the lonely and rocky island in the middle of lake AMSVARTNIR where Odin and the other Æsir bound the wolf Fenrir upon the hill, SIGLILNIN. This is where the son of the god Loki will remain captive until the time of Ragnarok when he will break free and join the side of the giants.

Source: Daly, *Norse Mythology A to Z*, 66; Grimes, *Norse Myths*, 286, Guerber, *Myths of the Norsemen*, 92

Lyonesse

Variations: Armenye, Leonais, Leonois, Leonnesse, Leonnoys, Liones, Lothian, Lyoness, Lyonnesse, Parmenie

A lost kingdom of Arthurian lore, Lyonesse was said to be located off the coast of Cornwall, Britain near the Isle of Scilly, but had been swallowed up by the sea. There is a rocky outcropping there now known as the Steven Stones and the City, as it is said by locals the salt-water there is so clear you can see the ancient town and its flowering fields intact on the ocean floor. This lost kingdom was said to be beautiful, having ripe orchards and 140 churches. One of its citizens, a man named Trevelyan, fearful of the dangerous inroads the ocean was making inland, moved his family to higher ground; not too long after, a great flood covered the city killing everyone but Trevelyan and his family.

Arthurian legends say Lyonesse is the kingdom of Tristan, the lover of Iseult; otherwise Lyonesse is marginal, as there is mention of only one of its districts, Surluse, and that it is ruled by Galahalt the lord of the Loingtaines.

Source: Evan-Wentz, *Fairy Faith in Celtic Countries*, 12; Jones, *Myths and Legends of Britain and Ireland*, 14–15; Lacy, *Arthurian Encyclopedia*, 344; Monaghan. *Encyclopedia of Celtic Mythology and Folklore*, 300

Lyr

In Norse mythology, Lyr ("Heat Holding") was Menglad's hall in JOTUNHEIM; it was constructed by the god Loki and the dwarfs Bari, Delling, Dori, Iri, Jari, Ori, Uni, Var, and Vegdrasil.

Source: Blumetti, *Book of Balder Rising,* 351; Crossley-Holland, *Norse Myths*, 124, 247

Ma-li-ga-si-ma

A lost continent of Chinese lore Ma-li-ga-si-ma was sunk to the bottom of the ocean due to the sins of the giants who lived upon it. Only the pious king Peiru-un and his family were able to escape the disaster as he was warned by the gods. He and his family went on to become the progenitors of the Chinese people.

Source: Blavatsky, *Secret Doctrine*, Volume 1, 365

Machanon

Variations: Machonon, Zebhul

The fourth of the seven HEAVENs of Jewish lore, Machanon is ruled by the angel Michael and is the home of the heavenly Jerusalem. According to Enoch, Machanon is where the GARDEN OF EDEN is located, not in SAGUN, the third HEAVEN.

Source: Godwin, *Godwin's Cabalistic Encyclopedia*, 349; Lewis, *Angels A to Z, 2nd Edition*, 332; Vohs, *Am I Going to Heaven?*, 36

Machon

Variations: Ma'on, Mathey

The fifth of the seven HEAVENs of Jewish lore, Machon ("Dwelling") is the home of Aaron, the avenging angels, and God; the northern region is home to the grigori (Watcher angels) and the southern region is filled with ministering angels who endlessly chant the praises of God.

Source: Lewis, *Angels A to Z, 2nd Edition*, 332–33; Webster, *Encyclopedia of Angels*, 85

Mag Findargat

The Irish OTHERWORLD, Mag Findargat ("Plain of White Silver") is an island where there grows an ancient tree with blossoms; upon this tree gather the birds of the island and each hour they chime out in harmony the time.

Source: Hewitt, *History and Chronology of the Myth-Making Age*, 63

Mag Mar

Variations: Mag Mor, Magh Mhor

A FAIRYLAND of Irish lore, Mag Mar ("Great Plain") is an OTHERWORLD where the dead walk incessantly; described as a great level field, Mag Mar was seen as a parallel dimension which could be accessed by mortals from this world.

Source: Arbois de Jubainville, *Irish Mythological Cycle and Celtic Mythology*, 15; Evan-Wentz, *Fairy Faith in Celtic Countries*, 335

Mag Mell

Variations: Mag Argatnél, Magh Meall ("plain of joy"), Magh Mhor, Tir na nÓg

A FAIRYLAND of Irish lore, Mag Mell ("Plain of Honey") is a FLOATING ISLAND far to the west and beneath the ocean. This OTHERWORLD PARADISE was accessible to only a select few, much the same way the ELYSIAN FIELDS and VALHALLA had a selection process.

Source: Arbois de Jubainville, *Irish Mythological Cycle and Celtic Mythology*, 15; Evan-Wentz, *Fairy Faith in Celtic Countries*, 335; Monaghan. *Encyclopedia of Celtic Mythology and Folklore*, 308

Mag Réin

The Irish OTHERWORLD, Mag Réin ("Palin of the Sea") is an island of order and organized thought and the beginning of wisdom. It is connected to to the OTHERWORLD island AIRCTHECH by a land bridge called CIUIN.

Source: Federation of European Sections, *Transactions of the Third Annual Congress*, 191; Nansen, *Northern Mists*, Volume 354

Mag Tuirid

Variations: Mag Tuirid, Magh Tuireadh, Moytirra, Moyturra

Mag Tuirid ("Plain of the Pillars") was the location of two mythological but significant battles in Irish lore; both battles favored the Tuatha de Danann.

Source: Monaghan. *Encyclopedia of Celtic Mythology and Folklore*, 309

Magnetic Mountain

Variations: Mountain of Loadstone (see LOADSTONE, MOUNTAIN OF)

Popular in medieval legends a magnetic mountain is a mountain upon an island which has the ability to draw the nails and other iron-works out of a ship if it came within its magnetic draw. Such a mountain is mentioned the German metrical romance "*Herzog Ernst von Schwaden*," the sixth voyage of *Sindbad the Sailor*, and in the third dervish of *The Porter and the Three Girls of Bagdad* in *One Thousand and One Arabian Nights* (see also MURUKEYYIN).

Source: Blamires, *Herzog Ernst and the Otherworld Voyage*, 41–46; Sprague de Camp, *Lands Beyond*, 143

Mahajwala

In Hindu mythology Mahajwala ("that of the great flame") is a partition in HELL (or NARAKA) ruled over by Yama; it is located beneath the earth and water where souls are punished for the sin of incest with either a daughter or daughter-in-law.

Source: Wilson, *Oriental Translation Fund*, Volume 52, 208; Wilson, *Vishńu Puráńa*, 215–16

Mahapadma

Variations: Mahāpadma

The eighth of the eight cold NARAKA (HELLS) named in Buddhism Mahapadma ("deep red lotus") as the souls here are described as looking like opened deep-red lotus flowers, as it is so cold their skin has split open leaving the body raw and bloody.

The length of time one stays in the COLD HELLS is very precise if not specific. For each person in the HELL there is a grain room filled with 80 bushels of sesame seeds. Once every 100 years, one seed is removed. The length of time for each descending HELL is 20 times the previous.

Source: Dowson, *Classical Dictionary of Hindu Mythology*, 394; Hastings, *Encyclopedia of Religion and Ethics Part*, Part 7, 133

Mahar-Loka

One of the eight regions of heavenly existence in Hindu mythology, Mahar-Loka, is the heavenly home of Bhrigu, the celestial spirits, and the other saints who co-exist with Brahma. Mahar-Loka is said to be located ten-million leagues above Dhruva; the inhabitants here are distinguished for the piety.

Source: Dowson, *Classical Dictionary of Hindu Mythology and Religion*, 179; Garrett, *Classical Dictionary of India*, 370

Mahararavam

According to Hindu and Vedic mythology Mahararavam is one of the NARAKAS (HELLS) located in a providence in the kingdom of Yama; it is filled with the instruments of torture and particularly vicious *ruru* serpents to punish those who deny legitimate heirs their rightful inheritance. Here sinners are bound securely to a floor of burning copper while animals tear their bodies apart.

Source: Parmeshwaranand, *Encyclopaedic Dictionary of Purāṇas*, 721–22

Maharaurava

Variations: Mahāraurava ("Piercing")

According to Hindu and Vedic mythology Maharaurava ("Great Howling") is the second of the twenty-eight NARAKAS (HELLS) located in a providence in the kingdom of Yama; it is filled with the instruments of torture Here sinners are bound securely to a floor of burning copper while animals the body apart.

In to Indian Buddhism, Maharaurava ("hot") is the fifth of the EIGHT HOT HELLS; it is known as the Great Screaming Hell. Here the souls who are punished are those who were liars in life.

Source: Becker, *Contribution to the Comparative Study of the Medieval Visions of Heaven and Hell*, 14; Prabhupāda, *Śrīmad Bhāgavatam*, 903; Par-

meshwaranand, *Encyclopaedic Dictionary of Purāṇas*, 721–22

Mahatala, Caverns of

Variations: Mahaatala

In Hindu lore the Caverns of Mahatala are believed to be the sixth of the seven underground levels in a vast cavernous system which stretches from Benares, India to Lake Manosarowar, Tibet. In all of the regions (ATALA, PATALA, RASATALA, SUTALA, TALATALA, and VITALA), there are beautiful cities built by the architect, Maya.

Source: Parmeshwaranand, *Encyclopaedic Dictionary of Purāṇas*, 1010–1012

Malebolge

In Dante Alighieri's *Inferno*, Malebolge is the eighth layer of HELL; it is described as an inverted hollow cone of concentric circles and having 10 *bolgia* ("divisions"). The eighth circle begins at the edge of a precipice that descends to the seventh circle and ends at the edge of the pit that descends to the ninth and lowest layer of HELL.

Although each of the 10 *bolgia* ("divisions") are not individually named, they are each assigned to punished a specific sinner of some sort of fraudulence. The first bolgia punishes pimps and seducers, the second, flatterers; the third simonists, those who sell church offices and profit by it; the fourth, classical diviners; the fifth is for those guilty of political grafting; the sixth, hypocrites; the seventh for thieves; the eighth, those who give fraudulent council; the ninth, creators of strife; and the tenth is for counterfeiters.

Among the damned of Malebolge are Aghinolfo da Romena, the wealthy counterfeiter of gold florins; Gianni Schicchi, a noted mimic; Jason the seducer of Hypsipyle; Manto, the false prophet; Mosca, a Florentine who brought bloodshed to the city; Pope Nicholas III; Puccio Sciancato, a Florentine who committed beautiful and graceful theft; Simon the Greek; Thais the flatterer with filthy disordered hair; the wife of the Egyptian official

Potiphar who tried to seduce Joseph, son of Jacob, and when rejected accused him of rape; and Tiresia the diviner.

Source: Kleiner, *Mismapping the Underworld*, 36–38; Lansing, *Dante Encyclopedia*, 585

Mam, Isle of

A FLOATING ISLAND similar to BRENDAN ISLE in the Atlantic Ocean, the Isle of Mam was located somewhere off the coast of Ireland; it was typically found on maps from the 15th to 17th century.

Source: Johnson, *Phantom Islands of the Atlantic*, 119

Manala (mä'-nä)

Variations: TUONELA

Manala is the OTHERWORLD where, according to Estonian mythology, common people go to after death; this land of eternal darkness is ruled by the god, Mana. The spirits who reside here are known as *manalanes*. Located beneath the sea, spirits will spend eternity in its lovely grottos sitting upon couches covered with sea-moss. The words TUONELA and Manala are used interchangeably even though they are different location in the afterlife.

Sins that qualify someone to send their afterlife in the gloomy prisons of Manala are disobedience to your parents, harming the innocent, speaking falsehoods, and wronging the weak. Here there are couches of fire covered with pillows of snakes and coverlets of vipers. Sinners here have no food to eat and the only thing to drink is the blood of adders.

Source: Eivind, xiv, 24, 91; Pentikäinen, *Kalevala Mythology*, 204, 262

Mandara, Forest of

In Hindu lore the Forest of Mandara is where the Tree of Desire grows.

Source: Rāya, *Mahabharata of Krishna-Dwaipayana Vyasa*, 48

Mandara, Mount *see* Mount Mandara

Manheim

Variations: Mannheimar

The realm of man, Manheim ("Home of Man") is the name of the earth in Norse mythology.

Source: Anderson, *Norse Mythology*, 452; Bennett, *Gods and Religions of Ancient and Modern Times*, Volume 1, 393

Mapcha Khabab

In Hindu mythology Mapcha Khabab ("River from the Peacock's Mouth") is one of the four rivers which runs out of MAPHAM YUMTSHO, the lake located at the bottom of Mount MERU; it flows to the south.

Source: McCue, *Trekking in Tibet*, 207

Mapham Yumtsho

In Hindu mythology Mapham Yumtsho is the lake located at the bottom of Mount MERU; from here flow four rivers towards the ocean, one to each of the four cardinal points, LANGCHEN KHABAB to the west, MAPCHA KHABAB to the south, SENGE KHABAB to the north, and TAMCHOK KHABAB to the east.

Source: McCue, *Trekking in Tibet*, 207

Marut-Loka

Variations: Diva-Loka

In Hindu mythology Marut-Loka is the heavenly home of the winds and Vaisyas. In the seven spheres of the earth, Marut-Loka is the third.

Source: Garrett, *Classical Dictionary of India*, 386; Wilson, *Vishńu Puráńa*, 48

Mauri-Gasima

Variations: MA-LI-GA-SI-MA

Once located near the island of Formosa, Mauri-Gasima sank into the sea as a consequence of the criminal and sinful acts of its inhabitants. According to Chinese lore, only the pious king Peiru-un and his family were able to escape the disaster; he and his family went on to become the progenitors of the Chinese people.

Source: Blavatsky, *Secret Doctrine*, Volume 1, 365; Brewer, *Dictionary of Phrase and Fable*, 562

Mbulu

The UNDERWORLD of Fijian mythology Mbulu is divided in regions; some sources say there are three, but are vague as to what differentness a soul going to one realm rather than another; both punishment and reward is dealt out, but neither has anything to do with morality. The road to reach Mbulu is long and difficult to travel; both the evil and the virtuous walk the same path.

In most regions of Mbulu the residents do everything they would have done in life, such as live in family units, quarrel among themselves, and plant crops.

Source: Frazer, *Belief in Immortality and the Worship of the Dead* 467; Williams, *Fiji and the Fijians*, 193–94

Mburotu

Variations: MBULU

In the Fijian UNDERWORLD, Mburotu is the equivalent of the Greeks ELYSIUM FIELDS; it is described as having an abundance of every desire, pleasant glades, scented groves, and an unclouded sky. Mburotu is filled with the truly good, those who have taken many lives and consumed the roasted flesh of their enemies.

Source: Frazer, *Belief in Immortality and the Worship of the Dead* 466–67; Williams, *Fiji and the Fijians*, 193–94

Meropis

A fictional island created by the fourth century BC Greek historian and writer Theopompus of Chios Meropis was intended to be a parody of Plato's ATLANTIS. A vast continent located beyond the stream of the Ocean, Meropis was populated with the idealized races of men, such as the Eusebians. Upon Meropis are two cities, Eusebes ("Pious Town") where the people live in opulence and never grow hungry and Machimos ("Fighting Town") where its population is born with weapons in hand and are constantly engaged in war. A third city is mentioned, ANOSTOS ("No Return"), located on the outermost border of Meropis; it is described as looking like a yawn-

ing abyss, is in a perpetual state of twilight, and is covered in red fumes and smoke.

Source: Hastings, *Encyclopædia of Religion and Ethics*, Volume 2, 697; Romm, *Edges of the Earth in Ancient Thought*, 67

Meru, Mount *see* Mount Meru

Mezzoramia

An earthly PARADISE said to be somewhere in the deserts of Africa, Mezzoramia is said to be accessible only be a narrow road. Gaudentio di Lucca, the hero of a romance of Simon Bering, found this legendary land of happiness and perfection and lived there, secluded from the rest of the world, for twenty-five years. The customs, government, and laws of Mezzoramia are idealized and civil.

Source: Brewer, *Reader's Handbook of Famous Names in Fiction*, 408, 702; Dunlop, *History of Fiction*, 420

Mictlan

In Aztec mythology Mictlan is the lowest layer of the UNDERWORLD, a dark region reserved for the souls of those who died of an accident, disease, natural causes, old age, or a circumstance not specifically covered by the other three underworlds. Mictlan is ruled by the god of the dead, Mictlantecutli, and his female companion Mictlanchuatl (Mictecacihuatl). To arrive in Mictlan the deceased must complete a long and arduous journey filled with obstacles to be overcome in nine separate stages.

First the dead needed to cross the river Apanohuaya and upon emerging must then, naked, pass between the mountains Tepetl Monamictia which are constantly crashing together and coming apart. Next, they must scale the mountain Iztepetl with its razor sharp obsidian surface. Following this ordeal the dead must then cross eight gorges (Cehuecayn) and eight valleys (Itzehecayan) where it is freezing cold, always snowing, and has a bitter wind constantly blowing. Next, the dead must walk down a path (Temiminaloyal) where a continuous rain of arrows falls; at completion, they will discover a jaguar has consumed their heart. The mysterious region called "where the flags wave" must be passed; here is a crocodile called Xochitonatl that signaled to the deceased they are nearly at the end of their journey. Finally, the dead need to cross the Chiconahuapan River ("Nine Rivers") to reach CHICONAMICTLAN ("Nine Hells") where they are received by Mictlantecutli. The lore tells us this journey takes about four years to complete but once it is over the deceased lose all attachment to the earth and disappear into darkness and nothingness. Immortality is only reserved for those who are destined to reside in the other realms.

Source: Leon-Portilla, *Aztec Thought and Culture*, 124; Moreno, *Handbook to Life in the Aztec World*, 165; Spence, *Introduction to Mythology*, 211

Mid-World

According to Manx lore Mid-World, where the fairies fly about in the air, is only 21 miles up from this world to the first HEAVEN.

Source: Evan-Wentz, *Fairy Faith in Celtic Countries*, 123

Midgard

Variations: Mana-Heim, Miðgarðr

In Norse mythology, Midgard ("mid-yard"), one of the NINE WORLDS, was the realm of mankind; it was located between GIMLE above and NIFLEHEIM below. Midgard is one of the three words that touch the roots of the tree YGGDRASIL. Situated in the middle of the universe, Midgard is bordered by mountains and the great sea, *úthaf*, so vast that to cross it is impossible. Jormungand, the Midgard serpent, lives in this sea. On the other side of this sea is the home of the giants, UTGARD ("Out-Yard"). North of Midgard is NIDAVELLIR ("Dark Home"), the home of the dwarfs; below is SVARTALFHEIM ("Land of the Dark Elves") home of the elves. The Rainbow Bridge, BIFROST, connects Midgard to ASGARD.

Source: Anderson, Norse Mythology, 453; Crossley-Holland, *Norse Myths*, xxi; Dunham, *History of Denmark, Sweden, and Norway*, Volume 52; Guerber, *Myths of the Norsemen*, 12

Mill of Frodi *see* Frodi, Mill of

Mimirsbrunnr Well

Variations: Mimir, Mimir's Well

In Norse mythology Mimirsbrunnr Well, the font of all wisdom and wit; it is located in MIDGARD at Mimir's Grove at the JOTUNHEIM root in the land of ODAINSAKER. One of the three wells which nourish the ash tree, YGGDRASIL, the water of this well was so clear that even the future could be seen it in (see HVERGELMIR WELL and URDARBRUNNR WELL). This spring was considered the headwater of memory, and desiring to have great wisdom god Odin exchanged one of his eyes for a drink from it. Mimirsbrunnr Well is guarded by the god Mimir himself.

Source: Anderson, *Norse Mythology*, 453; Crossley-Holland, *Norse Myths*, 247; Guerber, *Myths of the Norsemen*, 13, 30–31

The Mire of Clay

Variations: Tit Hayyaven

According to Jewish Cabalists, there are seven levels to HELL; ALADDON, the GATES OF DEATH, GEBEANOM, the Mire of Clay, the PIT OF CORRUPTION, the SHADOW OF DEATH, and SHEOL.

These realms are set one atop the other; ordinary fire is one-sixtieth the heat of the fire of GEBEANOM which is one-sixtieth the heat of the GATES OF DEATH, which is one-sixtieth the heat of the SHADOW OF DEATH, which is one-sixtieth the heat of the PIT OF CORRUPTION, which is one-sixtieth the heat of the Mire of Clay, which is one-sixtieth the heat of ALADDON, which is one-sixtieth the heat of SHEOL.

Source: Brewer, *Dictionary of Phrase and Fable*, 596; Mew, *Traditional Aspects of Hell*, 173

Misadventure, Forest of *see* Forest of Misadventure

Mitnal

Variations: Mitlan

Of the nine layers of the Mayan UNDER-

WORLD Mitnal is the darkest, deepest, and most dreadful section of XIBALBA ("HELL"); here souls are tormented by demons, hunger pains, and weariness. Mitnal is ruled over by Ah-Puch, the god of death; he is assisted by such entities as Blood Gatherer, Bone Scepter, Pus Master, Skull Scepter, and Stab Master.

Source: Crisafulli, *Go to Hell*, 78; de Landa, *Yucatan Before and After the Conquest*, 58

Mnemosyne

A river in the Greek UNDERWORLD, anyone who drank from Mnemosyne ("Memory") would attain omniscience and remember everything they encountered in life. Upon entering HADES, Mnemosyne is described as being off to the right, beneath a white cypress tree.

Source: Cahill, *Paradise Rediscovered*, 751; Hard, *Routledge Handbook of Greek Mythology*, 110–11

The Moon, Land of *see* Land of the Moon

Mount Mandara

This mythical mountain of Hindu lore was used by the god for the churning of the oceans in order to obtain *amrita*, the divine drink of immortality. Mount Mandara is the home of King Kubera; his bejeweled palace designed by the divine architect, Visrakarman lies in his capitol city of ALAKAPURI.

Source: Dalal, *Hinduism*, 240; Daniélou, *Myths and Gods of India*, 136

Mount Meru

Variations: Gang Rimpoche ("Precious Jewel of Snow"), Gang Ti-Se, Ti-Se

The spiritual center of the universe in Hindu mythology, Mount Meru is described as being 84,000 miles tall and having the entire universe revolving around it. Atop the mountain sits Lord Shiva and his consort, Parvati. It is also the home of Demchok, a multi-armed wrathful god worshiped in Tibetan Buddhism; with him lives his consort Dorje Phakmo.

The earthly manifestation of Mount Meru is Mount Kailash ("Silver Mountain").

Source: McCue, *Trekking in Tibet*, 207; Sprague de Camp, *Lands Beyond*, 282

Mount Olympus (oh-LIHM-puhs)

The mythological dwelling place of the Greek gods, the heavenly MOUNT OLYMPUS is shaped like an inverted mountain, its base is in the sky and its summit is pointed towards the earth. Full of breaks, forests, and glens, it never snows here nor are there any harsh elements to disturb the gods as they dine on ambrosia and enjoy sweet playing music.

Source: Anthon, *Classical Dictionary*, 923; Daly, *Greek and Roman Mythology, A to Z*, 106; Evans, *Dictionary of Mythology*, 193; Evslin, *Gods, Demigods, and Demons*, 159

Mount Ossa

According to Homer, the greatest of ancient Greek epic poets, MOUNT Ossa and MOUNT PELION were the two mountains the giants Ephialtes and Otus planed on piling on top of one another in order to then be able to climb up to MOUNT OLYMPUS. Before the plans of the brothers could be hatched the god, Apollo, shot them both dead with his bow and arrow (*Odyssey*, book xi 1).

Source: Baldwin, *Story of the Golden Age*, 80; Evans, *Dictionary of Mythology*, 198; Lee, *Ovid: Metamorphoses* I, 89–90

Mount Pelion

According to Homer, the greatest of ancient Greek epic poets, MOUNT Ossa and MOUNT PELION were the two mountains the giants Ephialtes and Otus planed on piling on top of one another in order to then be able to climb up to MOUNT OLYMPUS. Before the plans of the brothers could be hatched the god, Apollo, shot them both dead with his bow and arrow (*Odyssey*, book xi 1).

In Greek mythology the pelionides were the naiads of the springs of MOUNT PELION; they were the nurses to the infant centaurs (Kentauroi).

Source: Baldwin, *Story of the Golden Age*, 80;

Evans, *Dictionary of Mythology*, 198; Lee, *Ovid: Metamorphoses I*, 89–90

Mountain of Lodestone *see* Lodestone, Mountain of

Mountain of the Zughb

According to the ancient Persian fairytale, *Sindbad the Sailor* (750 CE), the Mountain of the Zughb was an island named in the third voyage of the fictional sailor's adventures; it was renowned for its population of people who were as hairy as apes.

Source: Burton, *Seven Voyages of Sinbad the Sailor,* 22; Sprague de Camp, *Lands Beyond*, 130

Moy Mell

Moy Mell ("Pleasant Plain") was a place from Irish folklore similar to HEAVEN, as it was a plain of never-ending pleasure, happiness, peace, and perpetual youth.

Sources: Jarvie, *Irish Folk and Fairy Tales*, 253; Wallace, *Folk-Lore of Ireland*, 90

Mu

Variations: Moo

A continent in the Pacific Ocean, Mu was said to have sunk beneath the waves 50,000 years ago taking its entire population of 64,000,000 people with it.

In 1864 French scholar Charles Étienne Brasseur de Bourbourg attempted to translate an ancient Mayan text called the *Troano Codex* (a treatise on Mayan astrology); largely he had little more than incoherent descriptions of a volcanic catastrophe however in there were two symbols he came across which he believed resembled the letters "M" and "U" of the alphabet created by Spanish Missionary Deigo de Landa who had once written a treatise on Mayan culture entitled *Relación de las Cosas de Yucatán* (*Account of the Affairs of Yucatan*). Brasseur assumed the letters were the name of the land destroyed by the volcanic eruption, and thus, the Island of Mu was created.

Since then, Brasseur's translation has been discredited; however it did dissuade Augustus Le Plongeon, a contemporary of Brasseur's and a great contributor to the ATLANTIS theory. By combining Brasseur's translation and inspired by some pictures he discovered on the walls of Chichen Itza he invented the romantic tale of two princes, Aac ("Turtle") and Coh ("Puma"), fighting for the hand of their sister Moo, the queen of ATLANTIS. According to Le Plongeon tale, Aac was murdered by Coh, a crime so heinous it cause the continent to sink; Moo fled to Egypt, changed her name to Isis and had the Sphinx built to commemorate her late brother and husband.

Source: Churchward, *Lost Continent of Mu*, 9, 337; Le Plongeon, *Queen Móo and the Egyptian Sphinx*, 227; Sprague de Camp, *Lands Beyond*, 15–17

Muirthemne

In Irish lore the great plain of Muirthemne was the location of the great defeat of Fir Bolg, one of the mythological races which was said to have once occupied Ireland; having lost this battle, the Great Route of Muirthemne ("Brislech mor Maige Muirthemne"), the Tuatha de Danann gain control of the land.

Source: Matthews, *Encyclopedia of Celtic Myth and Legend*, 468–69; Monaghan. *Encyclopedia of Celtic Mythology and Folklore*, 343

Murias

One of the four cities the legendary Tuatha de Danann of Celtic lore are said to originate, Murias was the place from where the Cauldron of Abundance (Dagda's Cauldron) came from (see FALIAS, FINDIAS, and GORIAS).

Source: Matthews, *Encyclopedia of Celtic Myth and Legend*, 45; Monaghan. *Encyclopedia of Celtic Mythology and Folklore*, 344

Murimuria

A part of the Fijian UNDERWORLD, Murimuria is where the soul of a man is judged by the god, Degei. The souls who do not go to BUROTU are thrown into a lake and eventually sink to the bottom, Murimuria, an inferior sort of HEAVEN. Here souls are punished for the sins they committed while alive; for instance those who have never taken a life are punished for their negligence by having to pound the mucky bottom of the lake with clubs and women who were not tattooed are chased by female ghosts who cut, scrape, and tear at them with sharp shells. Not having had one's ears pierced must carry for all time a log upon their shoulders on which laundry is beaten.

Source: Frazer, *Belief in Immortality and the Worship of the Dead*, 466; Williams, *Fiji and the Fijians*, 193

Murukeyyin

Variations: Mountain of Loadstone

A mountain of loadstone (see LOADSTONE, MOUNTAIN OF and MAGNETIC MOUNTAIN), Murukeyyin is located on a bleak island; its magnetic pull is so strong it will cause a ship to drift off course. As the ship near the island, its iron works will be pulled free and attached to the mountain. If the ship is so well built its ironworks do not detach the entire vessel will come crashing ashore. Any who survive being dashed upon the shore may well be eaten by the island's griffin population.

Source: Sprague de Camp, *Lands Beyond*, 139

Muspelheimr (mus'pels-him)

Variations: Abode of Muspel, Muspelheim ("Muspel land"), Muspell, Múspell, Muspells-Meim, Muspellsheimr

In Norse mythology Muspelheimr, one of the NINE WORLDS, was the abode of fire and the home of Surtur (Surtr) of the fiery sword Sviga Laevi, and his fiery djinn; this god had dominion over his demonic subjects, the Mighty Sons of Muspel (Muspel's Lytir). Five lesser roots of the tree Yggrdasyll grow in Muspelheimr.

Located far below LIOSALFAHEIM, directly opposite of NIFLHEIM, and due south of GINNUNGA-GAP, Muspelheim was possible uncreated (existing before time) and may not be destroyed; it was described as a land like a blazing hot inferno where firebrands made the wind and lava made the clouds. Muspelheimr is pop-

ulated by *muspells-lyoir* ("the people of Muspell") an array of fiends who will, during Ragnarok, destroy the world with fire.

Source: Bennett, *Gods and Religions of Ancient and Modern Times*, Volume 1, 394; Dunham, *History of Denmark, Sweden, and Norway*, Volume 52; Evans, *Dictionary of Mythology*, 178; Grimes, *Norse Myths*, 3; Guerber, *Myths of the Norsemen*, 2

Naastrand

Variations: Nastrand, Nastrond, Náströnd

A place of punishment in Norse mythology, Naastrand ("Shore of Corpses") is where the wicked will be sent after the battle of Ragnarok. Here there is a large and horrific looking structure built entirely of writing black snakes woven together; all of their heads are turned inward and each is continuously vomiting poison on the floor. The doors to this structure are facing north. Here those who committed adultery, murder, and perjury must wade through the halls. Dwarfs and giants, having no free will, will not be sent to Naastrand. Eventually, the wicked will be washed down into HVERGELMIR WELL, where the dragon of utter darkness, Nidhug, will consume them.

Source: Anderson, *Norse Mythology*, 430, 455; Bennett, *Gods and Religions of Ancient and Modern Times*, Volume 1, 394; Rydberg, *Teutonic Mythology: Gods and Goddesses of the Northland*, Volume 3, 1032

Nadi Vaitarani

One of the four kinds of sub-hells (*utsada*) to the EIGHT HOT HELLS in Indian Buddhism, Nadi Vaitarani ("Burning Hell") is described as a long, narrow river of boiling water where sinners are thrown into it and tossed about wildly by the currents. Should someone try to make their way to the bank and pull themselves out a guard will cut off their hands with a sword.

Source: Sadakata, *Buddhist Cosmology*, 51–52

Naga-Loka

Variations: Patala-loka

In Hindu mythology Naga-Loka ("World

of the Snakes") is located underground in a section of the CAVERNS OF PATALAS; its capitol city is called Bhogavati ("abode of snakes") and is ruled over by Vasuki. Naga-Loka has wide roads and is considered invincible, guarded on all sides by sharp-fanged and highly poisonous snakes. Here the nagas live in beautifully ornamented palaces. Typically Naga-Loka is said to be below ground but sometimes it is said to be located "to the south."

Source: Doniger, *Merriam-Webster's Encyclopedia of World Religions*, 776; Garrett, *Classical Dictionary of India*, 409; Vogel, *Indian Serpent-Lore*, 201

Nagrindr

Nagrindr ("Corpse Gate") is one of the named gates which lead into the realm of HEL, the land of the dead who died of disease or old age in Norse mythology. Nagrindr, like HEL-GRINDR, closes so fast it will catch the heel of anyone who passes through it.

Source: Daly, *Norse Mythology A to Z*, 111; Lindow, *Norse Mythology*, 172

Naherangi

Variations: Tuwarea

In Maori mythology, Naherangi is the tenth of the ten divisions of HEAVEN; in one version of the telling of the demigod Tawhaki there are twelve divisions but sometimes there are as many as fourteen and as few as two named. Naherangi is the highest of the HEAVENs and is inhabited by the greater god; it is presided over by the god Rehua.

Source: Craig, *Dictionary of Polynesian Mythology*, 56, 373; Grey, *Maori Lore*, 12; Mead, *Tāwhaki*, 58

Najrakantasali

According to Hindu and Vedic mythology Najrakantasali is one of the NARAKAS (HELLS) located in a providence in the kingdom of Yama; here those who had unnatural sexual intercourse with animals, particularly cows, are punished by being forced to embrace iron images filled with diamond needles.

Source: Parmeshwaranand, *Encyclopaedic Dictionary of Purāṇas*, 721

al Nār

The most common name for HELL in Islamic mythology, al Nār ("the fire") is divided into seven divisions; each section is reserved for a particular type of sin or sinner: HAWIAYA, for hypocrites; HUTAMA, for the Jewish people; JAHANNAM, for Muslims, JAHIM, for idolaters; LAGAM, Christians; SA'IR, worshippers of fire, the *sabaens*; and SAQAU, for the Magi.

Source: Esposito, *Oxford Dictionary of Islam*, 11; Knowles, *Nineteenth Century*, Volume 31, 438

Naraka

Variations: Niraya

The naraka of Buddhism, typically translated as HELL in English, differs from the hells of other religions as a person's soul is not sent to one of the naraka as a result of divine determination but rather it is based on the amount of karma one accumulated during life. Additionally, the length of time one remains in a naraka is not eternal but it can be for a very long time.

The narakas are a series of cavern-like layers below the mortal world; there are Eight Cold Narakas (see EIGHT COLD HELLS; ARBUDA, ATATA, HAHAVA, HUHUVA, MAHAPADMA, NIRARBUDA, PADMA, and UTPALA) and Eight Hot Narakas (see EIGHT HOT HELLS; AVICHI, KALASUTRAM, MAHARAURAVA, PRATAPANA, RAURAVA, SAMGHATA, SAMJIVA, and TAPANA). Each lifetime in a Narakas is twenty times the length of the one before it.

Source: Blo-gros-mtha'-yas, *Treasury of Knowledge*, 114; Hastings, *Encyclopedia of Religion and Ethics Part*, Part 7, 133; Mew, *Traditional Aspects of Hell*, 38–41, 98

Narekah

The HELL of serpents in Hindu mythology Narekah is a plain of black fire filled with the evil souls the djinn take there; it is the dominion of the god Eemen one of the eight Austatikcopauligaur who rules over one of the eight sides of the world.

Source: *Encyclopædia Metropolitana* 51, 135; Kindersley, *Specimens of Hindoo Literature*, 32; Spence, *Encyclopedia of Occultism and Parapsychology*, Volume 1, 253

Naut

Naut was one of the nine rivers from Norse mythology which flow from MIDGARD to NI-FLHEIM.

Source: Grimes, *Norse Myths*, 13; Guerber, *Myths of the Norsemen*, 13

Ne-no-Kuni

Variations: Ne-no-Katasukuni ("Firm or Hard-Packed Shoal Land of Origin"), Neno-kuni, Soko no Kuni

In ancient Shinto beliefs Ne-no-Kuni ("Land of Origin" or "Root Land") was a PARADISE believed to be located beneath the water or far off in the ocean. Although a shelter for snakes and wasps, Ne-no-Kuni also contains many items that assure sovereignty. The dwelling place of the daughter of the god Susano-O, Ne-no-Kuni is the land of the ancestors who will bring back prosperity and cleanse death of its natural pollution.

Source: Bonnefoy, *Asian Mythologies*, 270–71; Roberts, *Japanese Mythology A to Z*, 127

Neflhel

Variations: Nifl, Nifl-Hel ("Mist Hell")

The worst section of NEFLHEIM and the place where the goddess Hela has her home, ELIDNER, Nefhel ("to which men die from Hel") is a gloomy place of punishment, although was not originally so in the oldest poetry. One of the roots of the tree YGGDRASIL is here.

Source: Keary, *Outlines of Primitive Belief Among the Indo-European Races*, 57; Mortensen, *Handbook of Norse Mythology*, 144–45

Nemi, the Grove of *see* The Grove of Nemi

Neorxnawang

Variations: Neorxenawang, Neorxnawong

The Old English word neorxnawang ("Field of Contentment") translates as a Christian concept of PARADISE in Anglo-Saxon literature; it is something like a heavenly meadow where there is no work or worry.

Source: McKinnell, *Meeting the Other in Norse Myth and Legend*, 51; Simek, *Dictionary of Northern Mythology*, 229

Neritos

In Homer's *Iliad*, book II, Neritos, an obscure and unidentifiable island believed to have located in the Ionian Sea, was a part of the kingdom of Ithaca under the rulership of Odysseus (see AEGILIPS and CROCYLEIA).

Source: Earl of De Edward, *The Iliad*, 50; Page, *History and the Homeric Land*, 163

Neritum

In book II of Homer's *Iliad*, Neritum is a wooded mountain on the island of Ithaca in Odysseus's kingdom.

Source: Anthon, *Classical Dictionary*, 882; Smith, *New Classical Dictionary of Greek and Roman Biography*, 545

Neter-khertet

Variations: Khert Neter, TUAT

Neter-khertet ("Divine Place Underground") is the common name for the UNDERWORLD of Egyptian mythology.

Source: Budge, *Book of the Dead*, 205; Littleton, *Gods, Goddesses, and Mythology*, Volume 11, 1206

Ngā Atua

In some versions of the Maori legend of Tawhaki, Ngā Atua is the sixth of the twelve layers of HEAVEN; typically there are only ten named divisions but sometimes there are as many as fourteen and as few as two named. Ngā Atua is ruled over by Tawhaki himself.

Source: Craig, *Dictionary of Polynesian Mythology*, 56, 347; Mead, *Tāwhaki*, 58

Ngā-Roto

Variations: Ngāroto

In Maori mythology, Ngā-Roto is the third of the ten divisions of HEAVEN; in one version of the telling of the demigod Tawhaki there are twelve divisions but sometimes there are as many as fourteen and as few as two named. Ngā-Roto is the HEAVEN of lakes and is presided over by the god Maru.

Source: Craig, *Dictionary of Polynesian Mythology*, 56; Mead, *Tāwhaki*, 58

Ngā Tauira

In some versions of the Maori legend of Tawhaki, Ngā Tauira is the fifth of the twelve layers of HEAVEN; typically there are only ten named divisions but sometimes there are as many as fourteen and as few as two. Ngā Tauira is the HEAVEN where the inferior gods reside.

Source: Craig, *Dictionary of Polynesian Mythology*, 56, 347; Mead, *Tāwhaki*, 58

Nida Mountain (ne'da)

Variations: Nidafell

Nida Mountain will be the heavenly home to the dwarfs of Norse mythology after the battle of Ragnarok; there, ruled by Sindri, the dwarfs will have their own hall where they will drink their sparkling mead.

Source: Anderson, *Norse Mythology*, 455; Guerber, *Myths of the Norsemen*, 340

Nidafell

Variations: Niðafjöll ("Dark Mountains"), Nidafjöll, Nidavellir

Nidafell, a golden hall built by the Sindre (dwarfs) for the survivors of their race to live in after the battle of Ragnarok, will be built in the Nida Mountains, according to Norse mythology.

Source: Anderson, *Norse Mythology*, 455; Bennett, *Gods and Religions of Ancient and Modern Times*, Volume 1, 394

Nide's Plain

In Norse mythology the Nide's Plain was a hall of gleaming gold located at the base of the NIDA MOUNTAINS; those who lived in NIFLE-HEIM could see it.

Source: Grimes, *Norse Myths*, 291; Guerber, *Myths of the Norsemen*, 291

Nifleheim (nee-vel-haym or nifi-him)

Variations: Nifhel, Niflheim ("Cloud Home"), Niflheim, Nifl-heim, Niflheimr, Niflhel ("Cloud Death")

In Norse mythology, Nifleheim ("land of mist"), one of the NINE WORLDS, was the world of mist; it was the lowest of all the worlds and contained many poisonous fountains and rivers in which the evil are punished. Located directly opposite MUSPELHEIM and due north of GINNUNGA-GAP, Nifleheim was where HVERGELMIR WELL, the seething cauldron, bubbles out the twelve streams which are collectively known as the ELIVAGER. One of the roots of YGGDRASIL is here and the dragon Nidhug gnaws upon it.

Source: Anderson, *Norse Mythology*, 455; Bennett, *Gods and Religions of Ancient and Modern Times*, Volume 1, 395; Dunham, *History of Denmark, Sweden, and Norway*, Volume 52; Evans, *Dictionary of Mythology*, 185; Guerber, *Myths of the Norsemen*, 2

Niflhel

Variations: Nifelhel

In Norse mythology Niflhel ("misty Hel") was a region of HEL opposite Lake NIDAHELL where the goddess of death, Hel, sent the truly wicked. Damp fog rises up and constantly engulfs the area. Here the bed was named Care, the palace, Anguish; the table Famine; the threshold, Precipice, and the waiters, Delay and Slowness.

Source: Anderson, *Norse Mythology*, 387; Grimes, *Norse Myths*, 74, 291

Nikrintana

In Hindu mythology, Nikrintana ("cutting to pieces") is the fourth of the twenty-eight NARAKAS (HELLS) located in a providence in the kingdom of Yama; it is filled with the instruments of torture. Here, sinners are tied to a constantly spinning disk where they are sawed with black thread from head to foot by demons.

Source: Becker, *Contribution to the Comparative Study of the Medieval Visions of Heaven and Hell*, 14; Wilson, *Vishńu Puráńa*, 215–16

Nimindhara

Variations: Nemindhara

The Nimindhara Mountains are the seventh mountain chain surrounding SUMERU, the central would mountain in in Hindu cosmology; it is both 625 *yojanas* tall and wide. The measure of a single *yojanas* has never been clear, some scholars say it is approximately four and a half miles while other say it ranges between seven and nine miles.

Source: Howard, *Imagery of the Cosmological Buddha*, 66–68; Nagao, *Wisdom, Compassion, and the Search for Understanding*, 192

Nine Worlds

There are nine worlds in Norse mythology and all of them are connected by the great ash tree, YGGDRASIL, its branches creating a protective roof both sheltering and holding the worlds together. YGGDRASIL has nine roots, each one going to each one of the worlds; the three main roots go to JOTUNHEIM, MIDGARD, and NIFLHEIM while the lesser roots go to the other worlds.

The great god, Odin, from his throne, Hlidskialf, can see everything that is happening in all of the nine worlds with the assistance of his two ravens, Hugin and Munin.

The nine worlds are: ALFHEIM, ASGARD, HEL, JOTUNHEIM, MIDGARD, MUSPELHEIM, NIFLHEIM, SVARTALFHEIM, and VANAHEIM.

The nine worlds are broken into three groups of three. The first group contained, ALFHEIM, ASGARD, and VANAHEIM. The middle grouping of three contains JOTUNHEIM, MIDGARD, and SVARTALFHEIM. The final grouping was the Underworlds, HEL, MUSPELHEIM, and NIFLHEIM.

Source: Anderson, *Norse Myths*, 187; Daly, *Norse Mythology A to Z*, 73; Grimes, *Norse Myths*, 13

Nirarbuda

The second of the eight cold NARAKA (HELLS) named in Buddhism, nirarbuda ("Broken Blisters" or "Deeply Chapped"). Occupants of this NARAKA are described as looking like *arbudas* ("first month fetus" or "round mass").

The length of time one stays in the cold HELLS are very precise if not specific. For each person in the HELL there is a grain room filled with 80 bushels of sesame seeds. Once every 100 years one seed is removed. The length of time for each descending HELL is 20 times the previous.

Source: Faustino, *Heaven and Hell*, 30; Hastings, *Encyclopedia of Religion and Ethics Part*, Part 7, 133

No Return, Valley of *see* Valley of No Return

Noatun (no'a-toon)

Variations: Nôatûn

In Norse mythology Noatun ("Enclosure of Ships") located in ASGARD, was the home of the god of the winds and the sea near the shoreline, Niörd. Noatun was built near the seashore where the gulls and seals frequented. The monotonous cries of the seals, the roar of the ocean, and the shrieking of the gulls are persistent.

Source: Bennett, *Gods and Religions of Ancient and Modern Times*, Volume 1, 395; Dunham, *History of Denmark, Sweden, and Norway*, Volume 2, 55; Guerber, *Myths of the Norsemen*, 111–12, 114

Nonn

Variations: Nón, Nönn

Nonn ("strong"), one of the nine rivers from Norse mythology which flow from MIDGARD to NIFLHEIM.

Source: Grimes, *Norse Myths*, 291; Guerber, *Myths of the Norsemen*, 13

Noticia Rica

After the legendary tales of SIERRA DE LA PLATA began to spread, another lost city located deep in the jungles came into existence in eastern Peru, Noticia Rica ("Rich News"); rumors of lost Incan gold drove many expeditions to find it until the stories of PAITITI outgrew it in popularity amongst the treasure seekers.

Source: Magasich-airola, *America Magica*, 74, 89

Nuku-tere

In the mythology of the Pacific Islands, the swift moving Nuku-tere ("Floating Island") was a FLOATING ISLAND who was made stable when the god, Tane, stomped in into place.

Source: Craig, *Dictionary of Polynesian Mythology*, 114; Nunn, *Vanished Islands and Hidden Continents of the Pacific*, 92

Nysa

A beautiful mountain and valley, Nysa, of Greek lore, is where the five nymphs Bacche, Bromie, Erato, Macris, and Nysa (collectively known as the Nysiades) nursed and raised the god Dionysus, eventually becoming his followers.

Source: Hard, *Routledge Handbook of Greek Mythology*, 172; Lemprière, *Classical Dictionary*, 404; Rose, *Handbook of Greek Mythology*, 152

Nyt (nyt)

According to Norse mythology Nyt was one of the nine rivers which ran from ASGARD to MIDGARD; tt is also listed as one of the nine rivers which from MIDGARD to NIFLHEIM.

Source: Grimes, *Norse Myths* 13, Guerber, *Myths of the Norsemen*, 13; Sturlusonar, *Prose Edda of Snorri Sturluson*, 65

Oceanus

Variations: Ogen, Ogên, Ogênos, Ogenus, Okeanos, Ôkeanos ("River Ocean")

According to ancient Greek mythology Oceanus was one of the four rivers of the UNDERWORLD (see ACHERUSIAN STREAM, COCYTUS, and PYRIPHLEGETHON); it is the largest and outermost of the UNDERWORLD Rivers believed to encircle the earth, to be the fountain of all rivers, and the place where the moon and sun rose from and returned daily to rest in.

After crossing the river Oceanus the soul would find itself on the fertile shores of HADES, replete with popular and willow trees. The rivers PYRIPHLEGETHON and COCYTUS flow into the ACHERUSIAN near the site of a large unnamed boulder.

Source: Guthrie, *History of Greek Philosophy:* Volume 4, 361, 377; Westmorelands, *Ancient Greek Beliefs*, 705

Ochren

Variations: Coinchenn, Corrgend

A FAIRYLAND of Irish lore, Ochren ("Spoils") is also occasionally described as an OTHERWORLD located beneath the ocean where the fay entertain themselves by dancing in labyrinthine patterns.

Source: Bruce, *Arthurian Name Dictionary*, 94; Monaghan. *Encyclopedia of Celtic Mythology and Folklore*, 365

Odainsaker

In Norse mythology Odainsaker was the land of the god, Mimir; it was where MIMIRSBRUNNR WELL, the font of all knowledge, memory, wisdom, and wit was located. After Ragnarok the humans Lif and Lifthraser will settl e here.

Source: Grimes, *Norse Myths*, 14, 292; Guerber, *Myths of the Norsemen*, 14

Ogygia

Variations: Nympher, Ortygia

Named in Homer's *Odyssey*, (V, 99–101 and I, 50, 54) as well as in Plutarch's book "*De facie in orbe Lunae*," the island of Ogygia ("boss" or "navel") is located five days journey to the west of Britannia far out in the open sea. The home of the lovely-haired nymph Calypso, daughter of the titian Atlas, this island, described as being a well-wooded subtropical isle, was where Odysseus was detained for seven years, as the nymph wanted to marry him. Odysseus washed ashore upon Ogygia in Okuklja Bay and lived in a cave called Galicnjak.

Equidistant to Ogygia in the direction of the summer sunset are three additional unnamed islands; one of these islands is alleged to be the place where Kronos was kept prisoner by the god, Zeus.

Source: Mandzuka, *Demystifying the Odyssey*, 211, 209, 411; Sprague de Camp, *Lands Beyond*, 71, 218

Okolner (oo-kol-ner)

Variations: Ókólnir, Okolnir

After the battle of Ragnarok, the giants will have an ale hall called BRIMER located in Okolner ("Not Cool" or "Unfreezing") according to Norse mythology; until then good and virtuous being enjoy the hall as it known for its good drinks.

Source: Anderson, *Norse Mythology*, 430, 434; Bennett, *Gods and Religions of Ancient and Modern Times*, Volume 1, 395; Daly, *Norse Mythology A to Z*, 39

Olympus, Mount *see* Mount Olympus

Ophir

The location of the legendary mines of King Solomon, Ophir, was an ancient biblical country; the mines were a gift to the king from the Queen of Sheba. The mines of Ophir were known for its production of excellent quality gold. Apart from gold, it's most well-known export, Ophir also traded in apes, frankincense, ivory, myrrh, precious stones, sandalwood, and silver. The gold of Ophir is also spoken of in the Book of Job. The actual location of Ophir, if it ever existed, has been a matter of great debate; sites all over Africa, Arabia, and India have been suggested.

Source: Anthon, *Classical Dictionary*, 927; Ring, *International Dictionary of Historic Places*, 311

Ormet

Variations: Ormt

Ormet was one of the two rivers which ran beneath the BIFROST BRIDGE, the god Thor would wade across it, the river KORMT, and the stream KERLAUG each day to attend the daily meeting the gods held at the URARD FOUNTAIN.

Source: Grimes, *Norse Myths*, 16; Guerber, *Myths of the Norsemen*, 60

Ossa, Mount *see* Mount Ossa

Otherworld

Variations: ANNWFN ("Non-World"), Annwn, AVALON, ILDATHACH, MAG MELL, Mag Mon ("Plain of Sports"), MAG MOR, Mag Rein ("Plain of Sea"), PARADISE, Tech Duinn, Tir Na Mnan, Tir Tairngiri, Uffern

A place deep within the earth, a realm of the dead in Celtic traditions, the Otherworld is used almost interchangeably in the fairy tradition as a land where the fay dwell; there were oftentimes passageways in hills or mounds which connected our world to theirs. There were a number of Otherworld kingdoms as well, such as the LAND OF YOUTH and the PLAIN OF SILVER CLOUDS; in such places wells of knowledge and wisdom were found. It is a place separate and apart from our own reality in both time and space; the inside of a mound could be vastly larger than it would appear from the outside and the passage of time could mover either very quickly or very slowly. There was no illness or bad weather only beautiful days passed in joyful dance and song.

In the Irish tradition the Otherworld is described as a series of islands or land regions with different characteristics and inhabitants. The word *sid* was used to describe the beings who lived in the Otherworld; this included fairies as well as the old gods and goddesses of Ireland and the Tuatha de Danann. The *sid* were said to be human sized, very beautiful and exquisitely dressed in fine clothes and jewels.

Source: MacLeod, *Celtic Myth and Religion*, 34–39; Monaghan, *Encyclopedia of Celtic Mythology and Folklore*, 348, 371

Pactolus (PAK-toh-lus)

In the story of King Midas, ruler of Phrygia, the man who was given a boon by the god Dionysus so whatever he touched would be turned to gold, was eventually released of his curse when he accidently transformed his daughter, Marigold, into a golden statue. His cries of anguish were enough to convince the god to release him of the blessing; he told him to wash himself and his daughter in the river Pactoluse. Since that time, flecks of gold have been found in the sandy backs of the river.

Source: Evans, *Dictionary of Mythology*, 200; Fulgentius, *Fulgentius the Mythographer*, 75

Padma

The seventh of the eight cold NARAKA (HELLS) named in Buddhism, in Padma ("Lotus"), the souls are described as looking like opened red lotus flowers, as it is so cold their skin has split open leaving the body raw and bloody.

The length of time one stays in the EIGHT COLD HELLS is very precise if not specific. For each person in the HELL there is a grain room filled with 80 bushels of sesame seeds; once every 100 years one seed is removed. The length of time for each descending HELL is 20 times the previous.

Source: Faustino, *Heaven and Hell*, 30; Hastings, *Encyclopedia of Religion and Ethics Part*, Part 7, 133; Mew, *Traditional Aspects of Hell*, 98

Paititi

Variations: El Gran Paititi, Paipite, Paytiti

A legendary lost city or UTOPIAN society of Incain lore, Paititi ("Jaguar"), the Peruvian El Dorado (see EL DORADO), was said to be located on Apucatinti ("Lord of the Sun") Mountain although in the older legends, Paititi was said to be located by a lake. A shimmering city of golden temples Paititi was entered through via a huge golden gate adorned with solid gold crouching pumas; their eyes set with bright emeralds. The inhabitants were said to have achieved a level of spiritual enlightenment, some of which who were able to resist ageing and live hundreds if not thousands of years. The kingdom of Paititi was ruled over by a collection of mysterious white men whose king was known as the Tiger King; they lived in a white house by a lake.

Source: Childress, *Lost Cities and Ancient Mysteries of South America*, 115–16; Pinkham, *Return of the Serpents of Wisdom*, 58

Pandemonium

Variations: Pandæmonium

A city in HELL populated entirely by demons Pandemonium ("All Demons") was described in the epic poem *Paradise Lost* by the 17th century English poet John Milton; it was founded by Mammon, the fallen angel who found the necessary precious metals needed to build their demonic baroque palace and capitol city. The palace has a roof of fretted gold, golden pillars, and friezes with projecting sculptures. Milton describes Pandemonium as a place of worldly activities, demagoguery, and politics whose devils appear in the Infernal Court flaunting their self-important titles.

Source: Lewis, *Angels A to Z*, 233; Loewenstein, *Milton: Paradise Lost*, 69–70

Pankhaia, Island of

Variations: Panchaea

A mythical island located somewhere in the ocean beyond Arabia the island of Pankhaia was said to be inhabited by a lost Greek tribe led there by the god Zeus in the early days of his rule. A myrrh producing island this Utopian society has many temples and magnificent stone quarries. Its main waterway is called Water of the Sun. Three social classes exist, farmers (herdsmen), military, and priests.

In the Greek mythographer Euhemerus' fictionalized travel log, he explains the pious people of Pankhaia worship the god Zeus and relates the "true story" of how when Zeus was a mortal king, as was Cronus and Uranus, they were deified after their death. Panara, a notable city upon the island, enjoys unusual felicity; its only inhabitants are citizens of Pankhaia who live under laws of their own making; rather than having a king they elect three magistrates who have not authority over capital offence but render judgment on all other matters.

Source: Gagarin *Oxford Encyclopedia of Ancient Greece and Rome*, Volume 1, 109; Stephens, *Seeing Double*, 37

Panotti

Variations: Panotii, Panotioi

Said by Pliny the Elder, a Roman author, naturalist, natural philosopher, and army and naval commander, to be located off of Scythia, Panotti ("All Ears") is so named as its inhabitants had fan-shaped ears so large as to cover their whole body; at night they used one ear as a pillow and the other as a blanket. When freighted the people of Panotti would take an ear in each hand and flapping like like a bird, take flight into the air.

Source: Bovey, *Monsters and Grotesques in Medieval Manuscripts*, 10; Pliny the Elder, *Natural History of Pliny*, Volume 1, 343

Pantoroze, Land of

Variations: Pentexoire

A location in the kingdom of Prester John, the land of Pantoroze, as described by Sir John Mandeville, a doctor who claimed to have been there, as it being near a sea of gravel that ebbed and flowed as would the waves of the ocean.

Source: Mandeville, *Voiage and Travayle of Sir John Maundeville Knight*, 187–88; Sprague de Camp, *Lands Beyond*, 153

Papa

In Hindu mythology, Papa is one of the twenty-eight NARAKAS (HELLS) located in a providence in the kingdom of Yama; it is filled with the instruments of torture.

Source: Wilson, *Vishńu Puráńa*, 215–16

Paradise

Variations: Firdaws ("Paradise"), GARDEN OF EDEN, HEAVEN, al Jannah ("garden")

A realm of exceptional delight and happiness many religions include the notion of a full life beyond the grave where there is no suffering and all bodily delights are fulfilled. Buddhism, Christianity, and Islam have a primordially earthly paradise, such as the GARDEN OF EDEN, whereas in Hinduism paradise is a golden age of society at the beginning of each new cycle of human existence. In both Christianity and Islam paradise is a heavenly state of bliss with the divine; in Buddhism it is an eternal state of changelessness and peace.

Source: Doninger, *Merriam-Webster's Encyclopedia of World Religions*, 841; Gibb, *Concise Encyclopedia of Islam*, 268

Paradise of Fools

Variations: AL A'RAF, LIMBO, Paradise of Fools, Paradise of Infants

In the religious beliefs of the Hindus, Islamic, Roman Catholics, and Scandinavians the Paradise of Fools is a place located near PARADISE and PURGATORY; it is the realm where infants, the mentally disabled, and other such individuals who are incapable of committing sin are consigned to after death.

Source: Brewer, *Dictionary of Phrase and Fable*, 655; Demy, *Answers to Common Questions About Heaven and Eternity*, 58–59; Hughes, *Dictionary of Islam*, 20–21

Parmenie

Variations: Armenie, Armorica, Emenia, Ermonie, Hermonie, LYONESSE

In the medieval epic *Tristan and Iseult*, Parmenie was the homeland of Tristan; its capital city was CANOEL. Although the kingdom was left to Tristan by his father, King Rivalin, he never assumed power; rather he left his country in the stewardship of his foster-father Rual who in turn then left it to his sons.

Source: Bruce, *Arthurian Name Dictionary*, 101; Wagner, *Tristan and Isolde*, 207, 210

Parnassus (pahr-NASS-uhs)

One of the two sacred mountains of the Greek god Apollo, the caves of Parnassus is where the god's oracles resided. It was here the muses danced when not on the other sacred mountain, Helicon. Parnassus was a favorite location of the god Dionysus who would let his followers revel there when Apollo was not present.

Source: Evslin, *Gods, Demigods, and Demons*, 170; Mikalson, *Ancient Greek Religion*, 92

Paryavartanakam

Variations: Paryavartana

According to Hindu and Vedic mythology Paryavartanakam is the twenty-seventh of the twenty-eight NARAKAS (HELLS) located in a providence in the kingdom of Yama. Here, those who denied food to someone who came during mealtime. As soon as one arrives in this NARAKAS, their eyes are pulled out by crows.

Source: Parmeshwaranand, *Encyclopaedic Dictionary of Purāṇas*, 723

Patala, Caverns of

In Hindu lore the Caverns of Patalas are believed to be the seventh of the seven underground levels in a vast cavernous system which stretches from Benares, India to Lake Manosarowar, Tibet; it is populated by a race known as the Naga. In all of the regions (ATALA, MAHATALA, RASATALA, SUTALA, TALATALA, and VITALA), there are beautiful cities built by the architect, Maya.

The region of Patala is described as being 70,000 *yojans* high; it is unsure how long a single *yojans* is, sources vary between four and half miles to nine miles). This region remains at a constant and comfortable temperature, neither too cold nor too hot; the nagas to not feel the effects of the passage of time here. Living in Patala are the *nagalokadhipatis* ("chiefs of the serpent world"), as Asvadhara, Deveadatta, Dhanajaya Mahasikha, Dhrtarastra, Gulika, Kambala, Sankha, Sankhacuda, and Vasuki to name a few. Each of these great nagas have between five and 100 hoods; the luster of the diamonds on their hoods keep the region constantly illuminated.

Source: Dowson, *Classical Dictionary of Hindu Mythology, and Religion*, 233; Parmeshwaranand, *Encyclopaedic Dictionary of Purāṇas*, 1010–1012

Pathon, Isle of

A location in the kingdom of Prester John, the island of Pathon had snails on it so large their shells were used as houses according to as described by Sir John Mandeville, a doctor who claimed to have been there.

Source: Sprague de Camp, *Lands Beyond*, 153

Peirene (pye-REE-nee)

Variations: Hippoerene

A spring sacred to the muses Peirene was created when the winged horse, Pegasus struck the ground with his hoof; crystal clear water came forth. It was said anyone who drank from this spring became artistically inspired.

Source: Daly, *Greek and Roman Mythology, A to Z*, 112; Evslin, *Gods, Demigods, and Demons*, 171–72

Pelion, Mount *see* Mount Pelion

Pen Llwyn Diarwya

Mentioned in *The Mabinogi*, Pen Llwyn Diarwya was in the kingdom of Pwyll, Prince of Dyfed, lord of seven regions. According to the story he spent the night here while traveling to Glyn Cuch.

Source: Ford, *Mabinogi and Other Medieval Welsh Tales*, 37

Peng Lai

Variations: P'eng Lai, P'eng-Lai Shan, Penglai

A mythological island PARADISE in the East China Sea, Peng Lai was said to be the home to the Eight Immortals, as well as many other immortal individuals. Peng Lai was said to be made of jewels and gold, its trees were made of coral and pearls, its animals and birds were all glittering white. The epitomy of bliss, Peng Lai is where the mushroom of immortality grows.

There are four additional islands which the Immortals live on: DÀIYÚ, FĀNGZHÀNG, Yíngzhōu, and Yuánjiāo.

Source: Avant, *Mythological Reference*, 123; Roberts, *Chinese Mythology: A to Z*, 98

Perilous Bed

Variations: Adventurous Bed

In Arthurian legends the Perilous Bed, like a FLOATING ISLAND, did not have a fixed location but rather magically appeared to a knight during his quest for the Grail. The bed was described as looking inviting and overly soft but upon laying down upon it the knight would be punctured by scores of invisible knives. Eventually, Sir Gawain destroyed the Perilous Bed.

Source: Bruce, *Arthurian Name Dictionary*, 4;

Monaghan. *Encyclopedia of Celtic Mythology and Folklore*, 378

Perilous Ford

Located between the land of Queen Igraine's Canguin and Guiromelant's Orqueneseles in Arthurian lore, the Perilous Ford was so treacherous a locale that no knight had ever been able to cross it without losing their life. One day the Haughty Maid of Logres dared Sir Gawaine to jump his horse, Gringolet, across the Perilous Ford by claiming the Haughty Knight of the Rock did so daily for her amusement and pleasure. After When Gawain and Gringolet succeeded, Guiromelant confessed this was the first time anyone had ever attempted the feat and survived.

Source: Karr, *Arthurian Companion,* 394–95; Newell, *King Arthur and the Table Round,* 256

Perilous Seat

Variations: Adventurous Seat, Siege Perilous, Seige Perilleux

In Arthurian lore the Perilous Seat, much like the Celtic inauguration stone, recognizes true heroism; only the one who finds the Grail was able to sit upon it without disappearing. In some texts, Sir Percival sat upon the Perilous Seat after his first and fail encounter with the Fisher King causing the stone to crack under the weight of his unworthiness. Later the knight was able to restore the stone after he found the Grail.

Source: Bruce, *Arthurian Name Dictionary,* 4; Lacy, *Arthurian Encyclopedia,* 424; Monaghan. *Encyclopedia of Celtic Mythology and Folklore,* 379

Perilous Valley

Variations: Vale of False Lovers, Vale of No Return

Within the forest of Brocéliande, there was, according to Arthurian lore, a haunted vale that had been cursed by Morgan, the half-sister of King Arthur; this place was known as Perilous Valley. The spell was such that any man who had ever betrayed a woman would be unable to navigate his way through the area and remain hopelessly lost; to a faithless knight the region seemed to be filled with monsters but it was only a trick of their imagination. No matter how many knights entered into the forest as a group they would all soon be separated and lost. In the heart of Perilous Valley was a lake called the Fairy's Mirror from which nightmares rose up like mist.

Source: Markale, *Courtly Love,* 69; Monaghan. *Encyclopedia of Celtic Mythology and Folklore,* 379

Phaiakes

Variations: Phaeacians

Mentioned in Homer's *Odyssey,* the land of Phaiakes is under the rulership of King Alkinoos (Alcinous) and was located at the edge of the world where civilized lands meet uncivilized regions. It was here Odysseus arrived ten years after the fall of Troy, alone and completely destitute. After entertaining the king for three days straight with the tales of his adventure, Alkinoos gives Odysseus a ship so he may be able to go home.

Source: Mandzuka, *Demystifying the Odyssey,* 442, 461; Sprague de Camp, *Lands Beyond,* 49

Phantom Islands

Typically a phantom island is a land mass that once appeared on maps but was later removed once it was proven they did not exist. Sometimes a phantom island's disappearance is explained away by means of a natural catastrophe, such as with the volcanic eruption that was blamed for the destruction of Atlantis.

Legendary islands of Celtic lore which are said to appear and disappear in clouds of mist and are believed to be entrances to the Otherworld. Appearing on both lakes and oceans, typically on a seven year cycle, phantom islands could also appear once and never again.

Source: Babcock, *Legendary Islands of the Atlantic,* 174; Monaghan, *Encyclopedia of Celtic Mythology and Folklore,* 379

Phlegra

A narrow isthmus to the peninsula of Pallene was a country called Phlegra where it was said by the Greek geographer, historian, and philosopher Strabo (64 BC–AD 24), barbarous and lawless giants dwelled. There were four cities in Phlegra: Aphytis, Mende, Sana, and Scione. Hercules, on his way from Troy, destroyed the giants.

At one time a city known as Potidea was found here but later it was renamed Casaandreia after it was rebuilt by King Cassander.

Source: DeLoach, *Giants*, 234; Strabo, *Geography of Strabo*, Volume 1, 511

Pisacha-Loka

Variations: Pisachaloka

One of the eight regions of material existence in Hindu mythology, Pisacha-Loka is the realm of the Pisachas (demons, fiends, ghosts, and imps).

Source: Dowson, *Classical Dictionary of Hindu Mythology and Religion*, 180; Hoult, *Dictionary of Some Theosophical Terms*, 74, 99

Pison

Variations: Pishon

The first of the four rivers which flowed out of the GARDEN OF EDEN (Genesis 2: 11–12), Pison was said to compass the entire land of Havilah where there is bdellium, quality gold, and onyx stones.

Biblical and secular scholar alike heavily debate which modern river, if any, could be the biblical GIHON and Pison have been.

Source: McClintock, *Cyclopaedia of Biblical, Theological, and Ecclesiastical Literature*, Volume 3, 861–62

The Pit of Corruption

According to Jewish Cabalists, there are seven levels to HELL; ALADDON, the GATES OF DEATH, GEBEANOM, the MIRE OF CLAY, the Pit of Corruption, the SHADOW OF DEATH, and SHEOL.

These realms are set one atop the other; ordinary fire is one-sixtieth the heat of the fire of GEBEANOM which is one-sixtieth the heat of the GATES OF DEATH, which is one-sixtieth the heat of the SHADOW OF DEATH, which is one-sixtieth the heat of the PIT OF CORRUPTION, which is one-sixtieth the heat of the Mire of Clay, which is one-sixtieth the heat of ALADDON, which is one-sixtieth the heat of SHEOL.

Source: Brewer, *Dictionary of Phrase and Fable*, 596; Mew, *Traditional Aspects of Hell*, 173

Pitri-Loka

Variations: Land of the Spirits, Pitriloka, Prajapatys

In Hindu and Vedic mythology Pitri-Loka is ruled by the god, Yama. Located in the middle of three worlds, below the earth and above the Caverns of Atala (see ATALA, CAVERNS OF) the Agnisvattas stay here in a meditative trance to secure the prosperity of those who arrive here.

One of the eight regions of material existence in Hindu mythology, Pitri-Loka ("World of the Fathers"), is the realm of the Pitris, Prajapatis, and Rishis. In the seven spheres of the earth, Pitri-Loka is the first.

Source: Dalal, *Hinduism*, 306; Dalal, *Religions of India*, 398; Dowson, *Classical Dictionary of Hindu Mythology and Religion*, 179; Parmeshwaranand, *Encyclopaedic Dictionary of Purāṇas*, 720; Wilson, *Vishṅu Puráṅa*, 48

The Plain of Nide *see* Nide's Plain

Plain of Silver Clouds

Variations: Mag Argat-mel, MagArgatnél

The Plain of Silver Clouds from Celtic myths is a sacred plain in the OTHERWORLD.

Source: Macleod, *Celtic Myth and Religion*, 35; O'Conor, *Changing Ireland*, 58

Plains of Lethe

The ancient Greek tale, *The Myth of Er*, which appears at the end of Plato's *Republic*, tells the tale of Er, a person who was allowed to visit the UNDERWORLD where he is witness to the destiny of souls. First a soul must been judge and sent to either HEAVEN or HELL, after a certain amount of time the soul is allowed to choose a new body in which it will return to Earth in but first it must cross the Plains of Lethe, a journey which causes them to forget the time they spent in the UNDER-WORLD. After crossing the plain they must then drink from the river AMELES in order to forget the previous life they once had upon the earth. Only after completing all tasks is a soul allowed to be reincarnated.

Source: Plato, *Dialogues of Plato*, Volume 2, 116; Plato, *Plato's Republic* 196

Pohjola

Variations: Pohja ("The End of Things")

In Finnish mythology Pohjola ("North-land") is where the souls of the dead reside; it is located northwest of Finland, directly opposite of the opposite of the rising sun. Oftentimes it is used to describe the furthest reaches of the earth and a place difficult to both reach and leave. Pohjola is ruled over by Pohjola Akka ("Mistress of Pohjola"), a witch characterized by her crooked nose. This land is referred to as "the eater of men and drowner of heroes." There are numerous buildings and fortresses here and the region is populated with historical figures that fought one another in ancient times. Some of the place names mentioned in ancient songs are Kirjovuori ("colorful Mountain") and Tapomaki ("Tapo Hill").

Source: Lang, *Custom and Myth*, 149; Pentikäi-nen, *Kalevala Mythology*, 170, 172

Pou-turi

The seventh lowest of the UNDERWORLDS in Maori mythology, Pou-turi is ruled over by the goddess Rohe, the wife of the god Māui.

Source: Andersen, *Maori Life in Ao-Tea*, 561; Craig, *Dictionary of Polynesian Mythology*, 57

Pranarodham

Variations: Pranarodha

According to Hindu and Vedic mythology Pranarodham is the sixteenth of the twenty-eight NARAKAS (HELLS) located in a providence in the kingdom of Yama. Here brah-manas who kept asses, dogs, or mules into the

forest to hunt when it was necessary to do so. Sinners are hunted down by the servants of Yama who shot arrows into their limbs until they fall off.

Source: Garg, *Encyclopaedia of the Hindu World: Ar–Az,* Volume 1, 841; Parmeshwaranand, *Encyclopaedic Dictionary of Purāṇas*, 722; Wilson, *Vishńu Puráńa*, 215

Pratapana

Variations: Pratāpana

In to Indian Buddhism, Pratapana ("very hot") is the seventh of the EIGHT HOT HELLS; it is known as the Great Burning Hell. The length of time a soul remains in Pratapana is one half of an *antarakalpa*, about eight million years; however, it may be as short as one half of an *antahkalpa*, about fifty years.

Source: Mew, *Traditional Aspects of Hell*, 38–41; Pruden, *Abhidharmakośabhāṣyam*, Volume 1, 472

Prester John, Kingdom of

Variations: Land of Prester John, Presbyter Johannes

Originating in the early twelfth century and surviving into the seventeenth century, the Kingdom of Prester John was said to be an Asiatic Christian kingdom (although in the middle ages Prester John was believed to be in Ethiopia); originally the kingdom was said to be in Ethiopia and on occasion in India, but it eventually "settled" as being somewhere far off in Asia but not so far as China. Supposedly in 1122 the king of this land paid a visit to the Pope and amazed the court with wonders he described his land having. In the midst of his walled kingdom ran the river Pishon, one of the rivers of PARADISE; it had crystal-clear water which was filled with gold and precious stones such as amethysts, beryls, emerald, sapphires, and topazes. Only the devout and faithful lived in the Kingdom, for as soon as a heretic or non-believer hears true Christian doctrines he will either instantly convert or fall over dead. There is no greed, lying, poverty, or theft in Prester John. Some of the names of cities within Prester John were the

Isle of PATHON, Isle of SILO, ISLE ON THE RIVER RENEMAR, and the land of PANTOROZE.

The palace of the priest king has ceilings and joints made of a type of wood which cannot rot. Atop the building are two golden apples, each surrounded by crystals. The ceilings are strewn with sapphires and topazes in order to look like the sky. The floors are made of crystals. Some of the tables in the palace are made of gold while others are made of amethyst, but the legs of all are made of ivory. Each day 30,000 men eat lunch at the palace; among them are seven kings, 12 archbishops, 20 bishops, 62 dukes, and 365 counts.

In front of the royal palace is a public square where judicial duals are fought. The most interesting feature of this area is a mirror set atop a column; as one climbs up the 25 steps the mirror show the activity of the land and the adjacent provinces. It is guarded day and night by 12,000 soldiers.

The oldest Latin text describing Prester John listing its animals, including camels, crocodiles, Cyclopes, dog-faced baboons, dromedaries, elephants, fauns, giants, gryphons, hippopotamuses, humans with horns, panthers, phoenix, pygmies, red lions, silent cicadas, tigers, white bears, white lions, and wild human beings. This text also describes the land of Prester John as a land of milk and honey. It was said to have a forest, located at the base of Mount Olympus, that grew an abundance of pepper; from this forest flows a flagrante river and anyone who is fasting and drinks from it three times will never become sick and remain a youthful thirty-two years old. The text also describes an ocean of sand, always moving and shifting, which cannot be crossed and therefore it was unknown what lay on the other side.

Source: Curran, *Lost Lands, Forgotten Realms*, 139–148; Delumeau, *History of Paradise*, 71–77; Sprague de Camp, *Lands Beyond*, 155

Preta-Loka

Variations: Pitr-Loka

In Hindu mythology Preta-Loka ("place of the Pretas") is the loka of the *pretas* ("ghosts"); it is one of the lower ASTRAL PLANES.

Source: Garg, *Hand Book of Hindu Religion and Ethics*, 78, 93; Hoult, *Dictionary of Some Theosophical Terms*, 108

Promise, Land of *see* Land of Promise

Ptolomea

In Dante Alighieri's epic poem *Divina Commedia* ("Divine Comedy") (1320) the river Ptolomea is located in the third ring of the ninth circle of HELL; it was one of the four tributaries of the river (see ANTENORA, COCYTUS, and JUDECCA). Named for Ptolemy 1 of the Maccabees, captain of Jericho who killed his father-in-law and two sons while they were eating with him; traitors to the guest-host tradition are immersed in JUDECCA's icy waters all but for half of their face with their heads tilted back so their tears ice over their eyes.

Alighieri utilized names and locations from existing mythologies; many of the demons mentioned in the poem were pulled from established hierarchies for example. Because his work, which was meant to be an allegory for the soul's journey to the path of God was well read and accepted, the names and locations he created for the sake of good storytelling became accepted into mythology as well.

Source: Lansing, *Dante Encyclopedia*, 722; Zimmerman, *Inferno of Dante Alighieri*, xix, 232

Pulotu

Variations: Boolootoo, BULOTU

The UNDERWORLD of the mythology of western Polynesia, particularly in Samoa and Tonga, Pulotu is a PARADISE from which the gods came from and souls of the chiefs go to upon death (commoners are not believed to have souls). Pulotu is ruled by the god Hikuleo (Goolech). Some stories claim Pulotu is the starting place of a soul's journey to the UNDERWORLD and not the final destination.

Source: Craig, *Dictionary of Polynesian Mythology*, 218; Nunn, *Vanished Islands and Hidden Continents of the Pacific*, 105–06

Pumpkin Island

According to Lucian of Samosata's parody travel tales *True History* (second century AD) Pumpkin Island was populated by pirates who sailed the sea in vessels carved out of huge pumpkin shells.

Source: Davis, *Don't Know Much About Geography*, 48; Manguel, *Dictionary of Imaginary Places*, 118

Pure Land of the Western Paradise

Variations: Pure Land, Sukhavati

In the Mahayana tradition, Pure Land of the Western Paradise was where the god Amida-Nyorai resides; he promised that anyone who believed in him at the moment of their death would be taken into his realm, made into a Buddha, and enjoy an afterlife of luxury. Pure Land of the Western Paradise was described as being a colorful HEAVEN filled with bells, birds, streams, and trees.

Source: Whiting, *Religions for Today*, 239

Purgatory

Variations: AL A'RAF, ADHAB-ALGAL, ADLIVUN, BARZAKH, DIYU, HAMISTAGAN, JAHANNAM, LIMBO, PARADISE OF FOOLS

A concept held to be true by Christians, Jews, Mohammedans, and Pagans alike, purgatory is a realm where a soul will atone for offences it committed in life but did not merit eternal damnation; this restoration of the soul is necessary because nothing can be admitted into the presence of God which is in a state of any level of sin. The length of time a souls spends in purgatory depends on the amount of sin it has accumulated. This time, according to Maccabees (12:43–45, 56) can be shortened by the offering of acts of kindness, prayer, and sacrifices offered up in the deceased name.

Roman Catholics describe purgatory as a place where souls who died in a state of grace are detained because they are blemished with venial sin. Here the souls are cleansed and prepared for eternal bliss with God in HEAVEN. The suffering here is twofold, both from the physical transformation of the removal of sin as well as the separation from the presence of God.

Rabbinical teachings tell us on the Day of Judgment there will be three classes of souls; the righteous which will immediately ascend into HEAVEN, the damned who will immediately descend into GEHENNA, and a third whose sins and virtues counterbalance one another. It is these souls who will be dipped in and out of the fires of GEHENNA until they are purified and cleansed of all sin.

The Mohammedans idea of purgatory is AL A'RAF, a realm filled with souls not worthy of HEAVEN but neither deserving of HELL. On the Day of Judgment they will be summoned before God and lie prostrate before Him, will gain enough merit allowing them to pass into HEAVEN.

Source: Buck, *Theological Dictionary*, 504–05; Enns, *Moody Handbook of Theology*, 571; Hughes, *Dictionary of Islam*, 20–21; Singer, *Jewish Encyclopedia*, Volume 10, 274

Purvavudeha

In in Buddhist cosmology Purvavudeha and was described as being exactly round and lying directly east of SUMERU.

Source: Howard, *Imagery of the Cosmological Buddha*, 66

Puyavaha

Variations: Puyavaha

In Hindu mythology Puyavaha ("where matter flows") is a partition in HELL (or NARAKA) ruled over by Yama; it is located beneath the earth and water where souls are punished for the sin of eating sweetmeats mixed with rice alone, committing acts of violence, raises birds, cats, cocks, dogs, goats, or hogs. Also in this HELL are those Brahman who vends flesh, Lac, liquors, salt, or sesamum.

Source: Wilson, *Oriental Translation Fund*, Volume 52, 208; Wilson, *Vishńu Puráńa*, 215–16

Puyodakam

Variations: Puyoda

According to Hindu and Vedic mythology Puyodakam is the fifteenth of the twenty-eight

NARAKAS (HELLS) located in a providence in the kingdom of Yama. Described as a well filled with blood, excreta, phlegm, and urine, bramans who had intercourse with women outside of their caste system are sent here.

Source: Prabhupāda, *Śrīmad Bhāgavatam*, 903; Parmeshwaranand, *Encyclopaedic Dictionary of Purāṇas*, 722

Pyriphlegethon

Variations: Phlegethon ("fire-flaming")

According to ancient Greek mythology Pyriphlegethon ("blazing with fire") was one of the four rivers of the UNDERWORLD (see ACHERON, COCYTUS, and OCEANUS); it is associated with the eruptions of volcanoes. This river flows, boiling, through an especially hot region of the Underworld, where it forms into a vast boiling lake; eventually a small stream carries its waters on to TARTARUS. Both COCYTUS and Pyriphlegethon skirt along the ACHERUSIAN but neither enter into it.

The human souls who after their trial are deemed evil but curable spend about a year in TARTARUS before being sent up through both COCYTUS and Pyriphlegethon, passing thorough the water seeking forgiveness for the crimes the committed in life, the people they murdered or wronged.

Source: Evans, *Dictionary of Mythology*, 214; Evslin, *Gods, Demigods, and Demons*, 184; Guthrie, *History of Greek Philosophy: Volume 4*, 361, 377

Qimiujdrmiut

In the mythology of the Inuit, Qimiujdrmiut ("Dwellers of the Narrow Land") was one of the three locations where a person's spirit went to live; it is described as being a narrow strip of land located under the sea. The occupants of Qimiujdrmiut are those individual who died a natural death and only broke a few taboos in life; here they live without any hardship and hunt freely the numerous animals. One way to ensure the arrival of soul to Qimiujdrmiut is to lay out the deceased body on the ice rather than on the land.

Source: Leenaars, *Suicide in Canada*, 197; Lynge, *Mental Disorders in Greenland. Past and Present*, 13

Quivira

A legendary city said to be located in the American southwest, Quivira was one of the Seven Cities of Gold sought after by Spanish conquistadors. These cities were sought after in part because Catholic lore claimed that after the Muslim invasion of the Iberian peninsula of AD 714, seven bishops crossed the Atlantic Ocean with their flock and founded a Christian UTOPIA; these cities were referred to as *Ilha das Sete Cidades* ("Isle of the Seven Cities").

Source: Hendrickson, *Facts on File Dictionary of American Regionalisms*, 461; Smith, *Discovery of the Americas, 1492–1800*, 76, 107

Rainbow City

An abandoned extraterrestrial metropolis under the Antarctic ice, Rainbow City was first written about in 1946 by W. C. Hefferlin of the Borderland Sciences Research Associates, an occult-oriented group located in Vista, California, United States. According to the articles Hefferlin wrote, the occupants of Rainbow City came to Earth and settled in Antarctica, then a tropical PARADISE, when the atmosphere of Mars had become unbreathable. It was surrounded on all sides by hot springs. The greatest of the seven cities they founded here two and a half million years ago, Rainbow City was destroyed when the evil alien race known as the Vhujunka discovered them. The settelers were scattered over the earth and in the ensuing violence the axis of the earth was altered causing the Antarctica to become a polar region.

Source: Adam, *Hollow Earth Authentic*, 7; Clark, *Encyclopedia of Strange and Unexplained Physical Phenomena*, 153

Rakshasa-Loka

Variations: Rakshasaloka

One of the eight regions of material existence in Hindu mythology, Rakshasa-Loka ("World of Rakshasa") is the realm of the Rakshasa.

Source: Dalal, *Hinduism*, 225; Dowson, *Classical Dictionary of Hindu Mythology and Religion*, 180; Garrett, *Classical Dictionary of India*, 499

Rakshogana-Bhojana

Variations: Rakshoganabhojana

According to Hindu and Vedic mythology Rakshogana-Bhojana is one of the NARAKAS (HELLS) located in a providence in the kingdom of Yama. Those who reside here made sacrifices to Bhairava, Bhadra Kali, Rakshasas, or Ysha in life; upon their death, these sinners were taken to the home of Yamaraja where their victims have been transformed into Rakshasas; these demons would then cut them into pieces with axes and swords, dancing and singing while reveling in the bloodshed.

Source: Prapnnachari, *Crest Jewel*, 141; Wilson, *Vishńu Puráńa*, Volume 2, 215

Raksobhaksam

According to Hindu and Vedic mythology Raksobhaksam is one of the NARAKAS (HELLS) located in a providence in the kingdom of Yama. Here, those who are flesh eaters are punished. There are different compartments to this NARAKAS; those who perform human sacrifice and those who eat the flesh of once living creatures. All of the victims of the sinners gather together here and assault without mercy or relent, the souls who killed them.

Source: Parmeshwaranand, *Encyclopaedic Dictionary of Purāṇas*, 722

Rama Empire

Alleged to be a contemporary of ATLANTIS, the Rama Empire was described in ancient Indian text as having been at war with ATLANTIS, defending against weapons such as a fireball so large and destructive a single blast could destroy an entire city and a device known as Kapilla's Glance which could turn 50,000 men into ash in a matter of seconds.

Originally settled in India by the Nagas, the Rama Empire began to expand all over northern India; the aristocracy lived in the seven capital cities which were called the Rishi Cities and these priest kings were reputed to have great psychic powers. Although there is no complete list of the names of the seven cities it is generally accepted Deccan (Nagaour) was the main capital city of the empire and Harappa, Lothal, and Mohenjo-Daro were important trade centers.

The ancient Sanskirt epic *Mahabharata* (*Mahābhārata*), described the devastating war between ATLANTIS and the Rama Empire and the level of technology at use; there were descriptions of devices reminiscent of aerial chariots clad in iron with protruding wings, zeppelins called *vailixi* (*vimanas*, singular), and nuclear devastation.

Source: Childress, *Lost Cities of China, Central Asia, and India*, 240–44; Menon, *The Mahabharata*, 511–13, 524

Raquia

Variations: Raqia, Raqui ("Expanse")

Ruled by the angels Raphael and Zachariel, Raquia ("Expansive") is the second HEAVEN of Jewish lore. Raquia is where the fallen angels are imprisoned and the planets are fixed into place. According to Enoch, this is where the fallen angles are imprisoned in utter darkness as they await their final judgment.

Source: Lewis, *Angels A to Z, 2nd Edition*, 332; Vohs, *Am I Going to Heaven?*, 31; Webster, *Encyclopedia of Angels*, 85

Raro-henga (rah-roh-HENG-ah)

Variations: Rarohenga

In Polynesian mythology Raro-henga ("the underworld") is the UNDERWORLD region where a race of fair haired and skinned fairies known as the turehu are believed to live. Fond of dancing and eating only uncooked food, the turehu will occasionally venture into our realm and take a human spouse.

Source: Andersen, *Myths and Legends of the Polynesians*, 126, 288; Flood, *Pacific Island Legends*, 234

Rasatala, Caverns of

Variations: Rasaatala

In Hindu lore the Caverns of Rasatala are believed to be the fifth of the seven underground levels in a vast cavernous system which stretches from Benares, India to Lake Manosarowar, Tibet. In all of the regions (ATALA,

MAHATALA, PATALA, SUTALA, TALATALA, and VITALA), there are beautiful cities built by the architect, Maya.

Source: Parmeshwaranand, *Encyclopaedic Dictionary of Purāṇas*, 1010–1012

Rath

Variations: Burghs, Fairy Knowe, FAIRY FORT, Fairy Hill, Fairy Mound, Fairy Mount, Sithean ("house of the fairies"), Taigh Shidhe

In Ireland a rath is the traditional home of a fairy; it is described as looking like a mound of earth or one of the countries many prehistoric earthen mounds. The inside is called the BRUGH. Although Irish fay are typically only a few inches tall, inside the mounds, the space was vast; sometimes they are seen departing the rath mounted upon their tiny horses.

Source: *Bord*, Fairies, 3; Keightly, *World Guide to Gnomes, Fairies, Elves, and Other Little People*, 363; McCoy, *Witch's Guide to Faery Folk*, 42

Rath Chinneich

According to Irish lore, Rath Chinneich was the mythological location of the palace of one of the first settlers to Ireland, the Nemed.

Source: Keating, *Forus feasa air Éirinn*, 167; Monaghan, *Encyclopedia of Celtic Mythology and Folklore*, 391

Raurava

In Hindu mythology Raurava ("howling"), the dreadful HELL, is a partition in HELL (or *Naraka*) ruled over by Yama; it is located beneath the earth and water and is where souls are punished for lying or bearing false-witness through partiality. In this Hell, the sinners are forced to run over hot coals.

In to Indian Buddhism, Raurava is the fourth of the EIGHT HOT HELLS; it is known as the Screaming Hell souls here are punished for their sins of intoxication.

Source: Prabhupāda, *Śrimad Bhāgavatam*, 903; Becker, *Contribution to the Comparative Study of the Medieval Visions of Heaven and Hell*, 14; Mew, *Traditional Aspects of Hell*, 38–41; Wilson, *Oriental Translation Fund*, Volume 52, 207; Wilson, *Vishńu Puráńa*, 215–16

Rauravam

According to Hindu and Vedic mythology Rauravam is the third of the twenty-eight NARAKA (HELLS); here the souls of those who persecuted others as well as those who take another property and enjoy it are sent. Also in Rauravam are those women who, be they unmarried or widowed, shave their hair. Here the souls of the sinners are confronted by the images of those they wronged who torment them.

Source: Burgess, *Indian Antiquary*, Volume 3, 136; Parmeshwaranand, *Encyclopaedic Dictionary of Purāṇas*, 721

Rica de Oro

Variations: Armenian's Islands

An imaginary island sought after by Spanish conquistadors in the Pacific Ocean, the mythology of Rica de Oro ("Rich in Gold") and its sister island RICA DE PLATA began when a Portuguese ship, no date or name is given, was blown off course east of Japan and discovered this gold rich land populated by "white and civilized" people. First sought after in 1587 by Pedro de Unamuno, the Spanish continued the search on and off until 1741.

Source: Smith, *Discovery of the Americas, 1492–1800*, 131; Spate, *Spanish Lake*, 106

Rica de Plata

An imaginary island sought after by Spanish conquistadors in the Pacific Ocean, the story of Rica de Plata ("Rich in Silver") and its sister island RICA DE ORO began when a Portuguese ship, no date or name is given, was blown off course east of Japan and discovered this gold rich land populated by "white and civilized" people. First sought after in 1587 by Pedro de Unamuno, the Spanish continued the search on and off until 1741.

Source: Smith, *Discovery of the Americas, 1492–1800*, 131; Spate, *Spanish Lake*, 106

Rinn

According to Norse mythology Rinn was one of sixteen rivers which ran from ASGARD to MIDGARD.

Source: Grimes, *Norse Myths*, 13, 295; Guerber, *Myths of the Norsemen*, 13

Rinnandi

Variations: Rennandi

According to Norse mythology Rinnandi was one of sixteen rivers which ran from AS-GARD to MIDGARD.

Source: Grimes, *Norse Myths*, 13, 295; Guerber, *Myths of the Norsemen*, 13

River Renemar, Isle on the *see* Isle on the River Renemar

Rock of Canguin *see* Canguin, Rock of

Rodha

Variations: Bodha

In Hindu mythology Rodha ("that of obstruction") is a partition in HELL (or NARAKA) ruled over by Yama; it is located beneath the earth and water where souls are punished for the sin abortion, killing a cow, plundering a town, or strangling a man.

Source: Wilson, *Oriental Translation Fund*, Volume 52, 207; Wilson, *Vishńu Puráńa*, 215–16

Rudhirandha

Variations: Rudhirambhas

In Hindu mythology Rudhirandha ("whose wells are of blood") is a partition in HELL (or NARAKA) ruled over by Yama; it is located beneath the earth and water where souls are punished for the sins of being a boxer, a fisherman, a poisoner, a public performer, a seller of the acid Asclepias which is used in sacrifices, a soothsayer, a treacherous friend, a wrestler, an incendiary, an informer. Also found in this HELL are those individuals who attended secular affairs on the days of the Paruas or on the full or new moon; preformed a religious ceremony for rustics, or lived off the earnings of his wife's prostitution.

Source: Wilson, *Oriental Translation Fund*, Volume 52, 209; Wilson, *Vishńu Puráńa*, 215–16

Rusta

Variations: Rusat, Rusut

In Egyptian mythology Rusta was the Gate of Passage, the entranceway into the region of AMENTI known as the HALL OF TWO TRUTHS, the judgment place of the god Osiris. Rusta, similar to PURGATORY, is a place of rest for the dead.

Source: Bonwick, *Egyptian Belief and Modern Thought*, 46–50; Cooper, *Archaic Dictionary*, 474

Rutas

According to theosophical writings, the lost continent of Rutas once located in the Pacific Ocean east of India but was destroyed by a volcanic cataclysm and left behind what would become the country of Indonesia. The survivors of Rutas migrated to India and introduced Sanskirt to the language.

In the Brahminical traditions Rutas may have been named after one of Lemuria's chief deities, Rudra ("Cosmic Fire"). The people of Rutas were spiritually advanced sun-worshipers who, when their land was destroyed by a great flood, fled to India and founded the elite Brahman caste.

Source: JOSEPH, *Atlantis Encyclopedia*, 79; Nunn, *Vanished Islands and Hidden Continents of the Pacific*, 102–21

Saguenay, Kingdom of

Variations: Le Royaume du Saguenay

An Iroquoian legend as reported by French colonist in Canada during the sixteenth and seventeenth centuries the mythical Kingdom of Saguenay was sought after by the early French explorers of Canada as it was said to have not only great mines of copper, gold, silver, and rubies but also grew cloves, nutmeg, oranges, pepper, and pomegranates. In 1535, the explorer Jacques Cartier, fed by stories from his local guides, Donnacona and Taignoagny, sought the Kingdom of Saguenay which was alleged to be populated by winged people and unipeds. Many explorers combed the Canadian north over the years along the Saguenay River looking for this land of gold and silver mines in vain. Today, the Kingdom of Saguenay is generally accepted today as being mythical although some people have speculated it may have been an ancient pre–Columbian European settlement, such as the Norse settlement at L'Anse aux Meadows.

Source: Colombo, *Canadian Literary Landmarks*, 61; Hayes, *Historical Atlas of Canada*, 30–31; King, *Glorious Kingdom of Saguenay*, 31

Sagun

Variations: Shechakin, Shehaquim ("Sky")

The third of the seven HEAVENs of Jewish lore, Sagun is ruled by the angel Anahel and is the home of the Islamic angel of death, Izra'll. Here the wicked are tortured by angels; however, in the southern region of Sagun there is a beautiful PARADISE some sources say is the GARDEN OF EDEN, where the souls of the righteous reside.

Source: Lewis, *Angels A to Z, 2nd Edition*, 332; Webster, *Encyclopedia of Angels*, 85

Sa'ir

The fourth (or third, sources vary) of the seven Islamic HELLS, Sa'ir is reserved for worshippers of fire, the *sabaens* (see AL HUTAMAH, HAWIYAH, JAHANNAM, AL JAHIM, LAGAM, and SAQAU).

Source: Hughes, *Dictionary of Islam*, 170–71; Netton, *Popular Dictionary of Islam*, 221; Wagner, *How Islam Plans to Change the World*, 156; Wherry, *Comprehensive Commentary on the Quran*, 148

Salmali

According to Hindu and Vedic mythology Salmali is the twelfth of the twenty-eight NARAKAS (HELLS) located in a providence in the kingdom of Yama. This place is reserved for those men and women who committed adultery. For punishment a figure made of super-heated iron is placed before the sinner who is urged to embrace it; during the embrace, they are also flogged from behind.

Source: Parmeshwaranand, *Encyclopaedic Dictionary of Purāṇas*, 721

Salmydessus (sal-mi-DESS-us)

The mythological island of Salmydessus was the home of King Phineus who was persecuted by the harpies, creatures half bird and half woman. When the Greek hero Jason and his followers, the Argonauts arrived there, they drove the creatures far away to the Island of Turning (see TURNING, ISLAND OF). In gratitude the king advised them how to safely sail between the CLASHING ROCKS to reach the land where the Golden Fleece resided.

Source: Colum, *Golden Fleece and the Heroes Who Lived Before Achilles*, 51; Flaum, *Encyclopedia of Mythology*, 163

Salsabil

Variations: Salsabeel, Salsabiil

According to the Koran (76:17–18), Salsabil ("the softly flowing") was a spring or a fountain in al JANNA (PARADISE); it sourced from the roots of the tree, Tuba. The waters of these rivers are described as being like honey, milk, water, and wine and along the banks are precious gems.

Source: Hughes, *Dictionary of Islam*, 449, 563; Penrice, *Dictionary and Glossary of the Koran*, 63, 71

Samghata

Variations: Saṃghāta

In to Indian Buddhism, Samghata ("Crushing") is the third of the EIGHT HOT HELLS; it is known as the Hell of Crowding and the souls here are punished for the sins of sexual immorality and for those who have killed boar, deer, goats, hares, jackals, rats, sheep, and other living creatures. The sinners are piled up in a heap between two iron mountains which then crash together, smashing the sinners to death; as the mountains part, the sinners are restored and the process begins anew.

Source: Mew, *Traditional Aspects of Hell*, 38–41; Strong, *Experience of Buddhism*, 39; Yaldiz, *Along the Ancient Silk Routes*, 79

Samjiva

Variations: Sañjīva

In to Indian Buddhism, Samjiva ("Reviving")

is the first of the EIGHT HOT HELLS; it is known as the Hell of Repetitions and the souls here are punished by repeating the lives of those they have killed. Sinners are also hung upside down and are hacked to pieces with axes by the Watchmen of Yama; sometimes sinners will grow claws of iron and in their painful frenzy turn and attack other sinners.

Source: Mew, *Traditional Aspects of Hell*, 35; Yaldiz, *Along the Ancient Silk Routes*, 79

Sandamas

In Hindu mythology, Sandamas is one of the twenty-eight NARAKAS (HELLS) located in a providence in the kingdom of Yama; it is filled with the instruments of torture.

Source: Wilson, *Vishńu Puráńa*, 215–16

Sandansa

Variations: Sandarisa

In Hindu mythology Sandansa ("Hell of Pincers") is a partition in HELL (NARAKAS) ruled over by Yama; it is located beneath the earth and water where souls are punished for the sin of breaking a vow or breaking the rules of his orders.

Source: Garrett, *Classical Dictionary of India*, 547; Prabhupāda, *Śrīmad Bhāgavatam*, 903; Wilson, *Oriental Translation Fund*, Volume 52, 209

Saqar

Variations: Sakar ("Blazer"), Saqau

The fourth (fifth or seventh, sources vary) of the seven Islamic HELLS, Saqar is reserved for *magians* (atheists) (see AL HUTAMAH, HAWIYAH, JAHANNAM, AL JAHIM, LAGAM, and SA'IR).

Source: Hughes, *Dictionary of Islam*, 170–71; Wagner, *How Islam Plans to Change the World*, 156; Wherry, *Comprehensive Commentary on the Quran*, 148

Sarameyasanam

Variations: Sarameyadana

According to Hindu and Vedic mythology Sarameyasanam is the nineteenth of the twenty-eight NARAKAS (HELLS) located in a

providence in the kingdom of Yama; this NARAKAS is intended for those guilty of incendiarism, mass slaughter, poisoning food, and ruining the country. Here, sinners will find the only food to eat is dog flesh. Living here is a pack of 700 dogs, vicious as leopards, each one more ferocious than the next; they hunt out the souls here and attack them, rending them limb to limb.

Source: Garg, *Encyclopaedia of the Hindu World: Ar–Az*, Volume 1, 841; Knapp, *Secret Teachings of the Vedas*, n.p.; Parmeshwaranand, *Encyclopaedic Dictionary of Purāṇas*, 722

Sarpedon

The rocky isle of the gorgons, Sarpedon was located in the distant west not so far from the gardens of Hesperdae and the realm of the dead, according to ancient Greek mythology.

Source: Adams, *Universal Cyclopaedia*, Volume 5, 211; Hesiod, *Hesiod, the Homeric Hymns and Homerica*, 505

Sarras

A mythical island of Arthurian lore, Sarras was the destination of the knights who sought the Holy Grail; some text claim this was the location of Sir Galahad's death. Sir Galahad was said to have been commanded by Christ to remove the Holy Grail from CARBONEK CASTLE and relocate it to Sarras, the city where Joseph of Arimathea converted a pagan king over to Christianity.

Source: Manguel, *Dictionary of Imaginary Places*, 117; Monaghan. *Encyclopedia of Celtic Mythology and Folklore*, 409

Satya-Loka

Variations: BRAHMA-LOKA

One of the eight regions of heavenly existence in Hindu mythology, Satya-Loka, is the heavenly home the Brahma; souls here are exempt from rebirth. In the seven spheres of the earth, Satya-Loka is the seventh.

Source: Dowson, *Classical Dictionary of Hindu Mythology and Religion*, 179; Wilson, *Vishńu Puráńa*, 48

Satyrs, Island of the

According to the ancient Persian fairytale, *Sindbad the Sailor* (750 CE), the Island of the Satyrs was mentioned in the third voyage of the fictional sailor's adventures; he encountered it while traveling in the company of a group of merchants leaving out of Basra.

Source: Sprague de Camp, *Lands Beyond*, 129–20

Sawr-Loka

One of the eight regions of heavenly existence in Hindu mythology, Sawr-Loka, the HEAVEN of the god Indra, is located between the sun and the polar star.

Source: Dowson, *Classical Dictionary of Hindu Mythology and Religion*, 179

Scamander

Variations: Xanthus

A small but heavy flowing river that runs near Troy, the waters of Scamander were thought to be particularly beautiful; the goddesses Aphrodite and Athena bathed here and made a point to wash their hair here before they entered into the beauty contest held on Mount Ida.

Source: Evans, *Dictionary of Mythology*, 233; Westmoreland, *Ancient Greek Beliefs*, 342

Scheria

Variations: CORCYRA, Harpi ("Harp"), Phaeacia, Scherie

A region in Greek mythology, Scheria ("Continuous Shoreline") was first mentioned in Homer's *Odyssey* as being the home of the Phaiakians (Phaeacians) and the final stop of Odysseus's ten year long voyage returning to Ithaca. The harp-shaped island was described as having a rugged terrain and a rocky coastline, making it difficult to swim up to the shore. Scheria was Homer's model city, considerably similar to Plato's ATLANTIS.

The city on Scheria had towering walls even though it had never been attacked; its people kept to themselves, trading little with the outside world. Alkinos, the grandson of the god

of the sea, Poseidon, was the high king of Scheria, and he ruled over twelve lesser kings. Alkinos' castle had brazen walls, silver doors with golden handles, and a bronze threshold. The castle garden had two springs. The sailors in its navy were the best in the world and utilized the fastest ships known to man.

Source: Sprague de Camp, *Lands Beyond*, 41–42; Westmoreland, *Ancient Greek Beliefs*, 239

Schildburg

In German folklore, Schildburg is a proverbial town said to be inhabited by fools; it is similar to CHELM and SCHILDBURG. As the town has no cats, the population of Schildburg refuses to believe that cats exist as the town's motto was "If it isn't in Schildburg, it doesn't exist."

Source: Ben-Amos, *Folktales of the Jews*, 453; Walsh, *Heroes and Heroines of Fiction, Classical Mediæval, Legendary*, 279–80

Segais

Variations: CONNLA'S WELL, Segáis

In Irish lore Segais is the name of a secret well of wisdom and like all mystic wells it would impart this ability upon any who ate the fish swimming in it or drank the water from it. Segais was guarded by the sorcerer Nechtan and his three cupbearers, only they were allowed to visit the well. When the goddess Bóand once approached the well and waked around it three times counter-clockwise, its waters rose up and drowning her and carried her out to sea; from then on, the well was never able to contain the rushing water. The salmon Fintan who lived in the well was also taken out to sea where he was caught by Finnegas and eaten by Finn mac Cumhaill.

Source: Monaghan. *Encyclopedia of Celtic Mythology and Folklore*, 413; Mountain, *Celtic Encyclopedia*, 892

Segais, Well of *see* Well of Segais

Seisyllwch, the Seven Cantrefs

In the *Mabinogi*, a collection of eleven prose stories from medieval Welsh maunscripts, the seven *cantrefs* of Seisyllwch is the collective name for the various lands ruled over by Pryderi, son of Arawn the lord of the Underworld. In addition to the seven *cantrefs* of Dyfed he also ruled the four *cantrefs* of Ceredigion and the three *cantrefs* of Ystrad Tywi.

Source: Ford, *Mabinogi and Other Medieval Welsh Tales*, 56; Sullivan, *Mabinogi: a Book of Essays*, 309

Sekin

Variations: Sækin, Saskin, Sœkin, Sokin, Sökin, Søkin

According to Norse mythology Sekin was one of rivers which ran from ASGARD to MIDGARD.

Source: Grimes, *Norse Myths*, 296; Guerber, *Myths of the Norsemen*, 13

Senge Khabab

Variations: Khambab

In Hindu mythology Senge Khabab ("River from the Lion's Mouth") is one of the four rivers which runs out of MAPHAM YUMTSHO, the lake located at the bottom of Mount MERU; it flows to the north.

Source: McCue, *Trekking in Tibet*, 207

Seron

Variations: Idsheuan, the Place of Dispersion, Naxauana

The town built shortly after Noah's (Xisuthrus) ark came to rest on dry land in the mountains, Seron was the first city or town to be rebuilt after the Flood.

Source: Josephus, *Works of Flavius Josephus*, Volume 1, 17; Tomline, *Introduction to the Study of the Bible*, 29

Sessrymnir

Variations: Sesrumner, Sessrumnir

In Norse mythology Sessrymnir ("the roomy-seated") was the dwelling place of the beautiful and martial minded goddess, Freya; able to easily accommodate all of her guests, this hall was located in the realm of FOLKVANG. Every day Freya chooses half of those slain to reside here with her.

Source: Anderson, *Norse Mythology*, 457; Bennett, *Gods and Religions of Ancient and Modern Times*, Volume 1, 396; Guerber, *Myths of the Norsemen*, 131

The Seven Cantrefs *see* Seisyllwch, the Seven Cantrefs

Seven Cities of Gold

Variations: CÍBOLA

In the 16th century the Spanish of Mexico began to hear stories about the Seven Cities of Gold located hundreds of miles to the north, in what would now be the Texas, United States of America. The Spanish conquistador Francisco Coronado sought the seven cities he believed were founded by seven Catholic bishops who fled Europe, a legend which dated back to the eighth century.

One of the seven cities Qiviria (Quivara) was believed to be in a desert-like basin in Mexico called Jornada del Muerto ("Journey of Dead Men").

Source: Curran, *Lost Lands, Forgotten Realms*, 195–99; Grant, *American Nomads*, 67, 70

Seven Heavens

In the cosmology of Hinduism, Islam, and Judaism, HEAVEN is divided into seven sections or layers.

In the ancient Hindu texts *Atharvaveda* ("Knowledge") and the Puranas, there are fourteen worlds, seven of which are considered to be higher worlds, (the HEAVENs) and are called collectively *Vyahritis*. These seven Svarga ("HEAVENs") in their layered order are BHUR-LOKA, BHUVAR-LOKA, SAWR-LOKA, MAHAR-LOKA, JANA-LOKA, TAPAR-LOKA, and Satya-loka ("Vaikuntha").

The Koran mentions the existence of seven HEAVENs, and according to a *hadith* attributed to the Iman Ali names of them in order from lowest to highest as Rafi', Qaydum, Marum, Arfalun, Hay'oun, Arous, Ajma.'

In Hebrew lore there are seven layers or divisions to HEAVEN; each one has an angel to govern over it. The seven HEAVENs, in order from lowest to highest are SHAMAYIM, ruled over by the angel Gabriel; Raqia ruled over by the angels Raphael and Zachariel; SHE-HAQIM, ruled over by Anahel and three subordinate *sarim*: Jagniiel, Rabacyel, and Dalquiel; MACHONON, ruled over by the angel Michael; MACHON (Mathey), ruled over by Sandalphon (Aaron); ZEBUL, ruled over by Zachiel, assisted by Zebul (by day) and Sabath (by night); and ARABOTH, ruled over by the angel Cassiel.

Source: Dimmitt, *Classical Hindu Mythology*, 24–25; Heinen, *Islamic Cosmology*, 86, 141; Lewis, *Angels A to Z*, 331–333

Seven Hells

In Cabalistic lore there are seven layers or divisions to HELL; they are, in order from lowest to deepest, SHEOL, the Depths of the earth; ABADDON, the HELL of Perdition; TITAHION, the Clay of Death; BAR SHASKETH, the Pit of Destruction; TZELMOTH—Shadow of Death; SHAARI MOTH, Gates of death; and GEHINNON, HELL.

Source: Mathers, *Sorcerer and His Apprentice*, 24

Seven Lower Worlds

In the cosmology of Hinduism, the lower world is divided into seven sections or layers according to the ancient Hindu texts *Atharvaveda* ("Knowledge"). The seven lower worlds in their layered order are ATALA, VITALA, SUTALA, RASATALA, TALATALS, MAHATALA, and PATALA; collectively they are also sometimes referred to as Patala. These seven lower worlds are not NARAKAS (HELL); each is a beautiful PARADISE although they are occupied by demons and nagas.

Source: Dalal, *Hinduism*, 224; Lethaby, *Architecture, Mysticism and Myth*, 163

Shaari Moth

Variations: Sharre Moth

In Cabalistic lore Shaari Moth ("Gates of Death") is the third (or sixth, sources conflict) of the seven hells.

Source: Greer, *New Encyclopedia of the Occult*, 495; Mathers, *Sorcerer and His Apprentice*, 24

The Shadow of Death

Variations: TZELMOTH

According to Jewish Cabalists, there are seven levels to HELL; ALADDON, the GATES OF DEATH, GEBEANOM, the MIRE OF CLAY, the PIT OF CORRUPTION, the Shadow of Death, and SHEOL.

These realms are set one atop the other; ordinary fire is one-sixtieth the heat of the fire of GEBEANOM which is one-sixtieth the heat of the GATES OF DEATH, which is one-sixtieth the heat of the SHADOW OF DEATH, which is one-sixtieth the heat of the PIT OF CORRUPTION, which is one-sixtieth the heat of the Mire of Clay, which is one-sixtieth the heat of ALADDON, which is one-sixtieth the heat of SHEOL.

Source: Brewer, *Dictionary of Phrase and Fable*, 596; Mew, *Traditional Aspects of Hell*, 173

Shadows, Land of *see* Land of Shadows

Shad-u-kam

Variations: Shadukam, Shád-ú-kám

Shad-u-kam ("Pleasure and Delight") is one of the cities or provinces in DJINNESTAN, the Persian mythological equivalent of FAIRYLAND.

Source: Keightly, *World Guide to Gnomes, Fairies, Elves, and Other Little People*, 16; Smedley, *Occult Sciences*, 19, 775; Spence, *Encyclopædia of Occultism*, 177; Yardley, *Supernatural in Romantic Fiction*, 52

Shamayim

Variations: Vilon ("veil")

The first and lowest of the seven HEAVENS of Jewish mysticism, Shamayim ("Skies") is ruled over by the angel Gabriel; it boarders the earth and contains the clouds, the Upper Waters, and the wind. Shamayim is the home of some 200 astronomer angels who rule over the stars as well as Adam and Eve.

Source: Lewis, *Angels A to Z*, 332; Webster, *Encyclopedia of Angels*, 84; Vohs, *Am I Going to Heaven?*, 27

Shambhala

Variations: Aryavarsha, Belovodye, Chang Shambhala, Forbidden Land, His Tien, Janaidar, Land of Living Fire, Land of Radiant Spirits, Land of the Living Gods, Land of White Water, Land of Wonders, Shangri-La

According to Tibetan Buddhist legend Shambhala ("place of peace, tranquility") is a hidden kingdom said to be somewhere in the Himalayas. The kings enjoy of life of indulging in sensual pleasures and decadent wealth, however, they strive to remain kind to their subjects and seek enlightenment so the virtues of royalty may never decrease. The people of Shambhala are blessed with beauty and nearly perfect bodies; they never age or become ill nor do they know hunger or want. Every citizen is intelligent and virtuous, capable of reaching Nirvana in their lifetime. The laws of the land are mild; there are no beatings or imprisonment.

In the middle of Shambhala stands its capital city of KALAPA; to the south is a pleasure grove and a lake where the gods and mortals enjoy boat rides together.

Source: Lepage, *Shambhala*; 6–7; Znamenski, *Red Shambhala*, 1, 2

Shee Finnaha

The palace of King Lir, one of the Tuatha de Danann in Irish lore, Shee Finnaha is traditionally said to be located in Northern Ireland on the boraders of Armagh and Monaghan counties.

Source: Joyce, *Old Celtic Romances*, 2; Monaghan. *Encyclopedia of Celtic Mythology and Folklore*, 417

Sheep, Isle of

Variations: Faer-eyjar, the Ilonde of Sheep, Insula Arietum, Shepey

Described in the tales of Saint Brendan the legendary Isle of Sheep was located off the British coast on old maps; it was described in the *immram*, (Irish navigational story) *Navigatio Sancti Brendani* ("The Voyage of St. Brendan") as having sheep as large as an ox and *"there is never colde wether but ever sommer."*

Source: Bevan, *Mediæval Geography*, 172; Magasich-airola, *America Magica*, 138

Shehaqim

In Kabbalah Jewish mysticism, Shehaqim ("the HEAVENs, as in the sky") is the third of the seven HEAVENs; it is ruled over by the angel Anahel and his three subordinate *sarim* Dalquiel, Jagnieil, and Rabacyel. Located in this HEAVEN is the GARDEN OF EDEN and the Tree of Life; it is also where manna, the food angels eat, is produced. According to the second book of Enoch, HELL is located in the northern section of Shehaqim.

Source: Demy, *Answers to Common Questions About Heaven and Eternity*, 83; Vohs, *Am I Going to Heaven?*, 33–34

Sheol

According to Jewish Cabalists, there are seven levels to HELL; ALADDON, the GATES OF DEATH, GEBEANOM, the Mire of Clay, the PIT OF CORRUPTION, the SHADOW OF DEATH, and SHEOL.

These realms are set one atop the other; ordinary fire is one-sixtieth the heat of the fire of GEBEANOM which is one-sixtieth the heat of the GATES OF DEATH, which is one-sixtieth the heat of the SHADOW OF DEATH, which is one-sixtieth the heat of the PIT OF CORRUPTION, which is one-sixtieth the heat of the Mire of Clay, which is one-sixtieth the heat of ALADDON, which is one-sixtieth the heat of SHEOL.

Source: Brewer, *Dictionary of Phrase and Fable*, 596; Mew, *Traditional Aspects of Hell*, 173

Sid

Variations: Síd, Sidn, Síth

According to Norse mythology Sid was a river which originated from the droplets of water which fell off of the antlers of the hart, Eikthrynir, who stands atop the shield-roof of VALHALLA. Sid ran from HVERGELMIR to MIDGARD.

Source: Grimes, *Norse Myths*, 263, 296; Guerber, *Myths of the Norsemen*, 296

Sierra de la Plata

Said by the Guarani Indians to Spanish treasure hunters to be located deep in the forests of Brazil, Sierra de la Plata ("Silver Mountains") was a city ruled by a white king and abundantly rich with silver. The first reports of Sierra de la Plata came in 1515 but expeditions to discover it were never successful. In 1526 survivors of a shipwreck near Santa Caterina told their rescuers Sierra de la Plata was located "just up the river" and if they traveled there would be able to fill the hull of their ship with gold and silver; the city was never found. In the seventeenth century it was actively sought after by the Spanish but with met with no success.

Source: Magasich-airola, *America Magica,* 74, 89

Siglilnin

In Norse mythology, Siglilnin is the rocky hill upon the island in Lake AMSVARTNIR in NIFLEHEIM where Odin and the other Æsir bound the wolf Fenrir. At the time of Ragnarok Fenrir will break free and join the side of the giants.

Source: Grimes, *Norse Myths,* 78, 296; Guerber, *Myths of the Norsemen,* 299

Si'la

Variations: Island of the Si'la

An island in the sea of China, Si'la was reported by Arab geographers as being occupied by shaitans, cannibalistic demonic beings who were the offspring of humans and djinn.

Source: Hughes, *Dictionary of Islam,* 137

Silo, Isle of

According to John de Mandeville, a fourteenth century author and doctor, the Isle of Silo located in the Kingdom of PRESTER JOHN is home to two headed geese and white lions.

Source: de Camp, *Lands Beyond,* 153

Silver Clouds, Plain of the *see* Plain of the Silver Clouds

Sirat al-Jahim

Variations: al Sirat ("the Road")

In Islamic lore Sirat al-Jahim is a bridge that spans over HELL; it is described as having seven arches and its pathway is as thin as a hair and exceedingly sharp, akin to a razor's edge. Every soul who desires to go to HEAVEN must journey across this bridge; those without sin will be able to cross over easily while all others will fall into JAHANNAM.

Source: Hughes, *Dictionary of Islam,* 595; Netton, *Popular Dictionary of Islam,* 235

Sirenum Scopuli

According to the writings of the Roman poets Ovid and Virgil (*Aeneid,* book v.864) the Sirenum Scopuli there three small rocky islands and the home to the sirens of Greek mythology, creatures with the head of a woman and the body of a bird; the sirens would use their beautiful singing voices to lure sailors to turn their ships to their rocky shores and wreck their vessels.

Source: Addison, *Remarks on Several Parts of Italy,* 174; Carr, *Manual of Classical Mythology,* 364

Slid

Variations: Slíð, Slidr, Slíðr, Slith

A river of HEL in Norse Mythology, Slid ("Fearful"), runs from east to west through valleys of venom and near GIOLL and LEIPTER. It is full of knives, mud, and swords and the dead who are on their way to NIFLEHEIM have to wade through it.

Source: Anderson, *Norse Mythology,* 387; Grimes, *Norse Mythology,* 299

Slieve Gullion

In Irish mythology the mountain summit of Slieve Gullion is under the dominion of the fairy king, Cuilenn; within this realm is also the GREY LAKE OF CUILENN.

Source: Lincoln, *Death, War, and Sacrifice,* 56; Monaghan, *Encyclopedia of Celtic Mythology and Folklore,* 109

Sodom and Gomorrah

According to the biblical story of destruction told in the Old Testament (Genesis 18, 19) the cities of Sodom and Gomorrah were destroyed by God because He saw the cities as being filled with sin, although the specific sin is never named; an angelic messenger was sent to save the pious Lot who lived near Sodom who told the man to gather his family and flee into the mountains or run the risk of being destroyed by fire and flaming smoke. Lot did as he was instructed but his wife looked back at the destruction and was transformed into a pillar of salt. The Bible says at this time Bera was king of Sodom and Birsha was king of Gomorrah and these two kings, along with a few others, created an allegiance and made war upon their enemies; this collation failed.

Source: Beal, *Biblical Literacy*, 26–29; Piccardi, *Myth and Geology*, 134

Soequabeck

Variations: Soequabeck, Soequabkeck, Søkkaberkkr, Sökkvabekk, Sokkvabekkr, Sökkvabekkr, Sokvabek, Sökwabek, Soquabeck

In Norse mythology Soequabeck ("singing floor," "singing stream," or "sunken hall"), located in ASGARD, was the name of the crystal hall of the goddess of history and tradition, Saga; it was located one the sea where the waves broke against it. In this hall the god Odin would join Saga and drink mead with her from golden cups.

Source: Anderson, *Norse Mythology*, 458; Bennett, *Gods and Religions of Ancient and Modern Times*, Volume 1, 397; Dunham, *History of Denmark, Sweden, and Norway*, Volume 2, 55, 58; Guerber, *Myths of the Norsemen*, 299

Sokin

Variations: Sækin, SEKIN, Soekin, Sökin, Søkin

According to Norse mythology Sokin was one of rivers which ran from ASGARD to MIDGARD. It was created from the water dripping off of the antlers of Eikthryir as he stood atop the roof of VALHALLA eating leaves off YGGDRASYLL.

Source: Grimes, *Norse Myths*, 263; Guerber, *Myths of the Norsemen*, 13, 263

Soma-Loka

Variations: Somaloka

One of the eight regions of material existence in Hindu mythology, Soma-Loka ("World of Soma"), is the realm of the moon and the planets and its capitol city is called Somapura; it is ruled by the god Soma free from passions and sorrows. Those who live in this realm were those who in life always gave gifts but never received them, they were forgiving, hospitable, and never spoke ill of others.

Source: Dowson, *Classical Dictionary of Hindu Mythology and Religion*, 179; Wilson, *Vishṅu Puráṅa*, 186

Spring of Uppsah *see* Uppsah Spring

Strind

Variations: Strond

Strind was one of the nine rivers from Norse mythology which flow from MIDGARD to NIFLHEIM.

Source: Grimes, *Norse Myths* 13; Guerber, *Myths of the Norsemen*, 13

Strond

Variations: Sækin, Sekin, Soekin, Sökin, Søkin

According to Norse mythology Strond ("Border," "Coast," or "Edge") was one of the rivers which ran from MIDGARD to HEL.

Source: Guerber, *Myths of the Norsemen*, 299; Hamilton, *Spenser Encyclopedia*, 605

Styx (sticks)

The UNDERWORLD river of Greek mythology that bordered TARTARUS, the river Styx ("Hate") was named for the Titianess who is its presiding river-deity; it was given to her as a reward from the god Zeus, as she did not accompany the Titans when they fought against the Olympians. There are in all five rivers in HADES, the ACHERON ("Sorrow"), COCYTUS

("Lamentation"), LETHE ("Forgetfulness"), PYRIPHLEGETHON ("Fire"), and STYX ("Hate"); they form the boundary between upper and lower worlds.

Whenever one of the gods must make a sacred vow the messenger goddess Iris goes to TARTARUS and retrieves a vial of water from Styx; whoever vows upon it, the oath becomes inviolate. If the vow made was broken or done under false pretenses the god fell into a swoon for nine years; if after awakening they did not make good on the oath they were expelled from Olympus forever.

In the Roman telling of the pre-eminent Greek warrior of Troy, Achilles was the handsomest, most valiant, strongest, and swiftest person in his army; this was partially due to his mother being the divine nereid Thetis but also because shortly after his birth she dipped her child into the river Styx which rendered him invulnerable wherever the water touched his skin.

Source: Carr, *Manual of Classical Mythology*, 356; Evslin, *Gods, Demigods, and Demons*, n.p.; Hard, *Routledge Handbook of Greek Mythology*, 57, 456

Sucimukham

Variations: Sucimukha

According to Hindu and Vedic mythology Sucimukham is the twenty-eighth of the twenty-eight NARAKAS (HELLS) located in a providence in the kingdom of Yama. Here, those who in life were rich but miserly refusing to buy even the barest of necessities. Also, those who do not repay debts are found here. Here, these souls have thread stitched through their body similar to weavers making cloth.

Source: Parmeshwaranand, *Encyclopaedic Dictionary of Purāṇas*, 723

Sudarśana

Variations: Sudassana

The Sudarśana Mountains are the fifth mountain chain surrounding SUMERU, the central would mountain in in Hindu cosmology; it is both 5,000 *yojanas* tall and wide. The measure of a single *yojanas* has never been

clear, some scholars say it is approximately four and a half miles while other say it ranges between seven and nine miles.

Source: Howard, *Imagery of the Cosmological Buddha*, 66–68; Nagao, *Wisdom, Compassion, and the Search for Understanding*, 192

Sukara

Variations: Saukara

In Hindu mythology Sukara ("swine") is a partition in HELL (or *NARAKA*) ruled over by Yama; it is located beneath the earth and water where souls are punished for the sin of drinking wine, murdering a Brahma, or stealing gold. Also in this HELL is anyone who associated with anyone who committed any of these crimes.

Source: Wilson, *Oriental Translation Fund*, Volume 52, 208; Wilson, *Vishńu Puráńa*, 215–16

Sukaramukham

According to Hindu and Vedic mythology Sukaramukham is the eighth of the twenty-eight NARAKAS (HELLS) located in a providence in the kingdom of Yama; kings who neglected their duties and oppressed their subjects are found here. Souls here are crushed and beaten to a pulp; upon regaining consciousness and full recovery, the beatings continue.

Source: Prabhupāda, *Śrīmad Bhāgavatam*, 903; Parmeshwaranand, *Encyclopaedic Dictionary of Purāṇas*, 721

Sulaprotam

Variations: Sulaprota

According to Hindu and Vedic mythology Sulaprotam is the twenty-fourth of the twenty-eight NARAKAS (HELLS) located in a providence in the kingdom of Yama. Here those who have taken the lives of others who have done them no harm come to this NARAKAS. Each sinner is piked atop a trident and left there for the duration of their stay, suffering with intense hunger and thirst.

Source: Parmeshwaranand, *Encyclopaedic Dictionary of Purāṇas*, 722

Sumeru

Variations: Kangrinboqe, Meru, Pāli Neru, Sineru

The central world mountain in Buddhist cosmology Sumeru, ("excellent Meru" or "wonderful Meru") similar to Mount MERU, stands 80,000 *yojanas* tall according to Vasubandhu's *Abhidharmakośabhāṣyam*. Sumeru also descends an additional 80,000 *yojanas* beneath the surface of the earth and resting upon a layer of basal; shaped like an hourglass, the middle section of the mountain is about 20,000 *yojanas* square. The measure of a single *yojanas* has never been clear, some scholars say it is approximately four and a half miles while other say it ranges between seven and nine miles.

The square base of Sumeru is surrounded by an ocean which is surrounded by a wall of mountains, which is surrounded by another sea; in all there are seven seas and seven walls, each reduces in height and width as they near Sumeru (see AŚVAKARṆA, IṢADHARA, KHADIRAKA, NIMINDHARA, SUDARŚANA, VINADHARA, and YUGANDHARA). The outermost sea contains the continent of JAMBUDVIPA; it lies due south of Sumeru.

Source: Howard, *Imagery of the Cosmological Buddha*, 66–68; Nagao, *Wisdom, Compassion, and the Search for Understanding*, 192; Sadakata, *Buddhist Cosmology*, 26–27

Summer, Land of *see* Land of Summer

Summer Land

Variations: Summer Country

An OTHERWORLD from British mythology, Summer Land was described as always having flowers in bloom, fruit ripe and ready to eat off the trees, and nice weather. In some Arthurian texts, Summer Land was used to describe the home of the ogre Meleagant, the beast who held Queen Guinevere hostage until she was rescued by Sir Lancelot.

Source: Monaghan. *Encyclopedia of Celtic Mythology and Folklore*, 433

Sutala, Caverns of

In Hindu lore the Caverns of Sutala are believed to be the third of the seven underground levels in a vast cavernous system which stretches from Benares, India to Lake Manosarowar, Tibet. In all of the regions (ATALA, MAHATALA, PATALA, RASATALA, TALATALA and VITALA), there are beautiful cities built by the architect, Maya.

Source: Daniélou, *Myths and Gods of India*, 308; Parmeshwaranand, *Encyclopaedic Dictionary of Purāṇas*, 1010–1012

Svol

According to Norse mythology Svol was one of rivers which ran from ASGARD to MIDGARD. It was created from the water dripping off of the antlers of Eikthryir as he stood atop the roof of VALHALLA eating leaves off YGGDRASYLL.

Source: Grimes, *Norse Myths*, 263; Guerber, *Myths of the Norsemen*, 13, 263

Swabhojana

In Hindu mythology Swabhojan ("where they feed upon dogs") is a partition in HELL (or NARAKA) ruled over by Yama; it is located beneath the earth and water where souls are punished for the sin of being an adult who is given religious instructions by a child or was a religious student who fell asleep during the day and though unaware, was defiled.

Source: Wilson, *Oriental Translation Fund*, Volume 52, 209; Wilson, *Vishńu Puráńa*, 215–16

Swarga

Variations: Svarga, Swarga Loka

In Hindu cosmology, Swarga is one of the LOKA set above Mount MERU; it is a PARADISE where the righteous live before their next reincarnation. Swarga is ruled over by the god Indra; its capital is called AMARVAVTI, the gardens are known as NANDANA, and the palace is known as VAIJAYANTA.

Source: Chaturvedi, *Shiv Purana*, 124; Source: Dowson, *Classical Dictionary of Hindu Mythology and Religion*, 127

Swartalfaheim

Variations: Svart-alfa-heim, Svartálfaheim, Svartálfaheimr, Svartalffheim, Svartalfheimr, Svartalffheimr, Svartheim, Svarttalf-heimr

In Norse mythology, Swartalfaheim ("Dusk Alf Land"), one of the NINE WORLDS, was the home of the black dwarfs, or elves, and the spirits of darkness.

Source: Dunham, *History of Denmark, Sweden, and Norway*, Volume 53; Grimes, *Norse Myths*, 300; Keightly, *World Guide to Gnomes, Fairies, Elves, and Other Little People*, 68

Symplegades (sim-PLEG-uh-deez)

Variations: Blue Symplegades, CLASHING ROCKS, Cyaneae, Cyanei Montes, Insulae Cyaneae, Planctae, WANDERING ROCKS

Located at the entrance to Hellespont, Symplegades were the rocks which clashed together whenever a ship would try to pass between them; only the Argo, the vessel of Jason and the Argonauts, was able to make it through having lost only the tip of its stern. It is possible Symplegades is also the CLASHING ROCKS or WANDERING ROCKS mentioned in *The Odyssey*. Homer describes an azure cloud resting upon on of the rocks.

Source: Carr, *Manual of Classical Mythology*, 189, 282; Evans, *Dictionary of Mythology*, 244–45

Taenarum (TEE-nuh-rum)

An entrance to the Greek UNDERWORLD, Taenarum was said to be located in a cave in a peninsula of southern Greece. Taenarum was the entranceway chosen by Theseus and his cohort Peirithous when they attempted to abduct Persephone from Hades, the king of the dead. At the mouth of Taenarum the three headed canine guardian Cerberus guards the entranceway into the underworld; the dog was taken by the demigod Hercules and delivered to the court of King Euruystheus for his Twelfth Labor. Taenarum was also the site here the lyre player Arion was thrown into the ocean and rescued by a pod of dolphins. The Argonaut Euphemus was from the area of Taenarum.

Source: Daly, *Greek and Roman Mythology A to Z*, 238; Westmoreland, *Ancient Greek Beliefs*, 238, 692

Takama-ga-Hara

Variations: Takama-no-Har, Takamanohara

In ancient Shinto beliefs Takama-ga-Har ("High Plain of HEAVEN") was the dwelling place of the most eminent *kami* (the sacred spirits worshiped in Shinto); located in the sky, it was once connected to the earth by the floating bridge AMA-NO-UKI-HASHI. It is connected to ASHIHARA-NO-NAKATSUKUNI and YOMI by an axis called *ame no mihashira*.

Source: Ono, *Shinto*, 102; Picken, *Historical Dictionary of Shinto*, 293; Roberts, *Japanese Mythology A to Z*, 4

Takánakapsâlik

According to Inuit belief Takánakapsâlik is where the souls of the deceased who committed antisocial acts and ignored ritual prescriptions. Here, the Sea Spirit who has dominion over this realm may choose to send the spirit to another location or keep it captive forever.

Source: Leenaars, *Suicide in Canada*, 197

Tala

In Hindu mythology Tala ("Padlock") is a partition in HELL (*Naraka*) ruled over by Yama; it is located beneath the earth and water where souls are punished for the sin of committing adultery with the wife of his spiritual teacher or murdering a man of the second or third castes.

Source: Wilson, *Oriental Translation Fund*, Volume 52, 208; Wilson, *Vishńu Puráńa*, 215–16

Talatala, Caverns of

Variations: Talataala

In Hindu lore the Caverns of Talatals are believed to be the fourth of the seven underground levels in a vast cavernous system which stretches from Benares, India to Lake Manosarowar, Tibet. In all of the regions (ATALA, MAHATALA, PATALA, RASATALA, SUTALA and VITALA), there are beautiful cities built by the architect, Maya.

Source: Hastings, *Encyclopedia of Religion and Ethics*, Part 7, 160; Parmeshwaranand, *Encyclopaedic Dictionary of Purāṇas*, 1010–1012

Tamas

In Hindu mythology, Tamas ("darkness") is the third of the twenty-eight NARAKAS (HELLS) located in a providence in the kingdom of Yama; it is filled with the instruments of torture. Here, sinners experience the pains brought on by extreme cold, darkness, hunger, and thirst. A hailstorm known as Drihthelm breaks the bones of those condemned here, pressing out their blood and marrow.

Source: Becker, *Contribution to the Comparative Study of the Medieval Visions of Heaven and Hell*, 14; Wilson, *Vishńu Puráńa*, 215–16

Tamchok Khabab

In Hindu mythology Tamchok Khabab ("River from the Horse's Mouth") is one of the four rivers which runs out of MAPHAM YUMT-SHO, the lake located at the bottom of Mount MERU; it flows to the east.

Source: McCue, *Trekking in Tibet*, 207

Tamisra

Variations: Tamisram

According to Hindu and Vedic mythology Tamisra ("the darkness") is one of the twenty-eight NARAKAS (HELLS) located in a providence in the kingdom of Yama; it is filled with the instruments of torture; those who go to this HELL have stolen another property or woman. Here, sinner will be so severely beaten by the servants of Yama they may lose consciousness. A more deadly section to this Narakas is called Andha-Tamisra; it is reserved for those who rape their parton or their mentor's wife.

Source: Chaturvedi, *Devi Bhagwat Purana*, 90; Prabhupāda, *Śrīmad Bhāgavatam*, 903; Parmeshwaranand, *Encyclopaedic Dictionary of Purāṇas*, 721

Tapana

Variations: Tapa

In to Indian Buddhism, Tapana ("Hot") is the sixth of the EIGHT HOT HELLS; it is known as the Burning Hell; it is reserved for those who cling to and propagate falsehoods which they then use to rationalize their actions. Here the servants of Yama impale sinners with fiery spears until flames spout from their mouths and nostrils. The heat of Tapana is 16 times greater than it is in the previous HELL, MAHARAURAVA. A soul's stay in this NARAKAS (HELLS) is $5,308,416*10^{10}$ years long.

Source: Alexander, *Body, Mind, Spirit Miscellany*, 150; Dowson, *Classical Dictionary of Hindu Mythology and Religion*, 220; Mew, *Traditional Aspects of Hell*, 38–41

Tapar-Loka

Variations: Tapa-Loka, Tapaloka

One of the eight regions of heavenly existence in Hindu mythology, Tapar-Loka, is the heavenly home where the deities called Vairagis reside. In the seven spheres of the earth, Tapar-Loak is the sixth.

Source: Dowson, *Classical Dictionary of Hindu Mythology and Religion*, 179; Garrett, *Classical Dictionary of India*, 635; Wilson, *Vishńu Puráńa*, 48

Taptakumbha

In Hindu mythology Taptakumbha ("the HELL of heated cauldrons") is a partition in HELL (or NARAKA) ruled over by Yama; it is located beneath the earth and water where souls are punished for the sin of incestuous intercourse with his sister or murdering an ambassador. Sinners here are thrown headfirst into jars filled with boiling oil and iron dust. Skulls and bones instantly burst asunder, mangled limbs are devoured by vultures, and demons stir the liquid-soul concoction.

Source: Becker, *Contribution to the Comparative Study of the Medieval Visions of Heaven and Hell*, 14; Wilson, *Oriental Translation Fund*, Volume 52, 208; Wilson, *Vishńu Puráńa*, 215–16

Taptaloha

In Hindu mythology Taptaloha ("red-hot iron hell") is a partition in HELL (or NARAKA) ruled over by Yama; it is located beneath the earth and water where souls are punished for the sin of deserting his adherents, being a horse dealer, a jailer, or selling his wife.

Source: Parks, *Bibliotheca Sacra and American Biblical Repository*, Volume 15, 867; Wilson, *Oriental Translation Fund*, Volume 52, 208

Taptamurti

According to Hindu and Vedic mythology Taptamurti is the eleventh of the twenty-eight NARAKAS (HELLS) located in a providence in the kingdom of Yama; this HELL is reserved for those who plunder other's gold, jewels, money, and ornaments. Here, sinners are cast into iron furnaces which are always glowing red hot from their roaring fires.

Source: Parmeshwaranand, *Encyclopaedic Dictionary of Purāṇas*, 721

Taptasurmi

According to Hindu and Vedic mythology Taptasurmi is one of the HELLS (or *NARAKA*) created by Yama; it is reserved for those who have sexual intercourse with an unworthy member of the opposite sex. Offenders are beaten with whips and are forced to embrace a red-hot iron image of the illicit lover.

Source: Dange, *Bhāgavata Purāṇa*, 129; Prabhupāda, *Śrīmad Bhāgavatam*, 903

Tartarus

Variations: Tartaruchus, Tartaros ("deep place")

A realm appearing in both Greek and Roman as well as in the Old Testament, Tartarus is a fiery, Hell-like place where sinners are sent to be tormented.

In Greek mythology, Tartarus was a part of HADES, which also contains the ELYSIAN FIELDS; it was said to be a deep and gloomy pit located deep beneath the surface of the earth, a approximately 4733.22 miles deep, according to the calculations of the Greek poet Hesiod. The realm was encircled by a river of fire called PYRIPHLEGETHON. Plato wrote in the Socratic dialogue *Gorgias* (380 BC that souls were judged after death and those in need of punishment were sent to Tartarus.

There were three judges; Aeacus judged European souls, Minos was the deciding vote and judge of the Greek, and Rhadamanthus judged Asian souls. In addition to the souls who were sent here, many of the Titians were imprisoned here by the god Zeus; the prisoners were watched over by the Hecatonchires, three giants of incredible ferocity and strength.

There is also a deity named Tartarus in Greek mythology; he was the third force to manifest in the yawning void of Chaos.

In Roman mythology Tartarus was a place of punishment for the most evil of sinners; the Roman poet Virgil (70 BC–19 BC describes it as being very large, surrounded by the flaming river Phlegethon (see PYRIPHLEGETHON) and three wall; additionally it is guarded by a fifty-headed hydra who sits atop a gate surrounded by columns of solid adamantine.

In most translations of the bible, the word HELL is used to refer to the fiery place of punishment. The word Tartarus is found only once in the bible, in 2 Peter 2:4; there it said that God threw the angels who defied Him "into Tartarus, delivered them into pits of dense darkness to be reserved for judgment." The Book of Encoh, chapter 20 verse two says Tartarus is where God put the angels who cohabited with human women from Genesis six.

Source: Daly, *Greek and Roman Mythology, A to Z*, 137; Evans, *Dictionary of Mythology*, 248; Roman, *Encyclopedia of Greek and Roman Mythology*, 458–59

Tartessos

Variations: Tarshish

Said to be a very rich city located in the extreme west of Europe Tartessos was situated on the mouth of a large river but not near the seashore; much of their trade, primarily minerals, involved sailing. Little is known about the city itself except that it flourished for a long time and its main building was towering down from a hill top. Its temple to Hercules had two wells, one cold and one warm. The city nearest to Tartessos was Gades.

Many Atlantists—people who search for the lost city of ATLANTIS—claim that Tartessos was a colony of Atlantis, as much of what is known of it comes from the writings of the ancient Greeks such as Herodotus, Plato, and Strabo. Tartessos has been sought after in Sardinia and southwestern Spain.

Source: Forsyth, *Atlantis*, 102–04; Sprague de Camp, *Lands Beyond*, 41–42

Te Uranga-o-te-rā

The fifth lowest of the UNDERWORLDS in Maori mythology, Te Uranga-o-te-rā ("place at which the sun arrives") is ruled over by the goddess Rohe, the wife of the god Māui.

Source: Andersen, *Maori Life in Ao-tea*, 570; White, *Ancient History of the Maori*, 56

Tech Duinn

The land of the dead in Irish folklore Tech Duinn ("House of Donn") was described as a frightening place of darkness and dread; Donn was an UNDERWORLD god of death by drowning. Tech Duinn was the name of a rock island near the south-west of Ireland and was seen as being a meeting place for the dead.

Source: Maier, *Dictionary of Celtic Religion and Culture*, 262; Monaghan, *Encyclopedia of Celtic Mythology and Folklore*, 443

Tentagil

Variations: Tintagel, Tintagil

According to the Arthurian lore of Sir Thomas Malory's *Morte d'Arthur* (1485), castle Tentagil was the location where Uther Pendragon begot Arthur with Lady Igraine.

Source: Evans, *Dictionary of Mythology*, 250; Malory, *Le Morte Darthur*, 4, 5

Terabil, Castle

Variations: Castle Terrible, Dunheved Castle

In Arthurian lore the castle Terabil ("Terrible") was said to be in Launceston, Cornwall, ten miles from Tintagel; it was described as having a steep keep and a triple wall.

Source: Cooper, *Brewer's Book of Myth and Legend*, 48; Robbins, *Notes and Queries*, 41

Terra Australis

Terra Australis ("South Land") was a land mass assumed to exist by philosophers because they found it impossible to believe that a globe weighted down on top could maintain its equilibrium; therefore they placed it in the southern hemisphere; it appeared on European maps between the fifteenth and eighteenth centuries.

Source: Sprague de Camp, *Lands Beyond*, 191; Wilford, *The Mapmakers*, 139

Terrestrial Paradise

Commonly associated with gardens, such as the GARDEN OF EDEN, the terrestrial paradise is symbolic of heavenly order, an arcadian past, and a lost golden age. The Hereford map of the thirteenth century actually places the Terrestrial Paradise near India and draws it as a circular island. Not only is the island cut off from the mainland by the sea but also a battlement wall with one entranceway located in the west.

Source: Gould, *Curious Myths of the Middle Ages*, 234; Livingstone, *Geography and Enlightenment*, 67

Themiscyra

Said to be located at the mouth of the Thermodon River, Themiscyra was, according to the ancient Greek Historian Diodorus, founded by the Amazons who built a city on the Plains of Themiscyra which developed into a powerful kingdom. Eventually the nation was conquered by Hercules and his companions; the surviving Amazons were taken captive and loaded onto sailing vessels. While at sea, the Amazons rose up and slew every man on board to the last. Lacking the knowledge of navigation they floated adrift until they landed upon Cremni.

Source: Anthon, *Classical Dictionary*, 1313; Smith, *New Classical Dictionary of Greek and Roman Biography, Mythology and Geography*, Volume 2, 879

Thjodnuma

Thjodnuma ("Sweeping People Away") was

one of the nine rivers from Norse mythology which flow from MIDGARD to NIFLHEIM.

Source: Guerber, *Myths of the Norsemen*, 13; Sturlusonar, *Prose Edda of Snorri Sturluson*, 65

Tholl

According to Norse mythology Tholl was one of sixteen rivers which ran from ASGARD to MIDGARD.

Source: Guerber, *Myths of the Norsemen*, 13; Sturlusonar, *Prose Edda of Snorri Sturluson*, 65

Thrinakia

Variations: Isle Thrinakia, Island of Thrinakie, Thrinakie

In *The Odyssey* (xii, 127–131) Thrinakia was named as the small island location of the 350 immortal cattle that belonged to the god, Helios; the two nymphs and daughters of Helios, Lampetia and Phaethousa, tended the herd.

Source: Hard, *Routledge Handbook of Greek Mythology*, 44, 497; Sprague de Camp, *Lands Beyond*, 69–70

Thrudeim

Variations: Thrudheim ("Plains of Power"), Thrudheimr, Thrudvang, Thrudvangar, Thrudvangue, Thrudwang

The realm of the Norse god of thunder, Thor, Thrudeim ("Strength World") is located in the space between ASGARD and the earth; his home was called BILSKINIR.

Source: Crossley-Holland, *Norse Myths*, 251; Daly, *Norse Mythology A to Z*, 106; Dunham, *History of Denmark, Sweden, and Norway*, Volume 2, 55; Sturluson, *Younger Edda*, 50

Thrymheim

In Norse mythology Thrymheim ("Din World") located in ASGARD, was the home of the giants Skada (Skadi) and her father, Thjass (Thjazi). After Thjass died, Skada married Niörd (Njord) and the couple spent nine nights in Thrymheim and then nine nights in NOATUN, Niörd's residence. Subsequently the marriage broke up and Skada returned to her mountain home of Thrymheim.

Source: Bennett, *Gods and Religions of Ancient*

and Modern Times, Volume 1, 398; Dunham, *History of Denmark, Sweden, and Norway*, Volume 2, 55

Thule

Variations: Thila, Thoule, Thula, Thyïlea, Tile, Ultima Thule, Tyle

The northern most named location in the world of the ancient Greeks, very little is known about Thule due to its remoteness. The Greek explore and geographer, Pytheas, claimed the remote island of Thule lay six days sailing north of Britain. Pytheas traveled to Thule and wrote in his book, "About the Ocean," the nights there were only two or three hours long and in the summer time there was no nighttime at all. After the writing of Pytheas, no other Greek or Roman author learned anything more about Thule and these later writes, such as Strabo, doubted its existence. Thule began to take on a symbolic resonance representing the most distant region an explorer could travel.

Source: Cunliffe, *Extraordinary Voyage of Pytheas the Greek*, 126, 132; Romm, *Edges of the Earth in Ancient Thought*, 158, 198; Sprague de Camp, *Lost Continents*, 57

Thviti

Variations: Thvite, Tvit, Tviti

In Norse mythology, Thviti (Thwacker") is the boulder with is set deep into the earth to which Fenris Wolf (Fenriswulf) is bound to with the fetters, Gelgia. The other end of the fetters is bound to the rock, GIOLL.

Source: Grimes, *Norse Myths*, 303; Guerber, *Myths of the Norsemen*, 93

Thyn

According to Norse mythology Thyn ("Frothing") was one of sixteen rivers which ran from ASGARD to MIDGARD.

Source: Grimes, *Norse Myths*, 303; Guerber, *Myths of the Norsemen*, 13; Sturlusonar, *Prose Edda of Snorri Sturluson*, 65

Tír Fa Tonn

Variations: Tir fo Thuinn, Tìr fo Thonn

A FAIRYLAND or UNDERWORLD in Irish mythology, Tír Fa Tonn ("Land under the Waves"), was a land under a lake where mermaids and mermen resided.

Source: Hastings, *Encyclopædia of Religion and Ethics*, Volume 2, 609; Monaghan, *Encyclopedia of Celtic Mythology and Folklore*, 449

Tir-Innambeo

Under the rule of Fairy King Manannan, Tir-Innambeo ("The Land of the Living") was a beautiful and peaceful place; its inhabitants were principally women who lured away by noble men and youths by use of their love for them.

Source: Evan-Wentz, *Fairy Faith in Celtic Countries*, 334, 353

Tir na mBan

Variations: Tir na Ban

One of the many names given to the OTHERWORLD in Irish mythology, Tir na mBan ("Land of Women") was a FLOATING ISLAND ruled over by various fairy queens.

Source: Monaghan, *Encyclopedia of Celtic Mythology and Folklore*, 348; Mountain, *Celtic Encyclopedia*, Volume 5, 1339

Tir na nÓg (Teer nahn Ock)

Variations: Tir na nÓg, Tir-No-Nog

A FAIRYLAND or OTHERWORLD of Irish mythology, Tir na nÓg ("Land of Youth") was believed to be an island far off in the West.

Source: Monaghan, *Encyclopedia of Celtic Mythology and Folklore*, 347; Mountain, *Celtic Encyclopedia*, Volume 5, 1339

Tir-Na-Nog

Variations: Tir na nÓg, Tir-No-Nog

Tir na Nog ("Land of the Youth") was one of the many names given to the OTHERWORLD in Irish mythology; it is often confused with FAIRYLAND because this is the place where the Tuatha de Danann retreated to when they left this world; one sees nothing but harmony and beautiful forms there.

Source: Evan-Wentz, *Fairy Faith in Celtic Countries*, 334; Monaghan, *Encyclopedia of Celtic Mythology and Folklore*, 449

Tír Sorcha (cheer sor-achd)

Home of the Irish goddess Fand, Tír sorcha ("Land of Bliss" or "Shining Land") is where she lured the hero, Cuchulainn, with a promise of marriage, stealing him away from his wife Emer and concubine Ethne Ingubai.

Source: Arbois de Jubainville, *Irish Mythological Cycle and Celtic Mythology*, 183–84; Hastings, *Encyclopædia of Religion and Ethics*, Volume 2, 689

Tir Tairngiri

Variations: Tir-Rairngire, Tìr Tairnigir

The realm of the beautiful fairy queen, Niamh of Irish lore, Tir Tairngiri ("Land of Promise") was a small but ideal island having beautiful people, endlessly fruiting trees, and perfect weather.

Source: Hastings, *Encyclopædia of Religion and Ethics*, Volume 2, 689; Monaghan, *Encyclopedia of Celtic Mythology and Folklore*, 449

Titahion

Variations: Tit ha Yon ("Pit of Mire")

In Cabalistic lore Titahion ("Clay of Death") is the third (or fourth, sources conflict) of the seven HELLS.

Source: Greer, *New Encyclopedia of the Occult*, 488; Mathers, *Sorcerer and His Apprentice*, 24

Tlalocan

In Aztec mythology, Tlalocan ("Place of Tlaloc") was the heavenly PARADISE of the rain god Tlaloc; it was the place where the souls of those who died of Edema, lightning strike, physical disabilities, skin diseases, and sacrifices to Tlaloc went. Tlalocan was described as being filled with flowers and peaceful, its occupants passing the time with dancing, game play, and singing. After four years, the souls here returned to earth.

Source: Bingham, *South and Meso-American Mythology A to Z*, 126; Leon-Portilla, *Aztec Thought and Culture*, 125

Tokoyo-no-kumi

In ancient Shinto beliefs Tokoyo-no-kumi ("Land of the Mother") was the UTOPIAN world in which the purified spirits of the dead resided; those spirits that were impure went to the realm known as YOMI. Descriptions of Tokoyo-no-kumi are contradictory and vague at best but it is a land of eternal youth, not to be confused with YOMI, the land of the polluted dead.

Source: Bonnefoy, *Asian Mythologies*, 271; Picken, *Historical Dictionary of Shinto*, 302

Tomoanchan

Variations: the Land of Black and Red Ink, Tamoanchan

An Aztec PARADISE and supreme HEAVEN Tomoanchan is ruled over by the skeletal goddess Itzpapalotl. The god Quetzalcotal gathers up the bones of the dead and taking them to this realm gives them to his consort, Quilaztli; she takes the bones and grinds them up, placing the powder in sacred clay jars. Quetzalcotal would then offer a small blood sacrifice from himself pouring the libation over the ground bones; this would cause the people to be reborn back onto the earth.

Source: Leon-Portilla, *Aztec Thought and Culture*, 110–11; Moreno, *Handbook to Life in the Aztec World*, 7

Tonatiuhilhuicac

Variations: Chichihuacuaucho ("Orchard of the Gods")

In Aztec mythology, Tonatiuhilhuicac was a glorious HEAVEN for the fortunate souls who died in battle, women who died in childbirth (as they had a prisoner in their womb), and those who were offered up as a human sacrifice. This HEAVEN was said to be located in the western part of the sky.

Tonatiuhilhuicac was described as having an abundant landscape; of particular note were the trees whose branches grew breasts in order to wet-nurse the infants who died before they were weaned from their mothers. Some texts say after the child is able to be weaned

from the tree it will be reborn to a new mother while others claim they will be the people who will repopulate the earth after everyone else has been destroyed.

Source: Leon-Portilla, *Aztec Thought and Culture*, 126; Moreno, *Handbook to Life in the Aztec World*, 163

Tower of Babel *see* Babel, Tower of

Tree of Zaqqam *see* Zaqqam, Tree of

Trespasses, Bay of *see* Bay of Trespasses

Tuat

Variations: Tiaou, Tiau

An UNDERWORLD in Egyptian mythology Tuat is traditionally considered to be a place of rebirth; it is divided into twelve parts, one for each hour of the night; these divisions are called cities, fields, or *sekhet*. Originally neither a HEAVEN nor a HELL, Tuat was the place where the sun go, Ra passed through each evening on his journey to arise again in the eastern sky.

Tuat, unlike many other UNDERWORLDS, was not located beneath the earth but likely in the sky near the HEAVENS. Separated from our world by a mountain chain, it consisted of a valley surrounded by mountains; the mountains on one side divided Tuat from earth and the mountains on the other side divided it from the HEAVENS. Through the valley of Tuat runs a river and along the banks live devils, feinds, and monstrous beings of every shape and size.

Source: Budge, *Gods of the Egyptians*, Volume 1, 170–71, 176

Tuonela (tuo'-nay-la)

Variations: MANALA, Toonela

Tuonela is an OTHERWORLD, according to Estonian mythology where children and innocent people go to after death; it is ruled over by the god Tuoni. The descriptions of Tuonela vary greatly due to the cultural influence upon the Finnish people. In the nineteenth century epic poem compiled from folklore by compiled by Elias Lönnrot, *Kalevala*, Tuonela is surrounded by a river and the Maiden of Tuonela (Tuonen Piika or Tuonen Tytti) must ferry the dead across it. Life for the deceased here is very much as it was on earth, the dead even needing to drink, eat, and wear clothes.

Source: Eivind, *Finnish Legends for English Children*, xv; Pentikäinen, *Kalevala Mythology*, 206–07, 262

Turiruna

In the mythology of the Tiwi people there are four layers which make up the universe, ILARA, the subterranean world, the earth, JUWUKU the sky world, and the upper world known as Turiruna.

Source: Mountford, *The Tiwi*, 170

Turning, Island of

Variations: FLOATING ISLAND

In the ancient Greek story of Jason and the Argonauts, when the heroes arrived on the island of SALMYDESSUS they were meet by King Phineus, a man tormented daily by the harpies, cruel creatures half bird and half woman. Two of the Argonauts, Calais and Zetes, were descendants of the god of the North wind, Boreas, and had the ability of flight so they chased the harpies far, far, away. Eventually the weary creature landed on FLOATING ISLAND, but before the Argonauts could slay them the goddess Iris intervened and solicited a promise from the creatures never again to return to SALMYDESSUS. Thereafter FLOATING ISLAND's name was changed to the Island of Turning.

Source: Colum, *Golden Fleece and the Heroes Who Lived Before Achilles*, 51; Flaum, *Encyclopedia of Mythology*, 163

Twenty-Eight Hell Planets *see* **Hell Planets, Twenty-Eight**

Two Truths, Hall of *see* **Hall of Two Truths**

Tzelmoth

In Cabalistic lore Tzelmoth ("Shadow of Death") is the second (or fifth, sources conflict) of the seven HELLS.

Source: Greer, *New Encyclopedia of the Occult*, 495; Mathers, *Sorcerer and His Apprentice*, 24

Uca Pacha

In Incan mythology evil people would spend their afterlife in Uca Pacha ("Lower Earth"), a realm located at the center of the earth where there was constant cold, hunger, and pain. It was possible to avoid this fate if before death a person confessed their sins to a priest and did penance.

Source: Roza, *Incan Mythology and Other Myths of the Andes*, 17

Ulu- ka'a

Variations: Uala-ka'a

In the mythology of the Pacific Islands, Uluka'a was the FLOATING ISLAND of the gods; however in the story of Anelike it is an island of women that was reached one day by a young man who taught them how to cook food and later wed their chieftain.

Source: Beckwith, *Hawaiian Mythology*, 72; Craig, *Dictionary of Polynesian Mythology*, 86

Under the Waves, Land of *see* **Land Under the Waves**

Underworld

Most of the world's myths and religions include an existence beyond death that extends into an afterlife. While some mythologies describe this realm of the dead as being very similar to the world of the living others paint a grimmer picture of dark and gloomy pits where malcontent beings dwell. In many cases this realm is described as being somewhere up in the sky and described as a HEAVEN or PARADISE reserved for the gods or "good" souls whereas somewhere deep beneath the earth is an underworld for, at best, those condemned to eternal nothingness or in more extreme cases, is a HELL-like dimension filled with demonic beings to punish those who were "evil" during life.

Typically the underworld is described as being located beneath the surface of the earth, such as down into a cave, beneath the waves of the ocean, or under a mountain; common features include a ruling king or queen and indigenous spirits. In Western lore it is a common theme in heroic tales to have the hero descend into the underworld to achieve a goal, such as gaining knowledge, retrieving a loved one, or becoming immortal; it is common for the hero to fail in his quest. In many religions, especially Christian based one; the underworld is a place of damnation and suffering.

Source: Lewis, *Satanism Today*, 68; Stookey, *Thematic Guide to World Mythology*, 1–2

Underworld, Greek Rivers of the

In Greek mythology there are five rives of the UNDERWORLD: ACHERON the River of Woe or Sadness ("Grief-Flowing"), COCYTUS the river of lamentation ("to Weep"), LETHE the river of forgetfulness ("Black Oblivion"), PHLEGETHON the river of fire ("to burn"), and STYX the river of hate ("Loathe"); all of these rivers converge in a great marsh and work to keep separate the world of the living from the UNDERWORLD.

Source: Brewer, *Dictionary of Phrase and Fable*, 596; Daly, *Greek and Roman Mythology, A to Z*, 2, 34, 87, 145

Uppsah Spring

Variations: Urðarbrunnr Spring

The Norns of Norse mythology took the *aurr* (a mixture of ground gravel and water) from the Uppsah Spring to wash YGGDRASIL with in order to stave off decay.

Source: Anderson, *Norse Mythology*, 460; Grimes, *Norse Myths*, 305

Uppsala

Variations: Uppsalir

Uppsala is the land in MIDGARD where the god Freyr lives when he is not staying at ALF-HEIM.

Source: Grimes, *Norse Myths*, 305

Uranga-o-Te-Ra

The sixth lowest of the UNDERWORLDS in Maori mythology, Uranga-o-Te-Ra is ruled over by the goddess Rohe, the wife of the god Māui.

Source: Andersen, *Maori Life in Ao-tea*, 592

Urdarbrunnr Well

Variations: Urard Fountain, Urdbrunner ("Urd Fountain"), Urdar Well, Urd's Well, Uroarbrunnr, Well of the Weird

In Norse mythology, Urdarbrunnr Well is one of the three wells which nourish the ash tree, YGGDRASIL. Located in ASGARD, the waters of both HVERGELMIR and MIMIRSBRUNNR flow into it, making this the most sacred of the three wells; any item or person who was submerged into its water came out covered in a sacred white film. Urdarbrunnr supplied YGGDRASIL with its live giving energy allowing the tree to survive all of the continuous assaults upon it.

Source: Anderson, *Norse Mythology*, 460; Bennett, *Gods and Religions of Ancient and Modern Times*, Volume 1, 399; Guerber, *Myths of the Norsemen*, 15

Uruk

Variations: Rainbow City, Tiranna

In Sumerian mythology Uruk ("cattle pen" or "sheepfold") was the mythological capital city of the hero Gilgamesh; other kings include Enmerkar and Lugalbanda. The patrol deities of Uruk were the god Anu and the goddess Ishtar; Anu had a temple here called EANNA, it sat atop a ziggurat that he would stay in during her rare visits to earth.

Source: Chopra, *Academic Dictionary of Mythology*, 119, 239; Dalley, *Myths from Mesopotamia*, 330

Utgard

Variations: Utgaroa

In Norse mythology, Utgard ("Outer Yard"), one of the NINE WORLDS, lay beyond the vast sea and was the home to the giants. The worlds of MIDGARD and Utgard run parallel to one

Uthlanga

another. Utgard is also the name of the abode of the giant, Utgard-Loke.

Source: Anderson, *Norse Mythology*, 460; Dunham, *History of Denmark, Sweden, and Norway*, Volume 52

Uthlanga

Among the Kaffir tribes of Africa, Uthlanga ("Reed") is the primeval birthplace. Although its location is unknown, Uthlanga is described as looking like a land of reeds. The Basutos identify Uthlanga as a cavern located within the earth that is surrounded by a sea of reeds. It is not uncommon for the aristocracy to claim to be a descendant of the Uthlanga.

Source: Hastings, *Encyclopedia of Religion and Ethics*, Part 3, 364; Massey, *Ancient Egypt, the Light of the World*, 255

Utopia

Variations: Eutopia ("good place"), Outopia ("no place")

The novel, *Utopia* (1516), written by Sir Thomas More (1478–1535) an author, English lawyer, noted Renaissance humanist, social philosopher, and statesman depicted a fictional island with its own very unique customs and religion; here, More introduced to his readers the concept of a perfect society with perfect—utopian—beliefs and ideals.

Since publication of More's *Utopia*, the word *utopia* ("nowhere") has come to mean any place of idealized perfection, weather it refers to a regions climate and topography or to a society social structure with people behaving harmoniously with regards to culture, politics, religion, and secular activities.

As a colloquial, *utopia* means a good and idealized but non-existent society. Plato, the mathematician and philosopher of classical Greece, wrote perhaps the first utopian society in his *Republic* in the fourth century, BCE; in it he describes a Spartan utopia where childbirth is controlled by eugenics, good sand women are commonly owned, philosophers rule, slavery is taken for granted, and where there is no art, no dramas and very little poetry. Other authors and their utopian societies

are Johannes Valentinus Andreae's *Christianopolis* (1619), Francis Bacon's *New Atlantis* (1626), James Harrington's *Oceana*, (1656), and Thomas Hobbes's *Leviathan* (1651) to name but a few.

Source: Cuddon, *Dictionary of Literary Terms and Literary Theory*, 750; Levitas, *Concept of Utopia*, 1–7

Utpala

The sixth of the eight cold NARAKA (HELLS) named in Buddhism, Urpapa ("blue lotus") is described as being so cold the skin of its occupants turns blue and splits open into eight, thirty, or sixty pieces, much like the petals of a blue lotus nenuphar flower or water lily.

The length of time one stays in the EIGHT COLD HELLS is very precise if not specific. For each person in the HELL there is a grain room filled with 80 bushels of sesame seeds; once every 100 years one seed is removed. The length of time for each descending HELL is 20 times the previous.

Source: Faustino, *Heaven and Hell*, 30; Hastings, *Encyclopedia of Religion and Ethics Part*, Part 7, 133; Mew, *Traditional Aspects of Hell*, 98

Utsada

According to the writing in the *Abhidharmakosha* ("*Treasury of Abhidharma*") a Buddhist text written in the fourth century by the monk, Vasubandhu, each of the eight Hot Hells has an entranceway on each of their four sides; each of these entrances leads into four kinds of *utsada*, or sub-hell making the total 128. The four *utsada* are KSURAMARGA ("Razor Road"), KUKULA ("Heated by Burning Chaff"), KUNAPA ("Corpses and Dung"), and NADI VAITARANI ("Burning Hell").

Source: Nāgārjuna, *Nāgārjuna's Letter*, 107; Sadakata, *Buddhist Cosmology*, 51–52

Uttara Kuru

Variations: Uttarakuru

In Hindu mythology, Uttara Kuru was one of the four continents located in the outermost concentric circles surrounding Mount MERU (see GODHAVA, JAMBUDVIPA, and VIRAT-OLEHA). Located to the north, it was said to be huge and the country of the Hyperbpreans.

In in Buddhist cosmology Uttara Kuru was known as Uttarakuru and was described as being the shape of a square and lying directly north of SUMERU.

Source: Howard, *Imagery of the Cosmological Buddha*, 66; Kern, *Manual of Indian Buddhism*, 57; Sprague de Camp, *Lands Beyond*, 282

Uvdlormiut

In the mythology of the Inuit, Uvdlormiut ("People of the Day") was one of the three locations where a person's spirit went to live; this was HEAVEN, filled with those souls who died a violent death. This is a pleasant realm with many animals making for good hunting.

Source: Lynge, *Mental Disorders in Greenland. Past and Present*, 13

Vadgelmir

Variations: Vadgelmir

According to Norse mythology Vadgelmir was one of sixteen rivers which ran from AS-GARD to MIDGARD.

Source: Grimes, *Norse Myths*, 13, 305; Guerber, *Myths of the Norsemen*, 13

Vahnijwala

In Hindu mythology Vahnijwala ("Fiery Flame") is a partition in HELL (or *NARAKA*) ruled over by Yama; it is located beneath the earth and water where souls are punished for the sin of hunting deer or tending to sheep. Also in this HELL are potters.

Source: Wilson, *Oriental Translation Fund*, Volume 52, 209; Wilson, *Vishńu Puráńa*, 215–16

Vaikuntha

Variations: Param Padam ("Supreme Abode"), Paramapadam, Vishnupada ("Vishnu's Feet")

The abode of the god Vishnu of Hindu mythology, Vaikuntha ("Place of not Hindrance"), is located on Mount MERU; it has buildings made of precious gems, streets paved with gold, and was blessed by the celestial Ganga. Vishnu lives here with his consort, the goddess Laxmi. It is believed those who dwell in his HEAVEN enjoy bliss and freedom from karma.

Source: Dalal, *Religions of India*, 379; Williams, *Handbook of Hindu Mythology*, 196, 290

Vaitarani

Variations: Vaítarni

According to Hindu and Vedic mythology Vaitarani is the fourteenth twenty-eight NARAKAS (HELLS) located in a providence in the kingdom of Yama located beneath the earth; here adultery, those who destroyed a beehive or pillaged a phamet, and those kings who violated the orders of *sastras* are punished. Possibly the worst of all the NARAKAS, this place is filled with a river which runs with blood, bones, fat, flesh, hair, nails, urine, and all manner of human filth. Sinners here are hunted and attacked by the fractious beasts found here. In addition, these souls must eat and drink from the river.

Source: Prabhupāda, *Śrīmad Bhāgavatam*, 903; Parmeshwaranand, *Encyclopaedic Dictionary of Purāṇas*, 721; Wilson, *Oriental Translation Fund*, Volume 52, 209

Vajrakantaka-Salmali

Variations: Vajrakantakasalmali

According to Vedic mythology Vajrakantaka-Salmali ("a silk-cotton tree with thorns like thunderbolts) is a eight NARAKAS (HELLS) reserved for those individuals who have indiscriminate sex—even with animals. Here the agents of Yama hang the sinner on the cotton tree and then pull at him forcefully so the thorns will tear his body apart.

Source: Dange, *Bhāgavata Purāṇa*, 130; Prabhupāda, *Śrīmad Bhāgavatam Creative Impetus*, 919

Val sans Retour

In Arthurian lore the Val sans Retour ("Valley of No Return") is the place where Morgan le Fay has a chapel built that imprisons men who have been untrue to their lovers. Eventually the spell was broken by Sir Lancelot and when this happened, the castle and its walls disappeared.

Source: Brown, *Iwain*, 121; Lacy, *Text and Intertext in Medieval Arthurian Literature*, 96

Valaskiaf

Variations: Valaskjalf ("Shelf of the Slain")

In Norse mythology Valaskiaf ("Shelf of the Dead") located in ASGARD, was the home of the god Vale (Vile), a son of Odin by Rinda ("Frost"); however, some sources list it as the silver-roofed hall of the god Odin where he throne is located.

Source: Anderson, *Norse Mythology*, 460; Bennett, *Gods and Religions of Ancient and Modern Times*, Volume 1, 399; Dunham, *History of Denmark, Sweden, and Norway*, Volume 2, 55

Valgrind

Valgrind ("Carrion Gate") is one of the named gates in Norse mythology which lead into HEL, the realm of the dead who died of disease or old age.

Source: Anderson, *Norse Mythology*, 460; Bennett, *Gods and Religions of Ancient and Modern Times*, Volume 1, 399; Lindow, *Norse Mythology*, 172

Valhalla

Variations: Valhal, Valhöll

In Norse mythology, Valhalla ("Hall of the Slain") was built by the god Odin to receive those warriors who were slain in battle. Valkyries picked the deceased warriors, known as Einherjar, off the battlefield and carried them across BIFROST and into Valhalla. Here the Einherjar meet with legendary heroes and kings and together practice with Odin to prepare for Ragnarok.

Valhalla is described as having 640 doors, eachone large enough to admit 960 men at the same time. Everything here is made of solid gold; the ceiling is made of shields and spears.

Standing atop of Valhalla's roof of shields is the hart, Eikthryir, eating leaves off Yggdrasyll; the water dripping off of his antlers created

several rivers which flowed into MIDGARD, including EIKIN, FIMBULTHUL, FJORM, GEIRVIMUL, GIPUL, GOMEL, GOPUL, GUNNTHRA, SIND, SOKIN, SVOL, and VID.

Source: Bennett, *Gods and Religions of Ancient and Modern Times*, Volume 1, 399; Evans, *Dictionary of Mythology*, 266

Valley of Barahoot *see* Barahoot, Valley of

Valley of Diamonds

Variations: Mountains of Diamonds

According to the ancient Persian fairytale, *Sindbad the Sailor* (750 CE), the Valley of Diamonds was said to be located in the Far East; it was described as being a "huge valley barren of all vegetation and swarming with snakes that would have made but one gulp of an elephant."

Source: Burton, *Seven Voyages of Sinbad the Sailor*, 18; Sprague de Camp, *Lands Beyond*, 124

Valley of No Return

Variations: Valley of False Lovers

Valley of No Return from Arthurian lore was the home of DOLORUS TOWER; this valley was located next to the FOREST OF MISADVENTURE. Morgan le Fay has enchanted the valley so that anyone who has been unfaithful in love will become trapped there. Both Sir Gawain and his brother Sir Yvain become trapped there and Lancelot ventures there to save them. Although he is able to set them free he disturbs Morgan le Fay's sleep and is captured; his ring is sent to Arthur with the message that with his dying breath the knigh confessed the sin of his love for Queen Guinevere. Galehaut, distressed by the news, dies. On one of the furloughs he is granted Lancelot storms DOLORUS TOWER, kills Caradoc and liberates himself and the tower. Upon his return to Arthur's court he arranges for Galehaut to be buried at JOYOUS GARD so one day they will be able to lie together.

Source: Ashley, *Mammoth Book of King Arthur*, 457; Bruce, *Arthurian Name Dictionary*, 307

Vanaheim

Variations: Vindheim ("Wind Home"), Vanaheimar

In Norse mythology, Vanaheim, one of the NINE WORLDS, was the residence of the spirits of the air, the Vanir; it was located in the atmosphere beneath ASGARD. After the battle of Ragnarok, Vanaheim is where the sons of Balder and Hoder will live.

Source: Daly, *Norse Mythology A to Z*, 113; Dunham, *History of Denmark, Sweden, and Norway*, Volume 52

Vatarodham

Variations: Dandasuka

According to Hindu and Vedic mythology Vatarodham is the twenty-sixth of the twenty-eight NARAKAS (HELLS) located in a providence in the kingdom of Yama. Here, those who persecuted creatures who lived in the dense forests, hollow trunks of trees, and mountain peaks is made to suffer. This NARAKAS resembles caves, forests, and mountains and sinners here are tortured with fire, snake poison, and weapons.

Source: Dalal, *Hinduism*, 274; Parmeshwaranand, *Encyclopaedic Dictionary of Purāṇas*, 723

Vedhaka

In Hindu mythology Vedhaka ("Piercing") is a partition in the NARAKAS (HELLS) ruled over by Yama; it is located beneath the earth and water where souls are punished for making arrows.

Source: Garrett, *Classical Dictionary of India*, 706; Wilson, *Oriental Translation Fund*, Volume 52, 208

Vegsvinn

Variations: Vegsvin

Vegsvinn ("Way Knowing") was one of the nine rivers from Norse mythology which flow from MIDGARD to NIFLHEIM.

Source: Guerber, *Myths of the Norsemen*, 13; Sturlusonar, *Prose Edda of Snorri Sturluson*, 65

Venusberg

Variations: Hörselberg

In German mythology, Venusberg ("Venus Mountain") is the fictional mountain grotto where Sir Tannhauser found the court of Venus; he stayed there with her debauching himself until he was finally taken with remorse. He left Venusberg to seek out Pope Urban in Rome to beg for absolution of his sins.

Source: Brewer, *Character Sketches of Romance, Fiction and the* Drama, Volume 4, 75–76; Cicora, *Modern Myths and Wagnerian Deconstructions*, 62–63

Vid

According to Norse mythology Vid was one of rivers which ran from ASGARD to MIDGARD. It was created from the water dripping off of the antlers of Eikthryir as he stood atop the roof of VALHALLA eating leaves off YGGDRASYLL.

Source: Grimes, *Norse Myths*, 263; Guerber, *Myths of the Norsemen*, 13, 263

Vidi

Variations: Land-Vidi

Located in ASGARD, Vidi ("Willow Twig") is the hall of the god Vidar, done of the god Odin and the giantess Grid, in Norse mythology; this hall is described as being in a vast peaceful land covered in sapling trees, tall grass, and wildflowers.

Source: Avant, *Mythological Reference*, 411; Daly, *Norse Mythology A to Z*, 114

Vigrid

Variations: Oskopnis, Vigith, Vigridr, Vígríðr

According to Norse mythology and the *Poetic Edda*, the battle of Ragnarok will take place on a 100 square-mile field known as Vigrid.

Source: Bennett, *Gods and Religions of Ancient and Modern Times*, Volume 1, 400; Daly, *Norse Mythology A to Z*, 115; Evans, *Dictionary of Mythology*, 268

Ville au Camp

Variations: Ville-Okan

Ville au Camp is the underwater capital of the loas (zanges) of Vodou lore.

Source: Chopra, *Academic Dictionary of Mythology*, 301; Courlander, *Treasury of Afro-American Folklore*, 39

Vimer

Variations: Hemra, Veimer, Vimur

A river in Norse mythology Vimer is where the gods, Loki, Thjalfi, and Thor almost drown crossing in order to reach Geirridr's Garth when Geirridr's daughter Greip manifested before them in the water.

Source: Bennett, *Gods and Religions of Ancient and Modern Times*, Volume 1, 400; Grimes, *Norse Myths*, 309

Vimohana

Variations: Vilohita, Vimohand

In Hindu mythology Vimohana ("Place of Bewildering") is a partition in the NARAKAS (HELLS) ruled over by Yama; it is located beneath the earth and water where souls are punished for the sin of contemnor of prescribed observances or theft.

Source: Dalal, *Hinduism*, 274; Wilson, *Oriental Translation Fund*, Volume 52, 208

Vin

According to Norse mythology Vin was one of sixteen rivers which ran from ASGARD to MIDGARD.

Source: Guerber, *Myths of the Norsemen*, 13; Sturlusonar, *Prose Edda of Snorri Sturluson*, 65

Vina

Vina ("Dwina") was one of the nine rivers from Norse mythology which flow from MIDGARD to NIFLHEIM.

Source: Guerber, *Myths of the Norsemen*, 13; Sturlusonar, *Prose Edda of Snorri Sturluson*, 65

Vinadhar

Variations: Vinataka

The Vinadhar Mountains are the sixth mountain chain surrounding SUMERU, the central would mountain in in Hindu cosmol-

ogy; it is both 1,250 *yojanas* tall and wide. The measure of a single *yojanas* has never been clear, some scholars say it is approximately four and a half miles while other say it ranges between seven and nine miles.

Source: Howard, *Imagery of the Cosmological Buddha*, 66–68; Nagao, *Wisdom, Compassion, and the Search for Understanding*, 192

Vingalf

Variations: GIMLE, Vingolf, Vingulf

The mansion of bliss, Vingalf of Norse mythology is where the palace of the *asynjes* (the female gods of ASGARD); it is located near URDARBRUNNR WELL.

Source: Anderson, *Norse Mythology*, 461; Bennett, *Gods and Religions of Ancient and Modern Times*, Volume 1, 400; Evans, *Dictionary of Mythology*, 105

Virat-oleha

Variations: Purva Videha

In Hindu mythology, Virat-oleha was one of the four continents located in the outermost concentric circles surrounding Mount MERU (see GODHAVA, JAMBUDVIPA, and UTTARA KURU). Located to the east, its inhabitants were calm and virtuous.

Source: Kern, *Manual of Indian Buddhism*, 57; Sprague de Camp, *Lands Beyond*, 282

Visadana

Variations: Visamana

In Hindu mythology, Visadana is one of the twenty-eight NARAKAS (HELLS) located in a providence in the kingdom of Yama; it is filled with the instruments of torture.

Source: Wilson, *Vishñu Puráña*, 215–16

Visasanam

Variations: Visasana ("Murderous")

According to Hindu and Vedic mythology Visasanam is the seventeenth of the twenty-eight NARAKAS (HELLS) located beneath the earth and water in a providence in the kingdom of Yama. This NARAKAS is reserved for those sinners who perform *Yaga* by killing a cow to flaunt their wealth as well as for those who made making lances, swords, and other weapons. This HELL is also filled with those individuals who have made sacrifices to improper objects and uses the course of the stars as a means by which to predict the future. In Visasanam they will constantly flogged by the servants of Yama.

Source: Parmeshwaranand, *Encyclopaedic Dictionary of Purāṇas*, 722; Wilson, *Oriental Translation Fund*, Volume 52, 208

Vitala, Caverns of

In Hindu lore the Caverns of Vitala are believed to be the second of the seven underground levels in a vast cavernous system which stretches from Benares, India to Lake Manosarowar, Tibet. In all of the regions (ATALA, MAHATALA, PATALA, RASATALA, SUTALA, and TALATALA), there are beautiful cities built by the architect, Maya. This realm is ruled over by an aspect of Siva called Hātakeswara.

Source: Dowson, *Classical Dictionary of Hindu Mythology, and Religion*, 233; Parmeshwaranand, *Encyclopaedic Dictionary of Purāṇas*, 1010–1012

Vod

Variations: Vond

Vod was one of the nine rivers from Norse mythology which flow from MIDGARD to NIFLHEIM.

Source: Grimes, *Norse Myths*, 13; Guerber, *Myths of the Norsemen*, 13

Wails, Isle of

According to Homer, the greatest ancient Greek poet and the author of the *Odyessey*, the goddess Circe lived on the Isle of Wails with the Aiaiai, a collection of nymphs.

Source: Brann, *Homeric Moments*, 192

Wairua

Variations: Wai-Rua

In Maori mythology, Wairua is the ninth of the ten divisions of HEAVEN; in one version of the telling of the demigod Tawhaki there are twelve divisions but sometimes there are as many as fourteen and as few as two named. Wairua is the residence of the gods who are waiting upon those who are in the tenth HEAVEN, NAHERANGI.

Source: Craig, *Dictionary of Polynesian Mythology*, 56; Mead, *Tāwhaki*, 58

Waka-Maru

Variations: Wakamaru

In Maori mythology, Waka-maru is the second of the ten divisions of HEAVEN; in one version of the telling of the demigod Tawhaki there are twelve divisions but sometimes there are as many as fourteen and as few as two named. Waka-maru is the HEAVEN of rain and sunshine.

Source: Craig, *Dictionary of Polynesian Mythology*, 56; Mead, *Tāwhaki*, 58

The Wandering Island

In English mythology the enchantress Acrasia lived in the BOWER OF BLISS upon the FLOATING ISLAND, Wandering Island which is presented as an earthly PARADISE; here she transformed her lovers into monsters and kept them captive. Ultimately, she is destroyed by the knight, Sir Guyon.

Sources: Hamilton, *Spenser Encyclopedia*, 273; Tambling, *Allegory*, 59

The Wandering Rocks

Variations: Azure Islands, Crushers, Cyaneae, Plancta, Symplegades

A mythical strait in the world of the ancient Greeks, the Wandering Rocks would rush together so quickly and with such violent force that no ship had ever passed safely between them.

The Wandering Rocks from Homer's *The Odyssey* may very well have been inspired, if not outright borrowed, from Apollonius of Rhodes' older tale entitled *Argonautica*; it told the tale of Jason and the Argonauts on their quest to capture the Golden Fleece. The ancient Greek lyric poet Pindar claimed the Wandering Rocks to be living beings that could move as swiftly as a storm wind. One of the rocks was described as being tall enough to pierce HEAVEN with its top, having sides too smooth for a man to climb.

In *The Odyssey,* Odysseus was warned by the goddess Circe only one ship has ever successfully passed between the deadly strait, the *Argo.*

Source: Bloom, *The Odyssey,* 59; Woolsey, *Ancient City,* 75

Waves, Land Under the *see* Land Under the Waves

Well of Hvergelmir *see* Hvergelmir Well

Well of Mimirsbrunnr *see* Mimirsbrunnr Well

Well of Segais

Similar to CONNLA'S WELL of Irish lore, the Well of Segais was also a source of inspiration, surrounded by nine hazel trees, and contained salmon; anyone who drinks the water or eats the nuts or fish was gifted with supernatural knowledge. Only the god Dagda and his three cup bearers were allowed to drink from the well; the river goddess Boand drowned when she attempted to drink from the well, as the water of the well rose up and eventually created the river Boyne.

Source: Matson, *Celtic Mythology, A to Z,* 34, 118; Varner, *Sacred Wells,* 91–92

Well of Urdarbrunnr *see* Urdarbrunnr Well

Western Paradise *see* Pure Land of the Western Paradise

Women, Land of the *see* The Land of Women

Wrath's Hole

In the folklore of Cornwall, Britain, Bolster, a large and evil wrath (spirit) was harassing St. Agnes with lascivious and lude talk as he wanted her for his lover; the holy woman told the being she would comply but first it had to fill a small hole of her choosing with his blood. Bolster quickly agreed but was unaware the hole St. Agnes chose led to the ocean. When the wrath bled himself to death, St. Agnes pushed his body into the ocean.

Source: Brewer, *Character Sketches of Romance, Fiction and the Drama,* Volume 8, 264; Polwhele, *History of Cornwall,* Volume 1–3, 208

Wunderberg

Variations: Underberg

In fairy lore, Wunderberg is the primary haunt of the wild women; it is described as being located beneath the great moor near Salzburg. This hollowed-out region is outfitted with churches, gardens, monasteries, springs of gold and silver, and stately palaces. There is a staff of diminutive men who guard the treasures of Wunderberg.

Source: Keightly, *World Guide to Gnomes, Fairies, Elves, and Other Little People,* 234; Spence, *Encyclopedia of Occultism and Parapsychology,* Volume 1, 986

Xibalba

The collective name for the nine layers of the Mayan Underworld, Xibalba ("Place of Fear") was generally an unpleasant place. A soul had to travel through Xibalba, a real filled with topographical challenges such as deep chasm, a plane of scorpions, a region of spiked thorns, and raging rivers; each layer is ruled by its own god. Within Xibalba are places of torcher each with their own particular brand of punishment, such as House of Bats, House of Cold, House of Fire, House of Gloom, House of Jaguars, and House of Knives.

Source: Crisafulli, *Go to Hell,* 77–78; Stookey, *Thematic Guide to World Mythology,* 204

Xuan Pu

A mythical FAIRYLAND in Chinese lore, Xuan Pu is said to be located on the summit of Kunlun Mountain directly beneath the door which leads to HEAVEN.

Source: Sukhu, *SUNY Series in Chinese Philosophy and Culture*, 228

Yaaru (yah'roo)

Variations: AALU, AARU, Iaru

Similar to EDEN or the ELYSIAN FIELDS, Yaaru of the religion of the ancient Egyptians is a beautiful realm of the dead under the dominion of the god Osiris; here the deceased who when weighed in the Halls of Maat soul weighed less than a feather, enjoy their favorite activities. The fields of Yaaru, which is represented as a vast field of wheat, are tilled in order for the deceased to harvest food. Located in the East Yaaru is sometimes referred to as a grouping of islands.

Source: Avant, *Mythological Reference*, 167; Gardiner, *Gateways to the Otherworld*, 231

Yaksha-Loka

Variations: Yakshaloka

One of the eight regions of material existence in Hindu mythology, Yaksha-Loka ("World of Yaksha") is the realm of the Yaksha.

Source: Dowson, *Classical Dictionary of Hindu Mythology and Religion*, 180; Knappert, *Indian Mythology*, 152

Yamapuri

In Hindu and Vedic mythology Yamapuri is the city in the realm known as PITRILOKA where the god Yama lives in a huge palace called Kalichi. Yamapuri is 1,000 *yojanas* (approximately 4,545.45 miles) in size, on one side of the city is the Hindu god, Citragupta's mansion; south of this mansion is Jvaramandira ("House of Diseases"). Yama's personal home is 20 *yojanas* from Citragupta's mansion. The fort surrounding the city is made of iron and there is a single entrance on each of the cities four sides. There are exactly 100 streets in this city.

Source: Dalal, *Religions of India*, 398; Parmeshwaranand, *Encyclopaedic Dictionary of Purāṇas: A–C*, 720

Yao Chi

In Chinese lore Yao Chi ("Jade Pool") is located in the palace of Xi Wang Mu ("Queen Mother of the West"), the home of the immortals, in the mysterious western mountains surrounded by riches.

Source: Eberhard, *Dictionary of Chinese Symbols*, 185

Ydale

Variations: Ydaler, Ydalir

In Norse mythology Ydale ("Valley of Rain") located in ASGARD, was the home of the god of hunting, Uller.

Source: Bennett, *Gods and Religions of Ancient and Modern Times*, Volume 1, 400; Dunham, *History of Denmark, Sweden, and Norway*, Volume 2, 55

Yetzirah

Variations: Olam ha-Yetzirah

The third of the four Cabalistic worlds Yetzirah ("formation") is the world of interwoven form and force. Yetzirah's element is water; it's is associated with Vav of the Tetragrammation.

Source: Godwin, *Godwin's Cabalistic Encyclopedia*, 342; Greer, *New Encyclopedia of the Occult*, 180

Yggdrasil

Variations: Ash Tree of Existence, Mimameior, Tree of Existence, Ash Yggdrasil, Ygdrasil, Yggdrasill, Yggdrasyll, Yggdrasill

Standing in the cents of the NINE WORLDS of Norse mythology, the ash tree known as Yggdrasil ("bearer of Ygg"), bind these planes together as its roots spread out in the past, present, and future. It was created when Bestla and Bor planed its seed under a rock moments before the tidal wave of Ymir's blood washed over them, drowning the couple. The blood nourished the seed and the ash tree grew forth and matured quickly. When this mighty ash tree finally falls, the universe will be destroyed. There are three wells from which Yggdrasil draws its water from, HVERGELMIR WELL, MIMIRSBRUNNR WELL, and URDARBRUNNR WELL.

Nott, the daughter of the jotuns, Narfid and Nor, was born in the dales beneath Yggdrasil. When Odin needed to gain the knowledge and wisdom of the dead he sacrificed himself to himself and hung from the branches of Yggdrasil for nine days.

In the top-most branches of Yggdrasil lives the rusty-yellow eagle, Edgar; the hawk, Vedrfolnir built its nest blocking Edgar's view. The serpent (or dragon) Nidhoggr has entwined itself around the roots of the tree in the realm of NIFLHEIM. Here, he and his sons, Goinn, Grabakr, Grafvolludr, Moinn, Ofnir, and Svafnir chew of the roots of the mighty ash and eat the decease who are deposited there. The red squirrel Ratatoskr runs up and down the trunk of tree carrying gossip and rumors to Edgar and Nidhoggr in hopes of stirring-up trouble so they would attack the tree. There are four harts that graze beneath Yggdrasil, Dainn, Duneyrr, Durathorr, and Dvallinn; the honeydew that drips from the branches of Yggdrasil to their horns nourishes the bees.

Each day the Æsir cross the BIFROST bridge and gather beneath Yggdrasil to hold council with one another.

Source: Anderson, *Norse Mythology*, 74, 120, 190, 206, 370, 453; Evans, *Dictionary of Mythology*, 275; Grimes, *Norse Myths* 7, 15, 242, 261, 263, 281, 291–92

Yíngzhōu

Variations: Yingzhou

A mythological island PARADISE in the East China Sea, Yíngzhōu ("Sea Island") is one of four FLOATING ISLANDS the Immortals are believed to live upon (see FĀNGZHÀNG, YÍNGZHŌU, and YUÁNJIĀO). Each of these islands is 70,000 li apart from one another; each has a mountain on it rising 30,000 *li* (49,215,000 feet) high and at its top is a plain 90,000 *li* (147,645,000 feet). The palaces on each of these mountains is constructed of gold. At one point the islands were fixed into place on the back of 15 celestial sea turtles.

Source: Chen, *Chinese Myths and Legends*, 26–27; Roberts, *Chinese Mythology: A to Z*, 60

Ynys Gutrin

Variations: Island of Glass, Ynys Wydrin

A legendary place in Welsh lore, Ynys Gutrin ("Glass Island") cannot be seen with mortal eyes; this beautiful land was populated only by women. In various telling in Arthurian lore Morgan le Fay carried King Arthur to Ynys Gutrin after the Battle of CAMLAN so she could heal his wounds.

Source: Melrose, *Druids and King Arthur*, 54; Monaghan. *Encyclopedia of Celtic Mythology and Folklore*, 447

Yomi

Variations: Ne no Kuni ("Land of Roots"), Soko no Kuni ("Deep Land"), Yomi-no-kuni ("Land of Yomi"), Yomo-tsu-kuni ("World of Darkness")

In ancient Shinto beliefs Yomi was the filthy and polluted UNDERWORLD of the dead; spirits who were clean and pure resided in a HEAVEN known as TOKOYO-NO-KUMI. Once a soul has eaten the food of Yomi it cannot return to earth and is doomed to remain is a constant state of decomposition. Neither a HEAVEN to aspire to nor a HELL to be punished in, the souls of Yomi live out a perpetually gloomy shadow existence. Ruled over by the goddess Izanami no Mikoto, the Grand Deity of Yomi, the earthly entrance to this realm was believed to lie in the entrance to Yomi lies in Izumo province but was long ago sealed up by her husband Izanagi with a large boulder. Before this it was connected to ASHIHARA-NO-NAKATSUKUNI and TAKAMA-GA-HAR by an axis called *ame no mihashira*.

Source: Ono, *Shinto*, 102; Picken, *Historical Dictionary of Shinto*, 302; Roberts, *Japanese Mythology A to Z*, 127

Youdu

The capital of *Diyu* (HELL) in Chinese mythology, Youdu ("Dark Capitol") is located beneath the earth. According to beliefs, when a person dies their soul descends into this very dark UNDERWORLD where it is met by the god of Youdu, Houto.

Source: Yang, *Handbook of Chinese Mythology*, 236

Youth, Land of *see* Land of Youth

Yuánjiāo

Variations: Yuanqiao, Yuan Jia

A mythological island PARADISE in the East China Sea, Yuánjiāo ("Round Mountain") is one of four FLOATING ISLANDS the Immortals are believed to live upon (see FĀNGZHÀNG, YÍNGZHŌU, and YUÁNJIĀO). Each of these islands is 70,000 li apart from one another; each has a mountain on it rising 30,000 *li* (49,215,000 feet) high and at its top is a plain 90,000 *li* (147,645,000 feet). The palaces on each of these mountains is constructed of gold. At one point the islands were fixed into place on the back of 15 celestial sea turtles. When two of the celestial turtles were killed and eaten by a giant from Longhuo DÀIYÚ and YUÁNJIĀO became too unstable, drifted to the North Pole and eventually sank into the sea leaving more than 100 million immortals homeless.

Source: Chen, *Chinese Myths and Legends*, 26–27; Roberts, *Chinese Mythology: A to Z*, 60

Yugandhara

The Yugandhara Mountains are the second mountain chain surrounding SUMERU, the central would mountain in in Hindu cosmology; it is both 40,000 *yojanas* tall and wide. The measure of a single *yojanas* has never been clear, some scholars say it is approximately four and a half miles while other say it ranges between seven and nine miles.

Source: Howard, *Imagery of the Cosmological Buddha*, 66–68; Nagao, *Wisdom, Compassion, and the Search for Understanding*, 192

Z, Lost City of

Col. Percy Harrison Fawcett, a British surveyor, and his son, Jack, disappeared under unknown circumstances while looking for a lost city they named Z in the Mato Grosso region of Brazil in 1925. He believed that there was still an active civilization of highly advanced people living in the Brazilian Amazon; Fawcett imagined the city he named Z would be located in a valley about ten miles wide and would be approachable by a barreled roadway of stone and that there would be low, windowless houses and a step-pyramid.

Written by Portuguese explorer João da Silva Guimarães, he claimed he visited the city in 1753, described it in great detail but did not give its location. Guimarães claimed he and his expedition entered into a fissure in the side of a mountain and on the other side there discovered a great and ancient city that had many underground shafts all along its perimeter. Living in the city were two men described as having black hair, white skin, and wearing robes. This document is known as Manuscript 512 and housed at the National Library of Rio de Janeiro.

Source: Childress, *Lost Cities and Ancient Mysteries of South America*, 75, 120; Walton, *Guide to the Inner Earth*, 72

Zaqqam, Tree of

In Islamic mythology the Tree of Zaqqam is a bitter-smelling and horrific looking tree located in the pit of HELL; the flowers it bears resembles the heads of demons. Evil-doers will be forced to eat the barbed fruit of this tree which will burn their stomachs as if it were boiled oil or water.

Source: Hamdaan Publications, *Glorious Quran*, 441, 497, 547; Netton, *Popular Dictionary of Islam*, 264

Zebul

Variations: Makhon, Zebhul ("Lofty Place")

The sixth of the seven HEAVENs of Jewish mysticism, Zebul is ruled by night and during the Sabbath day by the angle who lent his name to this realm, Zebul; the rest of the time it is ruled by the angel Zachiel. Described as being stormy and always snowing, seven cherubim reside here who sing the praises of God; it is also home to seven phoenixes. Additionally, a multitude of other angelic beings also reside here, each studying from a wide array of subjects including astronomy, ecology, mankind, and the seasons.

Source: Lewis, *Angels A to Z, 2nd Edition*, 333; Vohs, *Am I Going to Heaven?*, 38; Webster, *Encyclopedia of Angels*, 85

Zerzura

Variations: ATLANTIS of the Sands, Oasis of Little Birds

A legendary oasis said to be located in the desert west of the Nile River in Egypt, Zerzura ("Oasis of Little Birds") has been mentioned in documents dating back as far as the thirteenth century; it has been described in the fifteenth century Arabic text *Kitab el Kanuz* ("*Book of Lost Treasures*") as being "a white city, white as a dove." The city within this oasis, also called Zerzura, is alleged to be filled with riches and guarded by a sleeping king and queen; those who find the city are free to take what treasure they can carry so long as they do not wake the royal couple.

Source: Piper, *Cartographic Fictions*, 107–08; Vivian, *Western Desert of Egypt*, 365–66

Zophos

An island mentioned in Homer's *Odyssey*, Zophos ("darkness" or "gloom") was said to be located between where the sun sets in the summertime and where it rises in the summertime, basically in the north and north-west of Ithaca.

Source: Goekoop, *Where on Earth Is Ithaca*, 125, 173; Sprague de Camp, *Lands Beyond*, 80

Zulal

A stream in PARADISE, Zulal ("Clear Water") is described as being a clear as a perfect crystal and as delicious as nectar according to the mythology of Islam; the spirits of the just drink from it.

Source: Brewer, *Dictionary of Phrase and Fable*, 1324

Bibliography

Acharya, Kala, Lalita Namjoshi, Harshadray N. Sanghrajka, and Shriram Mahadeo Bhatkhande. *Indian Philosophical Terms: Glossary and Sources.* Mumbai: Somaiya Publications, 2004.

Adam, Sadek. *Hollow Earth Authentic.* Pomeroy, WA: Health Research Books, 1999.

Adams, Charles, Kendal. *The Universal Cyclopaedia: Volume 5 of the Universal Cyclopaedia: A New Ed. Prepared by a Large Corps of Editors, Assisted by Eminent European and American Specialists, Under the Direction of Charles Kendall Adams President of the University of Wisconsin, Editor-in-Chief; Illustrated with Maps, Plans, Colored Plates, and Engravings.* New York: D. Appleton, 1900.

Addison, Joseph. *Remarks on Several Parts of Italy, etc. in the Years 1701, 1702, 1703.* Hague: Henry Scheurleer, 1718.

Agrippa von Nettesheim, Heinrich Cornelius, edited by Donald Tyson. *Three Books of Occult Philosophy.* St. Paul, MN: Llewellyn, 1993.

Aiyaṅgār, Maṇḍayam A. Nārāyaṇa. *Essays on Indo-Aryan Mythology*, Volume 1. Bangalore: Caxton Press, 1898.

Alexander, Jane. *The Body, Mind, Spirit Miscellany: The Ultimate Collection of Fascinations, Facts, Truths, and Insights.* New York: Sterling, 2009.

Andersen, Johannes Carl. *Maori Life in Ao-tea.* Christchurch: Whitcombe and Tombs, 1907.

_____. *Myths and Legends of the Polynesians.* Mineola: Courier Dover, 1995.

Anderson, Rasmus Björn. *Norse Mythology.* Chicago: S. C. Griggs, 1884.

Andreä, Johann Valentin. *Johann Valentin Andreae's Christianopolis: An Ideal State of the Seventeenth Century.* New York: Oxford University Press, 1916.

Andrews, Tamra. *Dictionary of Nature Myths: Legends of the Earth, Sea, and Sky.* Oxford: Oxford University Press, 2000.

Anthon, Charles. *A Classical Dictionary: Containing the Principle Proper Names Mentioned in Ancient Authors and Intended to Elucidate All the Important Points Connected with the Geography, History, Biography, Mythology, and Fine Arts of the Greeks and Romans. Together with an Account of Coins, Weights, and Measures, with Tabular Values of the Same*, Volume 1. Whitefish, MT: Kessinger, 2005.

Ara, Mitra. *Eschatology in the Indo-Iranian Traditions.* New York: Peter Lang, 2008.

Arbois de Jubainville, Henry. *The Irish Mythological Cycle and Celtic Mythology.* Dublin: Hodges, Figgis, 1903.

Archibald, Elizabeth, and Ad Putter. *The Cambridge Companion to the Arthurian Legend.* Cambridge: Cambridge University Press, 2009.

Ashe, Geoffrey. *Mythology of the British Isles.* London: Methuen, 1990.

_____. *The New Arthurian Encyclopedia.* New York: Garland, 1996.

Ashley, Michael. *The Mammoth Book of King Arthur.* New York: Running Press, 2005.

Ashliman, D. L. *Fairy Lore: A Handbook.* Westport, CT: Greenwood, 2005.

Avant, G. Rodney. *A Mythological Reference.* Bloomington, IN: AuthorHouse, 2005.

Babcock, William Henry, and the American Geographical Society of New York. *Legendary Islands of the Atlantic: A Study in Medieval Geography.* New York: American Geographical Society, 1922.

Baldwin, James. *A Story of the Golden Age.* New York: Scribner's, 1900.

Barber, Richard. *Legends of King Arthur.* Woodbridge: Boydell Press, 2001.

Baring-Gould, Sabine. *A Book of Folklore.* Whitefish, MT: Kessinger, 2004.

_____. *Curious Myths of the Middle Ages.* London: Rivingtons, 1868.

Baskin, Wade. *Dictionary of Satanism.* New York: Citadel Press, 1972.

Beal, Timothy. *Biblical Literacy.* New York: HarperCollins, 2009.

Bechtel, John Hendricks. *A Dictionary of Mythology.* Philadelphia: Penn, 1917.

Becker, Ernest Julius. *A Contribution to the Comparative Study of the Medieval Visions of Heaven and Hell: With Special Reference to the Middle-English Versions.* Baltimore: John Murphy, 1899.

Beckwith, Martha Warren. *Hawaiian Mythology.* Honolulu: University of Hawaii Press, 1976.

Begg, Ean C. M., and Deike Rich. *On the Trail of Merlin: A Guide to the Celtic Mystery Tradition.* London: Aquarian Press, 1991.

Belanger, Jeff, and KIrsten Dalley. *The Nightmare Encyclopedia: Your Darkest Dreams Interpreted.* New York: Career Press, 2005.

Belanger, Michelle. *Dictionary of Demons: Names of the Damned.* St. Paul, MN: Llewellyn, 2010.

Bell, John. *Bell's New Pantheon or Historical Dictionary of the Gods, Demi Gods, Heroes and Fabulous Personages of Antiquity 1790.* Whitefish, MT: Kessinger, 2003.

Belloni Du Chaillu, Paul. *The Viking Age: The Early History, Manners, and Customs of the Ancestors of the English-Speaking Nations,* Volume 1. New York: Scribner's, 1889.

Bellows, Henry Adams. *The Poetic Edda: The Mythological Poems.* Minneola: Courier Dover, 2012.

Ben-Amos, Dan, and Dov Noy. *Folktales of the Jews,* Volume 2: *Tales from Eastern Europe.* Philadelphia: Jewish Publication Society, 2007.

Bennett, De Robigne Mortimer. *The Gods and Religions of Ancient and Modern Times,* Volume 1. New York: D.M. Bennett, 1880.

Berndt, Ronald Murray. *Djanggawul: An Aboriginal Religious Cult of North-Eastern Arnhem Land.* New York: Routledge and Paul, 1952.

Bevan, William Latham, Henry Wright Phillott, and Francis Tebbs Havergal. *Mediæval Geography: An Essay in Illustration of the Hereford Mappa Mundi.* London: E. Stanford, 1873.

Bevan-Jones, Robert. *The Ancient Yew: A History of Taxus Baccata.* Bollington, UK: Windgatherer, 2002.

Bingham, Ann, and Jeremy Roberts. *South and Meso-American Mythology A to Z.* New York: Infobase, 2010.

Birrell, Anne. *Chinese Mythology: An Introduction.* Baltimore: Johns Hopkins Paperback Press, 1999.

Blamires, David Malcolm. *Herzog Ernst and the Otherworld Voyage: A Comparative Study.* Manchester: Manchester University Press, 1979.

Blavatsky, Helena Petrovna. *The Secret Doctrine,* Volume 1. Wheaton: Quest Books, 1993.

_____. *The Secret Doctrine: Cosmogenesis.* New York: Theosophical Publishing Society, 1893.

_____. *The Theosophical Glossary.* London: Theosophical Publishing Society, 1892.

Blo-gros-mtha'-yas, Koṅ-sprul, and Rinpoche Bokar. *The Treasury of Knowledge: Myriad Worlds. Book One.* Ithaca, NY: Snow Lion Publications, 2003.

Bloom, Harold, ed. *Homer's* The Odyssey. New York: Infobase, 2009.

Blumetti, Robert. *The Book of Balder Rising.* New York: iUniverse, 2004.

Bokenkamp, Stephen R. *Early Daoist Scriptures.* Berkeley: University of California Press, 1999.

Bonnefoy, Yves, editor. *Asian Mythologies.* Chicago: University of Chicago Press, 1993.

Bonwick, James. *Egyptian Belief and Modern Thought.* London: C. Kegan Paul, 1878.

Bord, Janet. *Fairies: Real Encounters with Little People.* New York: Carroll and Graf, 1997.

Bovey, Alixe. *Monsters and Grotesques in Medieval Manuscripts.* Toronto: University of Toronto Press, 2002.

Brener, Anne. *Mourning and Mitzvah: A Guided Journal for Walking the Mourner's Path Through Grief to Healing: With Over 60 Guided Exercises.* Woodstock, VT: Jewish Lights Publishing, 2001.

Brewer, Ebenezer Cobham. *Dictionary of Phrase and Fable: Giving the Derivation, Source, or Origin of Common Phrases, Allusions, and Words That Have a Tale to Tell.* London: Cassell, 1905.

_____. *The Reader's Handbook of Allusions, References, Plots, and Stories: With Three Appendices.* London: Chatto and Windus, 1896.

_____. *The Reader's Handbook of Famous Names in Fiction, Allusions, References, Proverbs, Plots, Stories, and Poems.* London: Chatto and Windus, 1902.

_____. *The Wordsworth Dictionary of Phrase and Fable.* Hertfordshire: Wordsworth Editions, 2001.

_____, and Marion Harland. *Character Sketches of Romance, Fiction and the Drama,* Volumes 1, 4 and 8. New York: Selmar Hess, 1901–1902.

Briggs, Katharine Mary. *An Encyclopedia of Fairies: Hobgoblins, Brownies, Bogies, and Other Supernatural Creatures.* New York: Pantheon, 1976.

Brodrick, Mary. *A Concise Dictionary of Egyptian Archaeology.* London: Methuen, 1902.

Brough, R. Clayton. *The Lost Tribes: History, Doctrine, Prophecies and Theories About Israel's Lost Ten Tribes.* Springville, UT: Cedar Fort, 2005.

Brown, Arthur Charles Lewis. *Iwain: A Study in the Origins of Arthurian Romance.* New York: Ardent Media, 1965.

Brown, Ju. *China, Japan, Korea: Culture and Customs.* North Charleston, SC: Ju Brown, 2006.

Brown, Robert. *The Great Dionysiak Myth.* London: Longmans, 1877.

Bruce, Christopher W. *The Arthurian Name Dictionary.* Boca Raton, FL: Taylor and Francis, 1999.

Buck, Charles. *A Theological Dictionary, Containing Definitions of All Religious Terms, a Comprehensive View of Every Article in the System of Divinity; An Impartial Account of All the Principal Dominations Which Have Subsisted in the Religious World from the Birth of Christ to Present Day: Together with an Accurate Statement of Most Remarkable Transactions and Events Recorded in*

Ecclesiastical History. Philadelphia: William W. Woodard, 1824.

Budge, Sir Ernest Alfred Wallis. *Babylonian Life and History.* Whitefish, MT: Kessinger, 2003.

_____. *Egyptian Religion and Magic.* Whitefish, MT: Kessinger, 2005.

_____. *The Gods of the Egyptians: Or, Studies in Egyptian Mythology*, Volume 1. London: Methuen, 1904.

_____, translator. *Book of the Dead.* Whitefish, MT: Kessinger, 2003.

Bühler, Johann Georg. *On the Indian Sect of the Jainas.* Cirencester: Echo Library, [1903].

Bunson, Margaret. *Encyclopedia of Ancient Egypt.* New York: Infobase, 2009.

Bunson, Matthew. *Angels A to Z: A Who's Who of the Heavenly Host.* New York: Random House Digital, 1996.

Burgess, Jonathan S. *The Death and Afterlife of Achilles.* Baltimore: Johns Hopkins University Press, 2011.

_____, and the Royal Anthropological Institute of Great Britain and Ireland. *Indian Antiquary*, Volume 3. Bombay: Swati Publications, 1971.

Burke, Oliver Joseph. *The South Isles of Aran: (County Galway).* London: Kegan Paul, Trench, 1887.

Burn, Robert. *Rome and the Campagna: An Historical and Topographical Description of the Site, Buildings, and Neighbourhood of Ancient Rome.* Cambridge: Deighton, Bell, 1876.

Burton, Lady Isabel, and Justin Huntly McCarthy; translated by Sir Richard Francis Burton. *Lady Burton's Edition of Her Husband's Arabian Nights: Translated Literally from the Arabic*, Volume 3. London:Waterlow, 1887.

Burton, Robert, and Sir Richard Burton. *The Seven Voyages of Sinbad the Sailor.* New York: Digireads.com, 2010.

Cahill, Michael A. *Paradise Rediscovered: The Roots of Civilisation.* Volume 1. Queensland: Interactive Publications, 2012.

Calvino, Italo. *Invisible Cities.* New York: Houghton Mifflin Harcourt, 2012.

Campion, Nicholas. *Astrology and Cosmology in the World's Religions.* New York: New York University Press, 2012.

Capers, Roberta M., and Jerrold Maddox. *Images and Imagination; An Introduction to Art.* New York: Ronald Press, 1965.

Carr, Thomas Swinburne. *A Manual of Classical Mythology; or, A Companion to the Greek and Latin Poets: Designed Chiefly to Explain Words, Phrases and Epithets, from the Fables and Traditions to Which They Refer.* London: Simpkin Marshall, 1846.

Carroll, Robert. *The Skeptic's Dictionary: A Collection of Strange Beliefs, Amusing Deceptions, and Dangerous Delusions.* Hoboken, NJ: John Wiley, 2011.

Carter, Lin. *Lost Worlds.* Rockville, MD: Wildside Press, 2008.

Castleden, Rodney. *King Arthur: The Truth Behind the Legend.* New York: Routledge, 2002.

Chagnon, Napoleon A. *Yąnomamö: Case Studies in Cultural Anthropology.* Belmont, CA: Cengage Learning, 2012.

Chamberlain, Basil Hall, and W. B. Mason. *A Handbook for Travellers in Japan: Including the Whole Empire from Yezo to Formosa.* London: John Murray, 1901.

Charles, R. H. *The Book of Enoch or 1 Enoch.* Pomeroy, WA: Health Research Books, 1964.

Chaturvedi, B. K. *Devi Bhagwat Purana.* New Delhi: Diamond Pocket Books, 2001.

_____. *Shiv Purana.* New Delhi: Diamond Pocket Books, 2004.

Chen, Lianshan. *Chinese Myths and Legends.* Cambridge: Cambridge University Press, 2011.

Chesney, Elizabeth A. *The Rabelais Encyclopedia.* Westport, CT: Greenwood, 2004.

Childress, David Hatcher. *Lost Cities and Ancient Mysteries of South America.* Kempton: Adventures Unlimited, 1986.

_____. *Lost Cities of China, Central Asia, and India.* Kempton: Adventures Unlimited, 1991.

_____. *Lost Cities of North and Central America.* Kempton: Adventures Unlimited, 1992.

Chisholm, Hugh. *The Encyclopedia Britannica: A Dictionary of Arts, Sciences, Literature and General Information*, Volume 12. New York: Encyclopedia Britannica, 1910.

Chodag, Tiley. *Tibet, the Land and the People.* Beijing: New World Press, 1988.

Chopra, Ramesh. *Academic Dictionary of Mythology.* Delhi: Gyan, 2005.

_____. *Encyclopaedic Dictionary of Religion: G–P.* Delhi: Gyan, 2005.

Christensen, Liana Joy. *Deadly Beautiful: Vanishing Killers of the Animal Kingdom.* Auckland: Exisle, 2011.

Christie, Anthony. *Chinese Mythology.* Feltham, UK: Hamlyn, 1968.

Churchward, James. *The Lost Continent of Mu* (1931). Whitefish, MT: Kessinger, 2003.

Cicora, Mary A. *Modern Myths and Wagnerian Deconstructions: Hermeneutic Approaches to Wagner's Music-Dramas.* Westport, CT: Greenwood, 2000.

Clark, Jerome. *Encyclopedia of Strange and Unexplained Physical Phenomena.* Detroit: Gale Research, 1993.

_____. *Hidden Realms, Lost Civilizations, and Beings from Other Worlds.* Canton: Visible Ink Press, 2010.

Clay, Albert T. *The Origin of Biblical Traditions Hebrew Legends in Babylonia and Israel Lectures on Biblical Archaeology.* Whitefish, MT: Kessinger, 2006.

Coale, Samuel. *The Mystery of Mysteries: Cultural Differences and Designs*. Bowling Green, OH: Popular Press, 2000.

Collectif. *Classical Mythology and Arthurian Romance*. Genève, FR: Slatkine, 1974.

Collocott, E. E. V. "Notes on the Tongan Religion," in *The Journal of the Polynesian Society* Volume 30 (1967): 152–63.

Colombo, John Robert. *Canadian Literary Landmarks*. Willowdale: Dundurn, 1984.

Colum, Padraic. *The Golden Fleece and the Heroes Who Lived Before Achilles*. New York: MacMillan, 1921.

_____, editor. *A Treasury of Irish Folklore*. New York: Random House, 1997.

Connolly, Peter. *The Ancient Greece of Odysseus*. Oxford: Oxford University Press, 1998.

Conway, Moncure Daniel. *Demonology and Devil-Lore*, Volume 1. New York: Henry Holt, 1881.

Conybeare, Frederick C. "The Testament of Solomon," *The Jewish Quarterly Review*, Volume 11 (October 1889): 1–45.

Cooper, Jean C., and Ebenezer Cobham Brewer. *Brewer's Book of Myth and Legend*. Oxford: Helicon, 1993.

Cooper, William Ricketts. *An Archaic Dictionary: Biographical, Historical, and Mythological: From the Egyptian, Assyrian, and Etruscan Monuments and Papyri*. London: Samuel Bagster, 1876.

_____. *The Horus Myth in Its Relation to Christianity*. London: Hardwicke and Bogue, 1877.

Cottae, Bwana. "On the Ivory Trail," in *The Best of Field and Stream: 100 Years of Great Writing from America's Premier Sporting Magazine*, edited by J. I. Merritt, and Margaret G. Nichols, 249–269, New York: Globe Pequot, 2002.

Cotterell, Arthur. *Encyclopedia of World Mythology*. New York: Barnes and Noble, 1999.

Courlander, Harold, editor. *A Treasury of Afro-American Folklore: The Oral Literature, Traditions, Recollections, Legends, Tales, Songs, Religious Beliefs, Customs, Sayings, and Humor of Peoples of African Descent in the Americas*. New York: Da Capo, 2002.

Courtney, Margaret Ann. *Cornish Feasts and Folk-Lore*. Penzance: Beare, 1890.

Cox, George William. *Popular Romances of the Middle Ages*. London: Longmans, Green, 1871.

Craig, Robert D. *Dictionary of Polynesian Mythology*. Westport, CT: Greenwood, 1989.

_____. *Handbook of Polynesian Mythology*. Santa Barbara, CA: ABC-CLIO, 2004.

Crisafulli, Chuck, and Kyra Thompson. *Go to Hell: A Heated History of the Underworld*. New York: Simon & Schuster, 2010.

Crossley-Holland, Kevin. *The Norse Myths*. New York: Random House Digital, 2012.

Cuddon, J. A. *Dictionary of Literary Terms and Literary Theory*. Malden, NJ: John Wiley, 2012.

Cunliffe, Barry. *The Extraordinary Voyage of Pytheas the Greek: The Man Who Discovered Britain*. New York: Bloomsbury, 2002.

Curran, Bob. *Lost Lands, Forgotten Realms: Sunken Continents, Vanished Cities, and the Kingdoms that History Misplaced*. Pompton Plains, NJ: Open Road Media, 2012.

Dalal, Roshen. *Hinduism: An Alphabetical Guide*. New York: Penguin Books India, 2011.

_____. *The Religions of India: A Concise Guide to Nine Major Faiths*. New York: Penguin Books India, 2010.

Dale, Rodney. *The Book of Where? A Gazetteer of Places Real and Imaginary*. New York: Collector's Reference Library, 2004.

Dalley, Stephanie, editor and translator. *Myths from Mesopotamia: Creation, the Flood, Gilgamesh, and Others*. Oxford: Oxford University Press, 1989.

Daly, Kathleen N. *Norse Mythology, A to Z*. New York: Infobase, 2009.

_____, and Marian Rengel. *Greek and Roman Mythology, A to Z*. New York: Infobase, 2009.

Dange, Sindhu S. *The Bhāgavata Purāṇa: Mytho-Social Study*. Delhi: Ajanta Publications, 1984.

Daniélou, Alain. *The Myths and Gods of India: The Classic Work on Hindu Polytheism from the Princeton Bollingen Series*. Rochester, VT: Inner Traditions/Bear, 1991.

Daniels, Cora Linn, and C. M. Stevans, editors. *Encyclopædia of Superstitions, Folklore, and the Occult Sciences of the World*. Doral, FL: Minerva Group, 2003.

Dante Alighieri, translated by John Donaldson Sinclair. *The Inferno: Volume 1 of the Divine Comedy of Dante Alighieri*. Oxford: Oxford University Press, 1961.

_____. Translated by Mark Musa. *Dante Alighieri's Divine Comedy: Inferno, Italian Text and Translation*. Bloomington: Indiana University Press, 1996.

Darrah, John. *Paganism in Arthurian Romance*. Woodbridge: Boydell and Brewer, 1997.

Das, Sarat Candra, and the Buddhist Text and Research Society, Calcutta. *Journal of the Buddhist Text Society of India*, Volumes 1–3. Calcutta: Baptist Mission Press, 1893.

Dasa, Philangi. *Swedenborg the Buddhist or the Higher Swedenborgianism, Its Secrets and Thibetan Origin*. Whitefish, MT: Kessinger, 2006.

Davis, Jeff, and Al Eufrasio. *Weird Washington: Your Travel Guide to the Evergreen State's Local Legends and Best Kept Secrets*. New York: Sterling, 2008.

Davis, Kenneth C. *Don't Know Much About Geography: Everything You Need to Know About the World but Never Learned*. New York: HarperCollins, 2013.

de Camp, L. Sprague. *Lost Continents: The Atlantis*

Theme in History, Science, and Literature. Mineola, NY: Courier Dover, 2012.

_____, and Willy Ley. *Lands Beyond*. New York: Barnes and Noble, 1993.

de Claremont, Lewis. *The Ancient's Book of Magic: Containing Secret Records of the Procedure and Practice of the Ancient Masters and Adepts 1940*. Whitefish, MT: Kessinger, 2004.

De Edward, Earl of Derby. *The Iliad*. Whitefish, MT: Kessinger, 2004.

Degidon, N. F. "As the Sun Went Down," in *New Catholic World*, Volume 85, edited by Paulest Fathers, 98–102. New York: Office of the Catholic World, 1907.

de Landa, Diego. *Yucatan Before and After the Conquest*. New York: Courier Dover, 1978.

DeLoach, Charles. *Giants: A Reference Guide from History, the Bible, and Recorded Legend*. Lanham, MD: Scarecrow, 1995.

Delumeau, Jean. *History of Paradise: The Garden of Eden in Myth and Tradition*. New York: Continuum, 2000.

Demy, Timothy J., and Thomas Ice. *Answers to Common Questions About Heaven and Eternity*. Grand Rapids, MI: Kregel, 2011.

Dennis, Geoffrey W. *The Encyclopedia of Jewish Myth, Magic, and Mysticism*. St. Paul, MN: Llewellyn, 2007.

Dimmitt, Cornelia. *Classical Hindu Mythology: A Reader in the Sanskrit Puranas*. Philadelphia: Temple University Press, 2012.

Diodorus Siculus, translated by George Booth. *The Historical Library of Diodorus the Sicilian: In Fifteen Books. To Which Are Added the Fragments of Diodorus, and Those Published by H. Valesius, I. Rhodomannus, and F. Ursinus*, Volume 1. London: W. M'Dowall, 1814.

Disraeli, Isaac, and Benjamin Disraeli (Earl of Beaconsfield). *Curiosities of Literature*, Volume 2. Boston: Veazie, 1861.

Doane, Thomas William. *Bible Myths, and Their Parallels in Other Religions: Being a Comparison of the Old and New Testament Myths and Miracles with Those of Heathen Nations of Antiquity, Considering Also Their Origin and Meaning*. New York: J. W. Bouton, 1884.

Donald, James. *Chambers's English Dictionary: Pronouncing, Explanatory, and Etymological; with Vocabularies of Scottish Words and Phrases, Americanisms, etc.* London: W. and R. Chambers, 1872.

Doninger, Wendy, editor. *Merriam-Webster's Encyclopedia of World Religions*. Springfield, MA: Merriam-Webster, 1999.

Douglas, Kenyon, J. *Forbidden History: Prehistoric Technologies, Extraterrestrial Intervention, and the Suppressed Origins of Civilization*. Rochester, VT: Inner Traditions/Bear, 2005.

Dowden, Ken, and Niall Livingstone. *A Companion to Greek Mythology*. West Sussex: John Wiley, 2011.

Dowson, John. *A Classical Dictionary of Hindu Mythology and Religion, Geography, History, and Literature*. London: Trübner, 1870.

Dunham, Samuel Astley. *History of Denmark, Sweden, and Norway*, Volume 2. London: Longman, Orme, Brown, Green and Longmans and John Taylor, 1839.

Dunlop, John T. *The History of Fiction: Being a Critical Account of the Most Celebrated Works of Fiction from the Earliest Greek Romances to the Novels of the Present Age*. London: Longman Brown, Green, and Longman, 1825.

Dyer, Thomas Firminger Thiselton. *Church-Lore Gleanings*. London: A. D. Innes, 1892.

Eason, Cassandra. *A Complete Guide to Faeries and Magical Beings: Explore the Mystical Realm of the Little People*. Boston: Weiser Books, 2002.

Eberhard, Wolfram. *Dictionary of Chinese Symbols: Hidden Symbols in Chinese Life and Thought*. New York: Psychology Press, 2002.

Eitel, E. J. *Hand-Book for the Student of Chinese Buddhism*. London: Trübner, 1870.

Eivind, R. *Finnish Legends for English Children*. London: T. Fisher Unwin, 1893.

Eller, Jack. *Introducing Anthropology of Religion: Culture to the Ultimate*. New York: Routledge, 2007.

Ellis, Peter Berresford. *A Brief History of the Druids*. New York: Running Press, 2002.

_____. *Celtic Myths and Legends*. New York: Running Press, 1999.

Elwell, Walter A., and Philip Wesley Comfort. *Tyndale Bible Dictionary*. Wheaton: Tyndale House, 2001.

Encyclopædia Metropolitana; or, System of Universal Knowledge. Glasgow: Richard Griffin, 1855.

Enns, Paul P. *The Moody Handbook of Theology*. Chicago: Moody, 2008.

Enterline, James Robert. *Erikson, Eskimos and Columbus: Medieval European Knowledge of America*. Baltimore: Johns Hopkins University Press, 2002.

Esposito, John L. *The Oxford Dictionary of Islam*. Oxford: Oxford University Press, 2003.

Evans, Bergen. *Dictionary of Mythology*. New York: Dell, 1970.

Evans-Wentz, W. Y. *The Fairy-Faith in Celtic Countries*. New York: Courier Dover Publications, 2003.

Evelyn-White, Hugh Gerard, and Homer. *Hesiod, the Homeric Hymns, and Homerica*. London: W. Heinemann, 1920.

Evslin, Bernard. *Gods, Demigods, and Demons: An Encyclopedia of Greek Mythology*. New York: Scholastic, 1975.

Faber, George Stanley. *The Origin of Pagan Idolatry Ascertained from Historical Testimony and Cir-*

cumstantial Evidence, Volume 2. London: A.J. Valpy, 1816.

Farmer, John Stephen, and W. E. Henley. *Slang and Its Analogues Past and Present: A Dictionary Historical and Comparative of the Heterodox Speech of All Classes of Society for More Than Three Hundred Years, with Synonyms in English, French, German, Italian and Etc. Compiled by J.S. Farmer [and W. E. Henley]*, Volume 2. London: Harrison, 1891.

Farrar, Janet, and Stewart Farrar. *The Witches' Goddess*. Cincinnati: David and Charles, 2012.

Faustino, Mara. *Heaven and Hell: A Compulsively Readable Compendium of Myth, Legend, Wisdom, and Wit for Saints and Sinners*. New York: Atlantic Monthly Press, 2004.

Feder, Kenneth L. *Encyclopedia of Dubious Archaeology: From Atlantis to the Walam Olum: From Atlantis to the Walam Olum*. Santa Barbara, CA: ABC-CLIO, 2010.

Federation of European Sections of the Theosophical Society. Congress. *Transactions of the Third Annual Congress of the Federation of the European Sections of the Theosophical Society Held in Paris July 3–6, 1906*. London: Published for the Council of the Federation, 1907.

Flaum, Eric, and David Pandy. *The Encyclopedia of Mythology: Gods, Heroes, and Legends of the Greeks and Romans*. Philadelphia: Courage Books, 1993.

Flood, Bo, Beret E. Strong, and William Flood. *Pacific Island Legends: Tales from Micronesia, Melanesia, Polynesia and Austrialia*. Honolulu: Bess Press, 1999.

Ford, Patrick K. *The Mabinogi and Other Medieval Welsh Tales*. Berkeley: University of California Press, 2008.

Forsyth, Phyllis Young. *Atlantis: The Making of Myth*. Montreal: Taylor and Francis, 1980.

Frankel, Ellen, and Betsy Patkin Teutsch. *The Encyclopedia of Jewish Symbols*. Lanham, MD: Rowman and Littlefield, 1992.

Frazer, Sir James George. *The Belief in Immortality and the Worship of the Dead: The Belief Among the Aborigines of Australia, the Torres Straits Islands, New Guinea and Melanesia*. London: MacMillan, 1913.

_____. *Folk-Lore in the Old Testament*, Volume 2, *Studies in Comparative Religion, Legend and Law*. London: Macmillan, 1919.

_____. *The Golden Bough: A Study in Magic and Religion*. Oxford: Oxford University Press, 1998.

Freese, John Henry, editor. *The Philosophy of the Immortality of the Soul and the Resurrection of the Human Body*. London: Emily Faithfull, 1864.

Froud, Brian, and Alan Lee. *Faeries*. New York: Harry N. Abrams, 1978.

Fulgentius, Fabius Planciades. *Fulgentius the Mythographer*. Athens: Ohio State University Press, 1971.

Gagarin, Michael, and Elaine Fantham, editors. *The Oxford Encyclopedia of Ancient Greece and Rome: Academy-Bible*, Volume 1. Oxford: Oxford University Press, 2009.

Galang, Zoilo M. *Encyclopedia of the Philippines: Literature*. Manila: E. Floro, 1950.

Gardiner, Philip. *Gateways to the Otherworld: The Secrets Beyond the Final Journey, from the Egyptian Underworld to the Gates in the Sky*. Franklin Lakes: Career Press, 2009.

Gardner, Marshall Blutcher. *A Journey to the Earth's Interior: Or, Have the Poles Really Been Discovered*. Aurora, IL: M. B. Gardner, 1920.

Garg, Ganga Ram. *Encyclopaedia of the Hindu World: A–Aj*, Volume 1. New Delhi: Concept, 1992.

_____. *Encyclopaedia of the Hindu World: Ak–Aq*, Volume 1. New Delhi: Concept, 1992.

_____. *Encyclopaedia of the Hindu World: Ar–Az*, Volume 1. New Delhi: Concept, 1992.

_____. *Hand Book of Hindu Religion and Ethics*. New Delhi: Mittal, 1998.

Garrett, John. *A Classical Dictionary of India: Illustrative of the Mythology, Philosophy, Literature, Antiquities, Arts, Manners, Customs etc. of the Hindus*. Madras: Higginbotham, 1871.

Gibb, Sir Hamilton Alexander Rosskeen, and J. H. Kramers. *Concise Encyclopedia of Islam*. Lieden: Brill Academic, 1991.

Gillies, John. "XXVII: From Alexander to Augustus" in *The History of Ancient Greece: Its Colonies and Conquests; from the Earliest Accounts till the Division of the Macedonian Empire in the East. Including the History of Literature, Philosophy, and the Fine Arts*, Volume 4, Part 2. London: T. Cadell and W. Davies, 1820.

Gilman, Daniel Coit, Harry Thurston Peck, and Frank Moore Colby. *The New International Encyclopædia*, Volume 6. New York: Dodd, Mead, 1903.

Glassé, Cyril. *Concise Encyclopedia of Islam*. Walnut Creek, CA: Altamira, 2003.

The Glorious Quran: English Translation. N.p.: Hamdaan Publications.

Godwin, David, and Aleister Crowley. *Godwin's Cabalistic Encyclopedia: A Complete Guide to Cabalistic Magick*. St. Paul, MN: Llewellyn, 1994.

Goekoop, Cees H. *Where on Earth Is Ithaca? A Quest for the Homeland of Odysseus*. Delft: Eburon Uitgeverij B.V., 2010.

Gould, L. M. *Miscellaneous Notes and Queries with Answers in All Departments of Literature*, Volume 2. Manchester: S. C. and L. M. Gould, 1885.

Gould, Sabine Baring. *Curious Myths of the Middle Ages*. N.p: N.p., 1866.

Grant, Michael, and John Hazel. *Routledge Who's Who in Classical Mythology*. New York: Psychology Press, 2002.

Grant, Richard. *American Nomads: Travels with Lost Conquistadors, Mountain Men, Cowboys, Indians, Hoboes, Truckers, and Bullriders*. New York: Grove Press, 2005.

Graves, Robert. *The Greek Myths: Classics Deluxe Edition*. New York: Penguin, 2012.

Greer, John Michael. *The New Encyclopedia of the Occult*. St. Paul, MN: Llewellyn, 2003.

Gregory, Lady, Finn MacCumhaill, and William Butler Yeats. *Gods and Fighting Men: The Story of Tuatha de Danann and of the Fianna of Ireland*. London: John Murray, 1905.

Grey, Sir George. *Maori Lore: The Traditions of the Maori People, with the More Important of Their Legends*. Wellington: J. Mackay, 1904.

Grimal, Pierre, editor. *Larousse World Mythology*, Secaucus, NJ: Chartwell Books, 1965.

Grimassi, Raven. *Encyclopedia of Wicca and Witchcraft*. St. Paul, MN: Llewellyn, 2000.

Grimes, Heilan Yvette. *The Norse Myths*. N.p.: Heilan Yvette Grimes, 2010.

Grimm, Jacob. *Teutonic Mythology*, Volume 2. London: George Bell, 1883.

Guerber, H. A. *Hammer of Thor—Norse Mythology and Legends—Special Edition*. El Paso: Special Edition Books, 2010.

_____. *Myths of the Norsemen: From the Eddas and Sagas*. New York: Dover Publications, Incorporated, 1992.

Guest, Edwin. *Origines Celticae (a Fragment) and Other Contributions to the History of Britain,* Volume 1. London: Macmillan, 1883.

Guest, Lady Charlotte, translator. *The Mabinogion*. Whitefish, MT: Kessinger, 2006.

Guiley, Rosemary Ellen. *The Encyclopedia of Demons and Demonology*. New York: Infobase, 2009.

_____. *The Encyclopedia of Magic and Alchemy*. New York: Infobase, 2006.

Guthrie, W. K. C., William Keith and Chambers Guthrie. *A History of Greek Philosophy: Volume 4, Plato: The Man and His Dialogues: Earlier Period*. Cambridge: Cambridge University Press, 1986.

Gwyndaf, Robin, editor. *Chwedlau Gwerin Cymru (Welsh Folk Tales)*. Cardiff: National Museum Wales, 1989.

Hager, Alan. *Encyclopedia of British Writers, 16th, 17th, and 18th Centuries*. New York: Infobase, 2009.

Hamilton, Albert Charles. *The Spenser Encyclopedia*. London: Routledge, 2004.

Hanauer, J. E. *Folklore of the Holy Land: Moslem, Christian, and Jewish*. Minneola, NY: Courier Dover, 1935.

Hansen, William F. *Handbook of Classical Mythology*. Santa Barbara, CA: ABC-CLIO, 2004.

Hard, Robin. *The Routledge Handbook of Greek Mythology: Based on H.J. Rose's "Handbook of Greek Mythology."* New York: Psychology Press, 2004.

Hartley, Christine. *The Western Mystery Tradition: The Esoteric Heritage of the West*. London: Aquarian, 1968.

Hastings, James, John Alexander Selbie, and Louis Herbert Gray. *Encyclopædia of Religion and Ethics*, Volume 2. New York: Charles Scribner, 1910.

_____. *Encyclopedia of Religion and Ethics*, Part 3. Whitefish, MT: Kessinger, 2003.

_____. *Encyclopedia of Religion and Ethics*, Part 7. Whitefish, MT: Kessinger, 2003.

Haughton, Brian. *Haunted Spaces, Sacred Places: A Field Guide to Stone Circles, Crop Circles, Ancient Tombs, and Supernatural Landscapes: Easy Read Large Bold Edition*. Franklin Lakes, NJ: Career Press, 2009.

Hayes, Derek. *Historical Atlas of Canada: Canada's History Illustrated with Original Maps*. Vancouver: Douglas and McIntyre, 2006.

Hazlewood, David, and James Calvert. *A Fijian and English and an English and Fijian Dictionary: With Examples of Common and Peculiar Modes of Expression and Uses of Words: Also, Containing Brief Hints on Native Customs, Proverbs, the Native Names of Natural Productions, and Notices of the Islands of Fiji, and a Grammar of the Language with Example of Native Idioms*. London: Sampson Low, Marston, 1872.

Heidel, Alexander. *Gilgamesh Epic and Old Testament Parallels*. Chicago: University of Chicago Press, 1963.

Heinen, Anton M., and Suyūṭī. *Islamic Cosmology: A Study of as-Suyūṭī's al-Hay'a as-Sanīya Fī L-Hay'a as-Sunnīya, with Critical Edition, Translation, and Commentary*. Beirut: Orient-Institut der Deutschen Morgenländischen Gesellschaft, 1982.

Henderson, Lizanne, and Edward J. Cowan. *Scottish Fairy Belief: A History*. Tonawanda, NY: Dundurn Press, 2001.

Hendrickson, Robert. *The Facts on File Dictionary of American Regionalisms*. New York: Infobase, 2000.

Herodotus, and William Beloe, translator. *Herodotus*, Volume 2. London: Leigh and S. Southeby, 1806.

Hesiod, and Hugh Gerard Evelyn-White, editor. *Hesiod, the Homeric Hymns and Homerica*. Cambridge: Harvard University Press, 1995.

Hewitt, James, Francis Katherinus. *History and Chronology of the Myth-Making Age*. London: J. Parker, 1901.

Hexham, Irving. *The Concise Dictionary of Religion*. Vancouver: Regent College, 1993.

Hiatt, Lester Richard. *Australian Aboriginal Concepts*. Canberra: Australian Institute of Aboriginal Studies, 1978.

Hill, Ordelle G. *Looking Westward: Poetry, Landscape, and Politics in Sir Gawain and the Green*

Knight. Cranbury, NJ: Associated University Presses, 2009.

Hodgson, J, F. C. Laird, and John Britton. *The Beauties of England and Wales; or, Original Delineations, Topographical, Historical, and Descriptive of Each County*, Volume XII, Part 1. London: Longman, 1813.

Horowitz, Wayne. *Mesopotamian Cosmic Geography*, Volume 8. Winona Lake, IN: Eisenbrauns, 1998.

Hoult, Powis. *A Dictionary of Some Theosophical Terms*. London: Theosophical Publishing Society, 1910.

Houtsma, M. Th., editor. *E. J. Brill's First Encyclopaedia of Islam: 1913–1936*. Leiden: Brill, 1993.

Howard, Angela Falco. *The Imagery of the Cosmological Buddha*. Lieden: Brill Archive, 1986.

Huber, Michael. *Mythematics: Solving the Twelve Labors of Hercules*. Princeton, NJ: Princeton University Press, 2009.

Hughes, Thomas Patrick. *A Dictionary of Islam: Being a Cyclopædia of the Doctrines, Rites, Ceremonies, and Customs, Together with the Technical and Theological Terms, of the Muhammadan Religion*. London: W. H. Allen, 1896.

Hyamson, Albert Montefiore. *A Dictionary of English Phrases: Phraseological Allusions, Catchwords, Stereotyped Modes of Speech and Metaphors, Nicknames, Sobriquets, Derivations from Personal Names, Etc., with Explanations and Thousands of Exact References to Their Sources or Early Usage*. London: Routledge, 1922.

Illes, Judika. *Encyclopedia of Spirits: The Ultimate Guide to the Magic of Fairies, Genies, Demons, Ghosts, Gods and Goddesses*. New York: HarperCollins, 2009.

Ingram, James. *An Inaugural Lecture on the Utility of Anglo-Saxon Literature*. Oxford: Cooke and Parker, 1807.

Jarvie, Gordon, editor. *Irish Folk and Fairy Tales*. Belfast: Blackstaff Press, 1992.

John, Ivor B. *Popular Studies in Mythology, Romance and Folklore*, Volumes 11–16. London: David Nutt, 1901.

Johnson, Donald S. *Phantom Islands of the Atlantic: The Legends of Seven Lands That Never Were*. New York: Avon Books, 1998.

Johnston, Ian C., and Homer. *The Odyssey: A New Translation*. Arlington, VA: Richer Resources Publications, 2007.

Jones, James Athearn. *Traditions of the North American Indians Being a Second and Revised Edition of Tales of an Indian Camp*, Volume One 1830. Whitefish, MT: Kessinger, 2005.

Jones, Richard. *Myths and Legends of Britain and Ireland*. Auckland: New Holland, 2006.

Joseph, Frank. *The Atlantis Encyclopedia*. Franklin Lakes: Career Press, 2005.

Josephus, Flavius, and William Whiston, translator. *The Works of Flavius Josephus: The Learned and Authentic Jewish Historian and Celebrated Warrior, to Which Are Added, Three Dissertations, Concerning Jesus Christ, John the Baptist, James the Just, God's Command to Abraham, Etc. with an Index to the Whole*, Volume 1. London: Lackington, Allen, 1806.

Jōya, Moku. *Quaint Customs and Manners of Japan*, Volume 3. Tokyo: Tokyo News Service, 1960.

Joyce, Patrick Weston. *Old Celtic Romances: Translated from the Gaelic by P. W. Joyce*. London: D. Nutt, 1894.

Kaplan, Rabbi Aryeh. *Innerspace: Introduction to Kabbalah, Meditation and Prophecy*. Jerusalem: Moznaim, 1990.

Karr, Phyllis Ann. *The Arthurian Companion: The Legendary World of Camelot and the Round Table*. Oakland, CA: Chaosium Books, 1997.

_____. *The King Arthur Companion: The Legendary World of Camelot and the Round Table as Revealed by the Tales Themselves*. Reston, VA: Reston, 1983.

Keary, Charles Francis. *Outlines of Primitive Belief Among the Indo-European Races*. New York: Scribner's, 1882.

Keating, Geoffrey. *Forus feasa air Éirinn, Keating's History of Ireland, Book 1, Part 1, ed. with Gaelic Text, tr., etc. by P.W. Joyce*. Dublin: M. H. Gill, 1880.

Keightley, Thomas. *The World Guide to Gnomes, Fairies, Elves and Other Little People*. New York: Random House Value, 1878.

Kennedy, Mike Dixon. *Encyclopedia of Russian and Slavic Myth and Legend*. Santa Barbara, CA: ABC-CLIO, 1998.

Kern, Hendrik. *Manual of Indian Buddhism*. Strassburg: Karl J. Trübner, 1896.

Kindersley, Nathaniel E. *Specimens of Hindoo Literature: Consisting of Translations from the Tamoul Language of Some Hindoo Works of Morality and Imagination with Explanatory Notes: To Which Are Prefixed Introductory Remarks on the Mythology, Literature, etc, of the Hindoos*. London: W. Bulmer, 1794.

King, Joseph Edward. *The Glorious Kingdom of Saguenay*. Toronto: University of Toronto Press, 1950.

King, Leonard William. *Babylonian Religion and Mythology*. London: Kegan Paul, Trench, Trübner, 1903.

Kirch, Patrick V. *Island Societies: Archaeological Approaches to Evolution and Transformation*. Melbourne: Cambridge University Press, 1986.

Kish, George. *A Source Book in Geography*. Cambridge: Harvard University Press, 1978.

Kleiner, John. *Mismapping the Underworld: Daring and Error in Dante's Comedy*. Stanford, CA: Stanford University Press, 1994.

Kluger; Rivkah Schärf, and H. Yehezkel Kluger.

The Archetypal Significance of Gilgamesh: A Modern Ancient Hero. Einsiedeln, CH: Daimon Verlag, 1991.

Knapp, Stephen. *The Heart of Hinduism: The Eastern Path to Freedom, Empowerment and Illumination.* New York: iUniverse, 2005.

_____. *The Secret Teachings of the Vedas.* Detroit: Jaico Publishing House, 1993.

Knappert, Jan. *Indian Mythology: An Encyclopedia of Myth and Legend.* London: Aquarian Press (HarperCollins), 1991.

_____. *Myths and Legends of the Swahili.* London: Heinemann Educational Books, 1970.

Knowles, James. *The Nineteenth Century,* Volume 31. London: Sampson Low, Marston, 1892.

Koch, John. *Celtic Culture: A Historical Encyclopedia,* Volume 1. Santa Barbara, CA: ABC-CLIO, 2006.

_____. *Celtic Culture: Aberdeen Breviary-Celticism.* Santa Barbara, CA: ABC-CLIO, 2006.

Kõiva, Enn O. *Using Estonian/American Based Culture Models for Multi-Cultural Studies: An Innovative Approach to Studying the Multi-Cultural, Multi-Ethnic Experience.* Andover, CT: Estonian/American Culture Models, 1979.

Kovacs, Maureen G., translator. *The Epic of Gilgamesh.* Stanford, CA: Stanford University Press, 1989.

Kraig, Donald Michael. *Modern Magic: Eleven Lessens in the High Magical Arts.* St. Paul, MN: Llewellyn, 2004.

Kramer, Samuel N. *Sumerian Mythology: A Study of Spiritual and Literary Achievement in the Third Millennium B.C.* Philadelphia: University of Pennsylvania Press, 1972.

_____. *The Sumerians: Their History, Culture and Character.* Chicago: University of Chicago Press, 1964.

Kremer, Don. *The Chronological Order of the Endtimes.* Bloomington, IN: AuthorHouse, 2010.

Lacy, Norris J., editor. *The Arthurian Encyclopedia.* New York: Garland, 1986.

_____, editor. *Text and Intertext in Medieval Arthurian Literature.* New York: Routledge, 2013.

Lane, Edward William. *The Manners and Customs of the Modern Egyptians.* London: J. M. Dent, 1908.

_____, translator. *Sindbad the Sailor: And, Ali Baba and the Forty Thieves.* New York: Scribners, 1895.

_____, translator. *The Thousand and One Nights: Commonly Called, in England, the Arabian Nights' Entertainments. A New Translation from the Arabic, with Copious Notes.* London: Charles Knight, 1839.

Lang, Andrew. *Custom and Myth.* London: Longmans, Green, 1884.

Lansing, Richard, editor. *Dante Encyclopedia.* New York: Routledge, 2010.

Larkin, Clarence. *The Book of Revelation.* Stilwell, KS: Digireads.com, 2007.

Larson, Laurence Marcellus, translator. *The King's Mirror: (Speculum Reagle—Konungs Skuggsjá).* New York: American-Scandinavian Foundation, 1917.

Latta, Jeffrey Blair. *The Franklin Conspiracy: Cover-Up, Betrayal, and the Astonishing Secret Behind the Lost Arctic Expedition.* Toronto: Dundurn, 2001.

Lebling, Robert. *Legends of the Fire Spirits: Jinn and Genies from Arabia to Zanzibar.* London: I.B. Tauris, 2010.

Lee, A.G., editor. *Ovid: Metamorphoses I.* Wauconda: Bolchazy-Carducci, 1953.

Leenaars, Antoon A., editor. *Suicide in Canada.* Toronto: University of Toronto Press, 1998.

Leick, Dr Gwendolyn. *A Dictionary of Ancient Near Eastern Mythology.* New York: Routledge, 2002.

Lemprière, John. *A Classical Dictionary: Containing a Copious Account of All the Proper Names Mentioned in Ancient Authors.* New York: E. Duyckinck, G. Long, 1825.

Leon-Portilla, Miguel. *Aztec Thought and Culture: A Study of the Ancient Nahuatl Mind.* Norman: University of Oklahoma Press, 2012.

Lepage, Victoria. *Shambhala: The Fascinating Truth Behind the Myth of Shangri-la.* Wheaton: Quest Books, 1996.

Le Plongeon, Augustus. *Queen Móo and the Egyptian Sphinx.* New York: Kegan Paul, Trench, Thuner, 1896.

Leslie, Forbes. *The Early Races of Scotland and Their Monuments.* Whitefish, MT: Kessinger, 2005.

Lethaby, W. R. *Architecture, Mysticism and Myth.* New York: Cosimo, 2005.

Levitas, Ruth. *The Concept of Utopia.* New York: Peter Lang, 2010.

Leviton, Richard. *Encyclopedia of Earth Myths: An Insider's A–Z Guide to Mythic People, Places, Objects, and Events Central to the Earth's Visionary Geography.* Charlottesville, VA: Hampton Roads, 2005.

_____. *The Geomantic Year: A Calendar of Earth-Focused Festivals That Align the Planet with the Galaxy.* New York: iUniverse, 2006.

_____. *The Gods in Their Cities: Geomantic Locales of the Ray Masters and Great White Brotherhood, and How to Interact with Them.* New York: iUniverse, 2006.

Lewis, Sir George Cornewall. *An Historical Survey of the Astronomy of the Ancients.* London: Parker, 1862.

Lewis, James R. *Satanism Today.* Santa Barbara, CA: ABC-CLIO, 2001.

_____, and Evelyn Dorothy Oliver. *Angels A to Z, 2nd Edition.* Canton, MI: Visible Ink Press, 2008.

Lilly, William. *Christian Astrology,* Book 3: *An*

Easie and Plaine Method Teaching How to Judge Upon Nativities. Bel Air, MD: Astrology Center of America, 2005.

Lincoln, Bruce. *Death, War, and Sacrifice: Studies in Ideology and Practice.* Chicago: University of Chicago Press, 1991.

Lindahl, Carl, John McNamara, and John Lindow. *Medieval Folklore: An Encyclopedia of Myths, Legends, Tales, Beliefs, and Customs,* Volume 1. Santa Barbara, CA: ABC-CLIO, 2000.

Lindow, John. *Norse Mythology: A Guide to Gods, Heroes, Rituals, and Beliefs.* Oxford: Oxford University Press, 2002.

Littleton, C. Scott, editor. *Gods, Goddesses, and Mythology,* Volumes 1, 5, 10 and 11. Tarrytown, NY: Marshall Cavendish Corporation, 2005.

Livingstone, David N., and Charles W. J. Withers. *Geography and Enlightenment.* Chicago: University of Chicago Press, 1999.

Lockyer, Herbert. *All the Doctrines of the Bible: A Study and Analysis of Major Bible Doctrines.* Grand Rapids, MI: Zondervan, 1988.

Loewenstein, David. *Milton: Paradise Lost.* Cambridge: Cambridge University Press, 2004.

Logan, Siobhan, and Dolores Logan. *Firebridge to Skyshore: A Northern Lights Journey.* Maryport, UK: Original Plus, 2009.

Lowenstein, Tom, and Piers Vitebsky. *Native American Myths and Beliefs.* New York: Rosen, 2011.

Lucian of Samosata, Henry Watson Fowler and Francis George Fowler, translators. *The Works of Lucian of Samosata: Complete with Exceptions Specified in the Preface.* Oxford: Clarendon Press, 1905.

Lurker, Manfred. *The Routledge Dictionary of Gods and Goddesses, Devils and Demons.* New York: Routledge, 2004.

Lynch, Patricia Ann, and Jeremy Roberts. *Native American Mythology A to Z.* New York: Infobase, 2010.

Lynge, Inge. *Mental Disorders in Greenland. Past and Present.* Copenhagen: Museum Tusculanum Press, 1997.

Maberry, Jonathan, and David F. Kramer. *The Cryptopedia: A Dictionary of the Weird, Strange and Downright Bizarre.* New York: Citadel Press, 2007.

Macintyre, Stuart. *A Concise History of Australia.* Cambridge: Cambridge University Press, 2009.

MacKenzie, Donald A. *Teutonic Myth and Legend.* Whitefish, MT: Kessinger, 2004.

MacKey, Albert G., and Harry LeRoy Haywood. *Encyclopedia of Freemasonry 1909.* Whitefish, MT: Kessinger, 2003.

MacLeod, Sharon Paice. *Celtic Myth and Religion: A Study of Traditional Belief, with Newly Translated Prayers, Poems and Songs.* Jefferson, NC: McFarland, 2011.

Macrone, Michael. *It's Greek to Me.* New York: HarperCollins, 1994.

Magasich-airola, Jorge, and Jean-marc De Beer. *America Magica: When Renaissance Europe Thought It Had Conquered Paradise.* London: Anthem Press, 2007.

Mahon, Michael Patrick. *Ireland's Fairy Lore.* Boston: Thomas J. Flynn, 1919.

Maier, Bernhard. *Dictionary of Celtic Religion and Culture.* Woodbridge: Boydell and Brewer, 1997.

Maier, John R. *Gilgamesh: A Reader.* Wauconda: Bolchazy-Carducci, 1997.

Malkowski, Edward F. *Before the Pharaohs: Egypt's Mysterious Prehistory.* Rochester, VT: Inner Traditions/Bear, 2006.

Malory, Sir Thomas. *Le Morte Darthur: The Winchester Manuscript.* Oxford: Oxford University Press, 1998.

Mandeville, Sir John. *The Voiage and Travayle of Sir John Maundeville Knight: Which Treateth of the Way Toward Hierusalem and of Marvayles of Inde with Other Islands and Countreys.* London: Pickering and Chatto, 1887.

Mandzuka, Zlatko. *Demystifying the Odyssey.* Bloomington, IN: AuthorHouse, 2013.

Manguel, Alberto, and Gianni Guadalupi. *The Dictionary of Imaginary Places: Newly Updated and Expanded.* Boston: Houghton Mifflin Harcourt, 2010.

Markale, Jean. *Courtly Love: The Path of Sexual Initiation.* Rochester, VT: Inner Traditions/Bear, 2000.

Martínez, Javier. "Onomacritus the Forger, Hipparchus' Scapegoat?" in *Fakes and Forgers of Classical Literature,* p. 225. Madrid: Ediciones Clásicas, 2011.

Massey, Gerald. *Ancient Egypt, the Light of the World: A Work of Reclamation and Restitution in Twelve Books,* Volume 1. London: T. Fisher Unwin, 1907.

Mathers, Samuel Liddell MacGregor, and John William Brodie-Innes. *The Sorcerer and His Apprentice: Unknown Hermetic Writings of S.L. MacGregor Mathers and J.W. Brodie-Innes.* London: Aquarian, 1983.

Matson, Gienna. *Celtic Mythology A to Z.* New York: Infobase, 2010.

Matthews, John, and Caitlin Matthews, editors. *The Encyclopaedia of Celtic Myth and Legend: A Definitive Sourcebook of Magic, Vision, and Lore.* Guilford, CT: Globe Pequot, 2004.

Matthews, W. H. *Mazes and Labyrinths: Their History and Development.* Whitefish, MT: Kessinger, 2003.

McClintock, John, and James Strong. *Cyclopaedia of Biblical, Theological, and Ecclesiastical Literature,* Volume 3. New York: Harper, 1894.

McCoy, Edain. *A Witch's Guide to Faery Folk: Reclaiming Our Working Relationship with Invisible Helpers.* St. Paul, MN: Llewellyn, 1994.

McCue, Gray. *Trekking in Tibet: A Traveler's Guide.* Seattle: Mountaineers Books, 1999.

McKinnell, John. *Meeting the Other in Norse Myth and Legend*. Cambridge: D.S. Brewer, 2005.

Mead, Sidney M. *Tāwhaki: The Deeds of a Demigod*. Auckland: Reed Consumer Books, 1996.

Mehr, Farhang. *The Zoroastrian Tradition: An Introduction to the Ancient Wisdom of Zarathustra*. Shaftesbury, Dorset: Element, 1991.

Melrose, Robin. *The Druids and King Arthur: A New View of Early Britain*. Jefferson, NC: McFarland, 2010.

Menegon, Eugenio. *Ancestors, Virgins, and Friars: Christianity as a Local Religion in Late Imperial China*. Cambridge, MA: Harvard University Press, 2009.

Menon, Ramesh. *The Mahabharata*. New York: iUniverse, 2006.

Mercatante, Anthony S. *Who's Who in Egyptian Mythology*. New York: Barnes and Noble, 1998.

Merriam-Webster's Encyclopedia of Literature. Springfield, MA: Merriam-Webster, 1995.

Merrick, James Lyman, and Muḥammad Bāqir ibn Muḥammad Taqī Majlisī. *Hayât al-qulûb*. Boston: Phillips, Sampson, 1850.

Mew, James. *Traditional Aspects of Hell (Ancient and Modern)*. London: Swan Sonnenschein, 1903.

Meyer, Marvin W., and James M. Robinson. *The Nag Hammadi Scriptures*. New York: HarperCollins, 2010.

Mikalson, Jon D. *Ancient Greek Religion*. Oxford: John Wiley, 2011.

Mills, Watson E., and Roger Aubrey Bullard. *Mercer Dictionary of the Bible*. Macon, GA: Mercer University Press, 1990.

Monaghan, Patricia. *The Encyclopedia of Celtic Mythology and Folklore*. New York: Infobase, 2009.

More, Brookes. *Gods and Heroes: And Myths from Ovid, Also Sonnets and Legends*. Fort Smith, AR: Thrash-Lick, 1916.

More, Sir Thomas (Saint), with George M. Logan, Robert M. Adams, Clarence H. Miller, editors. *More: Utopia: Latin Text and English Translation*. Cambridge: Cambridge University Press, 1995.

Moreno, Manuel Aguilar. *Handbook to Life in the Aztec World*. Oxford: Oxford University Press, 2007.

Morford, Mark Percy Owen. *Classical Mythology*. Oxford: Oxford University Press, 1999.

Morley, Henry. *Ideal Commonwealths: Plutarch's Lycurgus, More's Utopia, Bacon's New Atlantis, Campanella's City of the Sun and a Fragment of Hall's Mundus Alter et Idem*. London: George Rutledge, 2008.

Morris, James M., and Andrea L. Kross. *The A to Z of Utopianism*. Lanham, MD: Scarecrow, 2009.

Morris, Kenneth. *The Fates of the Princes of Dyfed*. Point Loma, CA: Aryan Theosophical Press, 1914.

Mortensen, Karl. *A Handbook of Norse Mythology*. New York: Thomas Y. Crowell, 1913.

Morus, Cenydd. *The Fates of the Princes of Dyfed 1914*. Whitefish, MT: Kessinger, 2004.

Mouhy, Charles de Fieux. *Lamekis, ou les Voyages Extraordinaires d'un Egyptien dans la Terre Intérieure, avec la Découverte de l'Isle des Silphides*. Amsterdam: Chez J. Neaulme, 1738.

Mountain, Harry. *The Celtic Encyclopedia*, Volume 5. Aveiro, PT: Universal-Publishers, 1998.

Mountford, Charles Pearcy. *The Tiwi: Their Art, Myth, and Ceremony*. London: Phoenix House, 1958.

Munn, Mark H. *The Mother of the Gods, Athens, and the Tyranny of Asia: A Study of Sovereignty in Ancient Religion*. Berkeley: University of California Press, 2006.

Muss-Arnolt, William. *A Concise Dictionary of the Assyrian Language*, Volume 1. Berlin: Reuther and Reichard, 1905.

Nagao, Gadjin Masato, and Jonathan A. Silk, editors. *Wisdom, Compassion, and the Search for Understanding: The Buddhist Studies Legacy of Gadjin M. Nagao*. Honolulu: University of Hawaii Press, 2000.

Nāgārjuna, Red-mda'-ba Gźon-nu-blo-gros. *Nāgārjuna's Letter: Nāgārjuna's "Letter to a Friend," with a Commentary by the Venerable Rendawa, Zhön-nu Lo-drö*. Dharamsala: Library of Tibetan Works and Archives, 1979.

Najovits, Simson R. *Egypt, Trunk of the Tree*, Volume 2. New York: Algora, 2003.

Nansen, Fridtjof. *In Northern Mists: Arctic Exploration in Early Times*, Volume 1. New York: Frederick A. Stokes, 1911.

Narváez, Peter. *The Good People: New Fairylore Essays*. Lexington: University Press of Kentucky, 1997.

Netton, Ian Richard. *A Popular Dictionary of Islam*. New York: Psychology Press, 1997.

Newell, William Wells, and Chrétien de Troyes. *King Arthur and the Table Round: Tales Chiefly After the Old French of Crestien of Troyes, with an Account of Arthurian Romance, and Notes by William Wells Newell*, Volume 2. Cambridge: Houghton, Mifflin, 1911.

Nunn, Patrick D. *Vanished Islands and Hidden Continents of the Pacific*. Honolulu: University of Hawaii Press, 2009.

O'Conor, Norreys Jephson. *Changing Ireland: Literary Backgrounds of the Irish Free State, 1889–1922*. London: Harvard University Press, 1924.

Olberding, Amy, editor. *Mortality in Traditional Chinese Thought*. Albany: SUNY Press, 2011.

Olcott, Frances Jenkins. *The Book of Elves and Fairies*. Minneola, NY: Courier Dover, 2002.

Olmos, Margarite Fernández, and Lizabeth. Paravisini-Gebert. *Sacred Possessions: Vodou, San-*

tería, Obeah, and the Caribbean. New Brunswick: Rutgers University Press, 1997.

Ono, Sokyo, *Shinto: The Kami Way*. Tokyo: Charles E. Tuttle, 1992.

Orbell, Margaret R. *The Concise Encyclopedia of Māori Myth and Legend*. Christchurch, NZ: Canterbury University Press, 1998.

Osborne, Harold. *South American Mythology*. "Library of the World's Myths and Legends." New York: Peter Bedrick Books. 1968.

Osborne, Roger. *Civilization: A New History of the Western World*. New York: Pegasus Books, 2006.

Ossendowski, Ferdynand Antoni. *Beasts, Men and Gods*. New York: E. P. Dutton, 1922.

Oswald, H. P. *Vodoo*. N.p.: Books on Demand, 2009.

Owen, W. *A New and Complete Dictionary of Arts and Sciences*, Volume 2. London: Hommer's Head, 1763.

Page, Denys. *History and the Homeric Land*. Berkeley: University of California Press, 1959.

Parker, Janet, and Julie Stanton, editors. *Mythology: Myths, Legends and Fantasies*. Cape Town, SA: Struik, 2007.

Parks, Edward A., and Samuel H. Taylor. *The Bibliotheca Sacra and American Biblical Repository*, Volume 15. Andover, MA: Warren F. Draper, 1858.

Parmeshwaranand, Swami. *Encyclopaedic Dictionary of Purāṇas*. New Delhi: Sarup, 2001.

_____. *Encyclopaedic Dictionary of Purāṇas: A–C*. New Delhi: Sarup, 2001.

Partington, Charled F. *The British Cyclopaedia of the Arts, Sciences, History, Geography, Literature, Natural History, and Biography*, Volume 3. London: William. S. Orr, 1838.

Patapios, Hieromonk, and Archbishop Chrysostomos. *Manna from Athos: The Issue of Frequent Communion on the Holy Mountain in the Late Eighteenth and Early Nineteenth Centuries*, Volume 2. Bern: Peter Lang, A.G., 2006.

Paulson, Ivar. *The Old Estonian Folk Religion*, Volume 108. Bloomfield: Indiana University Press, 1971.

Pausanias, and Sir James George Frazer, translator. *Pausania's Description of Greece*, Volume 4. London: Macmillan, 1898.

Penglase, Charles. *Greek Myths and Mesopotamia: Parallels and Influence in the Homeric Hymns and Hesiod*. London: Routledge, 2003.

Penrice, John. *A Dictionary and Glossary of the Koran: With Grammatical References and Explanations of the Text*. New York: Biblo and Tannen, 1969.

Pentikäinen, Juha. *Kalevala Mythology, Revised Edition*. Bloomington: Indiana University Press, 1999.

Piccardi, Luigi, and W. Bruce Masse. *Myth and Geology*. Trowbridge: Geological Society, 2007.

Picken, Stuart D. B. *Historical Dictionary of Shinto*. Lanham, MD: Scarecrow, 2010.

Pinch, Geraldine. *Egyptian Mythology: A Guide to the Gods, Goddesses, and Traditions of Ancient Egypt*. Oxford: Oxford University Press, 2002.

Pinkham, Mark Amaru. *The Return of the Serpents of Wisdom*. Kempton, IL: Adventures Unlimited Press, 1997.

Piper, Karen Lynnea. *Cartographic Fictions: Maps, Race, and Identity*. New Brunswick, NJ: Rutgers University Press, 2002.

Plato, and Benjamin Jowett, translator. *The Dialogues of Plato*, Volume 2. New York: Charles Scribner, 1907.

_____, and I. A. Richards, editor. *Plato's Republic*. London: Cambridge University Press Archive, 1966.

Pleij, Herman. *Dreaming of Cockaigne: Medieval Fantasies of the Perfect Life*. New York: Columbia University Press, 2003.

Pliny the Elder, translated by John Bostock and Henry Thomas Riley. *The Natural History of Pliny*, Volumes 1–2. London: George Bells, 1890.

_____, translated by Philemon Holland. *Pliny's Natural History. In Thirty-Seven Books*, Volumes 1–3. London: G. Barclay, 1848.

Polwhele, Richard. *The History of Cornwall, Civil, Military, Religious, Architectural, Agricultural, Commercial, Biographical, and Miscellaneous*, Volumes 1–3. London: Michel, 1816.

Porter, Deborah Lynn. *From Deluge to Discourse: Myth, History, and the Generation of Chinese Fiction*. Albany: SUNY Press, 1996.

Prabhupāda, A. C. Bhaktivedanta Swami. *Śrīmad Bhāgavatam: The Creative Impetus*. Los Angeles: Bhaktivedanta Book Trust, 1999.

_____, and Hridayananda Goswami. *Śrīmad-Bhāgavatam: With a Short Life Sketch of Lord Śrī Caitanya Mahāprabhu, the Ideal Preacher of Bhāgavata-Dharma, and the Original Sanskrit Text, Its Roman Transliteration, Synonyms, Translation and Elaborate Purports*, Volume 5, Part 2. Alachua: Bhaktivedanta Book Trust, 1989.

Prapnnachari, Srikrishna. *The Crest Jewel: Srimadbhagwata Mahapuran with Mahabharata*. N.p.: Srikrishna Prapnnachari, N.D.

Pritsak, Omeljan. *The Origin of Rus': Old Scandinavian Sources Other than the Sagas*. Cambridge: Harvard Ukrainian Research Institute, 1981.

Pruden, Leo M. *Abhidharmakosabhasyam*, Volume 1. Berkeley, CA: Asian Humanities Press, 1988.

Pyle, Howard. *The Story of King Arthur and His Knights*. New York: Scribner's, 1909.

Rabelais, François, and Sir Thomas Urquhart. *Five Books of the Lives, Heroic Deeds and Sayings of Gargantua and His Son Pantagruel;* Volume 2 of 5. London: Lawrence and Bullen, 1892.

Rabinowitz, Shelly, and James R. Lewis. *The Encyclopedia of Modern Witchcraft and Neo-paganism*. New York: Citadel Press, 2004.

Randolph, Keith. *Truth About Astral Projection*. St. Paul, MN: Llewellyn, 1983.

Rawlinson, George. *The History of Herodotus*, Volume 3. New York: D. Appleton, 1860.

Rāya, Pratāpacandra. *The Mahabharata of Krishna-Dwaipayana Vyasa: Bhishma parva*. New Delhi: Munshiram Manoharlal, 2001.

Reddall, Henry Frederic. *Fact, Fancy, and Fable: A New Handbook for Ready Reference on Subjects Commonly Omitted from Cyclopaedias; Comprising Personal Sobriquets, Familiar Phrases, Popular Appellations, Geographical Nicknames, Literary Pseudonyms, Mythological Characters, Red-letter Days, Political Slang, Contractions and Abbreviations, Technical Terms, Foreign Words and Phrases, Americanisms, etc.* Chicago: A. C. McClurg, 1892.

Reed, Alexander Wyclif, and Alice Inez Hames. *Myths and Legends of Fiji and Rotuma*. Wellington, Auckland: Reed, 1967.

Rees, Charlotte Harris. *Secret Maps of the Ancient World*. Bloomington, IN: AuthorHouse, 2008.

Remler, Pat. *Egyptian Mythology, A to Z*. New York: Infobase, 2010.

Rengarajan, T. *Glossary of Hinduism*. New Delhi: Oxford and IBH, 1999.

Rhys, Sir John. *Studies in the Arthurian Legend*. Oxford: Clarendon Press, 1891.

Ring, Trudy, Robert M. Salkin, and Sharon La Boda. *International Dictionary of Historic Places: Middle East and Africa*, Volume 4. London: Taylor and Francis, 1996.

Robbins, Alfred F. "Sir Thomas Malory's "Castle Terabil" in *Notes and Queries: For Readers and Writers, Collectors and Librarians* 41. London: Oxford University Press, 1892.

Roberts, Jeremy. *Chinese Mythology: A to Z*. New York: Infobase, 2009.

_____. *Japanese Mythology A to Z*. New York: Infobase, 2009.

Rolleston, Thomas William. *Celtic Myths and Legends*. Mineola, NY: Courier Dover, 1990.

Roman, Luke, and Mónica Román. *Encyclopedia of Greek and Roman Mythology*. New York: Infobase, 2010.

Romm, James S. *The Edges of the Earth in Ancient Thought: Geography, Exploration, and Fiction*. Princeton, NJ: Princeton University Press, 1994.

Rose, H. J. *A Handbook of Greek Mythology: Including Its Extension to Rome*. Whitefish, MT: Kessinger, 2006.

Rose, Seraphim. *The Soul After Death: Contemporary "After-Death" Experiences in the Light of the Orthodox Teaching on the Afterlife*. Platina, CA: Saint Herman of Alaska Brotherhood, 1980.

Roza, Greg. *Incan Mythology and Other Myths of the Andes*. New York: Rosen, 2007.

Ruck, Carl A. P., and Danny Staples. *The World of Classical Myth: Gods and Goddesses, Heroines and Heroes*. Durham: Carolina Academic Press, 1994.

Rydberg, Viktor, Rasmus Björn Anderson, and James William Buel. *Teutonic Mythology: Gods and Goddesses of the Northland*, Volume 3. London: Norrœna Society, 1907.

Sadakata, Akira. *Buddhist Cosmology*. Tokyo: Kirei, 1997.

Samuel, Gabrielle. *The Kabbalah Handbook: A Concise Encyclopedia of Terms and Concepts in Jewish Mysticism*. New York, Penguin, 2007.

Seigneuret, Jean Charles, editor. *Dictionary of Literary Themes and Motifs*. 1 (1988). A–J. Westport, CT: Greenwood, 1988.

Shaffer, Aaron. "Gilgamesh, the Cedar Forest, and Mesopotamian History," *Journal of the American Oriental Society* Vol. 103 (1983): 307–13.

Simek, Rudolf. *Dictionary of Northern Mythology*. Cambridge: D.S. Brewer, 2007.

Simpson, Pamela H. *Corn Palaces and Butter Queens: A History of Crop Art and Dairy Sculpture*. Minneapolis: University of Minnesota Press, 2012.

Singer, Isidore, and Cyrus Adler, editors. *The Jewish Encyclopedia: A Descriptive Record of the History, Religion, Literature, and Customs of the Jewish People from the Earliest Times to the Present Day*, Volume 10. New York: Funk and Wagnalls, 1907.

Skinner, Charles M. *Myths and Legends of America: Strange Tales from Our Country's History*. Tucson, AZ: Fireship Press, 2007.

Skyes, Edgerton, and Alan Kendall. *Who's Who in Non-Classical Mythology*. New York: Psychology Press, 2002.

Smedley, Edward, William Cooke Taylor, Henry Thompson, and Elihu Rich. *The Occult Sciences: Sketches of the Traditions and Superstitions of Past Times, and the Marvels of the Present Day*. London: R. Griffin, 1855.

Smith, Andrew Phillip. *A Dictionary of Gnosticism*. Wheaton: Quest Books, 2009.

Smith, Benjamin Eli. *The Century Cyclopedia of Names: A Pronouncing and Etymological Dictionary of Names in Geography, Biography, Mythology, History, Ethnology, Art, Archaeology, Fiction, etc., etc*, Volume 6. New York: Century, 1918.

Smith, Edward R. *The Burning Bush*. Hudson, NY: Anthroposophic Press, 1997.

Smith, Tom, and Maurice Isserman. *Discovery of the Americas, 1492–1800*. New York: Infobase, 2009.

Smith, William. *A New Classical Dictionary of Greek and Roman Biography, Mythology and Geography*, Volumes 1–2. Whitefish, MT: Kessinger, 2006.

Smith, Sir William. *Dictionary of Greek and Roman Geography*, Volume 1. London: John Murray, 1872.

_____. *A Dictionary of Greek and Roman Geography: Abacaenum-Hytanis*. London: John Murray, 1878.

Society of Biblical Archæology of London, England. *Transactions of the Society of Biblical Archæology*, Volume 5. London: Longmans, Green, Reader and Dyer, 1877.

Sommer, Heinrich Oskar, editor. *The Vulgate Version of the Arthurian Romances: Index of Names and Places to Volumes I–VII*, Volumes 1–8. Washington: Carnegie Institution, 1916.

Spate, Oskar Hermann Khristian. *The Spanish Lake*. Canberra: Australian National University Press, 2004.

Spence, Lewis. *A Dictionary of Medieval Romance and Romance Writers*. London: G. Routledge, 1913.

_____. *An Encyclopædia of Occultism: A Compendium of Information on the Occult Sciences, Occult Personalities, Psychic Science, Magic, Demonology, Spiritism and Mysticism*. New York: Dodd, Mead, 1920; New York: Cosimo, 2006.

_____. *An Introduction to Mythology*. New York: Cosimo, 2004.

_____. *The Magic Arts in Celtic Britain*. Mineola, NY: Courier Dover, 2012.

_____. *The Minor Traditions of British Mythology*. New York: Benjamin Bloom, 1972.

_____. *The Mysteries of Britain*. Pomeroy: Health Research Books, 1996.

_____. *The Mysteries of Egypt: Secret Rites and Traditions of the Nile*. New York: Cosimo, 2007.

_____, and Nandor Fodor. *Encyclopedia of Occultism and Parapsychology*, Volume 1: *A Compendium of Information on the Occult Sciences, Magic, Demonology, Superstitions, Spiritism, Mysticism, Metaphysics, Psychical Science, and Parapsychology; with Biographical and Bibliographical Notes and Comprehensive Indexes; in Two Volumes*. Detroit: Gale Research, 1991.

Sprague, Roderick. *Burial Terminology: A Guide for Researchers*. Lanham, MD: Rowman Altamira, 2005.

Spring, Samuel, and Gardiner Spring. *Giafar Al Barmeki: A Tale of the Court of Haroun Al Raschid*, Volume 2. New York: Harper, 1836.

Squire, Charles. *Celtic Myth and Legend*. Rockville, MD: Wildside Press, 2003.

_____. *Celtic Myth and Legend, Poetry and Romance*. Whitefish, MT: Kessinger, 2006.

Stepanich, Kisma K. *Faery Wicca*, Book One. St. Paul, MN: Llewellyn, 1997.

Stephens, Susan A. *Seeing Double: Intercultural Poetics in Ptolemaic Alexandria*. Berkeley: University of California Press, 2003.

Stookey, Lorena Laura. *Thematic Guide to World Mythology*. Westport, CT: Greenwood, 2004.

Stork, Mokhtar. *A-Z Guide to the Qur'an: A Must-Have Reference to Understanding the Contents of the Islamic Holy Book*. Singapore: Times Books International, 2000.

Strabo, translated by Hans Claude Hamilton and William Falconer. *The Geography of Strabo*, Volume 1. London: George Bell, 1892.

Strassburg, Gottfried von. *Tristan and Isolde: Gottfried Von Strassburg*. New York: Continuum, 1988.

Strong, John. *The Experience of Buddhism: Sources and Interpretations*. Belmont, CA: Thomson/Wadsworth, 2007.

Sturluson, Snorri. *The Younger Edda, Also Called Snorre's Edda of the Prose Edda: An English Version of the Foreword; the Fooling of Gylfe, the Afterword; Brage's Talk, the Afterword to Brage's Talk, and the Important Passages in the Poetical Diction (Skaldskaparmal)*. Chicago: S.C. Griggs, 1879.

Sturlusonar, Edda Snorra. *The Prose Edda of Snorri Sturluson: Tales from Norse Mythology*. Berkeley: University of California Press, 1964.

Sukhu, Gopal. *SUNY Series in Chinese Philosophy and Culture: Shaman and the Heresiarch: A New Interpretation of the Li Sao*. Albany: SUNY Press, 2012.

Sullivan, C. W. III, editor. *The Mabinogi: A Book of Essays*. New York: Psychology Press, 1996.

Swanson, Paul Loren, and Clark Chilson, editors. *Nanzan Guide to Japanese Religions*. Honolulu: University of Hawaii Press, 2006.

Sylvester, Herbert Milton. *Indian Wars of New England: The Land of the Abenake. The French Occupation. King Philip's War. St. Castin's War*. Boston: W.B. Clarke, 1910.

Tambling, Jeremy. *Allegory*. London: Routledge, 2009.

Taylor, John William. *The Coming of the Saints: Imaginations and Studies in Early Church History and Tradition*. New York: E. P. Dutton, 1907.

Temple, George. *A Glossary of Indian Terms Relating to Religion, Customs, Government, Land; and Other Terms and Words in Common Use: To Which Is Added a Glossary of Terms Used in District Work in the N. W. Provinces and Oudh, and Also Those Applied to Labourers*. London: Luzac, 1897.

Thesiger, Wilfrid. *The Marsh Arabs*. New York: Penguin 1967.

Thorburn, John E. *The Facts on File Companion to Classical Drama*. New York: Infobase, 2005.

Thorpe, Benjamin. *Edda Saemundar hinns Fróda: From the Old Norse or Icelandic*, Volume 2. London: Trübner, 1866.

_____. *Northern Mythology: Comprising the Principal Popular Traditions and Superstitions of Scandinavia, North Germany, and the Netherlands*, Volume 1. London: E. Lumley, 1851.

Tichelaar, Tyler. *King Arthur's Children: A Study in Fiction and Tradition*. London: Loving Healing Press, 2010.

Tomline, George. *An Introduction to the Study of the Bible: Being the Tenth Edition of the First*

Volume of the Elements of Christian Theology, etc. [With MS. Index.]. London: Cadell and Davies, 1813.

Tresidder, Jack. *The Complete Dictionary of Symbols.* Vancouver: Chronicle Books, 2005.

Tripp, Edward. *The Meridian Handbook of Classical Mythology.* New York: Penguin, 1974.

Turner, Patricia, and Charles Russell Coulter. *Dictionary of Ancient Deities.* New York: Oxford University Press, 2001.

Vallee, Jacques. "Taken by the Wind," in *Other Worlds, Other Universes*, edited by Brad Steiger and John White, 83–110. Mokelumne Hill, CA: Health Research Books, 1986.

Van Duzer, Chet A. *Floating Islands: A Global Bibliography —With an Edition and Translation of G. C. Munz's Exercitatio Academica de Insulis Natantibus (1711).* Los Altos Hills, CA: Cantor Press, 2004.

Van Scott, Miriam. *The Encyclopedia of Hell.* New York: Macmillan, 1999.

Varner, Gary R. *Sacred Wells: A Study in the History, Meaning, and Mythology of Holy Wells and Waters.* New York: Algora, 2009.

Verma, Dhirendra. *Word Origins:* Volume 15 of *English Language Learning Series.* New Delhi: Sterling, 1999.

Veṭṭammāṇi. *Purāṇic Encyclopaedia: A Comprehensive Dictionary with Special Reference to the Epic and Purāṇic Literature*, Volume 2. Delhi: Motilal Banarsidass, 1975.

Vivian, Cassandra. *The Western Desert of Egypt: An Explorer's Handbook.* Cairo: American University in Cairo Press, 2000.

Vogel, Jean Philippe. *Indian Serpent-Lore: Or, The Nāgas in Hindu Legend and Art.* New Delhi: Asian Educational Services, 1926.

Vohs, George. *Am I Going to Heaven?* New York: Strategic Book, 2009.

W. I. T., Frater. *Advanced Enochian Magick: A Manual of Theory, Training, and Practice for the Novice and the Adept.* Parker, CO: Outskirts Press, 2008.

Wagner, Richard, and Edward Ziegler. *Tristan and Isolde.* New York: Frederick A. Stokes, 1909.

Wägner, Wilhelm. *Asgard and the Gods: Tales and Traditions of Our Northern Ancestors: Told for Boys and Girls.* London: W. Swan Sonnenschein and Allen, 1880.

Wagner, William. *How Islam Plans to Change the World.* Grand Rapids, MI: Kregel, 2012.

Waite, Arthur Edward. *The Occult Sciences.* New York: Cosimo, 2007.

Wallace, Kathryn. *Folk-Lore of Ireland: Legends, Myths and Fairy Tales.* Chicago: J. S. Hyland, 1910.

Walsh, William Shepard. *Handy-Book of Literary Curiosities.* Philadelphia: J.B. Lippincott, 1909.

_____. *Heroes and Heroines of Fiction, Classical Mediæval, Legendary: Famous Characters and Famous Names in Novels, Romances, Poems and Dramas, Classified, Analyzed and Criticised, with Supplementary Citations from the Best Authorities.* Philadelphia: J.B. Lippincott, 1915.

Walton, Bruce A. *A Guide to the Inner Earth.* Pomeroy, WA: Health Research Books, 1983.

Ward, J. S. M., and W. G. Stirling. *Hung Society or the Society of Heaven and Earth 1925.* Whitefish, MT: Kessinger, 2003.

Waterhouse, Joseph. *The King and the People of Fiji: Containing a Life of Thakombau; with Notices of the Fijians, Their Manners, Customs, and Superstitions, Previous to the Great Religious Reformation in 1854.* London: Wesleyan Conference Office, 1866.

Watts, Linda S. *Encyclopedia of American Folklore.* New York: Infobase, 2006.

Webster, Richard. *Encyclopedia of Angels.* Woodbury: Llewellyn, 2009.

Wellington, Richard S Weiss. *Recipes for Immortality: Healing, Religion, and Community in South India: Healing, Religion, and Community in South India.* Oxford: Oxford University Press, 2009.

Westmoreland, Perry L. *Ancient Greek Beliefs.* San Ysidro, CA: Lee and Vance, 2007.

Westwood, Jennifer. *Mysterious Places: The World's Unexplained Symbolic Sites, Ancient Cities and Lost Lands.* New York: Barnes and Noble, 1987.

Wheeler, William Adolphus, and Charles Gardner Wheeler. *An Explanatory and Pronouncing Dictionary of the Noted Names of Fiction: Including Also Familiar Pseudonyms, Surnames Bestowed on Eminent Men, and Analogous Popular Appellations Often Referred to in Literature and Conversation.* Boston: Houghton, Mifflin, 1917.

Wherry, E. M. *A Comprehensive Commentary on the Quran: Comprising Sale's Translation and Preliminary Discourse, with Additional Notes and Emendations*, Volume 1. Whitefish Kessinger, 2006.

Whitcomb, Bill. *The Magician's Companion: A Practical and Encyclopedic Guide to Magical and Religious Symbolism.* St. Paul, MN: Llewellyn, 1993.

White, John. *The Ancient History of the Maori: His Mythology and Traditions.* Wellington: George Didsbury, 1888.

White, Pamela, John Stewart Bowman, and Maurice Isserman. *Exploration in the World of the Middle Ages, 500–1500.* New York: Infobase, 2005.

Whiting, Roger. *Religions for Today.* Glouester: Nelson Thornes, 1991.

Wiedemann, Alfred. *Religion of the Ancient Egyptians.* New York: George. P. Putnam, 1897.

Wiese, Bill. *Hell: Separate Truth from Fiction and Get Your Toughest Questions Answered.* Lake Mary, FL: Charisma Media, 2012.

Wilcockson, Michael. *A Student's Guide to A2 Religious Studies for the OCR Specification.* London: Rhinegold, 2004.

Wilford, John Noble. *The Mapmakers, the Story of the Great Pioneers in Cartography from Antiquity to Space Age.* New York: Vintage Books, 1982.

Wilkinson, Philip. *Myths and Legends: An Illustrated Guide to their Origins and Meanings.* New York: Penguin, 2009.

Williams, George M. *Handbook of Hindu Mythology.* Oxford: Oxford University Press, 2008.

Williams, Thomas. *Fiji and the Fijians.* New York: D. Appleton, 1859.

Williamson, Robert W. *Religious and Cosmic Beliefs of Central Polynesia.* Cambridge: Cambridge University Press Archive, 1933.

Wilson, Horace Hayman. *The Vishńu Puráńa: A System of Hindu Mythology and Tradition.* London: Trübner, 1865.

_____. *The Vishńu Puráńa: A System of Hindu Mythology and Tradition*, Volume 5, Part 2. London: Trubner, 1877.

_____, translator. *The Vishńu Puráńa: A System of Hindu Mythology and Tradition.* London: Oriental Translation Fund of Great Britain and Ireland, 1840.

_____, and Fitzedward Hall. *The Vishńu Puráńa: A System of Hindu Mythology and Tradition*, Volume 2. London: Trübner, 1865.

_____, and the Oriental Translation Fund. *Oriental Translation Fund*, Volume 52. London: Oriental Translation Fund, 1840.

Woolf, Alex. *From Pictland to Alba: Scotland, 789–1070.* Edinburgh: Edinburgh University Press, 2007.

Woolsey, John Martin. *The Ancient City: Discovery of the City That Cain Built and Discovery of the Most Ancient Site of the City of Thebes and the Lost Europa, the Princess of Tyre, and Origin of the Swiss Lake Dwellings.* Charlottesville, VA: J. M. Woolsey, 1911.

Yaldiz, Marianne. *Along the Ancient Silk Routes: Central Asian Art from the West Berlin State Museums; an Exhibition Lent by the Museum Für Indische Kunst, Staatliche Museen Preussischer Kulturbesitz, and Berlin.* New York: Metropolitan Museum of Art, 1982.

Yang, Lihui. *Handbook of Chinese Mythology.* New York: Oxford University Press, 2005.

Yardley, Edward. *The Supernatural in Romantic Fiction.* London: Longmans, Green, 1880.

Zimmerman, Seth. *The Inferno of Dante Alighieri.* New York: iUniverse, 2003.

Znamenski, Andrei. *Red Shambhala: Magic, Prophecy, and Geopolitics in the Heart of Asia.* Wheaton: Quest Books, 2011.

Index